GOTHIC SCULPTURE

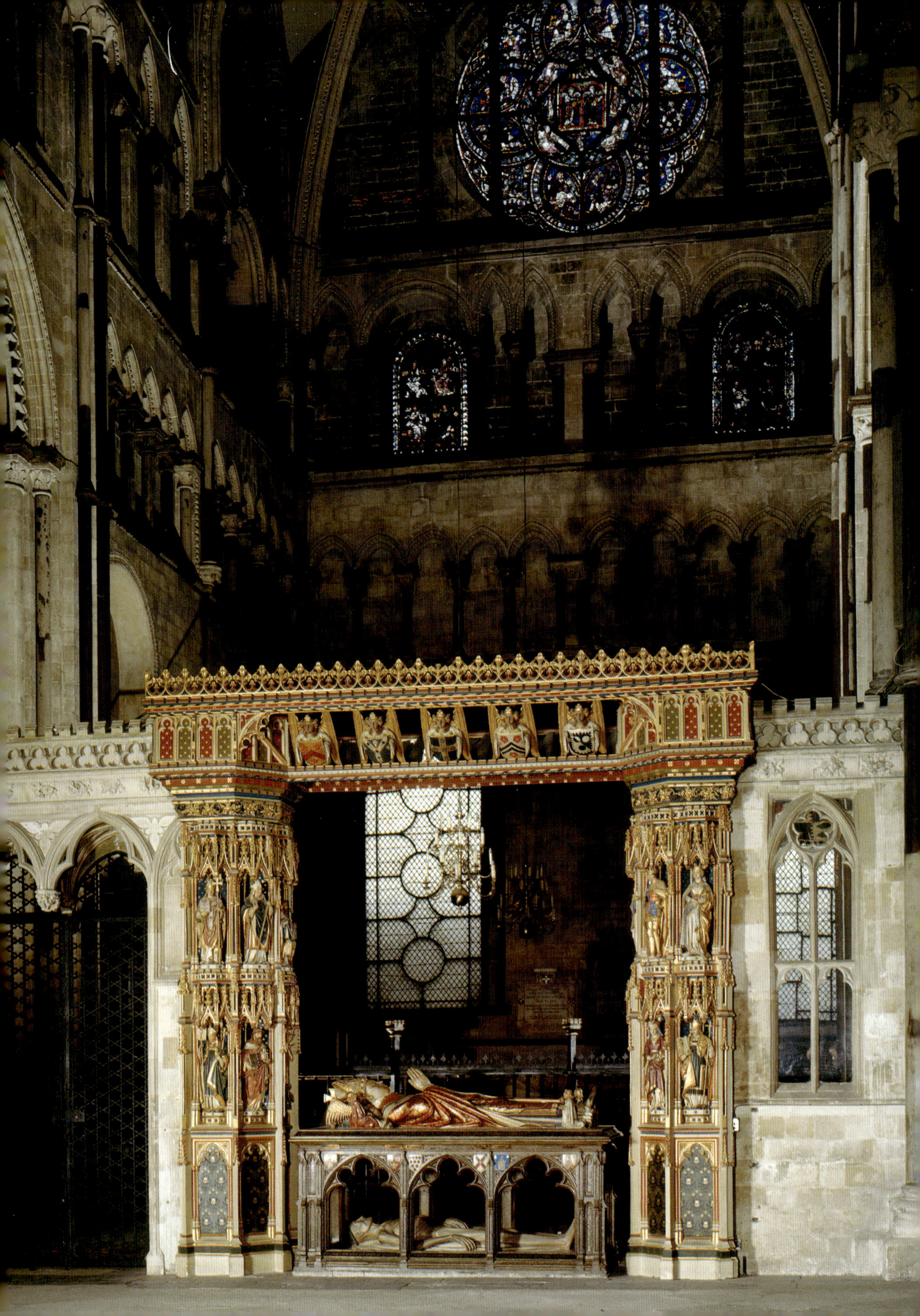

GOTHIC SCULPTURE

Paul Binski

Published for the Paul Mellon Centre for Studies in British Art by
Yale University Press • New Haven and London

A grant towards the cost of the illustrations for this book was generously provided by the Henry Moore Foundation.

ISBN 978-0300-241433 HB
Library of Congress Control Number: 2018955380

Designed by Emily Lees
Printed in Italy

MIX
Paper from responsible sources
FSC® C015829

frontispiece Canterbury Cathedral, choir, double-decker tomb of Archbishop Henry Chichele (d. 1443), raised around 1424–6, with north-east transept beyond (detail of pl. 112)
page vi Autun Cathedral (Sâone-et-Loire), west portal tympanum, detail of weighing of souls and inscriptions, about 1130 (detail of pl. 24)

Contents

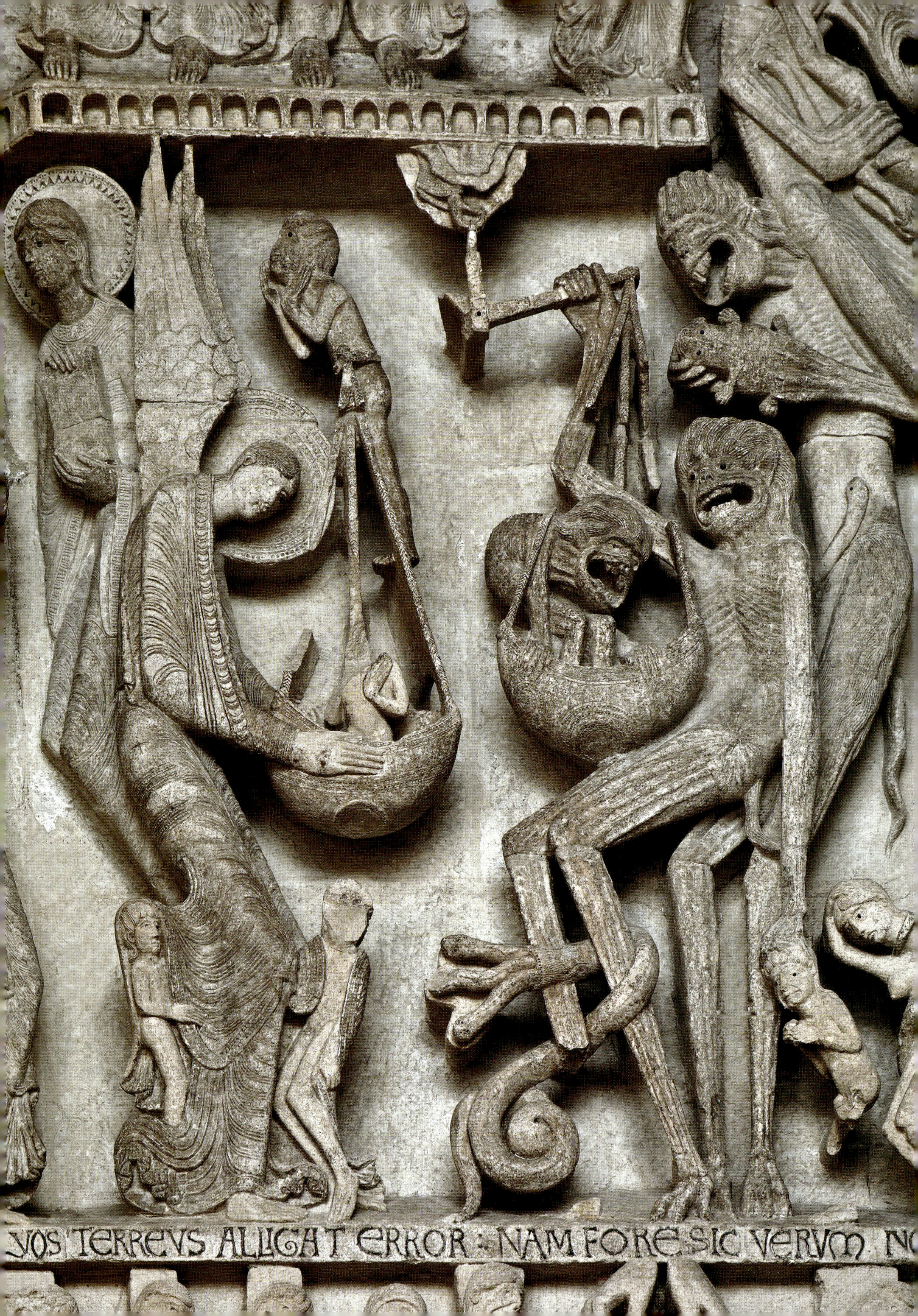
VOS TERREVS ALLIGAT ERROR : NAM FORE SIC VERVM

Acknowledgements

I acknowledge with gratitude all those who have helped me to get my ideas into order, especially my current brood of doctoral candidates, Anya Burgon, Rob Hawkins and Amy Jeffs, who read this text in draft and criticised it effectively and with charm. I have made every effort to keep the resulting book as short and as accessible as possible, in the hope that short texts are more likely to be read than long ones; and I take full responsibility for its errors. I hope that the many students I have taught in England and the United States since the early 1980s will allow me to dedicate this text to them with thanks for their vital role in keeping a professor on his toes for so many years.

I owe a particular debt to two people at the Paul Mellon Centre in London, Mark Hallett and Emily Lees, for the personal warmth and encouragement they have shown to me over more than one publishing venture, and for taking on the present book and making it a thing of beauty with their customary professionalism. As its text suggests, beauty is back, and its experience is enhanced by a level of production of which the Paul Mellon Centre is so very capable. I am delighted to acknowledge a grant from the Henry Moore Foundation in support of illustrating this study.

In the course of writing the book I have been encouraged by friends and colleagues, amongst whom I would like to mention especially a constant inspiration, Mary Carruthers, and also Julian Luxford, Sandy Heslop, Alex Marr and Jean-Pascal Pouzet. Jean-Claude Bonne, John Crook, Matt Kavaler, Kaja Kollandsrud, Chrystel Lupant and Tom Nickson were particularly saintly in their help with illustrations. I should also note that various aspects of this book have been presented in lectures in London (Courtauld Institute of Art), Oslo, Poitiers and Vienna.

Cambridge • 2018

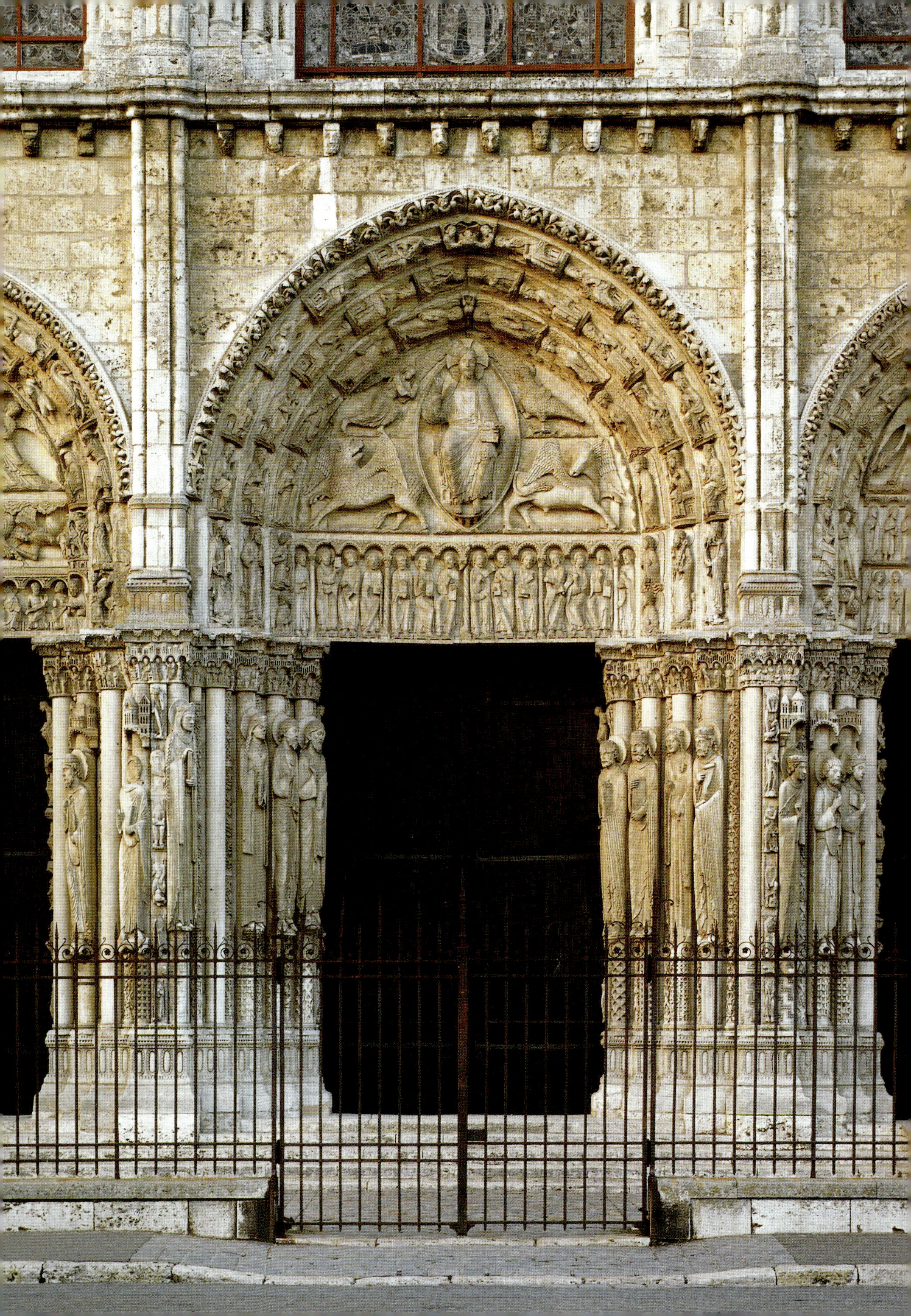

Introduction

By considering the many powers of sculpture I want to investigate the calculated eloquence of Gothic works of art more generally, particularly the way they engage us through their crafted substance and form. Sculpture, I hardly need say, stands out because its graspable nature lends it power, because it uses a wide variety of materials and because sculpting, carving and hewing were associated with a rich practical and figurative language of crafting. Sculpting embodied dangers, but it was also good to think with. When the great Roman rhetorician Quintilian criticised those who rush into written composition by hasty drafting, he called the unformed starting-point of raw material *silva*, a sort of primordial chaos, or forest; better, he said, to take care from the start and 'chisel' this material into shape accurately.[1] In Martianus Capella's widely read fifth-century *De Nuptiis Philologiae et Mercurii* – a medieval set text for the origin of the Liberal Arts – the personification of Grammar takes a pruning knife out of her toolbox in order to excise faults of pronunciation in the young.[2] The soul and body were things that could be crafted, improved on the model of sculpture. In his *Enneads* the philosopher Plotinus had spoken of the beautifying of the soul as if it were a polished and chiselled statue.[3] Later, in the same vein, the Parisian Dominican Hugh of St Cher (d. 1263) in his *Postilla* likened the process of filing, sawing and polishing ivory to the refining tribulations of the saints.[4] By being carved, chiselled, pruned and polished, a text or artefact has long been thought to become eloquent, and a human body virtuous. Sculpture had the metaphorical power to express rich and complex ideas long before Michelangelo's emergent marble *Slaves*.

1 Chartres Cathedral (Eure-et-Loir), west facade (detail of pl. 6)

My own toolbox is that of one kind of art historian, and I too have wielded my pruning knife in order to keep this book as short and I hope as accessible as possible. My text has conscious limitations. Although I make forays into the later Middle Ages, my primary concern is the period before about 1400. For brevity's sake it is not my aim to cover the whole field of medieval three-dimensional objects: I do not consider cast or beaten metal objects or seals, for example, because my interest is really the chisel. My focus is England and north-western Europe especially. This helps remedy the most obvious deficiency in the English evidence, the almost total post-medieval destruction of carved and painted wooden religious images, far better represented in Continental Europe. Nor can I hope to emulate the extraordinary specialised studies of Gothic sculpture which have emerged in the last two decades.[5] My concerns are not primarily with the cultic, miraculous or performative aspects of sculpture, important as these are: these aspects now dominate much of the literature on the subject and are better and fully treated elsewhere. Instead, I have carved and polished my own material with as much independence of mind as I can muster in order to confront specific difficulties which commentators on medieval sculpture and the arts more generally have created for themselves. What I have to say about the experience of Gothic sculpture necessarily has implications for the media generally.

To address these questions my study is divided into two parts. In the first part I focus on stone, and especially the large portals that developed from the later eleventh century in north-west Europe, concentrating on the twelfth and thirteenth centuries. I argue that such portals should be seen primarily as public monuments. Such portals, if I may be forgiven a shorthand distinction, have *functions* but they also have *purposes* or ends, and those ends I consider to be social, including not only admiration and pleasure but the attainment of conviction by means of artful persuasion. The sculpted figures on Romanesque and Gothic portals do not just convey doctrine but are conventionalised tools of eloquence which draw us in and move us, the spectators, but also get us to think and act. Such experiences are by their nature aesthetic, sensation-based. As in the verbal arts, 'figures' lead us through our experience of the artefact. There is at present a great deal of interest in the affective capacities of medieval art, which I share. Persuasion is the product of a melding of thought and sensation or, broadly speaking, emotion. Sensation colours thought, and thought colours sensation. My understanding of emotion is essentially cognitive, and for this I find support in the most widely accepted models of cognition and causation put to practical effect in the Middle Ages, which derived from Aristotle and Avicenna. Agency and intentionality develop in engaged, transactional situations. These transactions, like all aesthetic experience, are occasional (that is, dependent on context, situation and decorum), and because they are socially defined they limit the audience's horizon of experience. My emphasis therefore is less on individual response and psychology, more on social signification and hence, ultimately, the political force of images.

In reasserting the production as well as the reception of art, my stance towards public monumentality, the heroic enterprise and the technically surpassing resurfaces towards the end of Part I where I consider indexical representation or, for want of a better word, verism, of which celebrated examples in France and Germany date from the middle of the thirteenth century. Roland Barthes called this the 'reality effect'. By persisting with the idea of eloquence and its various strategies, I come to see this effect as serving the rhetorical order of panegyric or praise and not, as has become fashionable, the low or everyday style of speech, *sermo humilis*. I also see it as a technical possibility born of a comparatively specialised situation involving well-funded, ambitious and interconnected cathedral workshops in the middle of the thirteenth century which together formed what I call 'laboratories of the big effect'. I understand Gothic sculptural verism to be but one product of a culture of technical ambition and connectivity driven, of course, by power and realised within production itself. Sculpture cannot, and did not, stand alone, and by placing it in the context of power and technology, architecture included, we understand both its ideological capacity and its ability to form and limit imagination.

Some modern functional and empathetic readings of medieval works of art have tried to inject 'life' into them – in effect to re-enchant them – while also making problematical claims about emotion, thought and representation which descend, I suggest, from Romanticism and its preoccupations with sincerity. In confronting some of these claims I return the discussion to the way artifice itself shapes objects and subjects. At the heart of this idea of artifice is the ancient, and widely applicable, concept of *techne* (craft or art). From my 'classicist' as distinct from 'romantic' perspective, even experience itself is a crafted thing, rendered eloquent not by freedom but by skilled limitation or *askesis*.

If Part I offers a critique of the risks of emotivism, Part 2 interrogates the remagicking of art. Here, I am concerned not with exterior sculpture but with the no less social world of the interior artwork and its associated media, starting with wood. I continue my critique of post-medieval notions of authenticity, as opposed to my real concern, artifice. In particular, I have in mind two modern idols. The first, long since struck down, was post-Kantian aesthetic detachment, the straw man of image anthropology. The second idol, set up in its place and still standing, is the anaesthetic image of 'presence', of 'life', of the image as an excessive thing. Both, I think, may sometimes be substitutes for religion. In regard to the excessive image, I deliberately distance my discussion from animist and materialist theories which, to my mind, entail a form of reification of presence and 'stuff' without sufficient regard to historically defined representational thought and production. I argue against an undue suppression of human agency in the making and perception of things. Images may well be presences, but they are also representations, and to bypass that fact leads to a disregard for their crafting. Craft, and what I have called the human 'poetics' of materials, matter because they lend rationally guided eloquence to things: materials and style together possess intent. Materials matter fundamentally to craft, as art historians have long understood. But they are seldom innocent, thriving on reputations attributed to them by thinking, feeling subjects. Notions of eloquence lead us to useful critical style concepts such as the value, literal and figurative, of colour (the *colores* of rhetoric), surface, contrast (or *oppositio*), complexion, serious play (or *ludus*) and thus illusion, and *ekphrasis* – the vivid imagining of material things. My earlier thoughts about occasion and figuration continue to be relevant. Representation does not consist of substitution but of thoughtful conception and preconception. Medieval art, I argue, revels in illusion quite as much as in touch: it welcomes the undeceived depiction. Vivid mental image-making – often the most important form of medieval imagination understood as a composing faculty – was not a material thing at all.

Pursuing craft and transformation, in the last part of this study I take us for a walk in the woods and consider wildness, tending, turning and cultivation in the carving out of artistic eloquence. My final concern is an imaginary: the relationship of life, death and process. In death, our identity is lost in a final process of becoming, and so in considering macabre things I ponder fear, flesh and bone in the light of the same rhetorical orders as those explored earlier in the book.

2 Low relief panel with beasts and hunting scenes, detail from former *jubé* of Chartres Cathedral (detail of pl. 69)

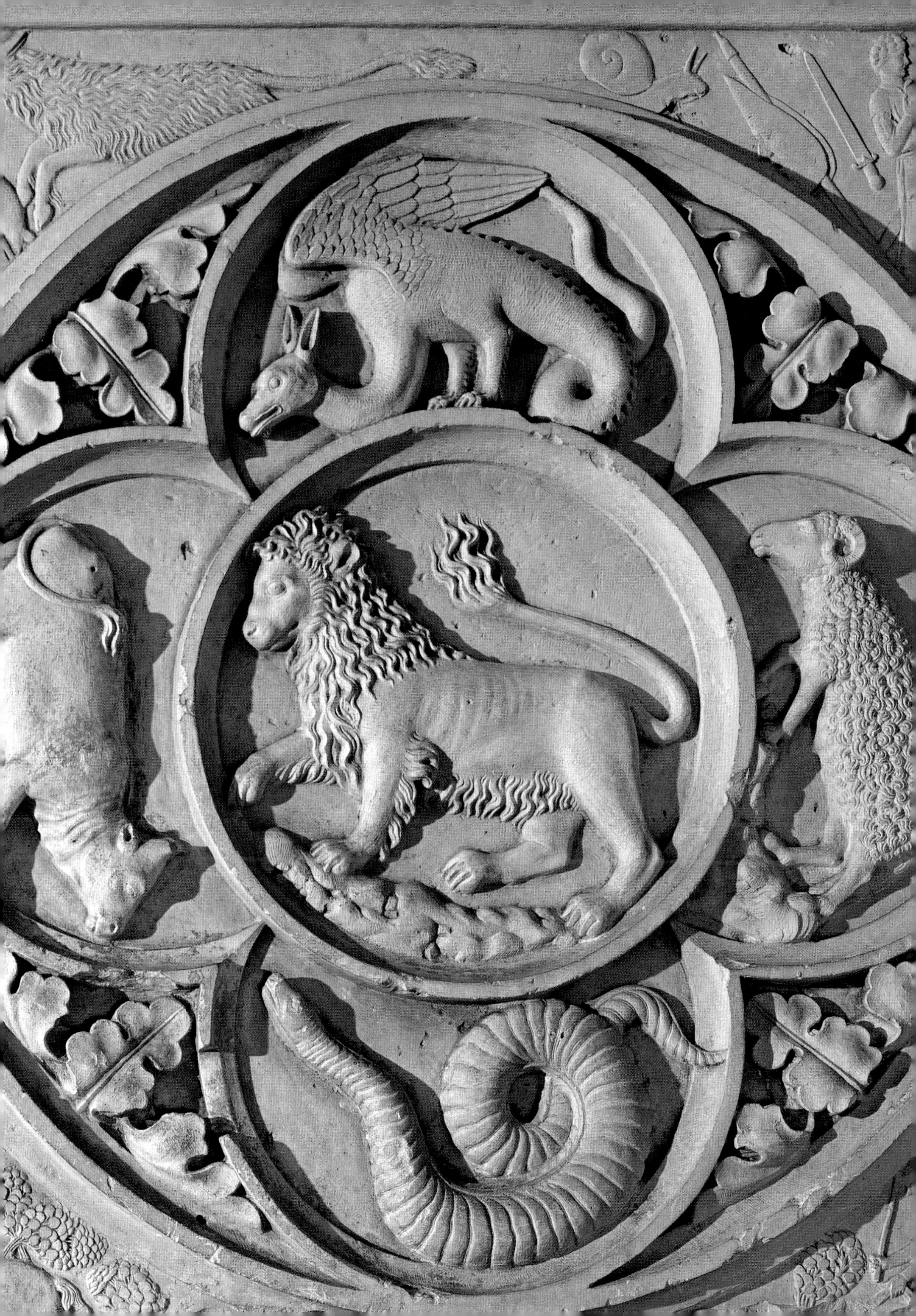

Part I

Stone

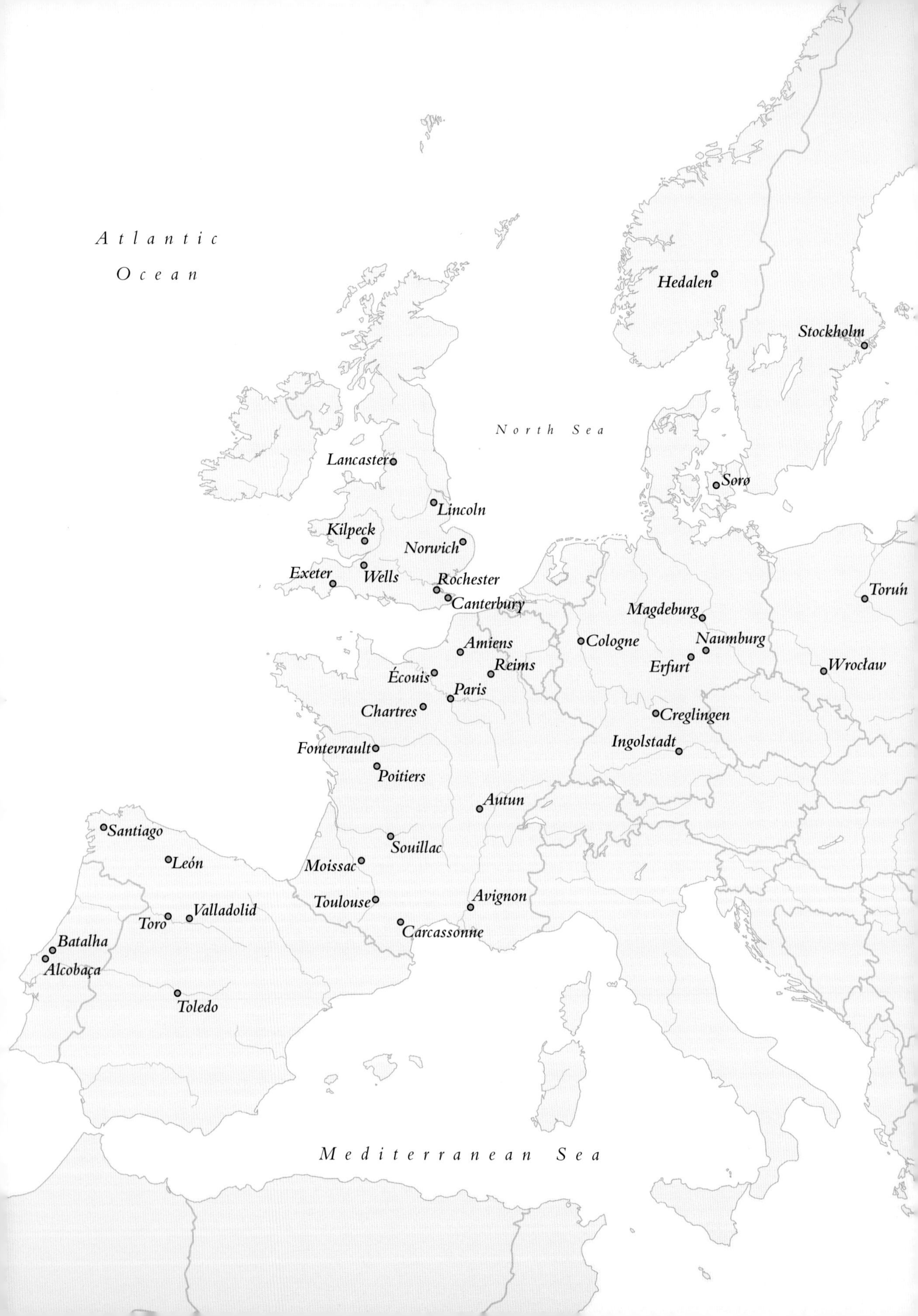
Atlantic Ocean
North Sea
Mediterranean Sea
Hedalen
Stockholm
Sorø
Lancaster
Lincoln
Kilpeck
Norwich
Exeter
Wells
Rochester
Canterbury
Magdeburg
Toruń
Amiens
Cologne
Naumburg
Erfurt
Reims
Wrocław
Écouis
Paris
Chartres
Creglingen
Ingolstadt
Fontevrault
Poitiers
Autun
Santiago
Souillac
León
Moissac
Toulouse
Avignon
Toro
Valladolid
Carcassonne
Batalha
Alcobaça
Toledo

I

OCCASION AND AGENCY

In a beautiful passage in his book *The Stones of Venice*, the critic John Ruskin anticipates our arrival in that great city by imagining it as if seen from above by migratory birds:

> Let us, for a moment, try to raise ourselves even above the level of their flight, and imagine the Mediterranean lying beneath us like an irregular lake ... Syria and Greece, Italy and Spain, laid like pieces of a golden pavement into the sea-blue, chased, as we stoop nearer to them, with bossy beaten work of mountain chains, and glowing softly with terraced gardens, and flowers heavy with frankincense'.[1]

Ruskin's interest was the Italian imagination and its appeal to the senses. But his literary device of flight to reconnoitre an entire situation was far older. It is an example of the ancient genre of *kataskopos*, the visionary bird's-eye view over the earth as if spread out like a map, at once general and specific.[2] Abbot Suger of Saint-Denis, the abbey near Paris often regarded as the birthplace of the Gothic style, and himself a great patron, uses it in his *De Administratione* of the 1140s when he writes of seeing himself mysteriously from above, as if on some strange and foreign shore.[3]

So when, like Ruskin, we look down and survey everything stretching out across our chosen region – north-western Europe between about 1100 and the later Middle Ages – what bejewelled sights present themselves (pl. 3)? The picture as a whole is wonderfully diverse: on many church buildings are great ensembles of sculpted relief work, strange, complex, at once fascinating and forbidding, often coloured and sparkling with

3 Map of the principal sites mentioned in the text

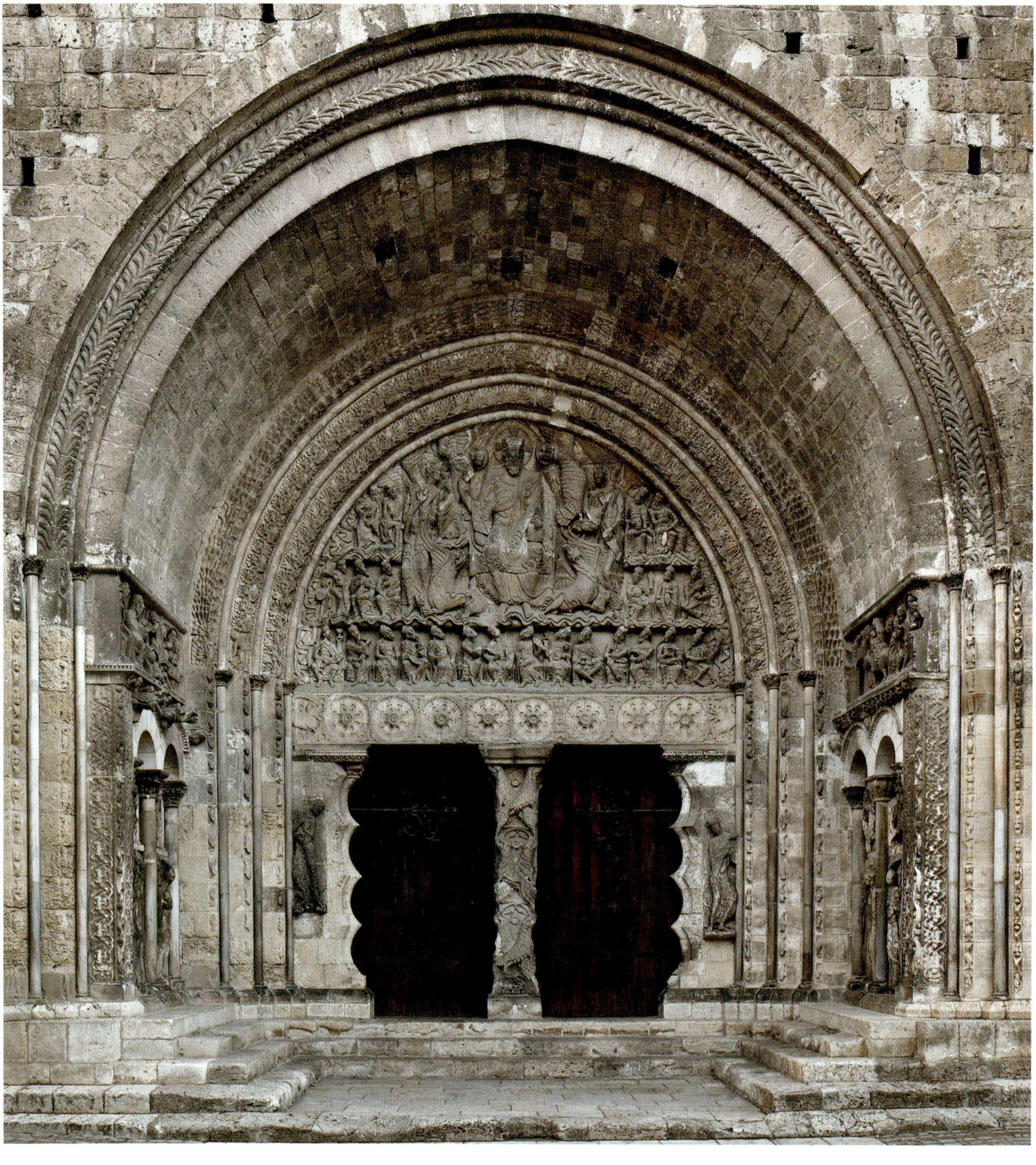

4 Moissac Abbey (Tarn-et-Garonne), south-west portal showing Apocalypse, early twelfth century

gold (pl. 4). There seems to be no agreement as to how a great church front might be decorated, where and how its figures and narratives might be displayed, and this extraordinary range and vitality is typical of much of what we see between Iberia and Hungary.[4] Sharpening our sense of time, we observe change: by the year 1300 there has been transformation. The doorways, like the churches, start to look more similar: swooping down and peering closely we now see sculpted arts shaped almost by a common sensibility, a shared canon of beauty, how things should look and be arranged. This currency reaches across much, though not all, of our landscape. To call it a *lingua franca*, a common speech for all, is not wrong: the agreed 'look' is provably French in origin and character.[5] By 1300 this common speech has become that of the French Rayonnant style. The Gothic church has become a type. For the associated arts this has consequences. What runs riot in the 1100s has been slowed, ordered, smoothed, tightened. The tremendous power and strangeness, wilfulness, of Romanesque art has been tempered. Variety is being edged out by a cooling cogency. Of course, the regional solution, local knowledge and practices, have not been suppressed entirely, nor could they be. International and regional differences can still be spotted by the trained eye. There were areas of 'resistance' to the new northern French format, which did not settle uniformly in, for instance, the south of France and some areas of the Holy Roman Empire.[6] Before the inception of Cologne Cathedral in 1248, sculpted portals in the Empire did not acquiesce to French formulas, yet by the time of late thirteenth-century Strasbourg (pl. 5), on the whole they did.[7] Whether in Castile – consider the cathedral of Burgos – or in the Ile-de-France and Champagne, or Burgundy or Alsace, and whether across the Rhine as far as Thuringia or way north to Trondheim, the arts towards 1300 tend to acquire a family resemblance which is more than that of a style.

What has changed above all is the architecture. The large-scale sculpted arts were framed and directed by the systems of shafts and arches, and precise ways of cutting ashlar stone, typical of the Romanesque and Gothic styles. The French Gothic portal is the result of what happens when doorways are cut into thick masonry walls framed on each side by a splayed surface (or 'jamb') sloping forward from the portal openings, so creating a deep and broad frame. These sloping surfaces have regular rows of shafts with arch-orders springing from them, as many orders as there are shafts, part answering calmly to part. These components, whether shafts or arches, then mutate into tall slim column-figures, or much smaller figures in relief on the curved under-surfaces of the arches (pl. 6). A spreading tympanum is formed from the flat arched field over the doors. This absolutely regular format, paradoxically, underlies the dynamism of sculpted figures on most Gothic doorways, which keep the axial core of the column while turning and relating to each other as if in dialogue.[8] The shaft and arch is to be the foundation for a new sociability. Even the earliest statement of such Gothic doorways, Suger's own west front at Saint-Denis certainly in place by 1144, showed off column figures with dynamically crossed legs, possessing within themselves an

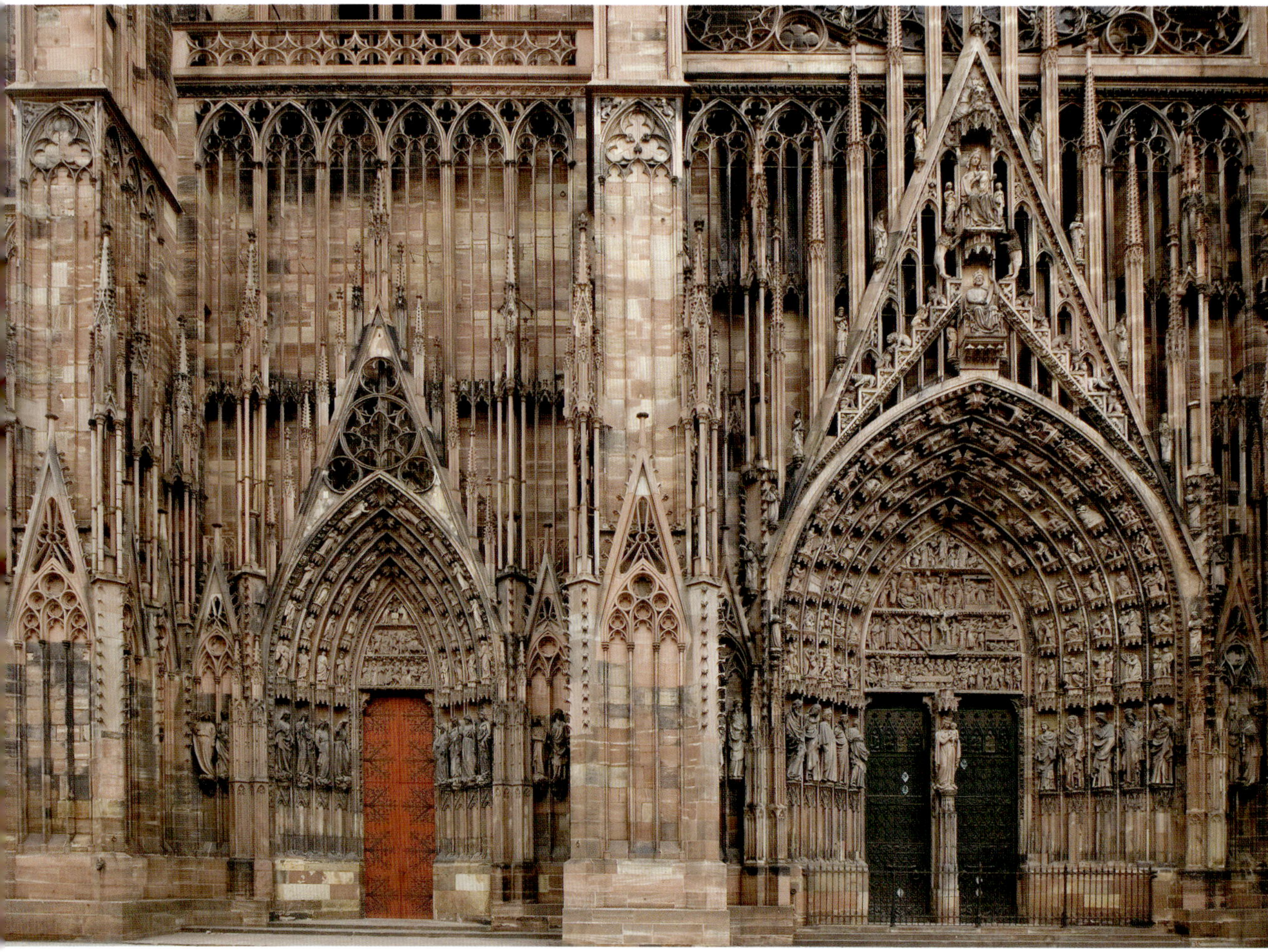

5 Strasbourg Cathedral (Alsace), west front, centre and north portal, begun 1277

apparent yet contained energy.[9] The Rayonnant idiom eventually calmed and universalised these effects throughout much of north-western Europe: Gothic had become a style.

One kingdom differed: England. During the formidable burst of creative energy in stone unleashed by the Norman Conquest in 1066, patrons of great stone buildings in England produced works of a scale and impact almost unmatched in Europe. Patrons in England had the energy, resources and imagination to outstrip their Continental neighbours, and England quickly produced a version of Gothic to match that of France. Indeed, at specific places before about 1200 – Lincoln and Rochester, for example – the idiom of carvings on church doorways was essentially similar to what we find in northern France.[10] The giant

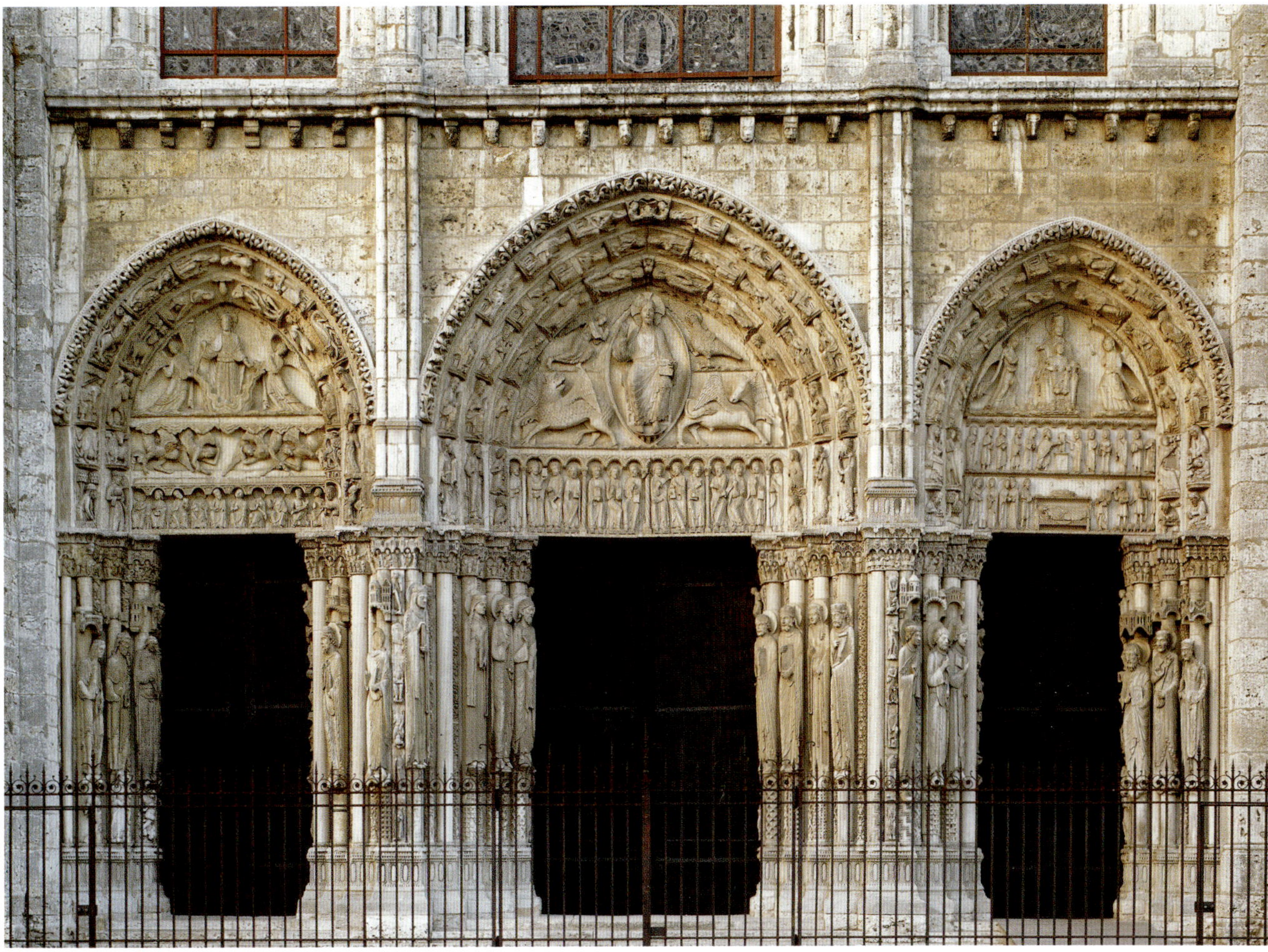

6 Chartres Cathedral (Eure-et-Loir), west facade, the Portail Royal, mid-twelfth century

Romanesque facade of Lincoln Cathedral, itself evoking the magnificence and scale of the triumphal arches of Rome itself, was planned and executed at the same time and in much the same way, armed as it was with column figures by the doors, as Abbot Suger's west front at Saint-Denis in the 1140s.[11] A portal strikingly like those on the west front of Chartres of *c.*1150 was executed at the west end of Rochester Cathedral (pl. 7) with the same Apocalyptic imagery.[12] But as regards general format and approach, the paths of England and France diverged from this point. By the mid-thirteenth century the large facades at Wells (pl. 9) and Peterborough ignore the French, and older English, emphasis on doors, in favour of colossal arches or screen-like ranks of much smaller tabernacles, the 'many mansions'

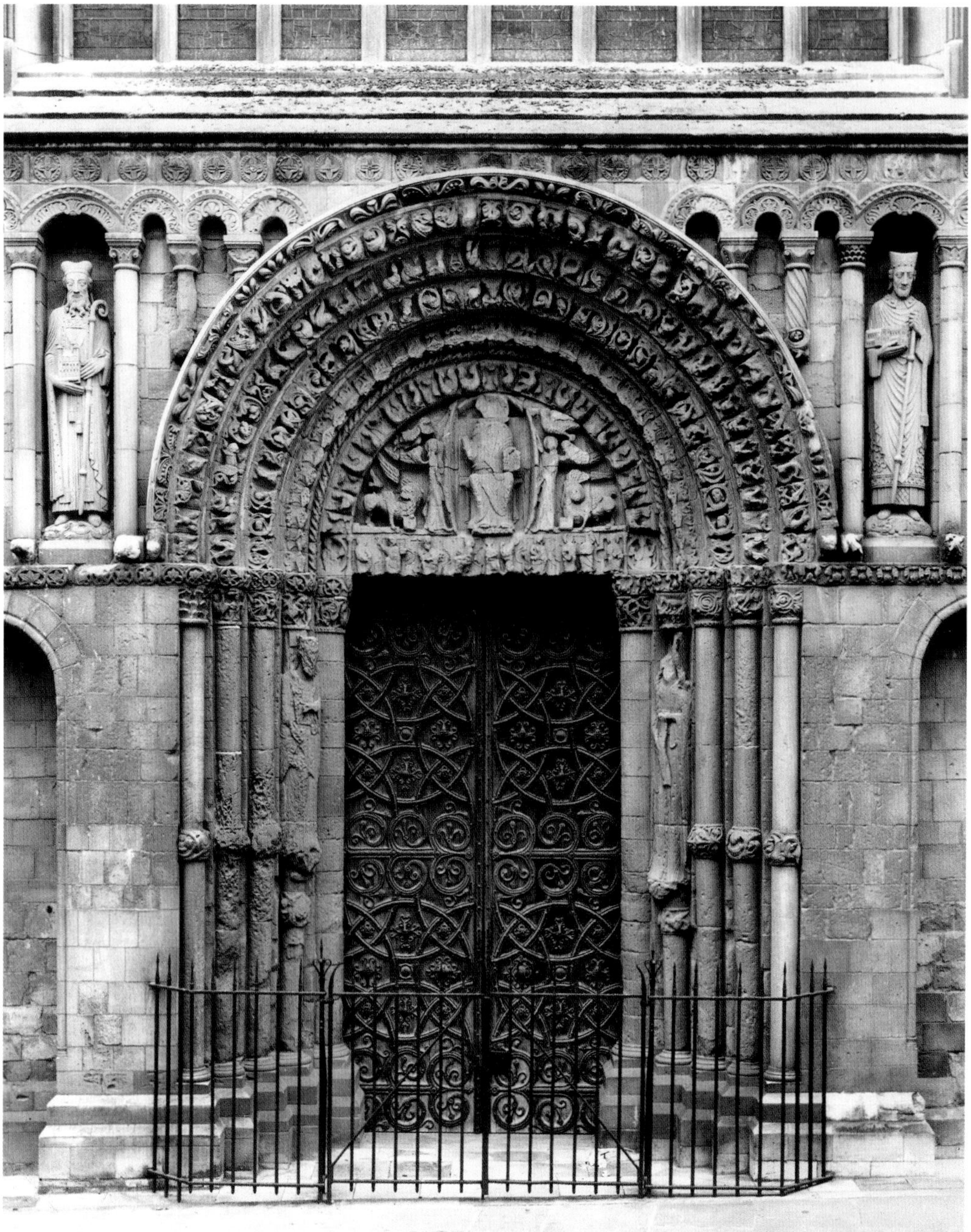

7 Rochester Cathedral, west portal with Christ in Majesty and column figures, third quarter twelfth century

facing page 8 Lincoln Cathedral, south east Judgement portal, *voussoirs*, about 1260

following pages 9 Wells Cathedral, west front, begun about 1220 (see also pl. 18) of the Bible.[13] The facade at Exeter Cathedral, in hand in the middle of the fourteenth century, persists with the Wells type of image-screen as a south-western English 'type'.[14] When a truly French-style High Gothic church was erected by Henry III (1216–1272) for Westminster Abbey, the overall northern French schema used for its main entrance, the great north transept facing the city of London, had giant porches but was adapted to display standing figures set in niches, an English more than a French practice.[15] It is likely that Henry admired the extraordinary sculpted work at Reims of the same period, yet the response of Henry's workmen to the portals of Reims (whose major north transept facade was finished before 1245) and of Amiens (see pl. 19), was independent. Loquacity in English sculpture was a matter of the brilliance of small-scale work, not the expansive outlook of the great portal: the delicate figural work on the archivolts of the Judgement porch on the south side of the Angel Choir at Lincoln (begun 1256; pl. 8) is as fine and charming as ivory but the format is in general that of the Westminster portals.[16] For some reason, possibly the fact that English cathedrals were often set in closes which isolated them from the urban public arena, and probably because the external buttressing systems of its Gothic churches did not encourage cavernous portals, the portal imaginary of England remained a thing apart from that often apparent in vastly impressive form on the Continent.[17] In England, sculpture was often turned inwards, a matter for the breathtaking and expensively finished interior: the greatest English 'copy' of Wells's facade is arguably spread around an interior, that of the Lady Chapel at Ely, begun in 1321 (compare pl. 79 for a detail).[18] The French type of portal simply never caught on.

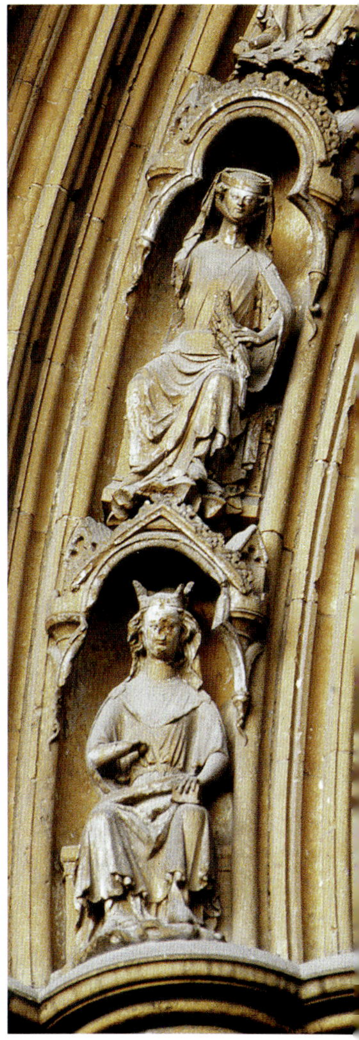

So we can overplay the absolute homogeneity of the northern European scheme. Great building did not necessarily open out giant portals. Nor should we forget resources. The creation of large sculpted and coloured doorways entailed a tremendous economic commitment. When the cathedrals of Chartres and Bourges were rebuilt on hitherto unimaginable scale from the 1190s, the commissioners were careful to retain the, in many ways outmoded, sculpted portals of the former twelfth-century buildings. Medieval art-making is beautifully efficient and unwasteful. But by 1300 only a few of the great new Gothic portal complexes had been finished. The really inventive projects in northern France, long engaged in a specialised conversation and exchange of ideas, a visual laboratory, had been pressed to completion in the 1260s. Tougher economic times lay ahead, and sculpted doorways, like towers, were expensive. Many would have to wait until the later part of the fifteenth century to realise their dreaming spires.

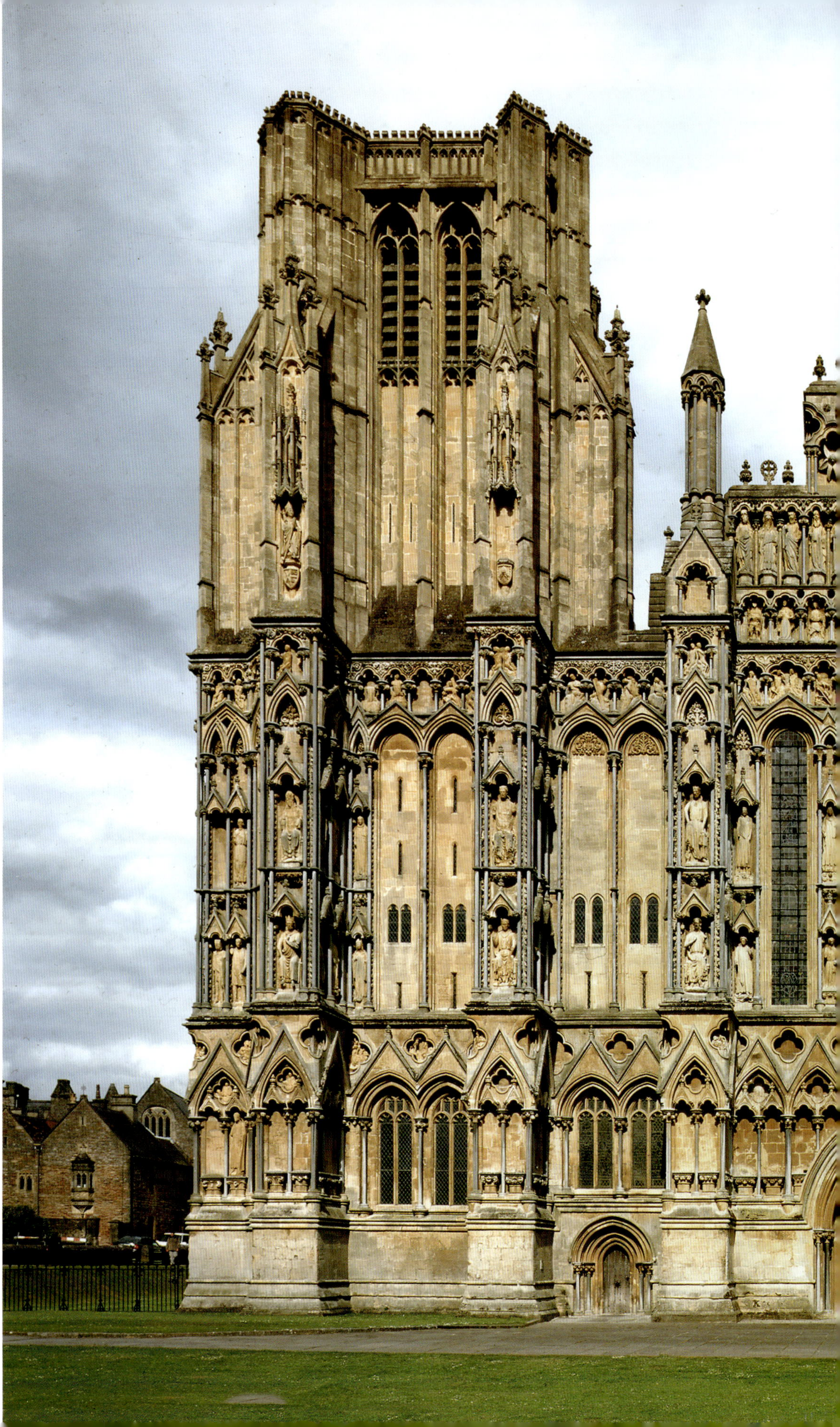

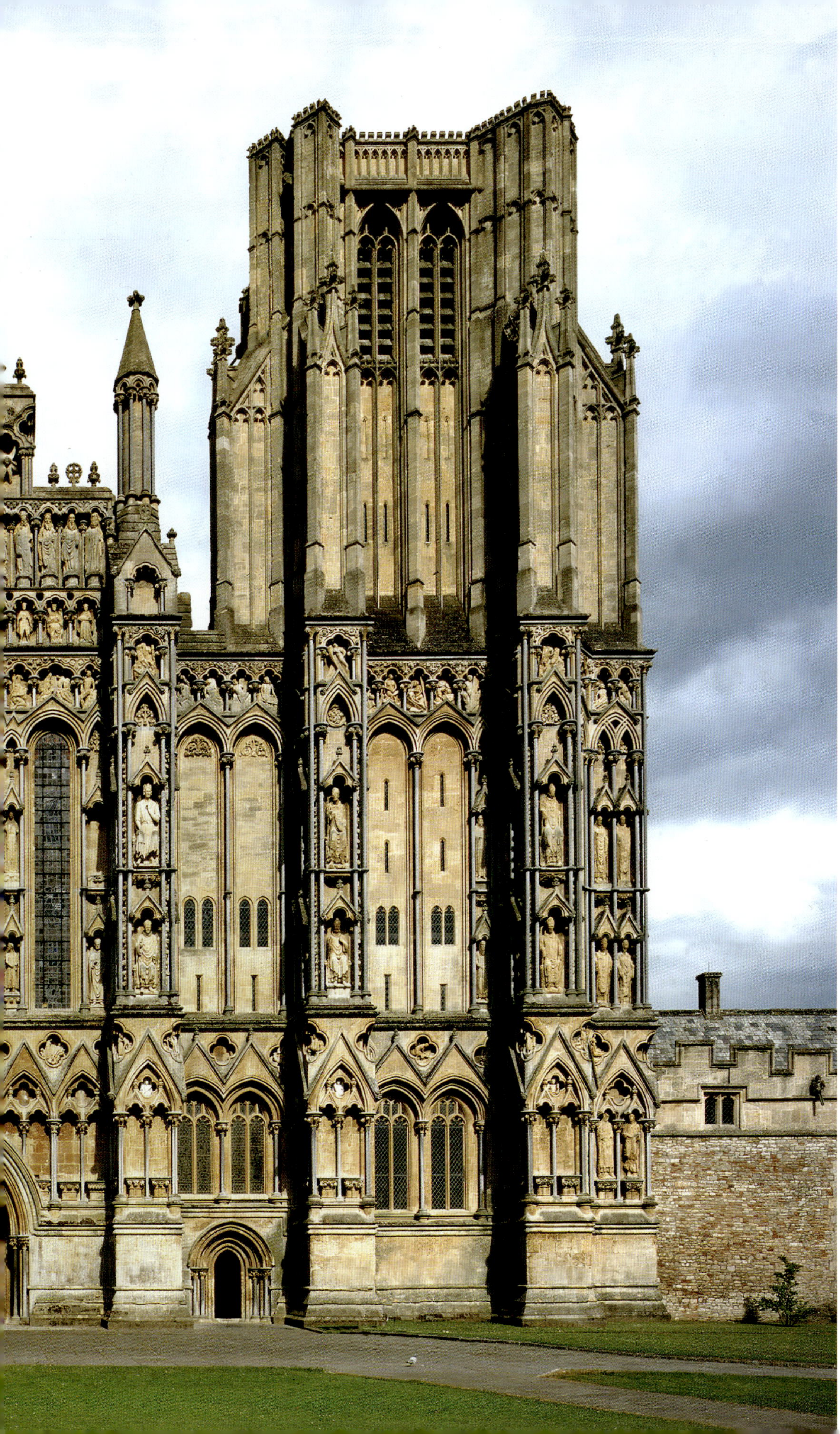

What are we to make of this complex landscape? The most widely read modern accounts of our doorways are of given and immutable truths, 'programmatic' in outlook, didactic, even propagandistic. Over these, the old school of iconography, top-down in outlook and heedless of context or human experience and engagement, long held sway.[19] Portals were there to transmit information. There has since been no shortage of alternative modern critical options for understanding portals and related sculptures – liturgical and performative, ideological, reformist, doctrinal, epigraphic, sensory, affective, sermonal and rhetorical.[20] Academic concern has, rightly, become more human, more social, orientated more towards reception than production. Indeed, the materials and technologies involved in making these artworks, to say nothing of their style, are now (if anything) secondary to cultural models of interpretation.[21] It is not clear to me that this ordering of things is necessarily quite right, because it obscures in what ways technical ability and change matter. Superb, regular, complex and hence eloquent stone-cutting was to Gothic what iron and steel construction were to Modernism.[22] By using the term 'artworks' I also persist in the belief that the charge that the Middle Ages were devoid of 'art', typically levelled by some (not all) forms of anthropology, is unhelpful.[23] I have no ambition at all to reconstruct the putative original audiences and emotions of the witnesses to these artworks. To reconstruct and, creator-like, revive something may be, as Mary Shelley long ago showed, to create a monster with its own will. Medieval art history is full of Frankenstein monsters gifted with life – of a sort. My concerns are not with 'authenticity'. But they are historical: and it would be true to say that I am more concerned with identifying that which is 'not inauthentic' than with breathing life into old things by means of what Carlo Ginzburg calls 'ventriloquism'.[24] While we have little option but to exercise our own historically positioned faculties and judgement, we can be perfectly aware that we are in fact doing so, and that medieval words and experiences were different from ours.[25]

ENTRANCE: OCCASION AND THE PUBLIC DOMAIN

To start to establish these horizons let us begin by asking what it might have been like to encounter a great Romanesque or Gothic sculpted entrance to a church. In considering this problem we have to admit, first, that in general the period lacks not only what we would recognise as a language of style – terms such as 'Romanesque' and 'Gothic' are post-medieval monikers – but also a language of experience, of the aesthetic or psychological exploration of artefacts.[26] It is striking to modern eyes that the self-evidently stupendous achievements of Gothic cathedral building, portals included, bear no relation to the thinness or absence of medieval written accounts of human experience of them.[27]

The difficulty that modern commentators have had in discussing the medieval experience of artefacts may explain the extraordinary rise of anthropologically, and so functionally based, accounts of artworks, giving them a life absent from discourse: while experience is a matter of subjective opinion or interpretation, function is a matter of firm knowledge, explanation. Or so it is claimed. Consider a favourite term of anthropology, 'liminality'. Portals are doorways, doorways have thresholds; and the Latin word for threshold, *limen*, furnished the name of liminality theory, the idea (formulated especially by Arnold van Gennep) that human life is itself marked by thresholds, major transitional experiences, rites of passage.[28] The threshold is a place of intensification and change. Crossing-points are held to be dangerous and charmed, bringing opportunity, requiring preparedness, promising rewards, addressing those who seek and then directing them. From its early period Christianity had sacramental thresholds marking rites of passage, baptism and death, and it is not coincidental that portal-like compositions with arches and figures featured on elaborate medieval tombs, and that doorways have ritual functions.[29] The Gospels are well stocked with door and passage images, such that from them alone we might in our minds' eyes summon up a great and forbidding entrance: 'I am the door. By me, if any man enter in, he shall be saved' (John 10:9); 'I am the way, and the truth, and the life' (John 14:6); 'he had opened the door of faith to the Gentiles' (Acts 14:26); 'that God may open unto us a door of speech [*ostium sermonis*] to speak the mystery of Christ' (Colossians 4:3); 'Behold, the judge standeth before the door' (James 5:9); 'and behold, a door was opened in heaven' (Revelation 4:1). These doors are either thrown nobly open in a gesture of revelation, or they are slammed shut, or at least perilously narrowed: we are to enter the kingdom of heaven through a narrow gate (*angusta porta*; Luke 13:24), from which we may even be turned away unrecognised, with much wailing and gnashing of teeth. The sculpted 'doors of speech' indeed bore bold and sometimes dramatic inscriptions in Latin through much of the twelfth century in Iberia, France and Italy.[30] Of these one of the most dramatic is that under the main lintel of the great Pórtico de la Gloria of Compostela Cathedral (pl. 10), drawn from Isaiah 6:1–4 and its vision of the Lord seated on a high throne: *et commota sunt superliminaria cardinum a voce clamantis* – 'and the lintels of the doors were moved at the voice of him that cried'.[31]

These tremendous, and undoubtedly imaginatively transcendent, biblical images are at heart ideas, literally mental images. What they do for us especially is to show how a portal offered an 'occasion'.[32] By this I mean something both specific and available to medieval thought. We now think of an occasion as something like a special event, an occurrence or 'happening' – and this is helpful. *Occasio*, or *Tempus*, was the Roman God of luck and opportunity, *occasio* coming from the Latin stem *ob-cadere*, a 'falling out'. Occasion is an important concept in rhetoric indicating the context or purpose for saying or writing something: some things are best said when a particular opportunity or context arises. The occasion

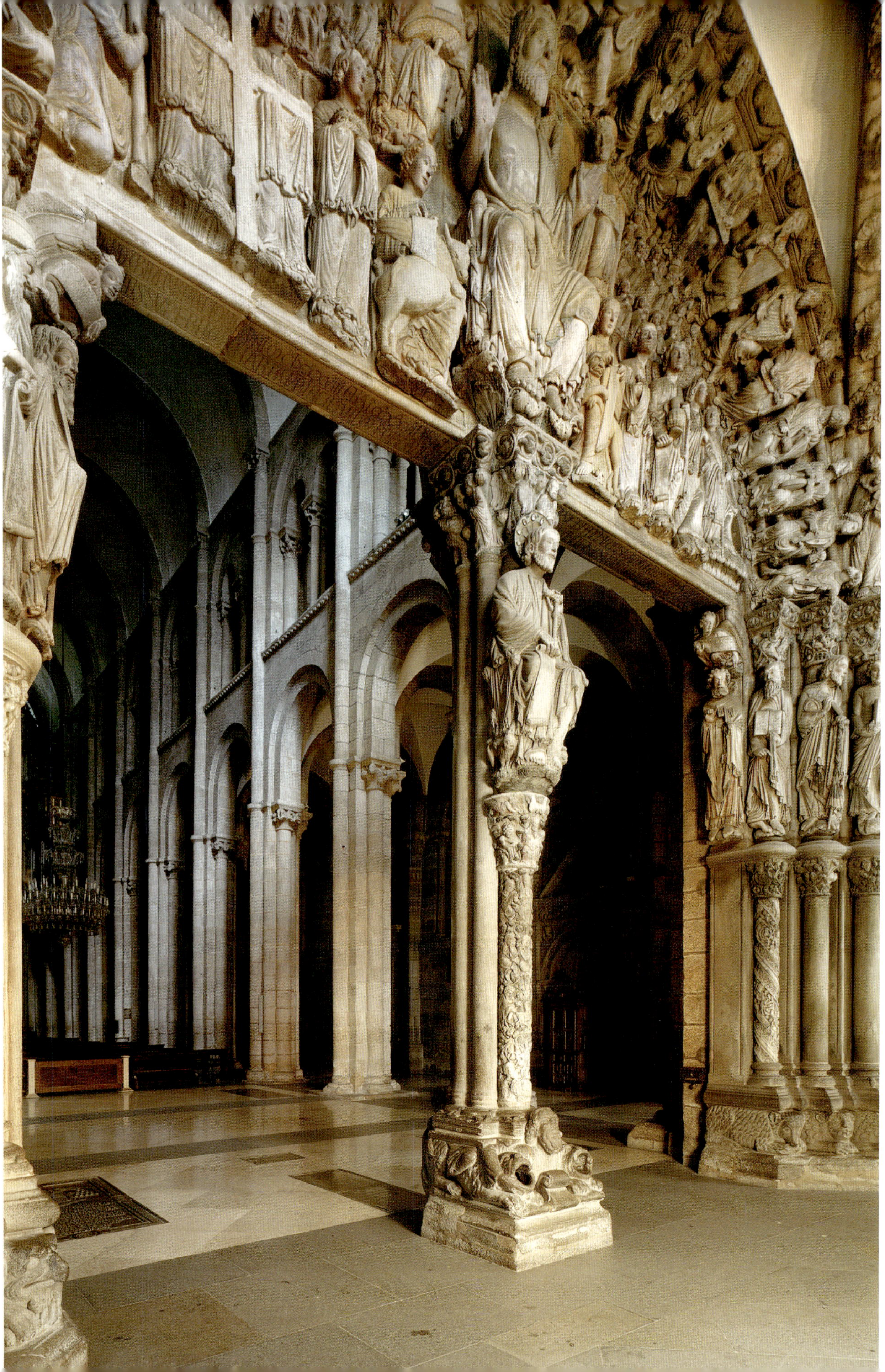

itself gives us a feeling for what is right or 'opportune' to say or write: it dynamically guides our sense of appropriateness, or decorum. An occasion is not a *state* but a *process* in which the artefact and the audience participate. For instance, liturgical and performative discussion of the great Royal Portal at the west end of Chartres (see pl. 6) stresses the connection between imagery and the public liturgy of the *introit*, the entrance of God into the world and of humankind into the Church.[33] A doorway, whether in a church facade or penetrating through a screen within it, brings us into the presence of Christ and his witnesses, the saints and prophets, and it may well favour us or not, as we deserve. But the door is not just a threshold but a starting-point: a large portal is encountered and gets things and us going. By means of its artificial surfaces it directs and gestures, moves things along. This is not simply a matter of the shifting external perception of an object changed by the physical movement of the spectator, important as that is: Kathryn Brush and Jacqueline Jung argue of medieval sculpture that movement should be included because it entails and shapes engagement, and engagement is fundamental to experience.[34] It is also a matter of movement within an artefact located in turn within a situation, and also of movement within the engaged spectator. Works of art are always experienced situationally, and the notion of occasion captures the way in which such situations themselves have agency and rationale.[35]

This idea of movement and direction (inward and outward) matters because in such encounters occasion may well bring with it a measure of *initial* disorientation prior to a sensation of relocation and redirection. I stress 'initial' because the study of reception of artworks seldom distinguishes between the very first, as it were innocent, encounter with a work of art and the habitual encounter. What prompts an initial movement at a threshold might be one of several things. One common in sculpted doorways would be with represented figures that are either substantially over life-size or large and near to us. Two good instances are Crucifixions: that made in the tenth century by Anglo-Saxon sculptors in high relief over the nave door of the church of St Swithun at Headbourne Worthy near Winchester, measuring about ten feet in height and looming directly over the narrow portal (pl. 11); and the even more assertive placement of the near life-size Crucifixion within the door of the west pulpitum or *lettner* of Naumburg Cathedral, dating to the mid-thirteenth century (pl. 12).[36] By the thirteenth century such large-scale Crucifixion groups were generally spectacularly elevated onto screens. Dramatically, Naumburg instead brings the Cross down to earth, overcomes distance, forces proximity to those passing through. In both cases the size and unavoidable proximity of the image creates a kind of obligation towards it. Again, the famous figures framing the doorways on the west front of Reims (see pl. 46) are almost double natural size, not exactly colossal figures but unusual in scale and also in their elevated placement. By such means they are 'magnified', as are our expectations of what is to follow.

10 Santiago de Compostela (Galicia), Pórtico de la Gloria, Christ in Majesty showing lintel inscriptions with date 1188

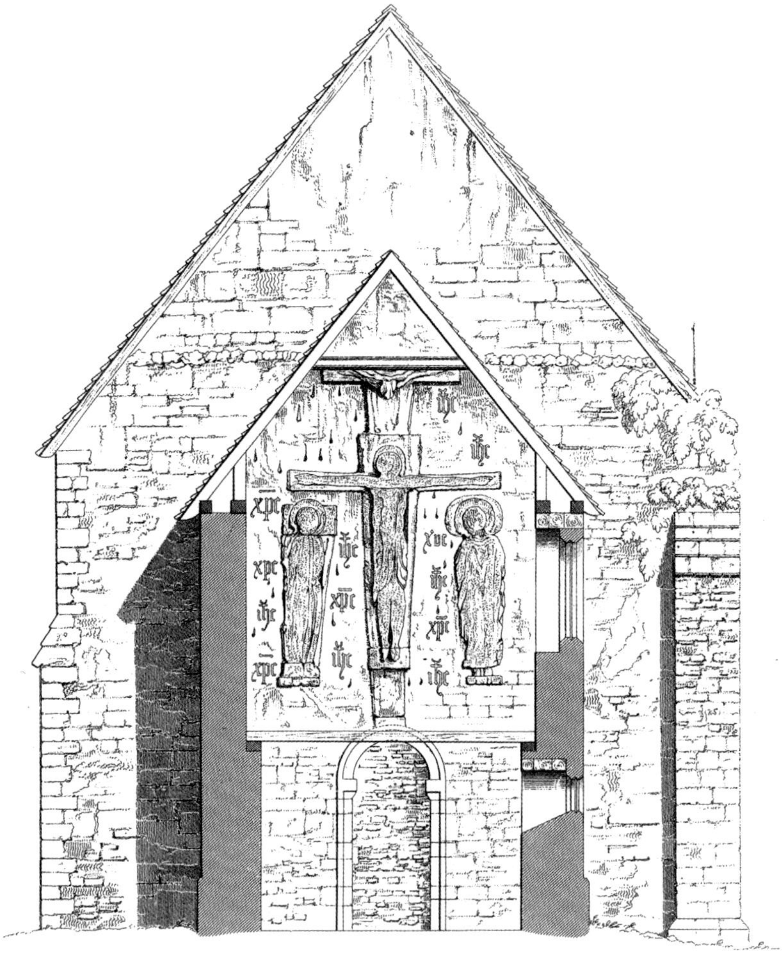

11 Headbourne Worthy (Hampshire), west end of parish church, engraving of 1844 showing pre-Conquest Rood, cut back at the Reformation

facing page 12 Naumburg Cathedral (Saxony-Anhalt), west choir screen, mid-thirteenth century

Another prompt to movement of mind and the passions is the generally smaller domain of ornament.[37] The powers of art exert themselves along with meaning or mimesis: we see simultaneously not just what something is or may be, but how it is done. Like large images, complex workmanship instantly creates a special situation or occasion which puts the unaccustomed spectator under pressure: art makes demands of us. Doorways in medieval art commonly witness extraordinary concentrations of the finest workmanship, whether on the door leaves themselves or – because more survive – on their frames. Not long after

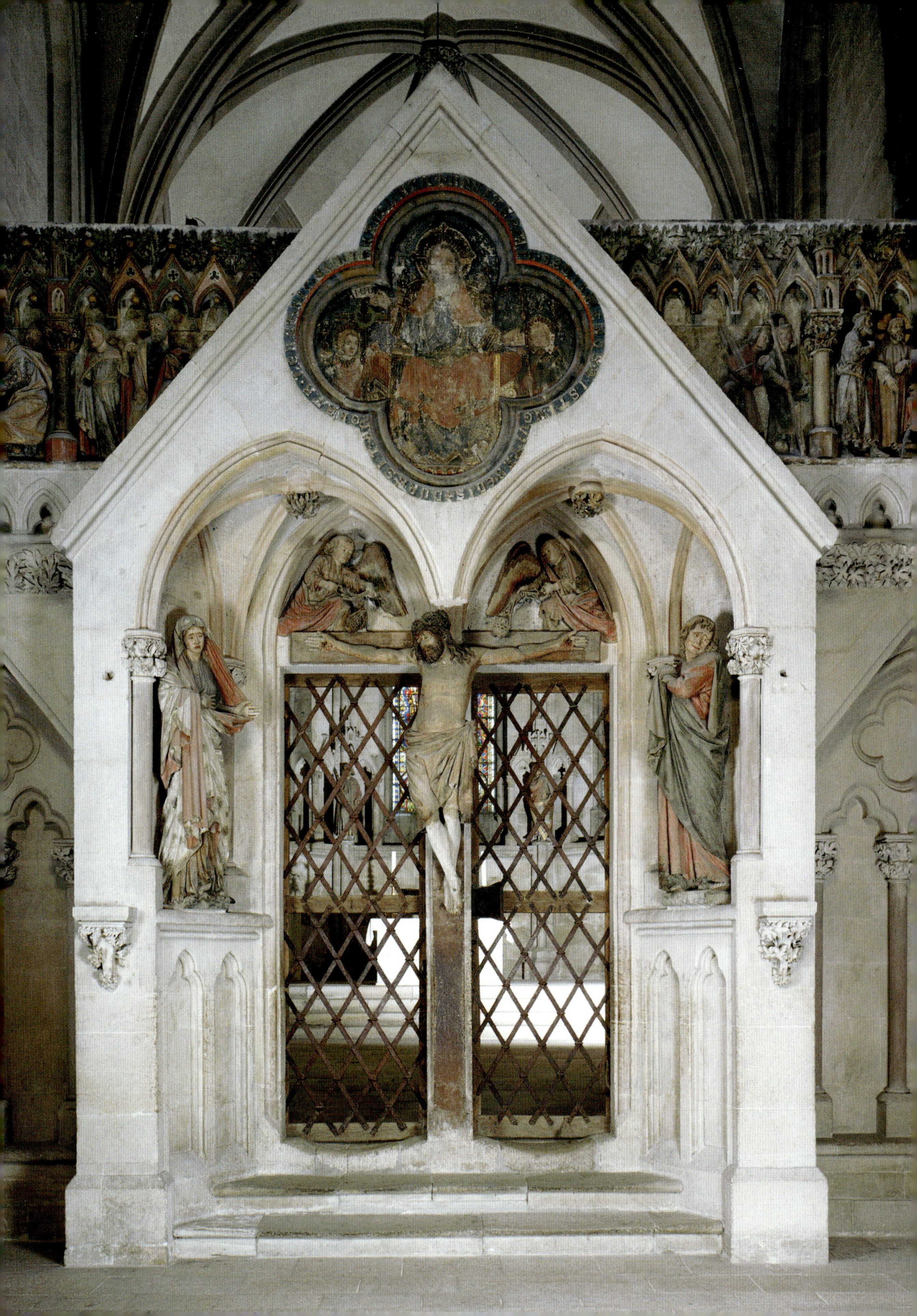

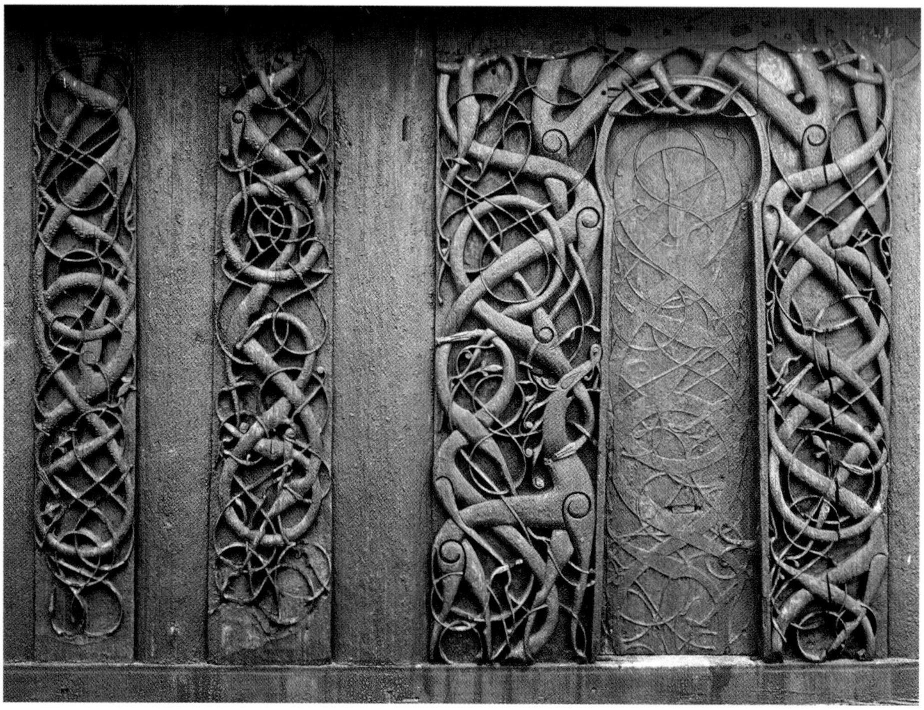

13 Urnes, Norway, stave church, north portal, eleventh century

facing page 14 Kilpeck (Herefordshire), parish church, south portal, mid-twelfth century

the Cross at Headbourne Worthy was made, Scandinavian woodcarvers were creating bravura concentrations of abstract ornamental and zoomorphic forms as on the eleventh-century wooden portal to the stave church at Urnes in Norway (pl. 13). The balanced yet dynamic weaving and tangling of forms of contrasting thickness and thinness at Urnes is instantly captivating, well described by George Henderson as conveying a 'hypnotic flow and ebb of sinuous snake-like necks and bodies and limbs, rubbery and smooth' with a 'chilly elegance'.[38] Technique, mastery, exquisite calculation assert themselves instantly, for the processes entailed are self-evidently difficult. The narrowness of the gate, at Urnes itself keyhole-shaped, stifling and perilous, intensifies the encounter. Here truly is the 'narrow gate' of Heaven. Such doors were themselves often covered in complex scrolling ironwork to extend the display of skill across their surface, as on the splendid forged forms on the doorway from Fåberg stave church, also in Norway.[39] This same balance of effects can be seen on the quite modestly scaled south doorway of the English parish church at Kilpeck in Herefordshire of *c.*1140 (pl. 14), where the door hinges complement the scrolled 'tree of life' detailing on the tympanum and the rubbery entanglements on the shafts.[40]

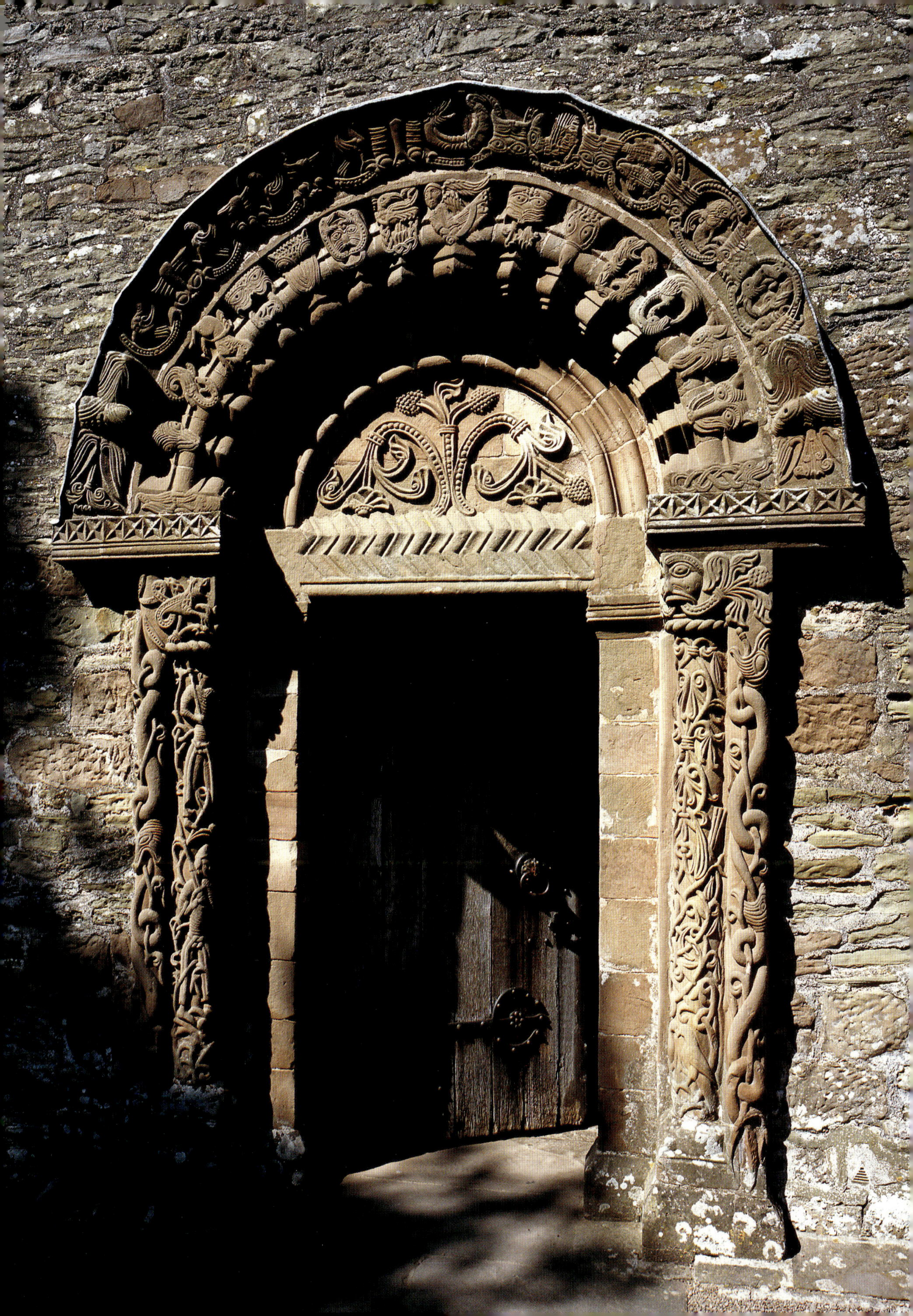

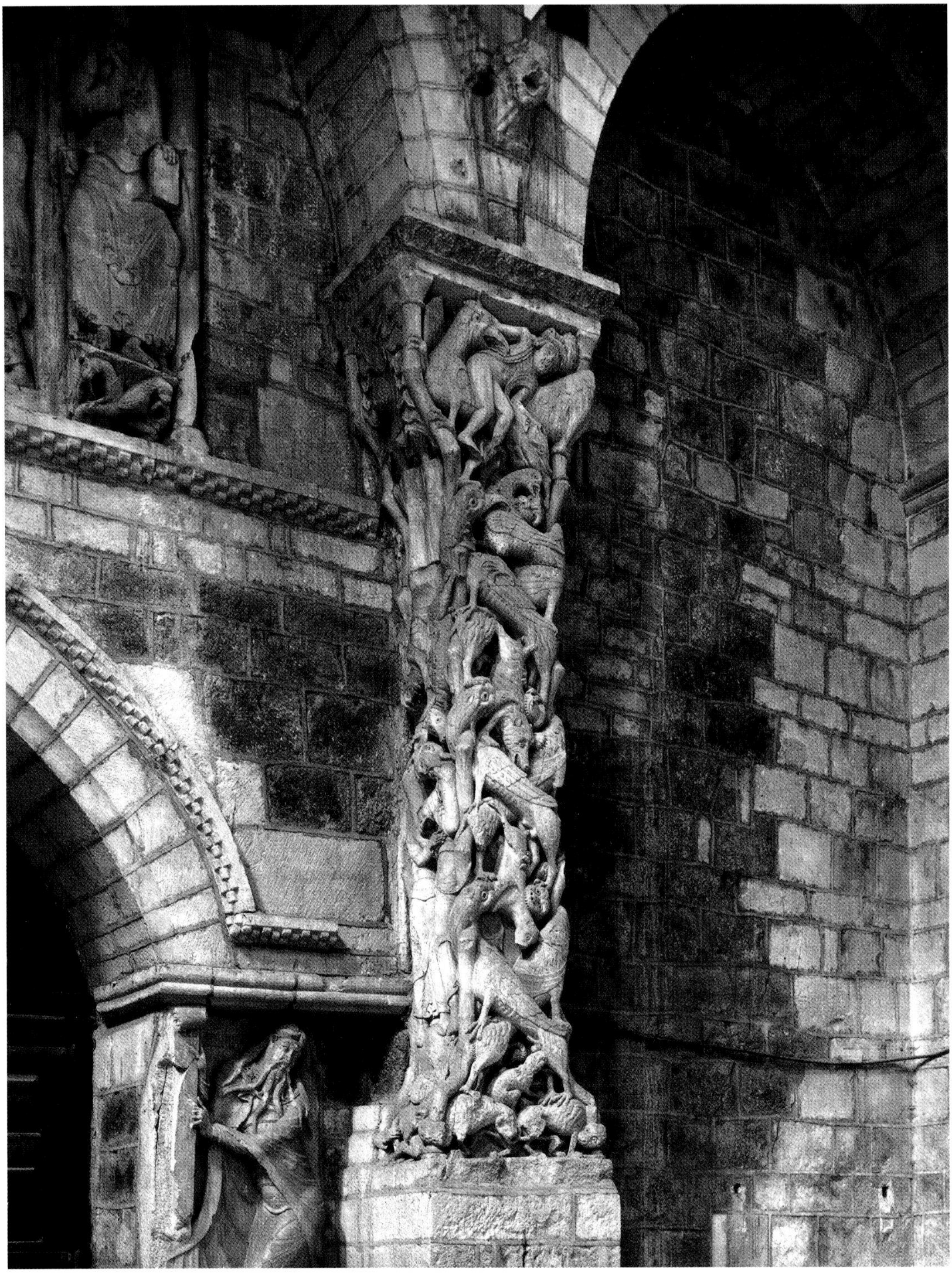

15 Souillac Abbey (Lot), inner west portal, trumeau with Isaiah (lower left) and story of Theophilus (top left), about 1120

The 'hypnotic' ebb and flow of such weaving might make us think of some ecstatic loss of sensibility, of some form of fear or enchantment, even that 'enchantment of technology' written of by Alfred Gell in an astute appreciation of the effects of artistic technique.[41] However, enchantment is a form of *force majeure* working on a possibly unwilling subject. The idea of the operation of spells, *incantatio*, had negative connotations in the Middle Ages just as the association of certain forms of linear art with 'transcendental' racial sensibility has an unfortunate history in modern art criticism of the psychological sort.[42] The whole point of magic is that it overcomes choice. Ornament, in contrast, helps to order perception, moving, emphasising and punctuating, creating a *ductus* or flow out of apparent disorder back into something more comprehensible and familiar.[43] This is a point made by structuralist analyses of carved ornament or of the hierarchical and compositional basics of large figurative sculptures which disturb then restore or assert order.[44] It is affirmed by the role of mobile, interlaced, even labyrinthine, literary structures which initially provoke amazement, understood in its Middle English sense as 'astonished, bewildered'.[45]

This is not an issue of medium or of style 'period'. The role of ornament is to energise, to engage, to give pleasure, to steer and to create an occasion as much as it is to subordinate or order things, as on the bravura displays on French Romanesque and earlier Gothic portals of the first half of the twelfth century at Moissac or Souillac or Chartres. On Chartres's great mid-twelfth-century west front (see pl. 6), the vertical expanses intervening between the column figures are all as wrought and busy, infested even, as any wood-carved or ivory object. Mary Carruthers writes of the role of ornament and emotion in kick-starting the 'way' in regard to the no less weird, seething and squirming art of the trumeau (the central column dividing two entrances) and its associated sculptures on the inner west wall of the abbey church of Souillac (pl. 15), working to create an inner animation or restlessness, a mood, which is but the prelude to meditation.[46] The comparable tangled metalwork art of the tall base of the early twelfth-century Gloucester candlestick associated with St Peter's Abbey at Gloucester also points forward to a kind of resolution or reordering by means of the text on its greasepan, which promotes the virtue of sustaining light over the shadow of vice.[47] This is a feature too of the great Apocalypse door at Moissac (*c.*1115 or earlier?) with its forbidding square-shouldered image of Christ (pl. 16 and see pl. 4), below which is an extraordinary knotted trumeau between the odd clamping jaw-like outer flanks of the portal, curved into strange and not entirely hospitable serrations.[48] The ensuing mood might be one of anxiety or puzzlement, partly because of the pile-up of writhing forms, partly because the language of perilous entanglement and ensnaring as a prelude to moral and spiritual work, fleshed out by the common Romanesque image of humans and animals trapped in coils of foliage in manuscript illuminations and sculptures, was deeply implicated in Christian discourse: Augustine himself had written of the *immensa silva*, the great dark thickets, of temptation and sin.[49]

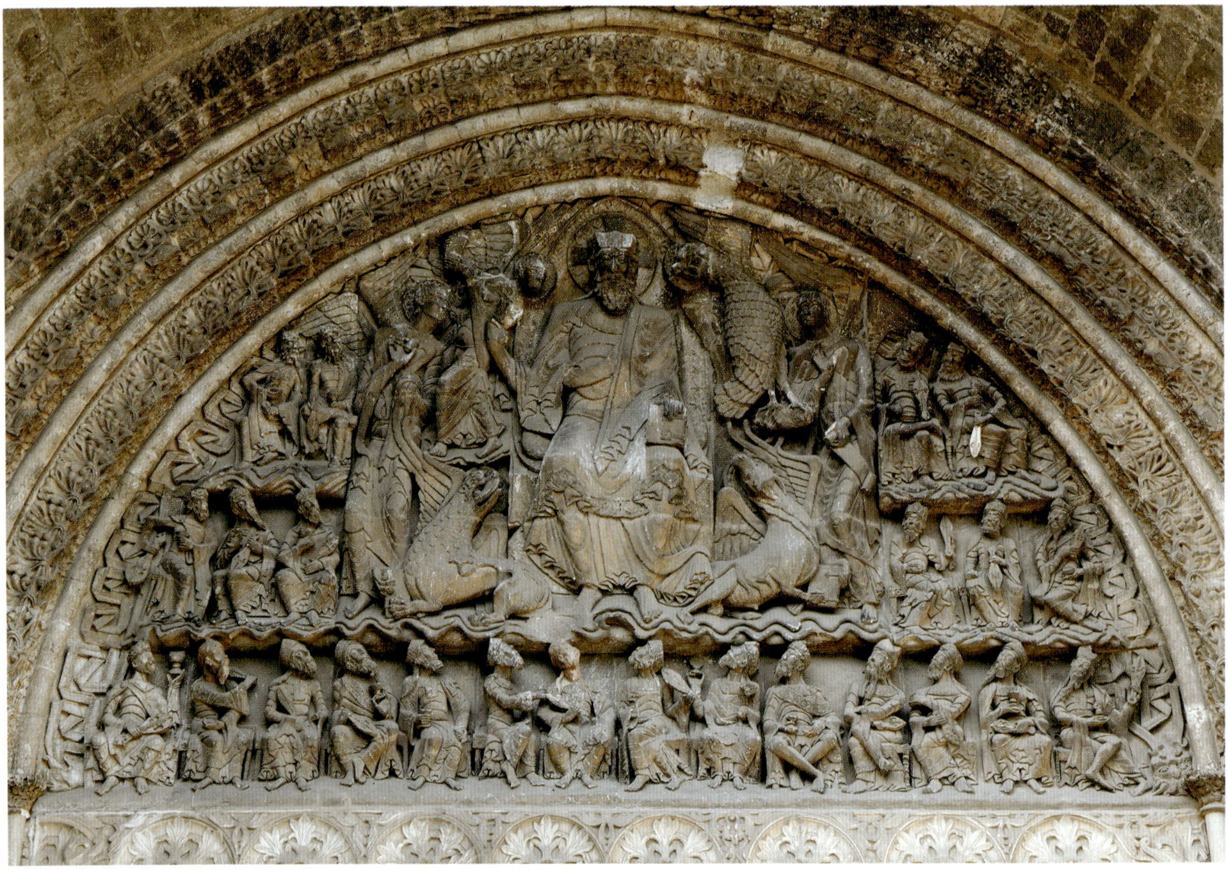

16 Moissac Abbey (Tarn-et-Garonne), south-west portal tympanum with Majesty of Christ, Evangelist symbols and Twenty-Four Elders, early twelfth century

facing page 17 Batalha Abbey, Portugal, junction of east end and entrance to the *capellas imperfeitas* or 'unfinished chapels', intended as a mausoleum for the Kings of Portugal but largely abandoned by 1517

But above all this was a larger continuity, for the culture of wonderful intricate effects around entrances was largely unbroken between the time of Urnes and the staggering portal arch in the *capellas imperfeitas* at the east end of the monastery of Santa Maria da Vitória at Batalha in Portugal, undertaken for King Dom Manuel I (d. 1521) in the early sixteenth century (pl. 17).[50] The total impact of these great doorways, to say nothing of their subject matter, can be both powerful and distancing in the sense that, momentarily, we step back before looking closer. That the eliciting of admiration and a sense of expectation was part of their intention is presumable. These experiences might relate to the workmanship provoking wonder, that initial questioning which precedes reasoned reflection

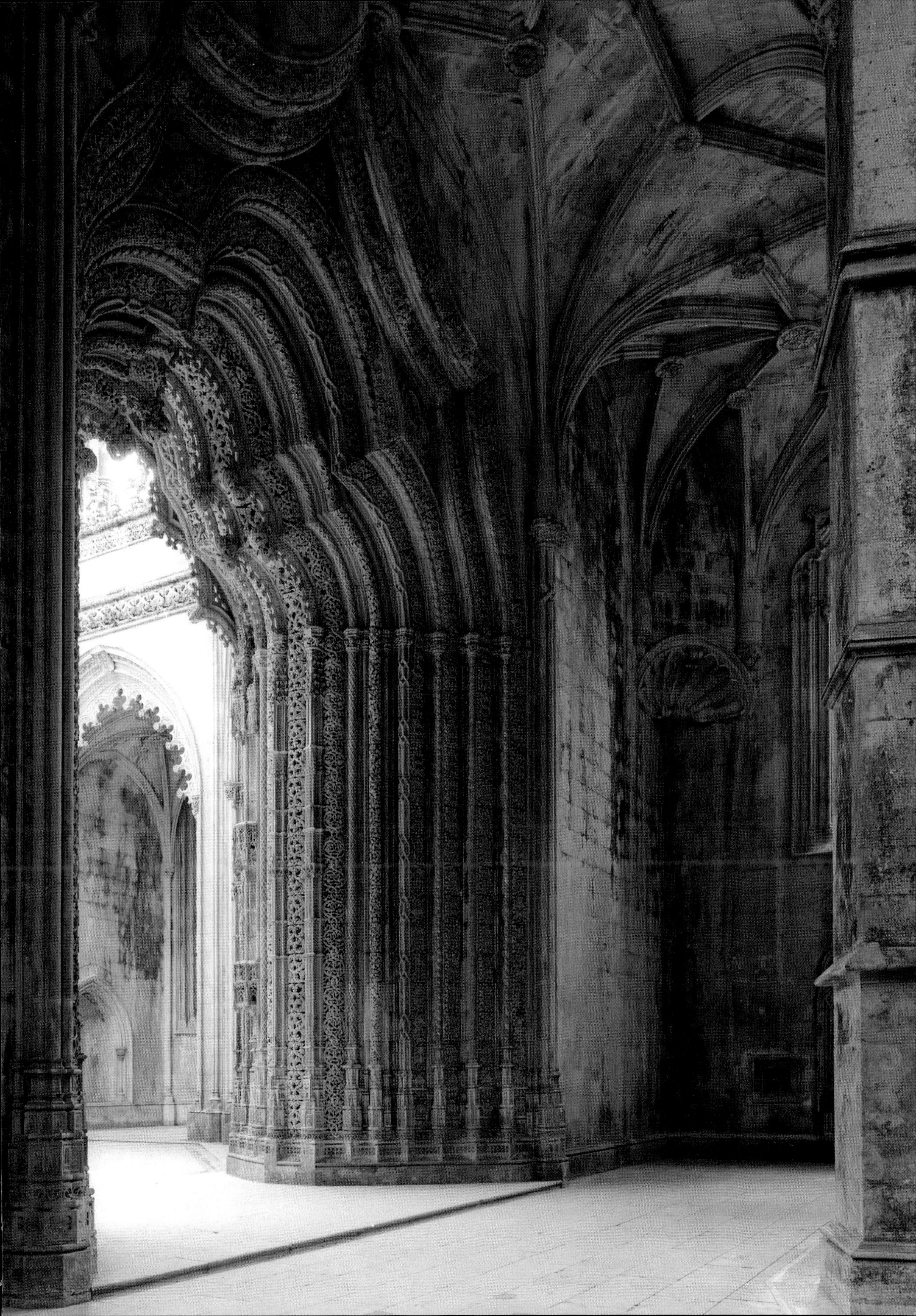

on 'how it was done'.[51] *Hoc opus eximium vario celamine mirum* – 'this extraordinary work, a marvel of varied relief' – as it says on the twelfth-century apse reliefs from Königslutter.[52] *Varietas* in particular always carried weight: one of the most valued aesthetic qualities of a complex work of art or literary text, a suitably governed variety is a medieval commonplace.[53] Variety and wonder-responses were associated. Ascetic critics understood this well, as did the rhetoricians, for whom virtue and vice were never far apart in matters regarding ornament, or indeed anything interesting aesthetically.[54] Ornament helped to guide attention, but within limits: too much, and we lose track and become subject to error and curiosity; too little, and the opportunity to guide, establish mood or just impress and dignify is lost too. Not surprisingly, some accounts of art in the course of the twelfth century connected the skill of artists to the risk of distraction or delusion. The moral position on variety 'gone wrong' to the point of *curiositas* was that by its distractive ability it threatened what we would now call 'mindfulness'. We might say that the peril of enchantment was played up by ascetic critics precisely in order to expose this difficulty. An instance is the account of the patronage of William, Bishop of Le Mans in the 1150s, which mentions a chamber he built and decorated for himself, evoked in a string of verbal commonplaces. Its workmanship surpassed the materials; next to it was a chapel with painted images, admirably (*ammirabili*) resembling living creatures, which held both the eyes and the minds of spectators enrapt in such a way that their pleasure made them forget their business there, so deluded (*delusi*) were they.[55]

That passage is not about sculpture but it helps us understand the simultaneous preoccupation, an ascetic preoccupation, with delight and distraction in the arts generally. Enchantment was precisely the risk – outright loss of judgement. More usually, reflection consisted of an active sensory and intellectual weighing up, a different matter from delusion. In its appreciation of the elegance and complexity of the marble used in the new choir of Lincoln Cathedral begun in the 1190s, the *Metrical Life of St Hugh of Lincoln* of *c.*1220 states that, on close inspection, the stone can 'suspend minds' in trying to decide what kind of stone was used, jasper or marble.[56] Ruskin, a great critic of Gothic, thought of complex ornament of this type as being not merely visible but 'sensible'.[57] Of all rhetorical experts, the one who most often supplies analogies to the non-verbal arts, Quintilian, notes that display oratory precisely sets out its wares as if for 'handling' (his chosen verb for this is *pertracto*).[58] So the fact that sculpture is actually or potentially tactile may matter to our apprehension of it: things are 'turned over' in the mind. In this process affective content need not be any more exact than mood, for affective content seldom is exact: affects (*affectus*) are more like movements and sensations than what we might call emotions or passions.[59]

The key issue in all these regards, I want to stress, is not enchantment but engagement. Engagement is a pledge requiring mindfulness, intention, will. This is not an issue of psychology, of personal emotion or taste, but of an affirmable, tangible social or public agency that acts on and with people. It is in the public domain and it can be agreed – and disagreed – about. This is why liminality theory does not exactly capture the experience or purpose of sculpted portals. Liminality theory is about special places or states of mind, and emphasises not the idea of continuity but of separation and change. It claims that in the midst of transition, human subjects are in an out of the ordinary condition, a bracketed off state, before they are reincorporated into a new state.[60] Because not every passage through a doorway was necessarily a sacramental event, a life threshold, such an idea is too ambitious to capture a sense of the ordinary social usage of doorways and of daily progress through them. Remarkable as they are and clearly always were, such portals do not automatically engender out of the ordinary experiences actively separate or discontinuous from the routine course of daily life and thought. They were things to get through, indivisibly connected by the thread of process and movement to what had gone before, and to what came next. They were socially and habitually embedded.

This processual thought brings me to the fundamental connection between engagement, experience and conviction or confidence, what Jean de Joinville, in his mid-thirteenth-century *Romans as Ymages*, called *ferme creance*.[61] Any disorientating sensation is but a prelude to reorientation (literally, directing us again towards the east). A portal should be seen in itself as an *exordium* or *introit*, an opening statement which establishes the occasion, direction, tone or mood for what follows.[62] The viewer is intended first to be captivated and suitably disposed. Rhetoricians spoke of this as *captatio benevolentiae*: so Cicero (*De Inventione* 1.15) tells us that by means of an exordium an audience should be made *benevolum, attentum, docilem* – well disposed, attentive and receptive (literally 'teachable'), an objective also set out in the medieval *artes praedicandi*, manuals of the arts of preaching.[63] This capturing requires arousal and so stimulus, sparkle, the fancy fly that leads the fish to the hook. As when a great medieval illuminated book is opened at its initiating pages and the first flashes of gold, colour and ornament are witnessed, there is a momentary standing-back in awe, a gasp of appreciation, *admiratio*. Curiosity follows, and curiosity is a thrusting forwards of attention in such a way as to take in, assimilate, what is perceived.[64] The artwork duly thrusts back. It is not difficult to pinpoint medieval sculptural genres that played consciously on opening and closing to enact a revelation: one such would be the dynamics of the shrine Madonna or *vièrge ouvrante*, a type of statue of the Virgin and Child the front of which opened up to reveal an image of the Trinity located mysteriously within.[65] So it is with the genre of the stone portal, for these effects are not solely monumental but pertain to all highly wrought things. That is why the omission of practical considerations of technique and crafting from the discussion of art agency is unhelpful. For one thing, a display of colour and artifice helps create a mood or predisposition as well as a feeling of expectancy, of anticipation.

Social, public perception matters: the very fact of monumentality, of great scale, is vital to understanding the occasion of portal sculpture. Here it is necessary to think of portals

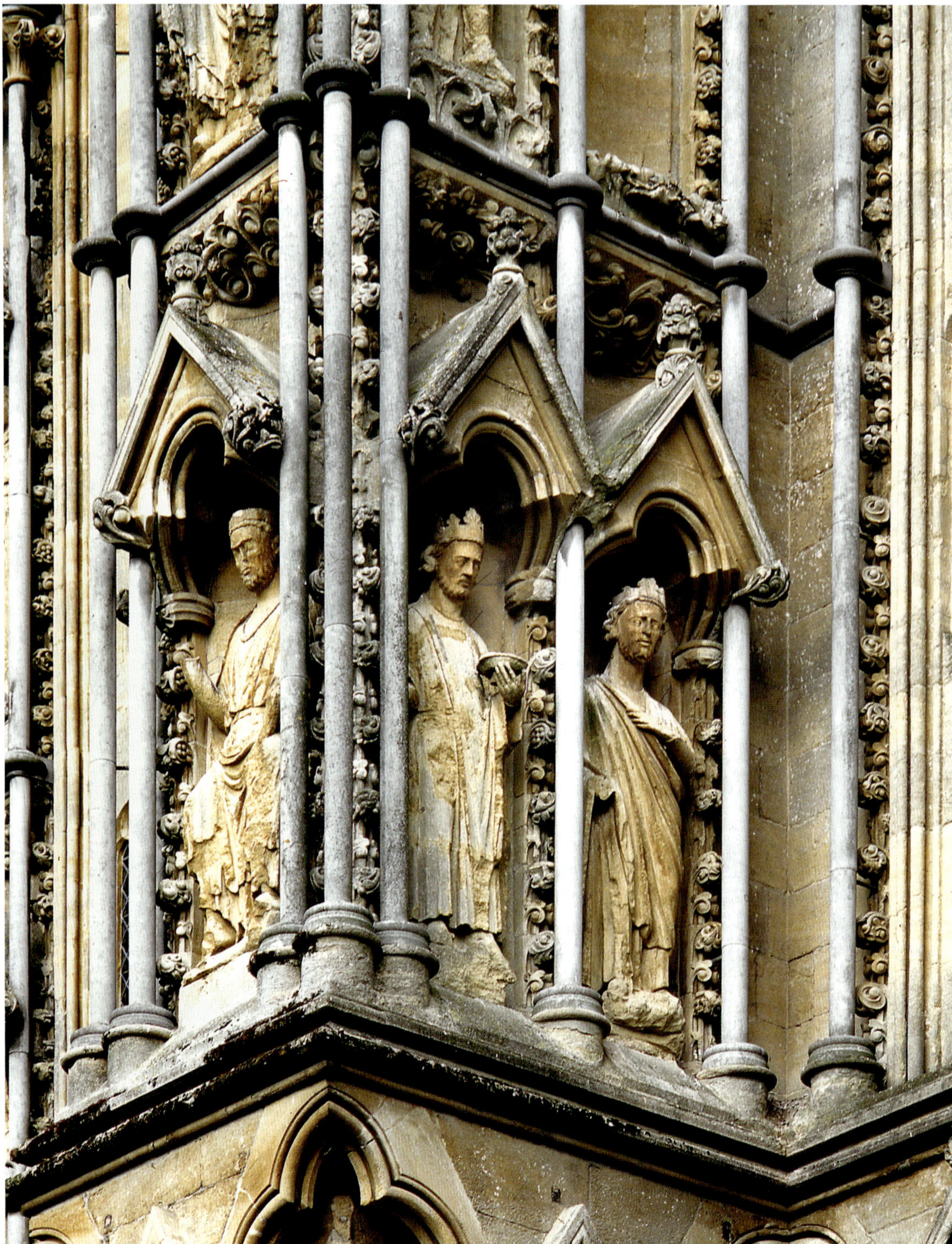

18 Wells Cathedral, west front, kings on north tower buttress

generically – as having a resemblance of kind – rather than formally, in terms of their specific 'looks'. Formal discussion of portal sculpture certainly matters because forms, materials and surfaces possess agency. But form has also been allowed too much priority in understanding the fundamental work that the portal, as a genre, actually does. Impress and splendour of a general type count here. We have only to stand awestruck before the giant looming caverns on the Gothic west front at Amiens Cathedral, a veritable mountain range of imagery, or gaze up at the great cliff face peppered with small, deep openings that is the west front of Wells (of the same years; pl. 18 and see pl. 9), to understand that monumentality is both uplifting and challenging. And at the same time we have to squint. Monumentality throws into relief the contrapuntal role the miniature has in the effect of such ensembles, for the great and small are always related tactically, and this is apparent in the enclosure within the huge architectural forms of great Gothic portals of numerous far smaller versions of the same architectural and other forms, amplifying and broadening the effect.[66] Telescopic changes of scale are initially fascinating, paradoxical. In writing of English artworks such as the punctured and inhabited facade at Wells, Jean Bony said poetically that 'overtones of dream or mystery always accompany the hollowing-out of masses of masonry'.[67] When discussing affliction and reading, Peter of Celle (d. 1183) said that the mind has greater expansive leisure within a small room than outside: 'the smaller the place the more extended the mind, for when the body is constrained the mind takes flight'.[68] In one of his astonishing sermons on the Song of Songs (no. 62), St Bernard of Clairvaux (d. 1153) actually engages in a flight of the mind to contemplate imaginatively the dove lodged in the clefts of the rock (Canticles 2:14) with the mental aid of an immense geological-theological image-stuffed stone formation of a type comparable to the great west front at Wells (see pl. 9); grand yet detailed, the vision paints for us the inhabited nooks and crannies which move the mind and heart and which fulfil our desire for incorporation into God:

> That wall of soft stone crumbles and gives way to the soul's desire, yields to pure contemplation and frequent prayer ... For 'to him who knocks it will be opened' [Matthew 7:8]. So it is within the power of each of us, even during our mortal life, to hollow out a place in the heavenly wall anywhere we like: as we like, now to visit the patriarchs, now to greet the prophets, now to mingle with the assembly of apostles, now to join the choirs of martyrs, even to run with the speed of mind that devotion gives us through the ranks and dwellings of the blessed angels, from the lowest even to the Cherubim and Seraphim. And if we stand and knock where we have been drawn, inwardly moved as the Spirit wills, [the door] will be opened to us at once ... God finds delight in such crannies; from them rings out the sound of gratitude, the sound of wonder and adoration.[69]

Isidore of Seville, to whom medieval scholars often turned for the sense of words in the Middle Ages, reminds readers when writing of tombs that a monument is so named

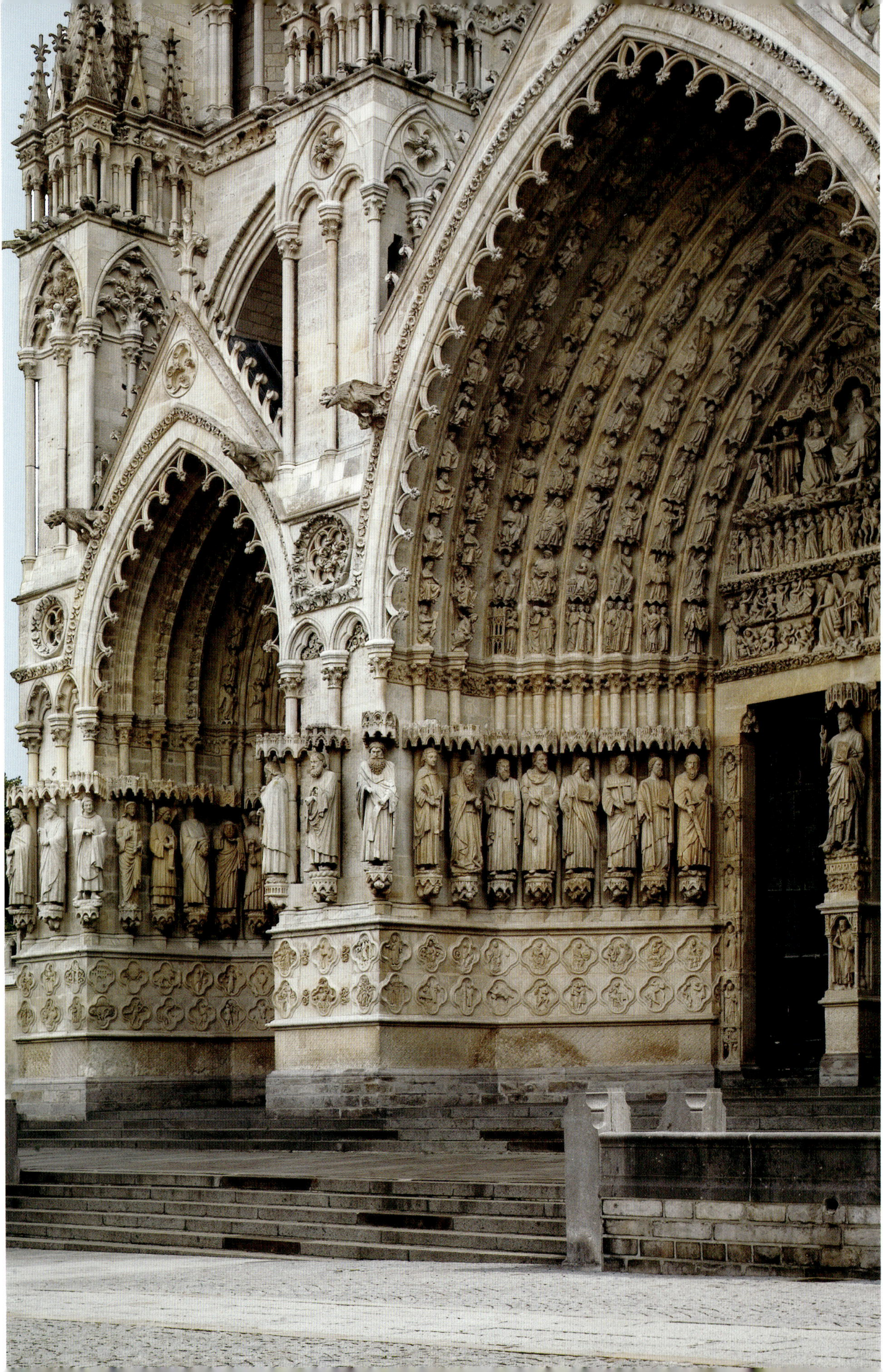

because it 'admonishes the mind to remember the deceased person .... Thus both "monument" and "memory" are so called from "the admonition of the mind (*mentis admonitio*)".'[70] Portals are not tombs, but it is not wrong to think of them monumentally, and in that sense Isidore's conception of mental admonition is helpful to us. Such facades may stand before us four-square and showily ornate like a Roman triumphal arch; they may, as at Lincoln, actually emulate the form and grandeur of triumphal arches; and as at Wells, these giant and mysterious complexes help serve the end of institutional self-affirmation.[71] The fact that these sculpted fronts are often thickly populated with images reminds us too of the major Christian tradition of likening the Church as a whole to a celestial city, in the tradition of Augustine and Beatus of Liébana.[72]

The point about such visions is not simply that their physical presence is city-like: their entire imaginary is social, experienced at all times and in all conditions, and in whatever mood we ourselves may be in. For what is personal psychology and mood in the face of the *ecclesia militans* and *ecclesia triumphans*, or the *ecclesia celestis*? It is in the light of this social imaginary that we can understand the way in which some facades, such as that at Wells, were designed to enhance liturgical occasions through, among other things, music, since at Wells (and also Salisbury and Lichfield) provision was made within the structure of the west wall for singers' galleries opening westwards with megaphone-like openings, projecting sung sound on such occasions as the singing of the Gloria Laus on Palm Sunday.[73]

Portals affect and create expectation; they promise something; they propose, regardless of their specific formal appearance. When the giant sculpted portals of Amiens were being completed towards the middle of the thirteenth century (pl. 19), one of the cathedral's canons, Richard de Fournival, compiled his *Bestiaire d'amours*, in which the faculty of memory has two gates (*portes*) of access, one of *painture* (sic) and the other of *parole*, sight and sound.[74] These doorways were loquacious and rhetorically 'intended' as their Gothic successors. That is why we can think authentically of 'portal talk' even though Gothic portals tend not to have as many boldly carved inscriptions as their Romanesque predecessors. Such doorways worked in the first instance in the public, not the private domain, the domain of the city rather than the family. Public liturgical experience is fundamental to this since, as Eric Palazzo has suggested, common and fundamental concepts such as the theology of the Eucharist were mediated by the senses in what he calls a 'sacramental effect', a form of general argument rooted in shared sensation.[75] For this reason rhetorical thought about invention and persuasion took interest in the *locus communis*, the commonplace or 'common topic', in essence a form of generally agreed argument that could be transferred to many cases.[76] Richard de Fournival's image of the portals as mnemonic devices is one such. The public monument was itself a *lieu commun* as well as a *lieu de mémoire*.[77] Place comes before person. 'We' have priority over 'you' or 'me'.

19 Amiens Cathedral (Somme), west front central (Last Judgement) and north (St Firmin) portals, 1220s–1240s

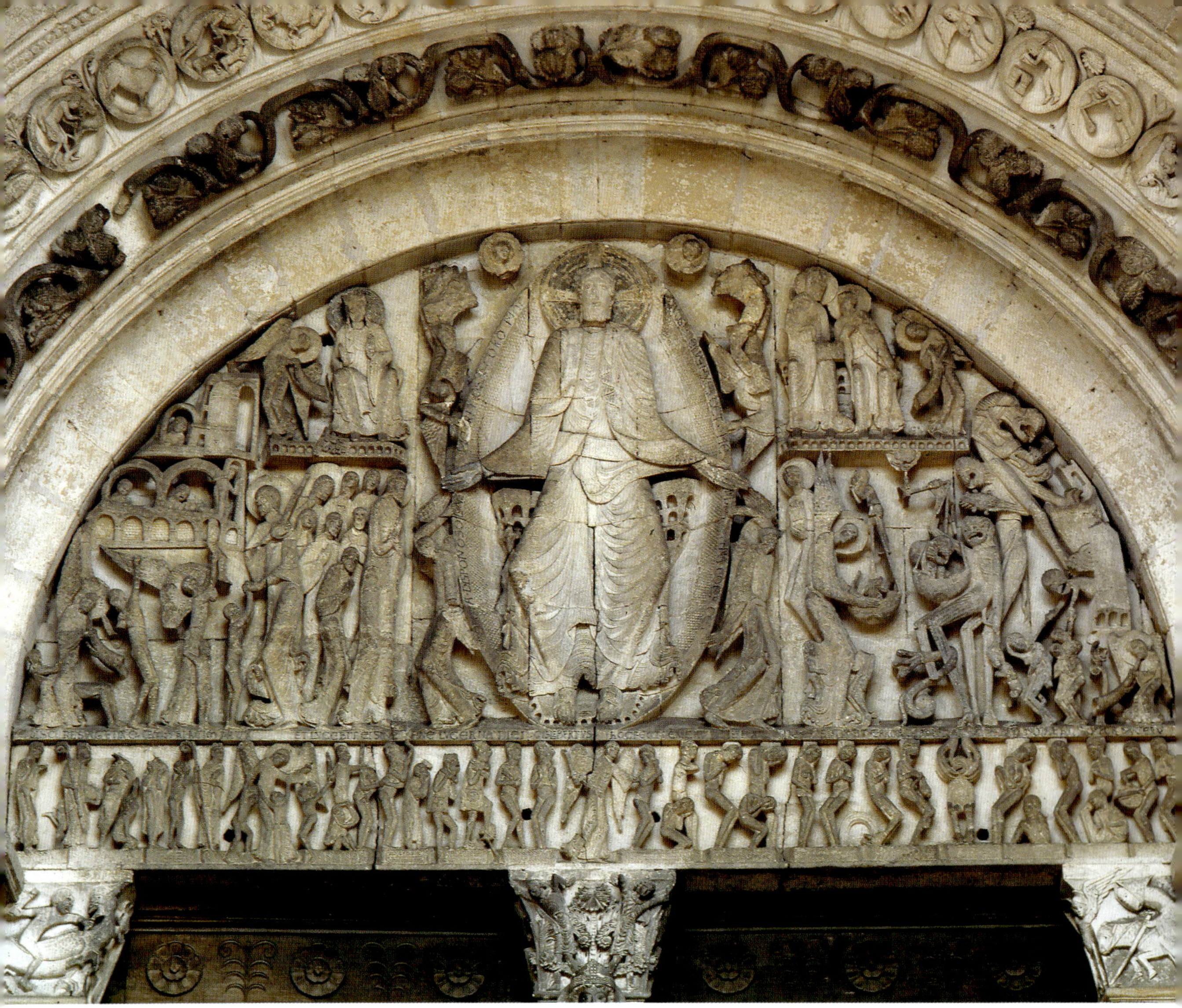

20 Autun Cathedral (Sâone-et-Loire), west portal tympanum with Last Judgement signed by Gislebertus, about 1130

I would like to press this point in order to stress not the ease but the artistic difficulty of planning and manufacturing any artwork intended for the public domain. In his brilliant and engaging lectures about Romanesque sculpture of the sort at Autun in Burgundy (pl. 20 and see pl. 24), Meyer Schapiro took it as axiomatic that the revival of monumentality was central to the rise of the great portals in the eleventh and twelfth centuries.[78] They were the natural companion of greatly enlarged stone churches. In stressing the importance of the new urban contexts of such portals, Schapiro also drew a distinction between the domain of monumental exterior sculpture and the liturgically dominated interior. The first was a space of what he calls 'free discourse', as opposed to the constraint of the interior world of liturgy, ritual.[79] This distinction tends to overlook the role that both *ludus* and convention play in all aesthetic experience, regardless of physical context.[80] Schapiro concedes that even the free externality of urban space was not entirely asocial, for it was a place of trade, the administration of justice, of marriage ceremonies: what characterised his notion of such external space was its secularity. He was not exactly concerned with the private and public, but with the modernist issues of freedom and constraint, the marginal and the central.[81] Yet of late, far more energy has been spent in privileging and pondering a private or personal sphere of creation, response or 'reception' and self-realisation. We have spent so long asking how medieval art might answer to personal moods and individual affects that we have forgotten to enquire just how difficult it is to create arts in the social domain, no matter how free or unfree.

One, though not the sole, reason for this has been the tacit acceptance by medievalists of an idea, a model, of the public and private spheres as historically separate things gifted with different potentialities (another is the economy of 'affect' to which I return later). This model has been described at length by Hans Belting. He maintains that the private image of the late Middle Ages followed the era of the public image and that 'whereas the private images served up one modernism after another, the old became a preserve of traditions in need of protection'.[82] In effect the public domain was doomed to conservatism. This admittedly broad thinking has landed us in difficulties. Aside from the historically problematical nature of the public–private distinction itself, the notion that the public arts of the Middle Ages were not progressive but conservative forces, and that private or personal consciousness could be hived off as automatically asocial, progressive and possessed of its own sphere of action, can and should be challenged. In her discussion of agency and social structure Sara Beckwith rightly reminds us that we should not make the 'assumption that the realm of the "subjective" and the realm of the "mystical" are automatically asocial', because in doing so we are 'in danger of making a very modern, post-Romantic opposition between self and society'.[83] In thinking anachronistically in this way, we overlook the manifest ability of richly conceived monumental artworks to operate at several levels for different audiences or 'interpretative communities', as well as the socio-aesthetic bonds of artifice or constraint (which I want to stress throughout these pages) that connect art and conduct and which rise above modern understandings of subjectivity.[84] Any account of the richness of these artworks should be free of progressive or teleological models of the 'rise of the individual' type. It should be alert to the plurality of all experience within forms of human activity such as art reception, where consensus is desirable but not compulsory: consensus in this case means agreement not about outcome but about what matters and what is engaging and credible.

In imagining social consensus we think especially of the public sphere of rhetorical engagement as envisioned by social theorists writing in the wake of Jürgen Habermas's formulations of the public sphere.[85] Habermas drew a distinction between pre-modern or feudal 'representational cultures', in which power showed itself through overwhelming effect, and the modern public sphere of critical debate. While greatness and totality of effect were undoubtedly objectives of the kind of medieval art we are considering here – perhaps supremely the giant forbidding entrances to the Gothic cathedrals – what is less clear is whether any artwork subject to daily experience is really merely 'representational' in this sense (that is, dazzling, overwhelming, beyond dispute). The domain of the common argument is also an ordinary social domain of reception, negotiation, judgement and conviction – agreeing as to what is worth thinking but also arguing about.[86] Admittedly, such concepts are generalised and cannot possess the type of social or institutional specificity that historical enquiry ideally seeks. Clearly, a public is not simply a populace; a public attends to things in a way that a populace, transient and indifferent, does not. The idea of attention entails a connection between what constitutes a public and what engages it: the public is constituted by the concerns, the experiences, that the work of art itself engenders. The public in this regard is an audience formed by tacit agreements about convention or custom, that which is *ad usum* or suitable to the task to hand. This audience is not just a mass to be impressed, or for that matter a collection of individuals: the social sphere of negotiation, conversation and debate requires some adjustment of personal subjectivity to the whole, some flattening of personal response. In showing the way through and guiding, artworks operate within a social and public world whose perceptions are formed by convention and memory. Jauss's notion of the 'horizon of expectation', which insists on the location of individual experience within larger social and cultural codes, captures something of the necessary mix of freedom and constraint in viewing, as does the notion of the 'interpretative community' which also emphasises shared beliefs.[87]

This is why Schapiro's characterisation of the public space of the portal as one of free externality is not quite satisfactory. It does not take into account the social value of the *locus communis*: that argument emerges from within the artwork, not in spite of it or just in front of it. This insight allows us to bear in mind the key but often forgotten issue of everyday convention, habit and familiarity which governed the experience of medieval artworks. Reception is not just a matter of the breathtaking first encounter, of the liminal transformation of being, but of habitual daily coexistence; indeed even the term 'reception', implying something actively given and passively received, does not quite capture the two-way dynamic of engagement. With such dynamic and reciprocal coexistence comes richness of discourse. Artworks, as well as being garrulous and persuasive, are for this reason not only occasional (that is, their aesthetic effects are contextual, not absolute) but also debatable.

Debate, even among different interpretative communities, requires common ground. While the nature of an audience should not be over-determined, law is one sign of what may constitute public understanding. Taken in itself, a legal maxim might be reductive. Even so, the entry around 1140 into Gratian's compilation of canon law (the law of the Church), the *Decretals*, of a section of Pope Gregory the Great's second letter on the validity of images was decisive in virtue of the wide circulation of the *Decretals* as a universal means of ready reference for canon law.[88] The Gregorian, and so patristic, doctrine which the *Decretals* embodies is concerned with the connection between the experience and the utility of art, what work images do, what use they are. It was the starting-point for all teaching on images in the Church. Necessarily elitist or condescending, the legal emphasis on the instrumental basis of images, founded on rhetorical ideas about seeing, reading or hearing and persuasion, and intended to work round the problem of idolatry, was clear-cut and continues to be stressed by art historians.[89] The rhetorical rather than disciplinary nature of these ideas needs emphasis. Gregory's second letter is one of the first and most durable statements of the instrumental role of art in making things, like words, 'present' (of images 'as' texts he uses the verb *praestare,* to stand 'in front' or 'before' us), so provoking affect and devotion: 'It is one thing to worship a picture, it is another by means of pictures to learn thoroughly [*addiscere*] the story that should be venerated. For what writing makes present to those reading, the same picturing makes present [*praestat*] to the uneducated'.

Gregory states specifically that by means of the sight of a deed (*ut ex visione rei gestae*) a congregation might feel the burning of compunction (*ardor compunctionis*) and then prostrate themselves humbly in devotion.[90] Note the order here, basically experience, emotion, conduct. Gregory's emphasis on the utility or instrumentality of art – images are not objects to be worshipped in themselves (idols), but tools to be used – guides us towards the work that images were thought to do, quite as much as towards the bodies of meaning or doctrine they might have conveyed. They are not simply propaganda, but starting-points of a complex sort in the establishment, celebration and enactment of values. Medieval discourse allowed that a text or artefact might bring pleasure but also have utility, benefit.[91] It recognised (even it did not always serve) ulterior purposes. This was diffused particularly widely in the language of means and ends of the pastoral church, as when, in the thirteenth century, the elevation of the Host was required at Mass since by it the devotion of the faithful might be excited or stirred up (*cum propter hoc excitetur devotio fidelium*).[92]

The issue, then, is far more complex than the stabilisation of meaning according to fixed schedules of the lowest common denominator. Sculpted work establishes an occasion for the delight and moral and spiritual work which it gets going in the audience in a purposeful and beneficial way, without dictating the outcome.

CHOICE AND CONVICTION

Portals, then, should be considered socially. Their experience creates a sensation or experience of something particular – the rhetorical notion of occasion and of the monumental – which prompts our thoughts and passions in a fruitful, expectant and above all engaged process. In Gregory's formulation, as in many instances throughout the Middle Ages, stirring up, inflaming or exciting is a dimension of the function of works of art (or 'equipment': *ornamenta*) which have faith, value and benefit as their end or purpose. To some, the great carved doorways of the Romanesque and Gothic periods indeed have an unarguable end: to assert doctrinal truth, as in the case of art historians who identify in some Romanesque facades, such as that at Saint-Gilles-du-Gard in Provence with its prominent display of the Crucifixion, an assertion of orthodox Christian belief against heresy.[93] But – at the risk of truism – no artwork really has the ability to make our minds up for us by itself. For all their magnificence, large artworks operating in complex public environments cannot decide, for decision is a matter of *voluntas*, human choice and will: human subject and art object work together, are dialogic. What such doorways can do, functionally speaking, is 'intend', direct or propose.

Is there evidence that portals of this type intended aesthetically and ethically as well as theologically? Although we have virtually no hard evidence of what engagement with portals was like in the great age of their manufacture, one or two pieces of evidence are admittedly striking. Notably, given that the French-style sculpted church portal never rooted itself firmly in England, these instances are English. One, perhaps quite specialised, type of engagement is the evocation of a basilica and portal, often held to be the Pórtico de la Gloria at Compostela Cathedral (see pl. 10), in the so-called Vision of Thurkhill dated 1206. St James at Compostela was a famous pilgrimage objective for the English. In the Vision, Thurkhill, an Essex peasant, is transported and has a vision of the condition of the recently dead at the church.[94] In this case Thurkhill is in a state of ecstasy (actually paralysed), standing outside himself in a condition of absolute dislocation or rapture; what is imparted to him is not so much *visio* (sight of the palpable and 'real') as spiritual *revelatio*.[95] Thurkhill's vision is by its nature outside the norm and cannot be described as a 'close reading' (sensory, experiential or embodied) of a portal: therefore we must leave it behind.

In contrast, a more practical example of *visio*, already known to art historians, comes from an event reported in the Plantagenet domain of western France. This is found in the *Magna Vita* of St Hugh of Lincoln, written by an English monk, Adam of Eynsham.[96] Hugh, who died in 1200 and was canonised in 1220, was also the subject of an informative Latin verse or 'metrical' life which contains an extraordinary description of the building of Lincoln Cathedral in the time of Hugh's service as bishop there from 1186.[97] The events related in the *Magna Vita* occurred right at the end of Hugh's life and concerned King John of England. The story, profoundly moralising, is that in 1199, the newly acceded John visited the abbey of Fontevrault with Hugh to see the tombs of John's Angevin ancestors in the church. Together they paused before the church's portal over which was sculpted a tremendous Last Judgement:

> When they reached the portal of the church and were about to enter, there was over it a representation of the Last Judgement showing the separation of the elect from the damned, a choice example of the human sculptor's art. The bishop drew the count, who was soon to be a king, by the hand to the left side of the Judge where there were kings in full regalia amongst the damned, about to hear the words, 'Go ye cursed into everlasting fire' [Matthew 25:41]. These were being carried off by their demon tormentors into Hell. The bishop then said, 'Fix your mind always on their howls and perpetual torment, and let your heart dwell upon their unceasing punishment; by frequently recalling their misfortunes you will learn the great risks those incur who for a short space of time are set over others as rulers'. He said also that such sculptures or pictures were at the entrances to churches for a very good reason, namely that those about to enter and pray to God in their need, should understand what would be their last and final extremity and so would pray for forgiveness for their sins. By such prayers they would be secure from torment and enjoy everlasting happiness. . . . Drawing the bishop with him, John crossed over to the opposite side and pointed out to him kings, made conspicuous by their splendid crowns, conducted in joy by angels to the King of Heaven. 'My lord bishop,' he said, 'you should have shown us these, whom we intend to imitate and whose company we desire to join.'[98]

The first point noted is that the representation was a fine instance of the human sculptor's art (*eleganter satis pro modulo humani exprimitur artificii opere sculptoris*). Thereby an occasion is created: the text becomes a set piece, to which the portal as something striking is an entry literally and figuratively. At first John seemed to get the point of the sculptures when he replied to Hugh that, having seen the saved kings he would imitate their example. That he was motivated by personal advantage and not fear is shown by the surrounding narratives in the *Vita* exemplifying John's superstition, avarice and greed: that the lessons offered by the portal did *not* result in the intended actions, because John was too essentially wicked for them to take hold.[99] When it came to the carrot and stick of moral incentive, John preferred the carrot. His apparent fearlessness in the face of this display is not a sign of courage but of moral stupidity or blindness. At this point the text goes on to refer to John's 'darkened mind' and cites Proverbs 18:3: 'The wicked man takes no heed, however great the evils that befall him.' In life, as we know, John went on to choose poorly.

That Hugh was able to give an account of the end or purpose of such a portal in straightforwardly Gregorian terms matters. The *Magna Vita* shows that around 1200 it could be assumed that such images were intended to impress both heart and mind, the bishop in this case saying that John should always summon up the sounds and sights before both his mind and the eyes of his heart (*vobis ante cordis oculos*), because by frequent recollection (*sedula recordatio*) he would get the message and translate it into action.[100] The portal thus has an

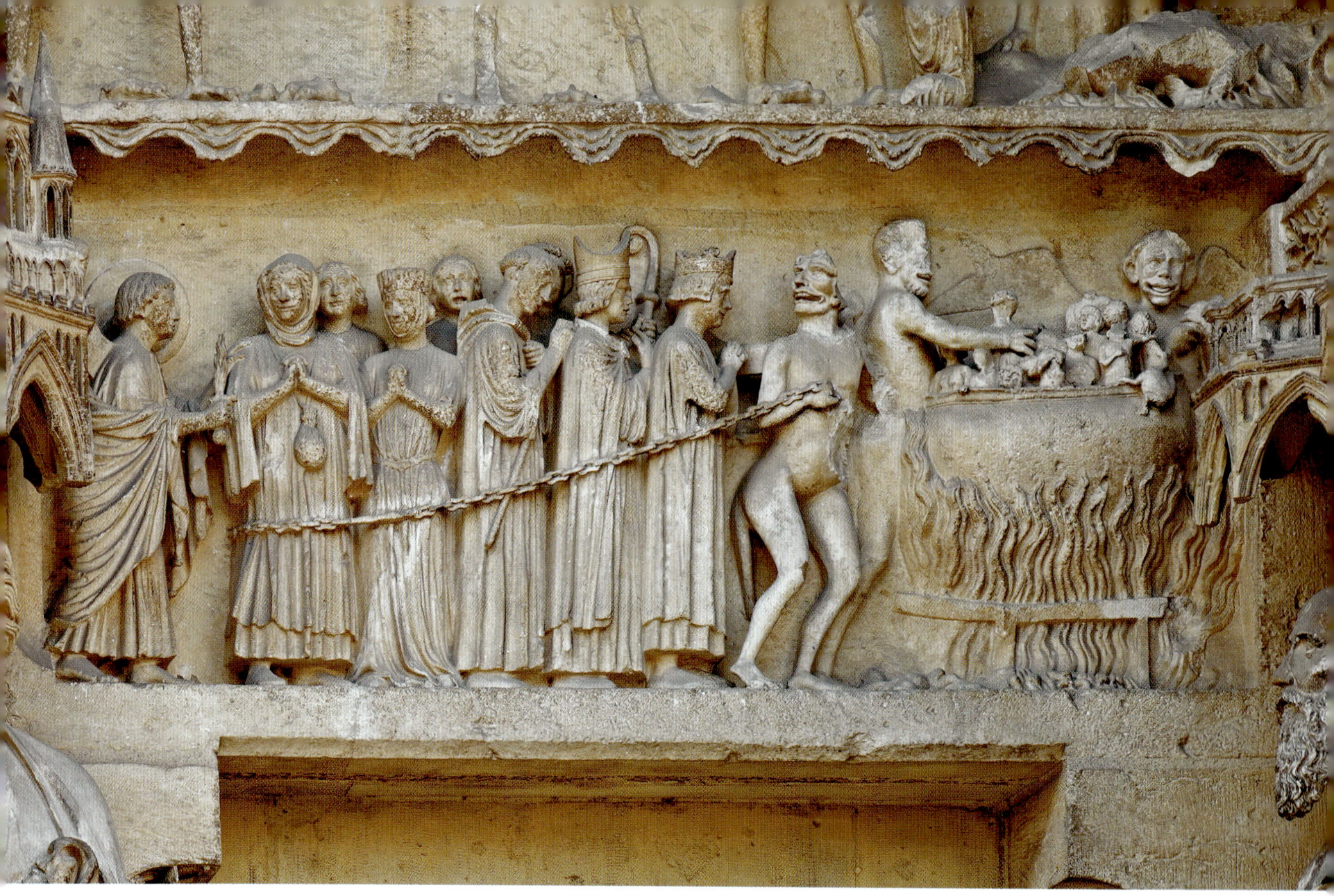

21 Reims Cathedral (Marne), north transept central portal, Last Judgement, detail of different social estates led to Hell, 1220s

facing page 22 Fontevrault Abbey (Maine-et-Loire), fragments of sculpture perhaps from a Last Judgement discovered in 1984, about 1200

end, which is the attainment of the felicity and salvation of its witnesses. That this particular work of art failed to make a moral impress is secondary: an artefact may have some sort of intrinsic aim, but that does not guarantee that this aim will be achieved.[101] Notably, in the step made from representation to memory, no mention at all is made of John's emotional response to the art. What John 'feels' about or towards this depiction is not mentioned.

Is this account 'realistic' rather than just conventional? Conventions inform life and thought. The detail of Hugh taking John by the hand and leading him round the sculpture and pointing out its features is a classic instance of an ekphrasis, a verbal-visual 'tour' around something.[102] Hugh acts as a travel companion. The elect on the great portal at Conques are themselves shown as being led by the hand happily onwards to Paradise.[103] Forming persuasive mental images and the importance of the impress of the eyes of the heart and mind were all established medieval and older commonplaces. This is what Isidore meant by *mentis admonitio*, the impact a monument makes on both the mind and heart, each possessing, so to speak, 'eyes'. The *Magna Vita* is evoking a form of Last Judgement which certainly existed in pictorial and sculptural art before 1200 and which deployed the different levels of society or social estates to get the point across; churchmen and kings appear in Last Judgements at Romanesque Conques, in the Winchester and Munich Psalters, at Gothic Chartres, Reims (pl. 21), Bourges, Mainz and elsewhere.[104] Whether or not such a portal ever existed at Fontevrault itself has not been established, for there is no trace of it now. However, in 1984 fragments of painted sculpture showing a group of souls being received blissfully into heaven, possibly from a Last Judgement and dating to around 1200, were discovered there, though whether these formed part of what the *Magna Vita* describes is unknown (pl. 22).[105] They certainly demonstrate the existence at the abbey of extremely fine sculpture at that time.

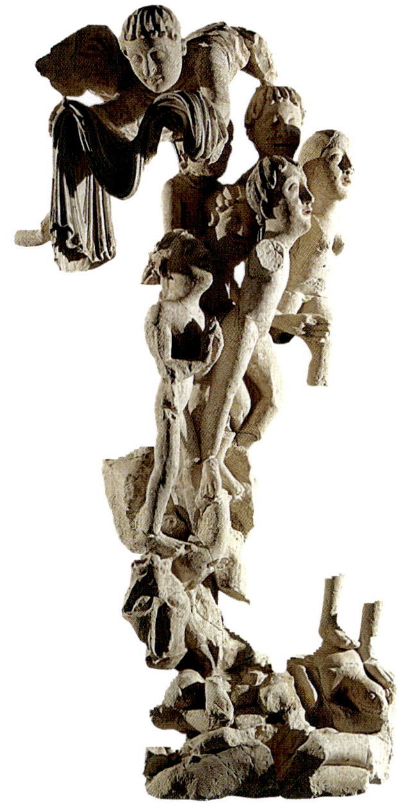

This vivid, and rare, example of a conversation before a Gothic artwork illustrates what is meant by rhetorical engagement, the text describing an occasion and then showing what it is to argue about an artefact and have an intention towards it. It suggests that by seeking evidence for response consistent with modern norms of self-awareness and psychology – in terms of which medieval sources necessarily fail – we may be looking in the wrong places. The account of John's experience makes no mention of his internal movements or affects, and the end to which this experience is directed is action, not feeling: prayer for forgiveness.

An encounter with an artefact entails the meeting of two bodies of artifice – the artefact, and the artificial and conventional character of its perception. This encounter is described effectively by rhetorical analysis; and it is within the classical and medieval heritage of rhetoric that we can begin to trace a language of experience more authentic not to us, but to our objects and subjects of study.[106] In classical rhetoric there were three general modes or divisions whose definition we owe to Aristotle; these were also known to the Middle Ages.[107] The first was judicial rhetoric, used in the courtroom for getting at truths, weighing up rights and wrongs, defending and prosecuting; its character was forensic, establishing and judging truth of some past state of affairs. Like any courtroom drama it might well inflame passions such as anger, yearning for justice. The second form was deliberative rhetoric. This was much more political in nature, warning or preaching in such a way as to appeal to reason and so persuade or dissuade an audience in forming 'policy', or deliberating rationally some course of action in a future state of affairs. The third form was demonstrative or epideictic (display) rhetoric, ceremonial in character and setting out praise (*laus*) and blame (*vituperatio*) in a show of eloquence, not intending to persuade or follow a course of action exactly, but rather to celebrate or denigrate. Pleasure in rhetorical skill itself mattered to this mode, catering to a human appetite for the beautiful and the good.

It is at first sight a little artificial to attempt to map this long-accepted scheme onto Gothic portals – or indeed any artworks – but in fact the exercise proves useful, and the ancient world had long conceded the value of the art-rhetoric analogy. There was one significant difference, however, between the beliefs of the ancient world and those of the Christian era. Christianity was a monotheistic revealed religion based on authority, not simply on the persuasive deployment of *ethos–logos–pathos* (the 'Aristotelian' formula of rhetoric describing the character of the speaker, the character of the words chosen and the audience's response). Christianity's truths were data, indisputable givens. In the case of a Last Judgement scene such as that at the centre of Chartres Cathedral's south transept, with its stern central judging figure of Christ, its intercessors, pleading, verdict and sentencing all drawn principally from Chapter 25 of St Matthew's Gospel, it would be natural to think first of judicial rhetoric and so of the courtroom. What we actually witness in such cases, however, is not so much judicial process as the authoritative demonstration of an inevitable outcome already revealed by the Christian doctrine of the Last Things, or eschatology. From this there is no escape by argument, or for that matter proof by argument. The future outcome is already something memorable.[108]

Indeed, the judicial dimension of such portals precisely underscores the importance of public occasion and the *locus communis* I set out a moment ago. The best indication of this is when a convention becomes widespread, literally a generally transferrable argument. For instance, a wide spectrum of any population is presumably alert to the experience of colour. Consider the widespread phenomenon of the 'red door', a major church doorway painted red, and associated actually and proverbially with judicial activity in the vicinity of the doorway. Instances of this are known at Xanten, Würzburg, Paderborn, Magdeburg – to which I shall return – Bamberg and Paris (the so-called *porte rouge* of Notre-Dame).[109] In such cases colour, as well as being memorable, has metaphorical power, for red is the colour of authority, martyrdom and punishment.[110] It works apotropaically and it 'colours' experience, offering a daily warning. Significant sculpted portals could frame judicial proceedings, as in the case of the south transept portal of Strasbourg Cathedral associated with a law court and including images of Solomon, Ecclesia and Synagoga (see pl. 36).[111]

Display and deliberative rhetoric also mattered. Display rhetoric can be found in all forms of Christian praise of the good (and the related condemnation of the bad) especially in writing about the beauties and virtues of saints. The Christian lyrical and liturgical tradition makes much use of it, as in the Laudes Mariae which celebrate the beauty and nobility of the Virgin Mary.[112] Typical of display rhetoric is the use of comparison, what the Greeks called *synkrisis*. At Fontevrault, for example, images of Heaven and Hell compare the best outcome with the worst possible, in such a way as to make us yearn for the good. Hugh makes full use of *synkrisis* in taking John by the hand to witness his certain future depending on his conduct. John acknowledges this when he says he would prefer to follow the example of the good kings taken to Heaven as shown on the portal. Comparison of the greater and the lesser, the better and the worse, was as central to medieval moral demonstration as it was to the classical conception of tragedy. Typology, the comparison of the Old with the New Law as an exposition of an already decided divine plan, was a fundamental way of structuring medieval images.[113]

Above all it is a fundamental way of dramatising choice. For authoritative prescription or 'advice' of the sort apparent in these doors recognises free will. John, the future king, is free to choose as he will, and might be – and in life in fact was – prone to *emulatio perversa*, 'deliberate emulation of the bad', to quote a caption in the series of wall paintings about moral subjects in the Aula Gotica at S. Quattro Coronati in Rome of the middle years of the thirteenth century.[114] As the well-known if cynical Ovidian quip put it, *Video meliora proboque, deteriora sequor*, 'I see the better and approve of it, but I follow the worse' (*Metamorphoses* 7:21). To overcome this human tendency, portals often include guiding narratives or personifications to flesh out and render vivid the issue of choice, such as the parable of Dives and Lazarus together with the torments of *Luxuria* (lust) before the Apocalyptic Christ at Moissac (pl. 23 and see pl. 73), the Wise and Foolish Virgins at Magdeburg Cathedral of the mid-thirteenth century (see pl. 31) or the Virtues and Vices.[115] The Bible figures girding the portal, the saintly company of heaven, the witnesses who stand at the threshold of all well-furnished (or well 'ornamented') portals, even the morally inferior or downright bad, are instances of ethical comparison which disincentivise bad behaviour. Good clear contrast was necessary to this, which is why the binary left–right arrangement of a doorway could also be a form of moral structuring, based ultimately on such liturgical texts as Psalm 109, *Dixit Dominus Domino meo sede a dextris meis*, 'the Lord said to my Lord: Sit thou at my right hand'. And it could also be the case that as demonstrations, the figures themselves, by their very outward appearance, could display or appear to display the idea of virtue, for outer form imitates inner truth, or its fiction. For this idea again there is firm evidence, again English in origin, and we will return to it shortly when we think about *figurae*.

But the key thing is that while the artworks depict outcomes and offer arguments, authoritative incentives, they do not and cannot of themselves dictate choice, though they might help it along and guide its range. The artwork's function is to direct, to create a mood and disposition through its crafting or handling, which we handle or weigh up in turn. The artwork creates a form of demonstrative experience. This two-way 'intending' requires the powers of sensation and reasoning of its audience. Any deliberative rhetorical model, whether ancient or Christian, will use the vital link of reason and passion in demonstrating and directing us through what is palpable to the senses, or 'sensible' as Ruskin put it. Whereas in Roman art, as on sarcophagi, display was given over to panegyric or artful praise

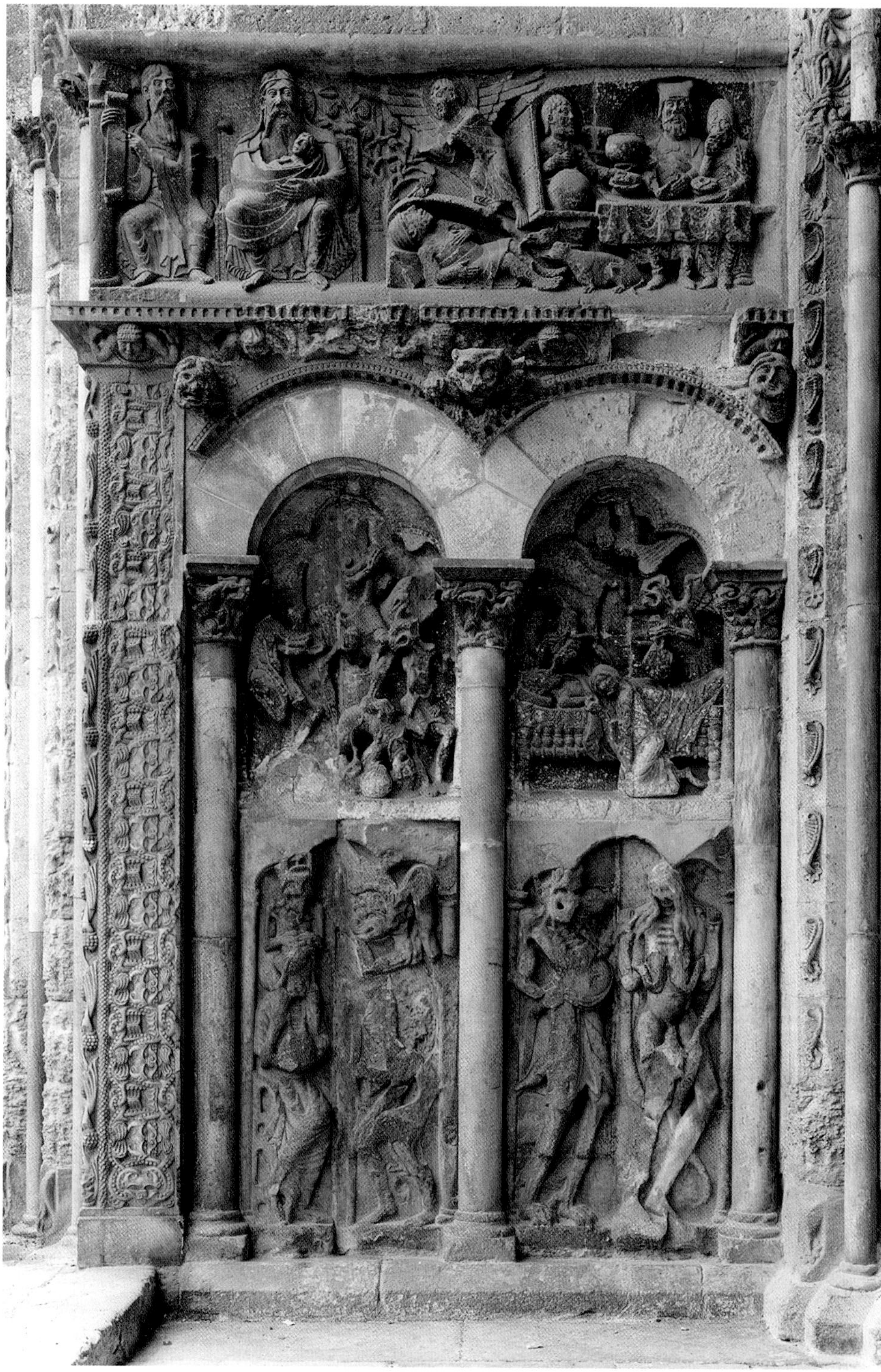

23 Moissac Abbey (Tarn-et-Garonne), south-west portal, left flank panels with the parable of Dives and Lazarus (top two tiers) and *Luxuria* tormented by a demon (lower right). For the context see pl. 4, lower left

of the dead, from an early point Christian art drew on all three modes of judicial, display and demonstrative rhetoric.[116] Put broadly, the classical panegyric expressed the pre-Christian notion of happiness as lying in past reputation. Here choice was over. The Christian dispensation was prospective, concerning the happiness of future salvation. It was possible to bear this future state in mind, indeed recollect it even though it had not yet happened: around 1235 Boncompagno da Signa, a Bolognese professor of rhetoric, wrote about the 'memory of Paradise' and the 'memory of Hell' in his discussion of rhetorical *memoria*.[117] This method reminds us a little of what St Hugh said to John at Fontevrault about careful recollection of states that actually lay in the future, after death. Here choice, driven and organised by vivid imagination, fuelled by appropriate passions, furnished and clarified by memory and deliberation, and leading to confident belief, sound judgement and action, was fundamental.

The witnessing public are above all not just listeners but arbitrators who judge the things to come.[118] The role of such artworks is social: through artifice (handling, colour, form) to create an experience which may variously guide and dispose, move or create delight and which, by engaging thought, may bring about judgement, conviction and action. Let us call this last the 'conviction purpose' of such art: works of art are instrumental in the sense that they may bring about convictions and actions.[119] This purpose is necessarily value-laden: we have confidence *in* something or are persuaded *by* something which we might consider as the 'end' of the experience. Unlike a fully or freely playful activity, conviction is not solely preoccupied by delight as a thing in itself, but is 'in earnest'. Clearly, such conviction is not just intellectual because it is guided by aesthetic experience. It requires a form of consent, a confident or trusting consent to believe, which involves both body and mind, sensory experience, emotion and thought.[120] Such estimation and consent is reasonable, not the product of a blinding flash. The body-language of such artworks may sometimes be dramatic and affective, involving a gut instinct or feeling. But it does not follow that everyday engagement was always dazzling, enchanting or enthralling, and so beyond choice or will, rational engagement and responsibility. As already said, it required consenting adults, and habit. It was precisely about mindfulness and intention, for which mood and affect prepared the way. Artefacts, to my mind at least, operate as a rule as forms of soft power which bring about change by altering the preferences of others by consent, not by force. They warm up an audience rather than over-heating or even blinding it.

Within this mindful situation, the affects have undoubted force. In the medieval Christian theological and artistic dispensation we have only to contemplate the role of fear. Fear is an especially, though not solely, prospective emotion: we cannot always fear what has occurred in the past, but we certainly can and do fear what might or is about to happen. The issue is what role fear itself plays. Consider the imagery and language of the great Last Judgement portal of about 1130 at Autun in Burgundy (pl. 24 and see pl. 20), with its inscription beneath Christ and above the damned:

TERREAT HIC TERROR QUOS TERREUS ALLIGAT ERROR
NAM FORE SIC VERUM NOTAT HIC HORROR SPECIERUM

May terror here terrify those whom worldly error ensnares
For thus here on the door truth depicts the horror of these sights[121]

The word-play on *terror* and *terreus* (lit: 'earthly') will have been enjoyable only to a small, literate, section of the community which responded to this doorway, a reminder that such inscriptions often involve complexities and ambiguities as well as certainties – though here certainty is key.[122] For true terror is an experience beyond experience, so to speak, a kind of paralysis or deprivation of sensation in the encounter with something unutterably weird and alien.[123] The gestural imagery of witness might be apparent at Moissac, which shows little figures at the base of the second order of archivolts to either side of the tympanum (see pl. 4) apparently responding to its fearsome image of Christ by recoiling and casting their arms up and backwards as if astonished, enraptured or even blinded, probably in allusion to the text in Revelation 4:5, the throne emitting lightning and voices and thunders.[124] *Terror* originates in the Latin word *terreo*, to quake or tremble. The experience of terror, as undergone for instance by the patriarch Jacob at Bethel (Genesis 28:17), was connected with prophecy.[125] The sensation of horror, referred to secondly at Autun, is in contrast embodied, 'sensible', coming from within rather than without. The subjunctive *terreat* implies a desired or possible end, and the plan is clearly that the experience of terror should at the very least be contemplated or 'entertained' in mind. Extraordinary as terror and (to a lesser extent) horror may be, such experiences as awe and dread work to incentivise, to point or indicate, to alter conduct or affirm belief: fear is part of the exercise of justice, is a beginning of wisdom, a prologue to virtue – as proposed in Augustine's stages of contemplation and as developed by the moral theology of the schools of the twelfth and thirteenth centuries.[126] The incitement of fear is a technique, and its deployment is instrumental.

What I want to underline here is that there is no reason to think that such artworks usually had the 'expression' of emotion as their end or purpose, Romantic-fashion, or emotion as their object of study. This means–ends point will need further thought.[127] For the present all I need to say is that while I would be the first to emphasise the affective role of medieval art (and have frequently done so), I find myself dissatisfied with the view that the goal of the more expressive sculpted portal images of the thirteenth century was more to understand the 'empathetic' responses that this outcome engendered than to call attention to a generally recognisable moral predicament.[128] Of course emotion and response matter: these artworks had a design on the beholder. The question is where at this time we locate emotion and in what relation to the economy of means and ends. My understanding is that (causally speaking) emotion was primary, not secondary: it was a matter of means, not outcome or end. Without pressing the means–ends distinction too far, it helps to see emotional stimulus

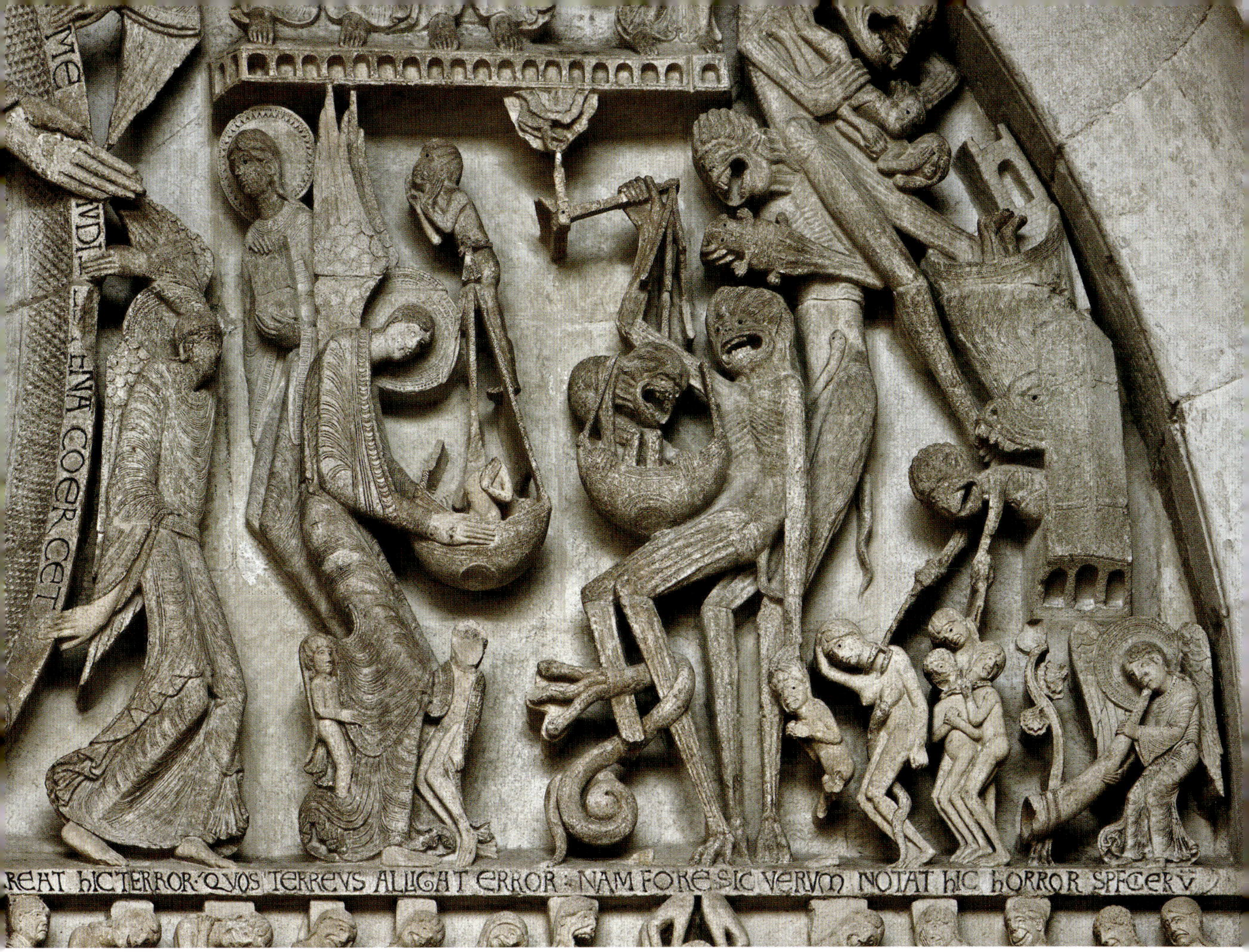

24 Autun Cathedral (Sâone-et-Loire), west portal tympanum, detail of weighing of souls and inscriptions, about 1130

as an aspect of the function of such artworks, of the work that they did, but as a much less clear part of their purpose or aim. Modern cognitive models of the emotions also remind us that persuasion has a sensory 'base' which melds reason and emotion. As Carruthers says of persuasion, 'It is deeply misleading to think that only "emotions" are involved with it, or that oratory makes "emotional appeals" *instead of* or *along with* [original emphases] rational ones. Historians need to discard their assumptions that reason and emotion are wholly different things.'[129]

We will return to these issues later, but for the moment a telling question within this economy of means and ends is how sculpted representation persuasively served the conviction purpose, and that takes us from basic points about the public domain and context to the related questions of affect and mimesis.

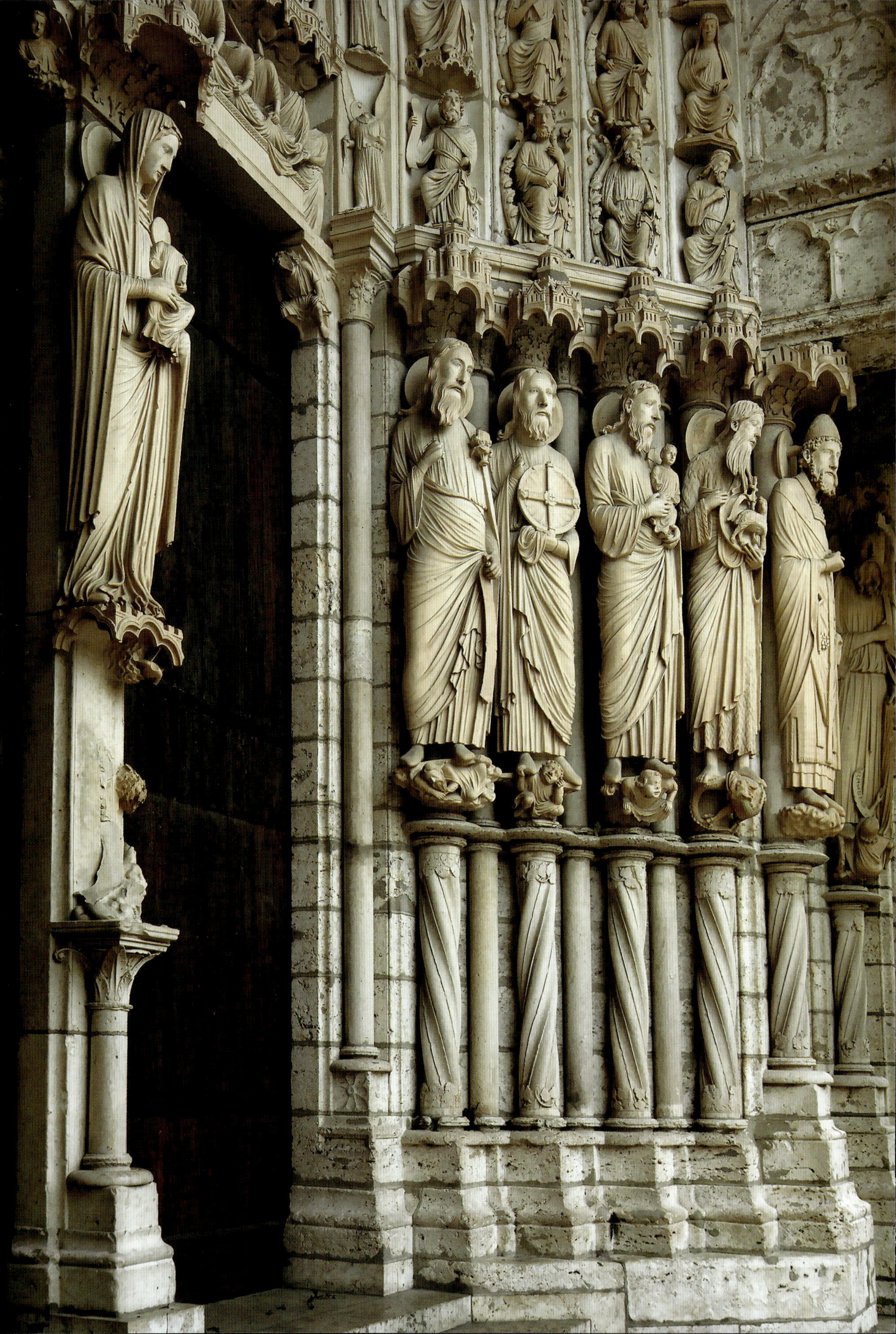

2

FIGURE AND AFFECT

The sculpted arts of the Church in the twelfth and thirteenth centuries were by their nature and intent drawn into the increasingly explicit, thoroughly reasoned, comprehensive and ambitious mission of moral and religious reform (pl. 25), driven in part by the moral theology of the schools of northern Europe, Paris especially, by monastic theory and practice and by the new ethics of courts. Those who commissioned the sculptures – in general the educated 'clerical' class – were those who formulated ideals of conduct and belief. A central objective of this mission, captured by historians of ethics, courtliness and theology, was the proper disciplinary reconciliation of inner and outer 'form'.[1] This worked by *imitatio*. The outer self in ancient and medieval doctrine was the mirror, the imitation, of the inner self; but the inner too could be regulated through the apprehension of properly formed ideas, practices or things of which it in turn became the likeness. Key to this ebb and flow of imitation was, in effect, a form of standardisation. The local had become more subordinate to the universal, the heterodox to the orthodox; waywardness of invention was captured and channelled towards a more 'ethical' world view; if we wish, an epic mindset started to yield to something more fundamentally directive and conformist. This ambition of overarching control is identified by some social and cultural historians with the age of the clericy, of bureaucracy, of papal supremacy, of the Crusades and Inquisition, of scholastic knowledge, of religious orthodoxy itself.[2] The clerical mentality was formed in the

25 Chartres Cathedral (Eure-et-Loir), north transept central portal of the Coronation of the Virgin, showing St Anne (on the trumeau) with Old Testament figures on the jambs, early thirteenth century

environment of the new universities and schools of the twelfth and thirteenth centuries. Its bureaucratic eye, suspicious of the local, the 'low' and the jongleuric (the lively, theatrical and playful), drew up the pastoral checklist, the inventory, of intolerance. The drawbridge followed. The Fourth Lateran Council of 1215, for some (following Michel Foucault), was the moment of truth in this narrative of the subordination of the local and individual.[3] That this process was social, religious and aesthetic goes without saying, for our period was deeply engaged in thought about the relation of inner and outer form. We are obliged to judge by appearances, for they matter now as they did then. That there was an issue of social class at work here is arguable: John Grandisson, a noble bishop of Exeter in the fourteenth century, mentioned in 1339 the way that peasant parishioners in country churches 'festooned' their altars in a way quite wrong for the urbane, clear and lucid, altars of great churches.[4] Our image of the smoothed out and constrained arts is an image of a certain sort of power and hierarchy at work, one that worked itself out in the 'look' of things and especially persons. Self-regulation was culturally determined, educable, codified and artificial. It could be accomplished by the exertion of techniques of one kind or another; art was one such technique.

There are difficulties with this model – arguably one of repression or control – yet we cannot set it aside not least because it might touch on the history of the emotions, itself a burgeoning field of study.[5] Underlying the regime of moral artifice and education as identified by the historians of civility was the ancient notion of imitation and emulation (*mimesis*, *zelos*) in the formation of character (*ethos*).[6] Good character should be 'sensible', embodied, palpable, a thing displayed: the tactility or apparent tactility of sculpture made it an especially vital medium of the convincing and so the exemplary.[7]

Although it is not my aim to insist on a universalising 'ethical poetic' in medieval representation of the sort once mooted for medieval textuality by J. B. Allen,[8] it is nevertheless striking that the earliest reference we have to Gothic art as embodying *moralitas* pertains to sculpture. It comes from an English grammarian and practitioner of the *ars poetriae* writing in Paris, John of Garland, and is found in his *Morale Scolarium*, in effect an early manual of conduct aimed at students in the schools dating to the early 1240s. In its thirtieth chapter it reiterates the norms of properly regulated clerical conduct and suggests an exemplar for imitation: *Templi sculpturas morum dic esse figuras / Vivas picturas in te gere non perituras*, 'Declare our churches' sculptures models of civility,/ Living pictures, to be borne in mind indelibly'.[9] It is clear from a second occurrence of this couplet, in John of Garland's *Carmen de Misteriis Ecclesie*, that the intended reference is to portal sculpture, the portal being Christ who spreads out the heavens, the column figures beneath being the Doctors of the Church.[10] Therefore carved images could exemplify conduct (*mores*) and so be open to moral scrutiny. Again, the background is Gregorian and rhetorical, and we note the emphasis on 'living' images and on the indelible assimilation or recollection of their exemplarity. In the eulogy of Paris of 1323 written by Jean de Jandun, Jean used the same trope when he praised the gallery of kings, called *ydola*, in the great hall of the royal palace as appearing at first sight as if alive (*quasi viva*).[11]

John of Garland's couplet conveys little or nothing about the exact way in which such sculptures conveyed virtue. This was, presumably, open to interpretation. But the view that projecting sculpted images embodied virtue was summarised by the liturgist Durandus in his late thirteenth-century *Rationale* when he stated that 'projecting sculptures are seen to be coming out of the walls of the church' because the virtues are thereby seen to be 'naturally' manifest and their works diligently pursued by the faithful, action following conviction.[12] In fact sculpted, modelled and painted images, including wax seals, had been cited as offering ethical direction through imitation by such twelfth-century authorities as Hugh of St Victor (*De Institutione Novitiorum*) and Alan of Lille (*Anticlaudianus*).[13] It is striking that to both John of Garland and Durandus, ethical demonstration (in itself a cliché of the period) seems especially associated with relief sculpture, particularly modelling – that shaping or forming which carried with it the ultimate imprint of God.[14] Such images might be small or precious, and they might convey doctrine. In the Pontigny Life of St Edmund of Abingdon (d. 1240), Archbishop of Canterbury, we read that Edmund, while sitting at his desk and studying, had before his face a most beautiful (*venustissima*) ivory image of the Virgin Mary (compare pl. 63), since what holy scripture could express in letters, a sculpture might clearly (*apertius*) demonstrate and readily impress on the mind by means of its *figura* or outer form.[15] Mary was a source of doctrine as well as virtue. This ultimately Gregorian vision finds a distinct later medieval echo in the visions of Tondal as depicted around 1475 by Simon Marmion and an associate (Los Angeles, J. Paul Getty Museum, Ms 30, fol. 33v), in which the soul of Tondal is brought before the bad, but not very bad, ensconced in a wall in heaven rather like statues (pl. 26); the manuscript also shows Tondal brought to the glorified martyrs and the pure inhabiting a great golden wall (fol. 38v), somewhat in the fashion of St Bernard's sermons on the Song of Songs (pl. 27).[16]

Sculpture, then, allows things to be 'set forth'. Important to this setting forth is the appearance of the carved figures themselves. Rhetorically speaking, the Latin term *figurae*, 'figures', used by John of Garland and many others, belongs less to the faculty of invention than to the faculty of style. A portal is furnished with human representations which should be vivid and governed or disciplined by their style, so possessing clarity, intelligibility and decorum or fittingness (pl. 28). By 'style' is not meant the modern analytical examination of form, but an older rhetorical idea of style as the furnishing or equipping of an argument by ornament. Ornaments are not things of pretty superficial skin, add-ons, as in post-medieval aesthetics, but words or forms chosen and disposed to work in a certain context to a certain argumentative end. In language they might include figures of speech such as metaphor.[17] The term 'figure' is used in many of the non-verbal arts: music analysis recognises the importance of

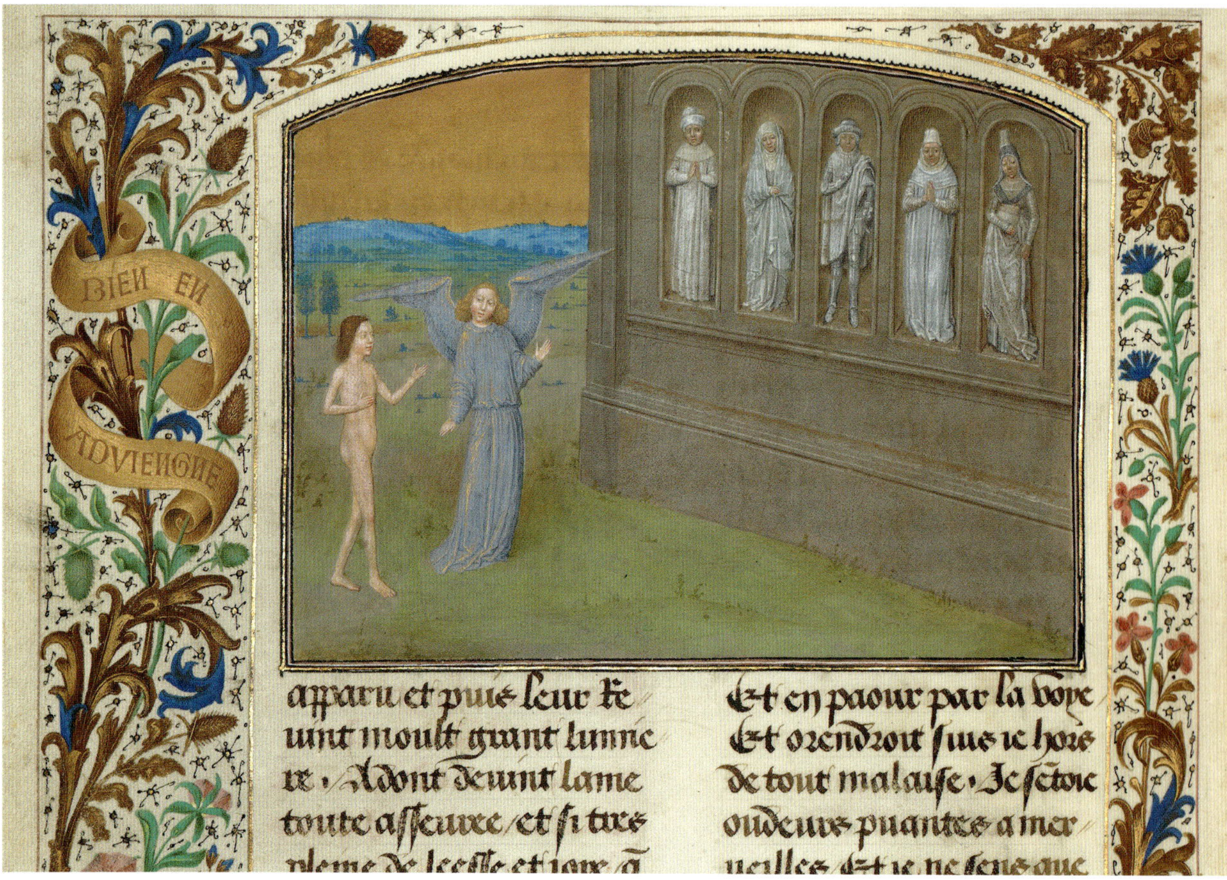

26 Visions of Tondal, Tondal encounters the bad, but not very bad, about 1475
(Los Angeles, J. Paul Getty Museum, MS 30, fol. 33v)

'figuration' by means of formulaic groupings of notes, apparent in their shape and contour as much to the eye as the ear.

In essence, figures are conventional patterns which lead us through a composition or work of art. In the verbal and the 'figurative' arts, *figura* is related to the Greek *schema*, meaning 'attitude', posture, while supplying what Isidore calls 'figures of speech', *eloquium figurae*.[18] One starting-point for such postures or movements were Euclidian geometrical figures (circles, squares, triangles) which worked as points of origin for invention, or 'topics'.[19] When, around 1230 or earlier, the north-eastern French artistic compiler Villard de Honnecourt included numerous geometrically based drawings of humans and animals and sculptures in the famous portfolio which bears his name, he was assembling *figurae* or *schemata* which might be used on different occasions.[20] These attitudes, as well as being

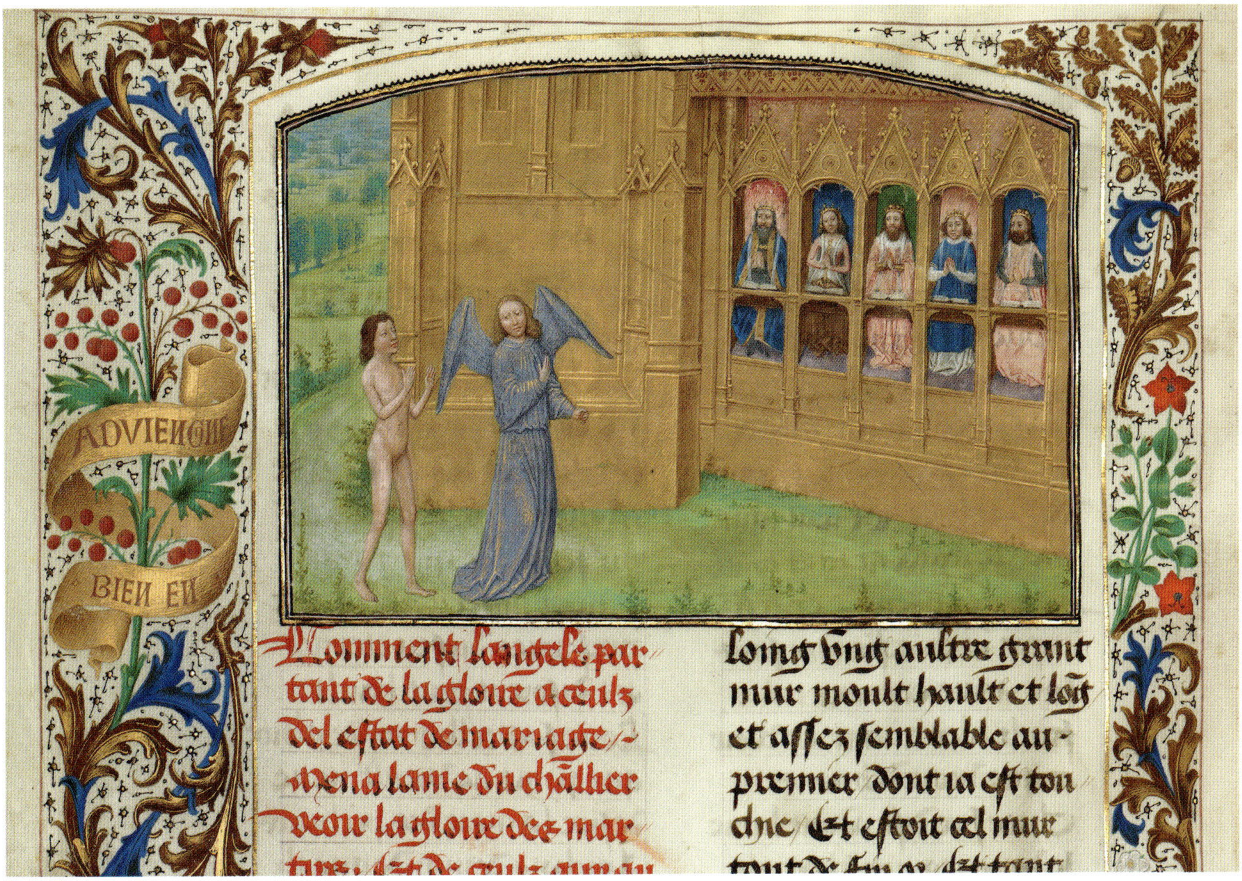

27 Visions of Tondal, Tondal before the glorified martyrs, about 1475 (Los Angeles, J. Paul Getty Museum, MS 30, fol. 38v)

admirably crafted in themselves, would lend variety, movement and subtlety to a composition, helping our way through it. Ornaments and figures, as rhetorical 'colours', are features of the style or clothing of a work which give it experiential force, persuasive ability, and through them writers and artists speak.[21] Onulf of Speyer, a twelfth-century rhetorician, thought of rhetorical colours as being *figurae verborum* as fragrant as flowers.[22] Marchetto of Padua, the early fourteenth-century musical theorist, related the subtle colours imparted by certain intervals in music to the grammatical colours that produce beauty of thought.[23] The association of the *colores* with beauty, delicacy and nuance was widespread and is useful to our understanding of moral delicacy, though it also hinted at a danger which some rhetoricians had already spotted in thinking about the way speakers can 'colour' an argument, that the colours could be a 'gloss', could mislead.[24]

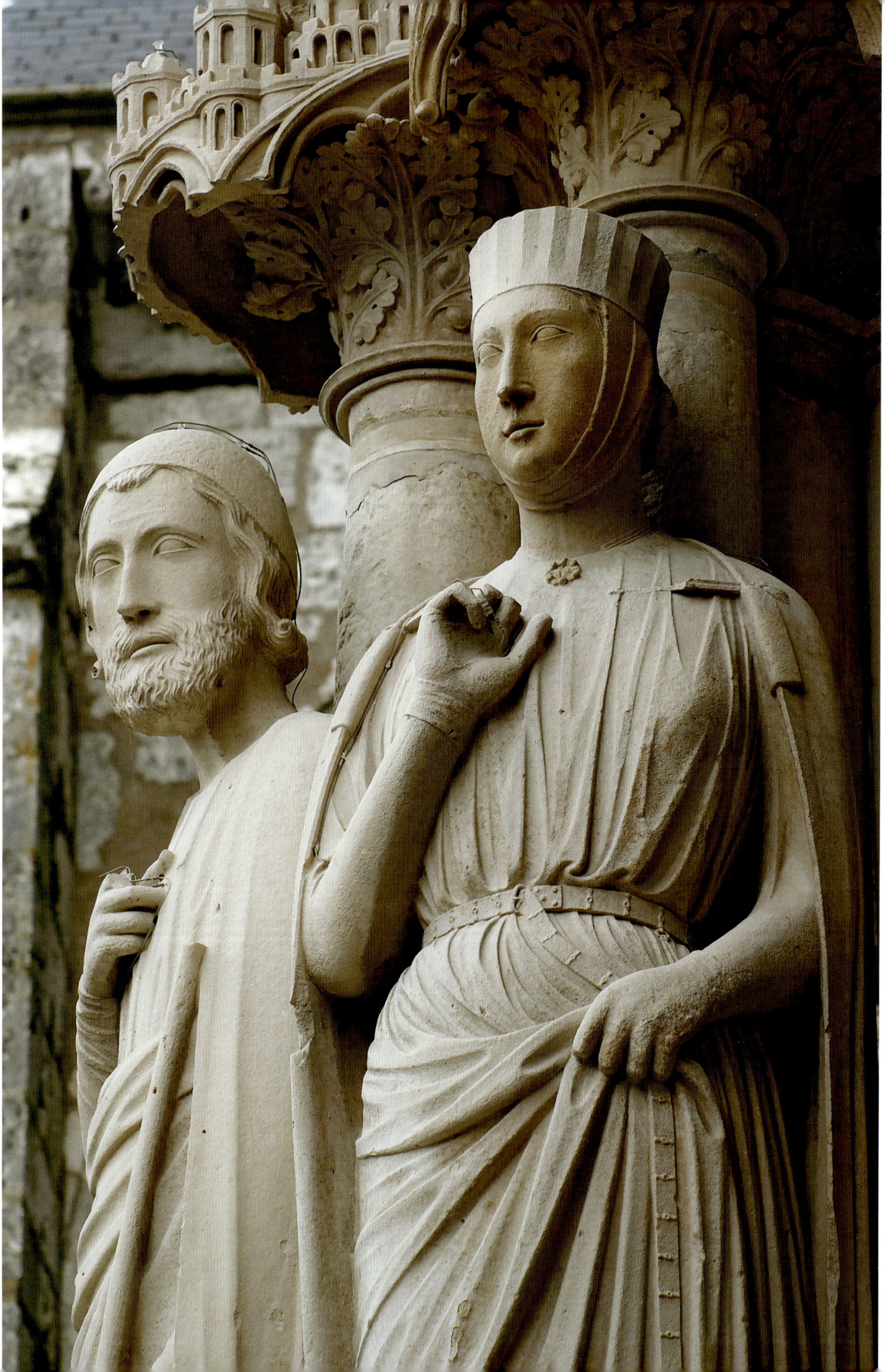

Colours and figures in a work lent it direction and persuasive power: style was an agent of experience. The colours might include the physical posture, attitude and gestures of a figure, the look on its face or 'cheer', the scrolls, books and other attributes figures might carry, their clothing – for clothing signals identity, class and moral outlook or *munditia*. The culturally determined and codified nature of speech and particularly gesture has been forcefully described by Jean-Claude Schmitt, who has traced thinking about external and internal form from the ancient world to the Middle Ages; Roland Recht too acknowledges that the notion of natural or spontaneous gesture has to be abandoned.[25] From the portal to the altar, and from the altar to the courtroom, gesture and attitude were all formalised, if not wholly codified; action could assist thought.[26] The literal colouration of the images with paint also mattered, for the evidence that most, perhaps all, portals were as brightly coloured and gilded as the carved wooden images inside churches is strong.[27] This was certainly true of the facades at Salisbury and Wells.[28] We can see all these effects spread out yet working together on the late twelfth-century Pórtico de la Gloria at Compostela (see pl. 10) or in the thirteenth century at the collegiate church of Toro, also in Iberia (pl. 29).[29] Paintwork of this order was almost as costly as the sculptures themselves. Choice pigments associated colouration with elegance, the word *elegantia* being connected to 'election', selection from the best.[30] In his 1323 eulogy of Paris, Jean de Jandun praised the Sainte-Chapelle for the 'most choice' colouring of its painted work, *picturarum electissimi colores*.[31] Elegance was also related to clarity. In 1253 Henry III of England ordered wall paintings in the Palace of Westminster to be executed with the 'best colours that it was possible to find' so that the pictures might be done 'distinctly and clearly', *distincte et aperte*, a verbal formula derived from rhetorical *elocutio* and its emphasis of good clear diction, including the public speech of clergy in church.[32] His pictures were elegant and loud and clear.

Clarity and elegance – modern notions of style and mimesis or verism aside – were fundamental to lending life to images in order to bring them indelibly before the mind, to cite John of Garland's more or less classical formulation again. The key tool of vividness was *enargeia*, in Latin *evidentia* or *demonstratio*, directed as much to quality of thought as to quality of speech, injecting a sort of energy and life well suited to the description of actions such that they could be witnessed and judged actively, as forms of evidence.[33] It is more than just clarity, but is something which thrust itself onto the viewer.[34] We recall that Gregory the Great had captured this idea in his use of the word *praestare*, to stand forward. Durandus, as just seen, remarks on sculptures seeming to come out of the wall by analogy with the instilling of virtue into the faithful. As in some amazingly vivid dream, *enargeia* is the means of making the viewer feel present without necessarily grasping the totality of a scene, creating a mood and sensation of reality which carries tremendous conviction.[35] As Richard de Fournival put it in his *Bestiaire d'amours*, shortly after writing of the two gates

28 Chartres Cathedral (Eure-et-Loir), north transept central portal, left jamb, Old Testament figures, early thirteenth century

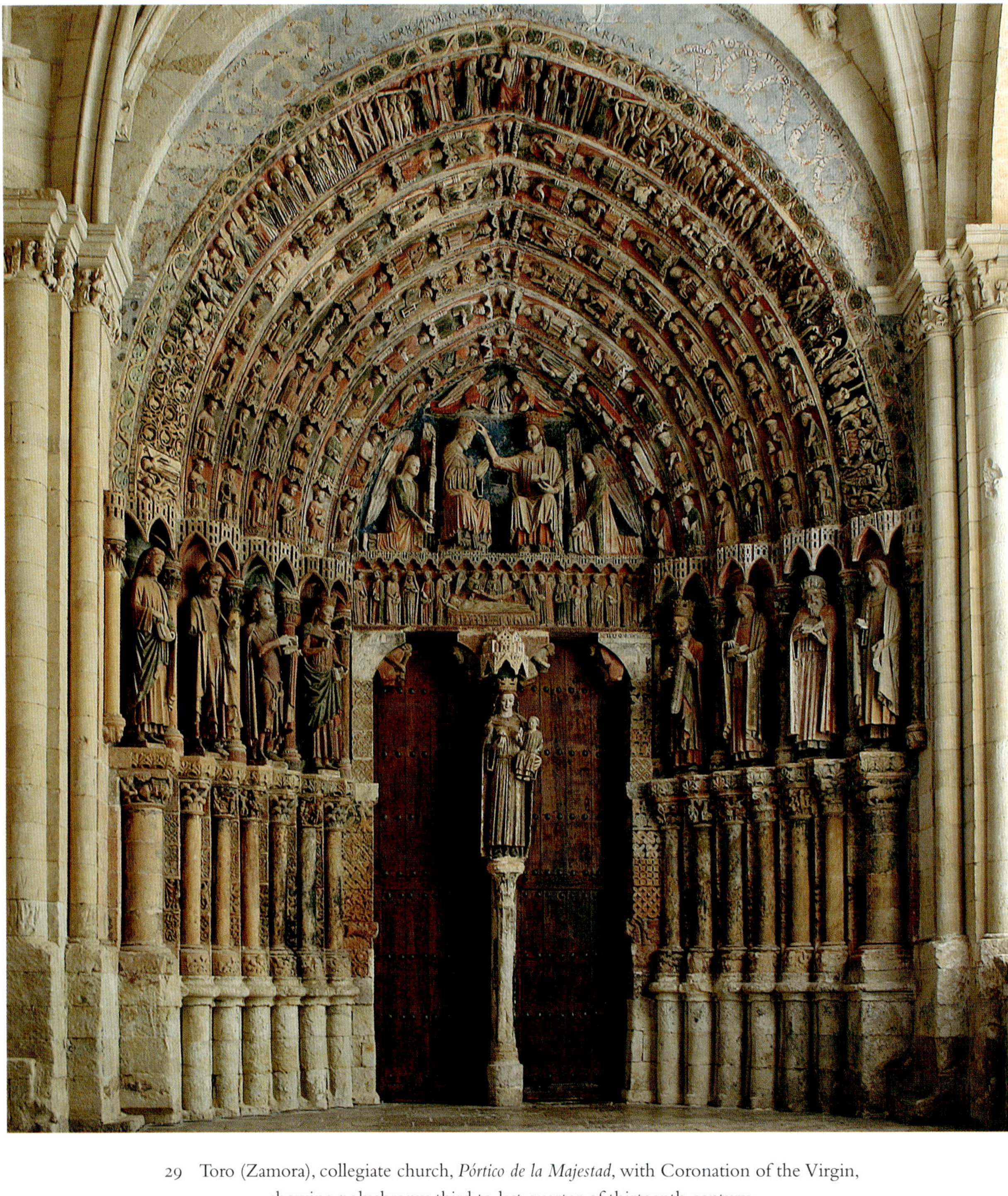

29 Toro (Zamora), collegiate church, *Pórtico de la Majestad*, with Coronation of the Virgin, showing polychromy, third to last quarter of thirteenth century

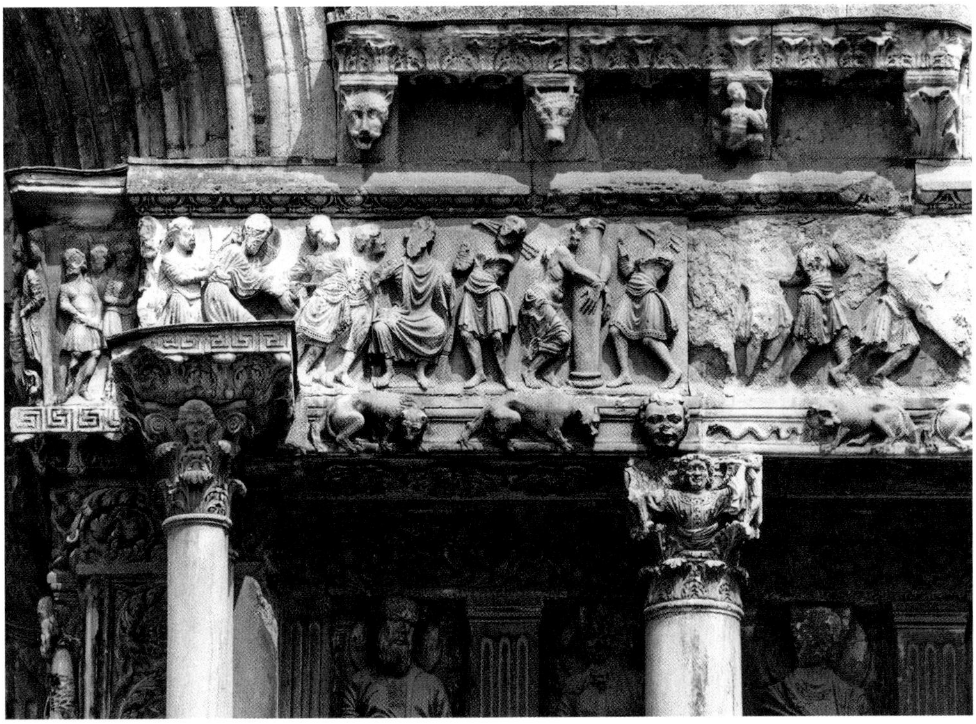

30 Saint-Gilles-du-Gard Abbey (Gard), west front, main lintel between central and southern portals showing Flagellation of Christ, mid- or third quarter twelfth century

of sight and sound, texts and their illustrations act on us as if the things shown were actually 'present' (*com s'il fussent present*).[36]

This assertiveness is not simply an attribute of that elusive concept, realism, which I will try (imperfectly) to distinguish from mimetic correspondence to the truth, naturalism or 'indexicality' (in the sense of photographic 'truth').[37] Mimesis is not central to realism, because realism may be a particular capacity, partly or even wholly non-representational, to portray the world convincingly. It is more like a force of actualisation and provocation, getting the audience to respond and think back, prodding it to complete the picture, but dictating neither response nor solution.[38] It is to be judged not by its correspondence but by its effect on an audience. Understood in this light, the agency and sheer actualising force, the realism, of much Romanesque sculpture would certainly be the equal of its mimetically accomplished Gothic successors because the ideas are just as vivid. Consider the Romanesque facade of Saint-Gilles-du-Gard in Provence, on the frieze of which is an astonishingly closely observed scene of the Flagellation of Christ (pl. 30); at the Crucifixion the onlookers include Synagoga falling violently yet abstractedly away in defeat, showing the same demonstrative language of posture as the small figures at Moissac.[39] The Pórtico de la Gloria at Compostela of the 1180s (see pl. 10), linked as we saw earlier to a more transcendental imaginary, is probably the finest instance of the physical animation, typically bodily (the implicit turning or spiralling of jamb figures), that had already appeared in northern France (Saint-Denis, Senlis) and at Souillac (see pl. 74). This foreshadowed the 'indexical' attributes of post-1200 Gothic sculpture (formal attributes which connect an image mimetically to a referent 'out there' in the world, with which it can be compared) that have preoccupied art historians.[40] Throughout the post-classical world the verbal concept range of imitation, contrivance and substitution had always been nuanced regardless of the representational regime at work.[41] The conflation of two separate ideas, that images may be drawn *from* life or brought *to* life, has led to the assumption that the greater an image's objective truth content or mimetic prowess, the greater its liveliness. Experience teaches otherwise. As many skilled artists have found to their cost, the force of an image does not necessarily depend on some agreed mimetic accomplishment. Art may be correct but dead. Were this not the case, the notion that an image might in some sense live could not have been a commonplace, a convention, of writing about art established long before the Gothic era. But this was precisely the convention, as Byzantine and earlier sources prove in regard to modes of representation whose indexicality differs significantly from those of much Gothic art.[42]

Rhetorical colouration and figuration is not causally or necessarily tied to any particular set of representational conventions. As already stated, it is impossible to sustain the idea that the age of body eloquence in figurative art only dawned in the 'naturalistic' thirteenth century. The body had remained a vehicle for speech under the rhetorically influenced classical system of ethics which articulated moral thinking throughout the high and late Middle Ages. Such speech might be typological and conventional, serving the figurative ends of theology, as Ilene Forsyth has shown in relation to the resemblance of opposites as cues to rumination, as at Moissac.[43] The composition and disposition of figures provided cues to ordering, hierarchy, significance and tone throughout the twelfth century.[44] Equally, it cannot be denied that the crafting of bodies saw significant shifts in priority in this period. Between the installations of the Pórtico de la Gloria at Compostela in the 1180s and the sculptures on the west facade of Reims (see pls 10 and 47), 'portal talk' focused increasingly on action, variegation and apparent mobility of facial expression, posture and gesture, while other surface effects such as those created by the garments of the figures were subject to simplification and selection of effect by means of the 'broad-fold' style (see pls 41, 47, 49 and 63). The product, at least to modern eyes, was a refocusing on those parts of the body conventionally regarded as especially expressive or significatory, such as heads and hands.[45] That there may have been underlying textual or discursive reasons for this shift in priorities is possible, but a significant causal question remains as to why it happened when and where

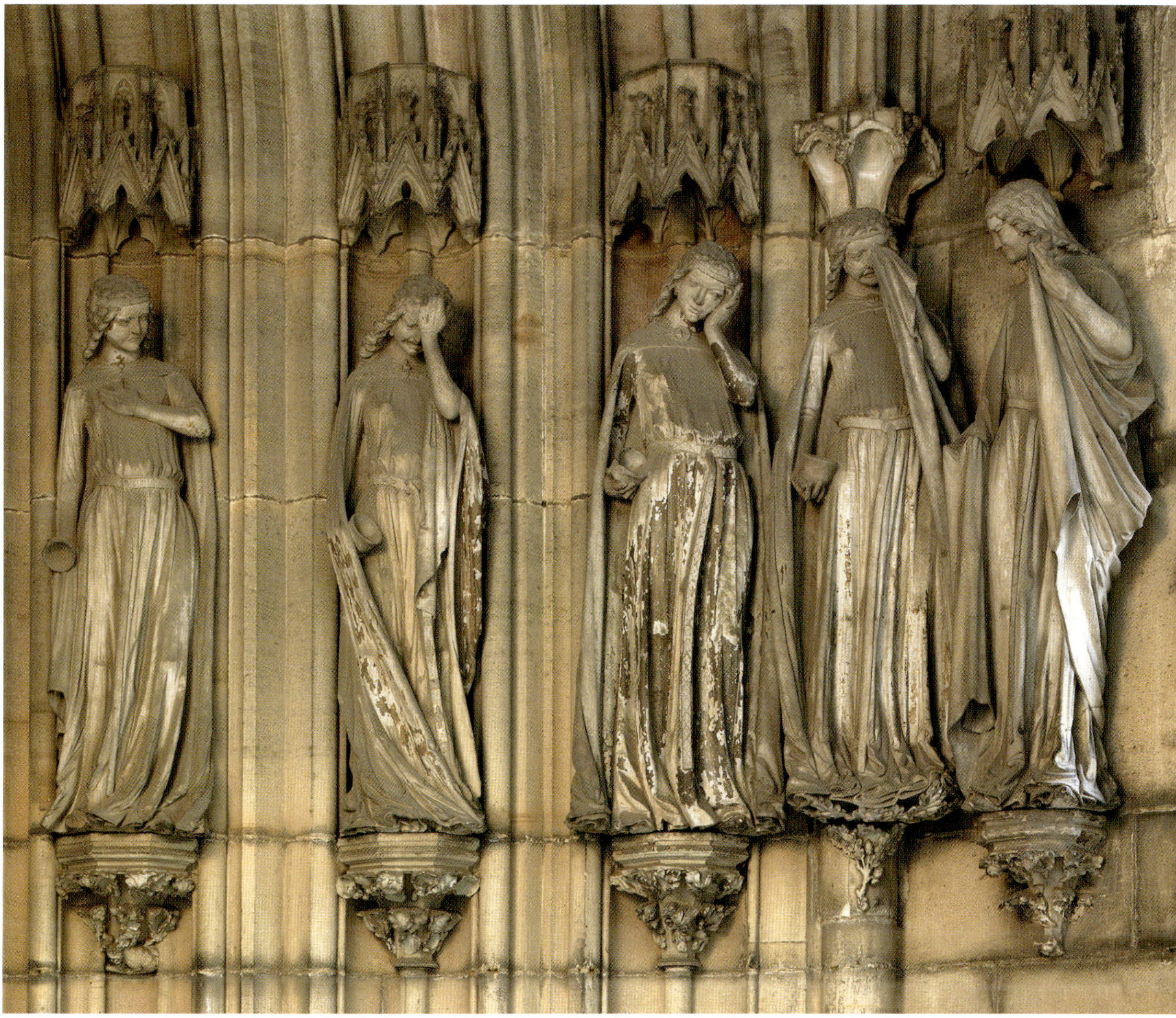

31 Magdeburg Cathedral (Saxony-Anhalt), north transept, Foolish Virgins, figures 1240s, setting later

it did. As it is, between the execution of the smaller sculptures on the upper parts of the exterior of the choir of Reims Cathedral, probably in the 1220s and certainly before 1241, the creation of the Fürstenportal at Bamberg Cathedral by the 1230s, the portal of the Wise and Foolish Virgins at Magdeburg by the 1240s (pl. 31), the founder images at Naumburg around 1250 and the west facade of Reims (see pls 41 and 47), the direction of change becomes distinct and is concentrated on a relatively small number of outstanding and also mutually informing projects strongly energised by the workshops at Reims.[46] Only at some

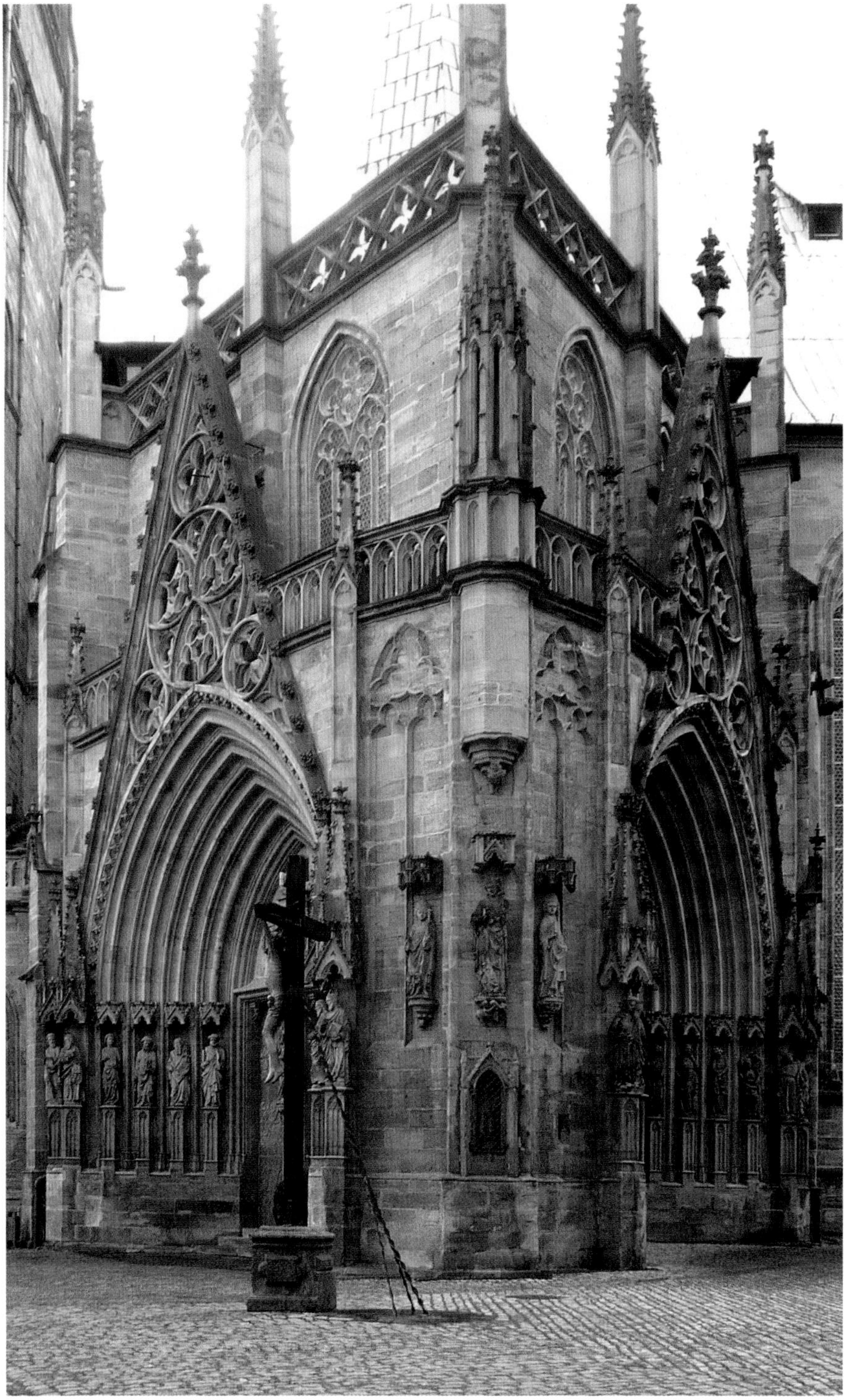

32 Erfurt Cathedral (Thuringia), north portals viewed from north, about 1330

point after the 1230s did the changes in idiom brought about by this relatively specialised conversation between great projects become more widespread in other media and contexts. In suggesting that this narrative of change may be associated with a post-medieval privileging of 'naturalism' we cannot, equally, overlook the fact that this new mode of presenting the human figure was to be influential, and has to be examined more deeply. I will return to it presently.

The later stages of a development should also be considered because they illuminate a number of issues in the use of *figurae* as expressive conventions. By the time the remarkable new north portal of Erfurt Cathedral in Thuringia was furnished with images of the Wise and Foolish Virgins, around 1330, this look was beginning to show signs of stress. The portal has an unusual triangular plan creating a wedge-like projection from the north transept, part of a reconstruction of the east end under way from the late thirteenth century.[47] Each side has a portal, which means the two portals can be seen simultaneously directly from the north (pl. 32). We choose our path accordingly. The north-eastern portal has a Crucifixion, Virgin and Child and Apostles, calm and decorous. The south-western portal jambs have the Wise and Foolish Virgins, Ecclesia and Synagoga and the tympanum has a form of Dëesis with Mary and John the Baptist. The Foolish Virgins, together with Synagoga, are a veritable compendium of theatrical gesture or *gesticulatio*, with discomposed and literally downcast facial features and arms and hands raised to cheeks in despair or flung up and wrung together, as can be perceived despite numerous later restorations (pl. 33). The Wise Virgins with Ecclesia are throughout contrasting models of smirking complacency (pl. 34). This is obvious *synkrisis*, comparison, brought home by a process of amplification from the Vulgate terms for wise and foolish, *prudentes* and *fatuae* in Matthew 25:2. Bodies and faces work together as *imagines verborum*, the faces of the written word.[48]

These qualities are made present aesthetically, mimetically, in the dispositions or *schemata* of the figures: the idea of 'mime' is helpful here. They also have the thrusting quality of ostentation and hence, to some eyes perhaps, a sort of forwardness or vulgarity not softened by the technical coarseness of the work (at least by the smooth standards of Cologne or Paris): the near-contemporary upper Rhenish programmes of Wise and Foolish Virgins at Strasbourg, Freiburg, Basel and (later) Berne are more restrained.[49] It is notable that the bodily affects are not derived from Matthew 25, which is itself non-affective in language, but either from the reference at the very end of Matthew 24 to 'weeping and gnashing of teeth' (*fletus et stridor dentium*) or from Luke 13:24–8 in which Jesus speaks of the narrow gate (*angusta portica*), the refusal of the master saying 'I know you not whence you are' (Luke 13:25, 27; compare Matthew 25:12) and finally the weeping and gnashing of teeth (Luke 13:28).

In fact at Erfurt the affects, as significant actions, are conventional in three ways. First, they arose by imitation, because it is intrinsically likely that the canons of Erfurt were moved to imitate the similar north portal of Magdeburg Cathedral where a set of fine Wise

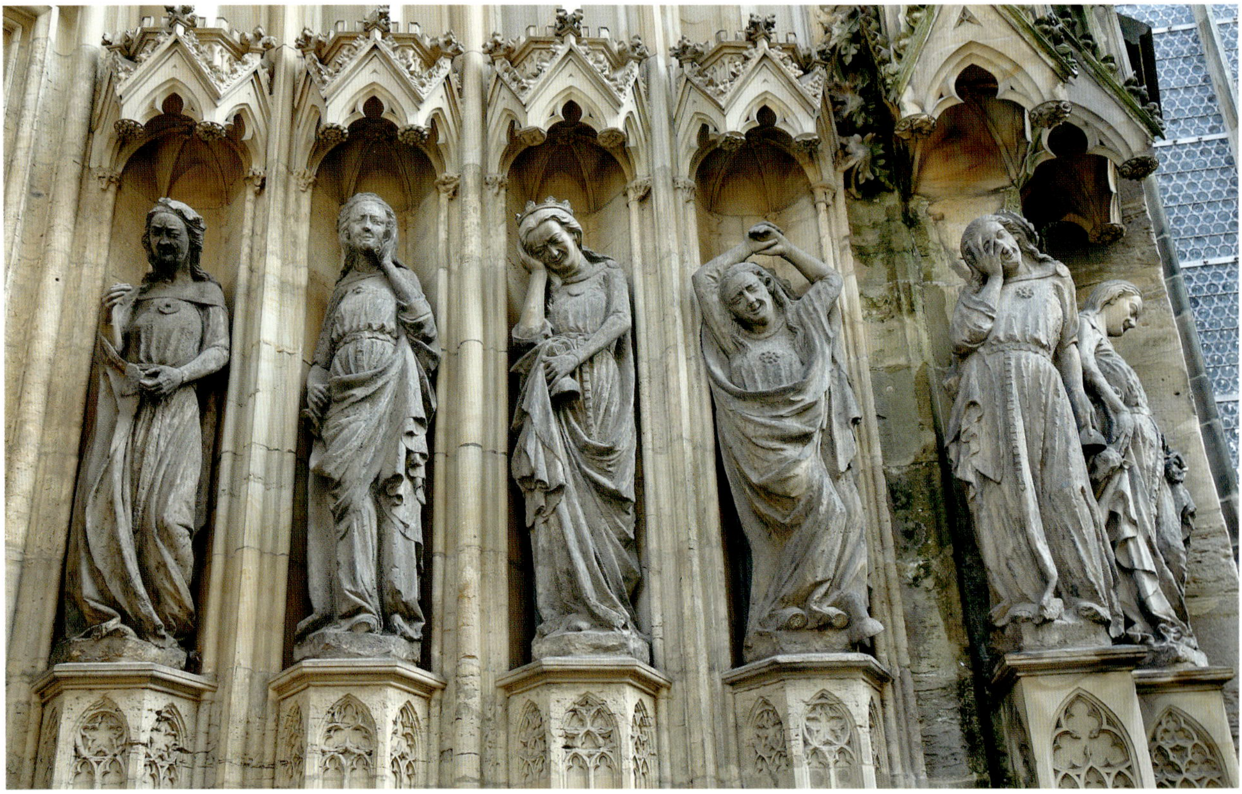

33 Erfurt Cathedral, north portal, Foolish Virgins with Synagoga to right

and Foolish Virgins of mid-thirteenth-century origin had recently been reinstalled in a more modern setting along with Ecclesia and Synagoga (see pl. 31).[50] In scale (under life-size) and confrontation the two sets of figures are clearly similar and the language of gestures comparable, though the contents of the tympana differ. The derivation may go back further. At Magdeburg the portal was not necessarily the first instance of the selection of the Wise and Foolish Virgins as a stand-alone topic; in September 1242 Henry III had commissioned a set of paintings of the Wise and Foolish Virgins for the queen's chapel at Windsor, at a time when French influence on styles and topics at the English court, and from Reims especially, was strong.[51] The possibility of some common north-eastern French model for these and for Magdeburg can at least be hypothesised.

A second aspect of the artificiality of the gestures lies in their varying genealogies. The Wise and Foolish Virgins appear much earlier on the archivolts of the technically superb early Romanesque portal of Saint-Pierre at Aulnay. Again, they are not a stand-alone topic subject to amplification as at Magdeburg and Erfurt, but are combined with the Psycho-

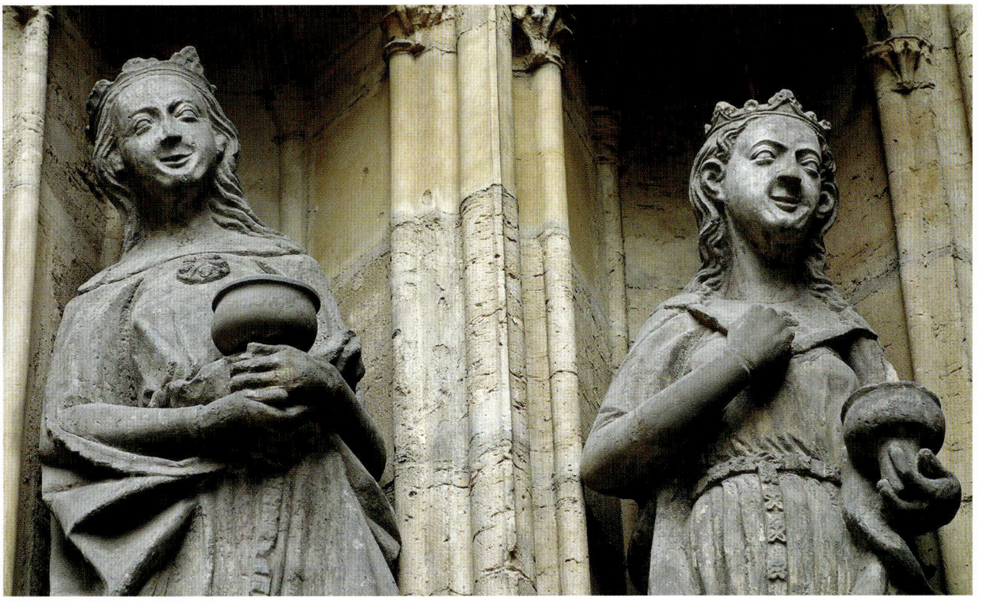

34 Erfurt Cathedral, north portal, Wise Virgins

machia (combat of the Virtues and Vices), a Zodiac and Labours of the Months.[52] But at Aulnay one of the Foolish Virgins raises her hand to her cheek in grief or despair in the same fashion as her later Gothic sisters at Magdeburg. The gesture is not unlike that sometimes performed in grief by the Virgin Mary or St John at the foot of the Cross, as on the small Romanesque cast figurine known as the Ushaw Virgin.[53] The 'rationale' of gesture remains essentially the same at an interval of perhaps two centuries: the bodily display rules as such seem not to have changed significantly.[54] At Erfurt, however, there intervenes a second type of attitude in which the arms are thrown up over the head and the hands wrung together. This has a different genealogy. It is a conventional threnodic gesture of despair, derived via French pictorial court art from central Italy and painters such as Duccio: the Parisian artist Jean Pucelle uses it for one of the mourners in the Entombment of Christ on folio 82v of the Hours of Jeanne d'Evreux of the 1320s (pl. 35).[55] It places Erfurt's version, around 1330, in the middle of a current of exchanges with central Italy in figurative art, paintings especially, apparent also at Strasbourg and Klosterneuburg in these years, as well as France and England.[56] It also raises the question whether, as at late medieval Troyes, painters were not involved in the design of the portal figures in the first place.[57]

The final conventional issue is also significatory: though *synkrisis* denotes contrast it can work, as Forsyth indicates, by typological resemblance. As one of the captions in the twelfth-century typological windows at Saint-Denis puts it, the Virgins might have an outer

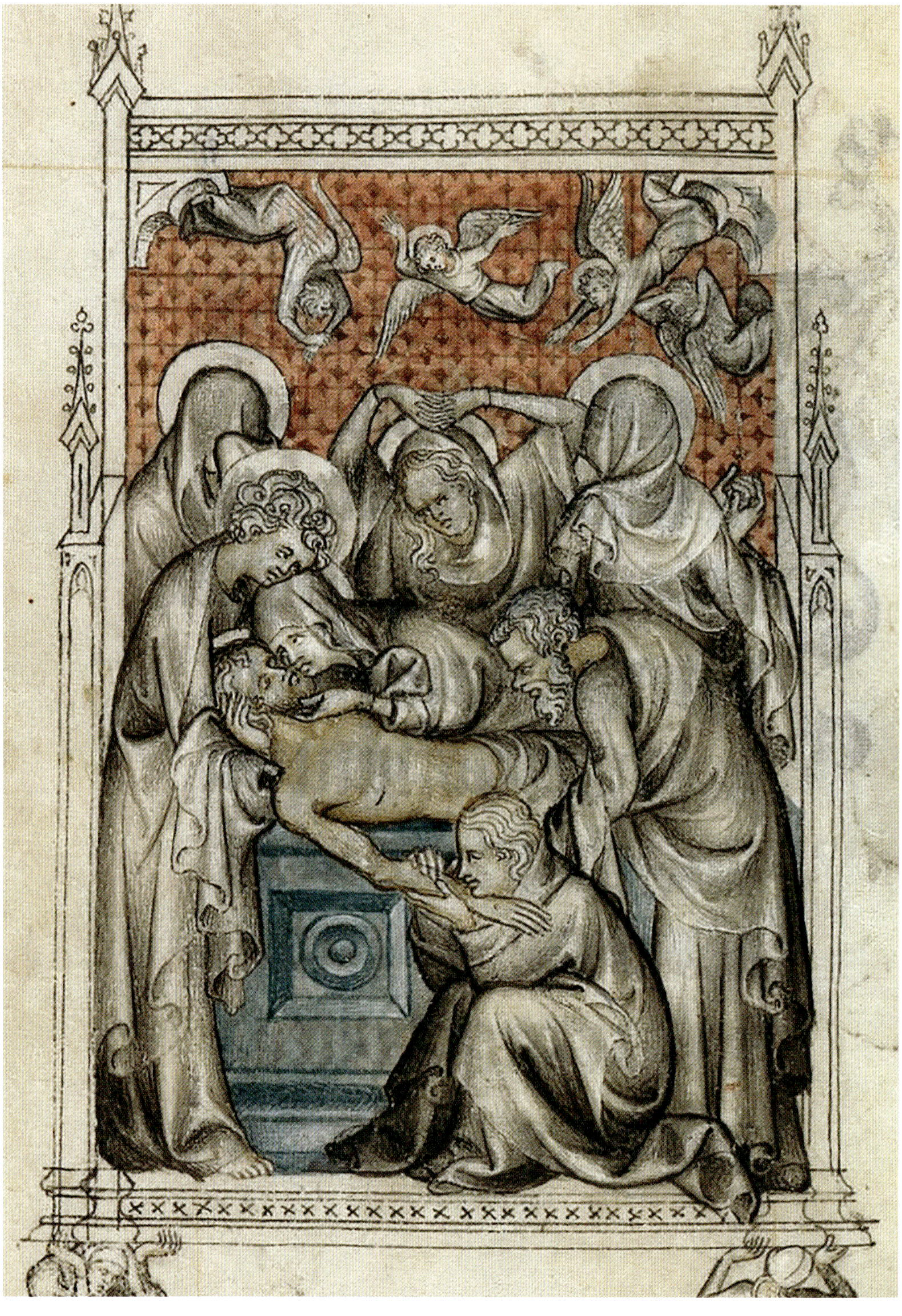

35 Entombment of Christ, Hours of Queen Jeanne d'Evreux, about 1324–8 (New York, The Cloisters Collection, MS 54.1.2, fol. 82v)

family or sororal resemblance, but their moral ends (that is, causes) differ: *Forma facit similis, causaque dissimilis*.[58] This formal continuity is not a matter of nuance but of the ordinary rhetoric of antithesis.[59] Outward similarity conceals an essential difference. That this type of imaginative beholding deployed *enargeia* and memory I have already suggested from other sources; but at Erfurt what strikes particularly is the ratchet effect in comparison with Magdeburg.[60] That some discomfort might arise from this over-amplification of gesture will be true to many who dislike distracting hand-waving or exaggerated gesture, and see it as a sign of discomposure – *gesticulatio*, not communicative *gestus*.[61] The effects are amplified and upgraded in order to continue working. What has changed is not their kind, but their degree. Such thinking was of course insensitive in holding that there was some correlation between affective response and sheer quantity and intensity of description. It was not unfamiliar to thirteenth-century clerics familiar with the (ultimately rhetorical) idea that to maintain attention in an audience they must bring about a striking change of activity. A well-known instance is supplied by the Spanish Bishop Lucas of Tuy writing probably in the 1220s. In criticising new-fangled, and to him heretical, three-nail Crucifixes with one nail going through Christ's overlapping feet (in fact the usual Gothic formula), Bishop Lucas put words into his adversaries' mouths to the effect that the new type of Cross was intended to provoke audiences by the sight of its greater pain, so allaying boredom at traditional depictions.[62] His text plays off *fastidium* (boredom or nausea) with inflaming (*excitatio*) in a way consistent with the value of *varietas* in stimulating pleasure and preventing tedium.[63]

A deployment of striking extremes, strong contrasts and marked visual effects brings to mind the contemporary work of another cathedral canon, Thomas Bradwardine (d. 1349) of Oxford, London and Lincoln, whose treatise on artificial memory draws on the *Ad Herennium*. In writing about memory location, Thomas passes to the furnishing of mind locations with memorable images. Their size should be average but their qualities telling:

> Their quality truly should be wondrous and intense, because such things are impressed in memory more deeply and are better retained. However such things are for the best part not averages but extremes, as the most beautiful or ugly, delightful or sad, worthy of respect or something ridiculous or derisory, a thing of great dignity or vileness, or wounded with greatly opened wounds with a remarkably lively flowing of blood, or in another way made extremely ugly, strange of clothing and all bizarre of equipment, the colour also very brilliant and intense, such as intense glowing red, and the whole colour strongly altering the appearance. The whole image also should have some other detail or movement, that thus more effectively than through what is routine or at rest, they may be commended to memory.[64]

Bradwardine's strongly sensory imagery, summoning up a brilliant red and striking movement, relates directly to the colour language of portals – we might recall the 'red doors' noted earlier – and to the gestures and postures of *figurae*. His mental images have that impressive and vivid actuality arising from *enargeia*: the whole point is their memorable and rather pushy out of the ordinariness.[65] What we see at Erfurt answers well to this schedule of syncretistic formal and affective contrast, between qualities of joy or sadness, or the ridiculous and the dignified.

Bradwardine thinks of emotions such as joy or sadness as qualities of a thing or image. But a work of art, having no life and hence no conscious inner life – at least to rationalists – cannot truly have such qualities. Inner emotional states are the private objects of thought or feeling of living subjects which, according to some schools of thought, cannot be observed empirically. That, at any rate, is the belief of behaviourism, which maintains that we can truly read only public dispositions not private ones – that the only domain of emotional analysis is what is on show.[66] Whatever our views about behaviourism as such, this insight is useful to us because reading an image's emotions is, indeed can only be, a form of behaviourist interpretation: an image is not actually joyful or sad but behaves, or appears to behave, joyfully or sadly. What is involved in this semblance is not actual behaviour, conduct, but the fixed vestiges or signs of conduct. In such thinking, mental states can be thought of not as objects but as adverbs.[67] Joy, happiness, grief, despair are actions or aspects of actions as much as fixed states, and we attribute them *to* images. This is what our earlier encounter at Fontevrault suggested: that the good and bad kings in the Last Judgement were acting out affects, albeit permanently frozen in stone.

Emotions in medieval discourse are by their nature movements within persons, rather than within voiceless things. While both persons and artworks might possess those tools of eloquence, namely an expressive face (*vultus*) and gestures (*gestus*), only persons have a voice (*vox*), to single out the three 'tongues' of delivery in medieval rhetoric.[68] So, despite scholastic clarity on the nature of the affects and the virtue of charity and pity in and between humans, it is a slightly larger step to try to work out which of these passions might be acted out by carved images of Wise and Foolish Virgins of the sort at Magdeburg or Erfurt. The basis, as noted, must be the accounts in Matthew 24–5 and Luke 13:24–8. Perhaps we might think first of joy or hope as opposed to sadness or, better, despair – emotions borne by both the face and the body as *imagines verborum*. Something on the spectrum of joy or complacency coupled to the extremity of despair seems 'about right', granted that basic emotions have an involuntary, and probably universal, aspect. We might better think of these states as actions: 'joying' as opposed to 'despairing' for example. Such actions may point to an affect and provoke it, or they may act as cues or emphases for scriptural reminiscence.[69] We are not wrong in thinking of the ability of these faces and gestures to be not just expressive but expressive of something.[70] But we can see straight away that involved in this guessing-game about *figurae* at the more subtle, symbolic, level is an act of estimation.[71] To cite Michael Baxandall's sensitive discussion of the issue, this act should resist brutalisation by the imposition of a schedule of terms.[72] The act, itself socially, culturally and historically determined, stands at the precarious boundary between the natural and the artificial, and is borne out less by responses to Gothic art than the substantial evidence in Greek *ekphraseis* that a single image could be thought to represent different, even contradictory emotions as a sign of artistic prowess.[73]

But even if we could reasonably estimate what the passions depicted might be, what passions in the audience (if any) might have greeted these depictions in turn? A modern psychological account of this exchange would almost certainly be guided by the ideas of empathy and sympathy. The sight of a (real) weeping or grieving woman surely moves us towards her naturally or spontaneously. Whether we feel sympathy or empathy, however, is moot. Sympathy (a term of early modern origin) is a form of agreement with another person which maintains a distance between the subjects involved. If I sympathise, I 'feel for' another, but I do not necessarily feel the same. Sympathy is a form of acknowledgement of the other person as a separate feeling subject. In contrast, empathy (a solely modern term first systematically explored through the German psychological word *Einfühlung*) is a feeling 'at one with' another which overcomes this distance in a fuller, more total psychological and especially bodily comprehension and identification. If I empathise with another, I feel the same as the other in a kind of unity. Empathy is the faculty whereby we are brought into another's subjective awareness, so as to have a first-person perspective on someone else's world. It is therefore an ambitious concept. It does not simply entail an affective movement towards something but an actual entry into their state of mind and body. Such entry is premised on a modern concept of the autonomous or unitary self encountering and penetrating another such self. We are familiar with such established medieval notions as affect, charity, pity (see pl. 88), compassion (that is, sympathy), friendship and the theological and mystical concept of co-inherence, which are for the most part separable from the notion of empathy properly understood.[74] Exactly how common a truly empathetic response was in medieval literature or art is worth some reflection.

To suggest therefore that an audience, modern or medieval, could empathise with a carved figure is to make an ambitious and essentially naturalistic claim: rather than a sensation being produced in a subject by the artwork, it is in some sense objectified by or within the artwork and then 'transmitted' to the subject. Underlying this claim is a 'hydraulic' understanding of emotions which sees them as universal, transparent, unwilled and uncontrollable emanations, involuntary signs, rather than as symbolic, acculturated dispositions.[75] Images could thereby transparently (and trans-historically) body forth emotions which produce the same emotions in audiences in a way that should be sincere, beyond dispute, rather as in Expressionist aesthetics or what modern criticism has called Expressive Realism.[76]

Unfortunately, this process is not necessarily beyond dispute. The problem of emotional participation and response to texts and artefacts is both extraordinarily difficult and interesting. A significant, but sometimes unacknowledged, difficulty of empathetic readings of public sculptures is that it is by no means clear that we respond with emotions to artefacts in exactly the same way that we respond to or participate in real life. No matter how moving, plausible or convincing images of the Wise and (especially) the Foolish Virgins may be, for example, we can see that a represented person might be pitiable without necessarily feeling pity ourselves. In looking at the Foolish Virgins we might 'entertain' pity without feeling pity exactly as a 'naturalistic' emotion. The belief that they are pitiable does not require a corresponding emotion or internal movement. Kendall Walton has examined this question of emotional participation in fictions or make-believe by means of the notion of 'quasi emotion', which is to say a form of emotion which is akin to, but not identical with, emotion felt in regard to non-fictional states. He says: 'skepticism concerning . . . psychological attitudes purportedly aimed at fictional objects is in order as well. We should be wary of the idea that people literally pity Willy Loman or grieve for Anna Karenina'.[77] While we may see emotion demonstrated, and even entertain those emotions – think about them, or experience them in the way we might experience an emotion if reading about it – we do not necessarily feel them: we are not hustled by them into action as we might be in real life. This issue is related to the difficulty we have in giving accounts of emotional responses to art. The gap between art and life is meaningful: emotion is something encountered imaginatively as well as experienced physically.

A reasonable initial objection to this line of thought about quasi-emotion is that there is surely a difference of degree and kind between the decline of a Brooklyn salesman, Willy Loman, and Christ dying for humankind on the Cross, where the issue is faith in something fully historical, what C. S. Lewis once called a 'true myth', and not fiction or make-believe. This objection has some force.[78] Little hangs on a fiction but, to believers at least, much hangs on the Cross (see pls 39, 62 and 67). Yet this also exposes a difficulty inherent in the now widespread tendency to dissolve the art–life boundary. It is that the horror of the Crucifixion experienced actually could never be reduced to art: faced with the terrible reality, all images would seem powerless. Fictional situations or objects clearly differ not just in whether or not they are consequential but in regard to their intensity and probably also their nature, and this creates a difficulty for the universalising (and I think reductive) claim of some image anthropology that we react to texts or artefacts just as we do to people or real-life situations: that life and fiction are the same.[79]

In fact the notion of entertained or quasi-emotion, though derived from a theory of fiction and make-believe, also admits something we can identify in medieval imagination at exactly the period we are considering, the mid-thirteenth century. This is the idea of 'cogitation'. Cogitation in the rhetorical and medieval sense is not bald reasoning but an active or moving process of mind and feeling (*cogitatio*, from *con* + *agito*, 'move, rouse') in thinking about a subject as if it were a creative, meditative or compositorial activity involving will, desire.[80] All such processes require some sort of guidance, habit, even prescription, and they certainly require time and reflection rather than knee-jerk response. An excellent instance is provided by the influential pastoral text the *Speculum Ecclesie* composed by Edmund of Abingdon (whose ivory statuette of the Virgin Mary we have already encountered), in the early years of the thirteenth century and so circulating at the high point of Gothic 'verism'; it was translated into French.[81] Writing in the tradition of St Anselm's affective devotional literature, Edmund advises the readers or listeners at each of the Hours of the liturgical day to ponder a pair of events from the Life of Christ: for example, at Matins, the Nativity and Betrayal, at Sext the Crucifixion and Incarnation. 'Ponder' is a fair translation of Edmund's repeated phrase at the outset of each meditation, *debes cogitare* or 'penser' in the French.[82] Consider chapter 20 of the *Speculum*:

> Before Matins you should first ponder the Lord's Nativity, and after that His Passion. About the Nativity, you should ponder diligently the time, place and hour in which our *sweet* Lord Jesus Christ was born. The time was midwinter, when it was *coldest*; the hour was midnight, the *hardest* hour; the place was in the middle of the street in a wall-less house. . . . Here you should ponder Mary's diligent care for her boy; and of how Joseph her husband had great *joy* [my emphases].

Edmund here sets out a basic plot or circumstances, but his language is sensory, full of adjectives picking out sensations and pointing to affects: how Joseph had great joy, *habuit magnum gaudium*, for instance. It leads us through cogitation and compunction (that 'pricking' of the conscience, *ardor compunctionis*, we read about earlier in Pope Gregory's letters), to self-reform. Sensory and affective language is used to help move the sensations, give them shape, vigour and memorability. It would be wrong not to think of the rigours of the season, the wall-less shack and Mary's tenderness as moving. However, things are indicated, not entered into or replicated internally or empathetically. The objects of cogitation are not the reading or listening subject's inward movement of sensations, but the outward affective actions of the Gospel events being conjured up and contemplated. Sensory as is Edmund of Abingdon's language, it is also remarkably unprescriptive, a form of cueing. This is why it is compositorial: it offers a starting-point for us as composers, just as our portals offer starting-points, get things going. Much of this is recognisable in the account of John at Fontevrault discussed earlier. We are being presented with an instrumental movement towards what Edmund calls *cognicio tui*, self-knowledge in regard to the outcome of all sinful and mortal things, which has as its beneficial goal or utility what he calls the 'perfection of life'.[83] Reason and emotion are not wholly different things but combine in the experiencing subject in a way that is active and conventional, which requires and inculcates habit but which, precisely because it is educable, also allows the sort of distancing apparent in entertained emotion. This is not emotional self-examination in the modern sense: the purpose or endpoint is not a state of being but action developed from self-knowledge that involves a complex of ideas combining contemplation and cognition.[84]

At stake then is the relation of emotion and moral assessment, and so action. There is no necessary ensuing connection between exciting emotion in people and making them sororal or charitable. Empathy (properly understood), as opposed to rational compassion, anger or admiration, is not *ipso facto* a constitutive precondition for positive moral judgement.[85] This point is illustrated by the well-known discussion in the 94th *questio* in the supplement to Part 3 of Thomas Aquinas's *Summa Theologiae* which ponders the question whether the blessed in heaven, or mortals, might justifiably pity, or rejoice at the sight of, the torments of the damned in Hell (see pls 21 and 24). In his reply to the latter problem, Aquinas cites Psalm 57:11, 'The just shall rejoice when he shall see the revenge: he shall wash his hands in the blood of the sinner', and goes on to respond that while to rejoice in the suffering of another for its own sake is really hatred, to rejoice at the suffering of another as a sign of a good (that is, something 'annexed' to the good) is not hatred.[86] So, by implication, rejoicing at the plight of the Foolish Virgins, who are usually placed on the side of the damned and to whom the door is shut and who grieve eternally, would not necessarily be bad (or in modern terms, malicious or sadistic) if that rejoicing ended, say, in good things such as shame, pity or repentance and the triumph of God's justice. Intention is all.

Holding that emotions do not automatically entail beliefs does not mean that emotion and belief are totally separate, however: the cognitive model of persuasion argues against that, as we can now see. Indeed, this model is owed ultimately to Aristotle, and also Avicenna: emotion and belief are, and should be, connected, though it is typical of the Aristotelian model that it thinks about this relationship as more detached than the penetrative model of modern empathy. Edmund of Abingdon and Thomas Aquinas were both as Aristotelian as the general tenor of much thirteenth-century pastoral thought.[87] Hence the Thomist concern just stated about whether pity or joy might appropriately accompany the sight of suffering. The very fact that this question can be posed is interesting. It seems odd, from a modern perspective, to think of 'appropriate' emotion. This is why I have often used the word 'affect' to indicate something other than emotion or psychology. The oldest doctrines about emotions, owed chiefly to Plato, saw them as passive and not active: emotion is, so to speak, a 'suffering' not a 'doing'. In the widely accepted Aristotelian and Avicennan formulation carried into medieval Christian ethics, however, emotions are inherently manifestations of an attitude or assessment open to praise or blame; affects are not just spontaneous and natural activities of the emotions but are embodied movements (hence the word 'emotion', from the Latin *emoveo*) of sensation and will, changes which arise because will and the passions shape each another.[88] We are drawn towards, or repelled from, something. Because affects are embodied they are apparent externally.

In his 94th *questio* just mentioned, Aquinas pinpoints this issue of intentionality: passions that are not simply wilful have *intent towards* something, because an intention is an aim. We get some way to understanding this by thinking about 'attitude' as both a mindset and physical stance. We have an attitude 'to' or 'towards' something. Affects can be taught, crafted, because a disposition is not just an appetite but something educable, like a habit, and also something in itself capable of argument.[89] So, as the moral theologians of the twelfth century argued, moral virtue requires not the expression of emotion but its regulation. And the purpose or end of that regulation is what Aquinas came to call a 'good disposition of the mind', *bona dispositio mentis*. This disposition, or attitude, is an appropriate bending of affect or striving towards the good or delightful, and away from what is fearful, and that process begins by being well captivated in the first place.

To repeat: the medieval artwork does not exist 'for the sake' of emotion in the way that a post-medieval or Romantic one might. The affective attaining of a good disposition of mind is purposeful, instrumental, a means and not an end. It involves a willed feeling of rightness or decorum, a feeling which, precisely because it is willed, is also educable and social. To return to our example of a viewer's experience of the Foolish Virgins, that disposition of mind might entail pity or it might entail a form of rejoicing at the operation of the greater good of God's justice. In other words, one perfectly legitimate response to such displays might have been that the Foolish Virgins were just improvident young women who had rightly got their just deserts. This last idea might seem incongruous and unempathetic, even cruel, nowadays, but only if we persist with the naturalistic and essentially modern view of interiority, emotion and moral destiny that I am trying to clarify. There is a risk in retrofitting the twelfth and thirteenth centuries with insights gleaned not just from modern emotional 'styles' but even from later medieval or even post-medieval devotional conduct also documented in connection with other art forms, such as religious drama.[90] What was true of the era of Margery Kempe (d. about or after 1438) or Lydwine of Schiedam (d. 1433), to say nothing of the Counter-Reformation, was not necessarily true of the era of Louis IX (d. 1270).

Indeed, emotions were provably bound together with thoughts and conduct that we might now deem actually incongruous. The late fourteenth-century dramatic feast of the Presentation of the Virgin associated with Philippe de Mézières includes a striking passage during the drama in which Synagoga (as at Strasbourg, pl. 36), facing up to the truth and inclining her head to her left and as if miserable (*tristis*), turning round and appearing to cry, is promptly expelled weeping and wailing from the dramatic arena arranged in the church, in such a way that it takes a while for the audience to quieten down their laughter at her plight: despite her eloquent behaviour, Synagoga's pathetic state is ridiculed, not empathised with.[91] What, in such a case mixing *ludus* and *seria*, is an appropriate passion or *bona passio*?[92] The 'appropriate' affects towards the Foolish Virgins and their apparent plight

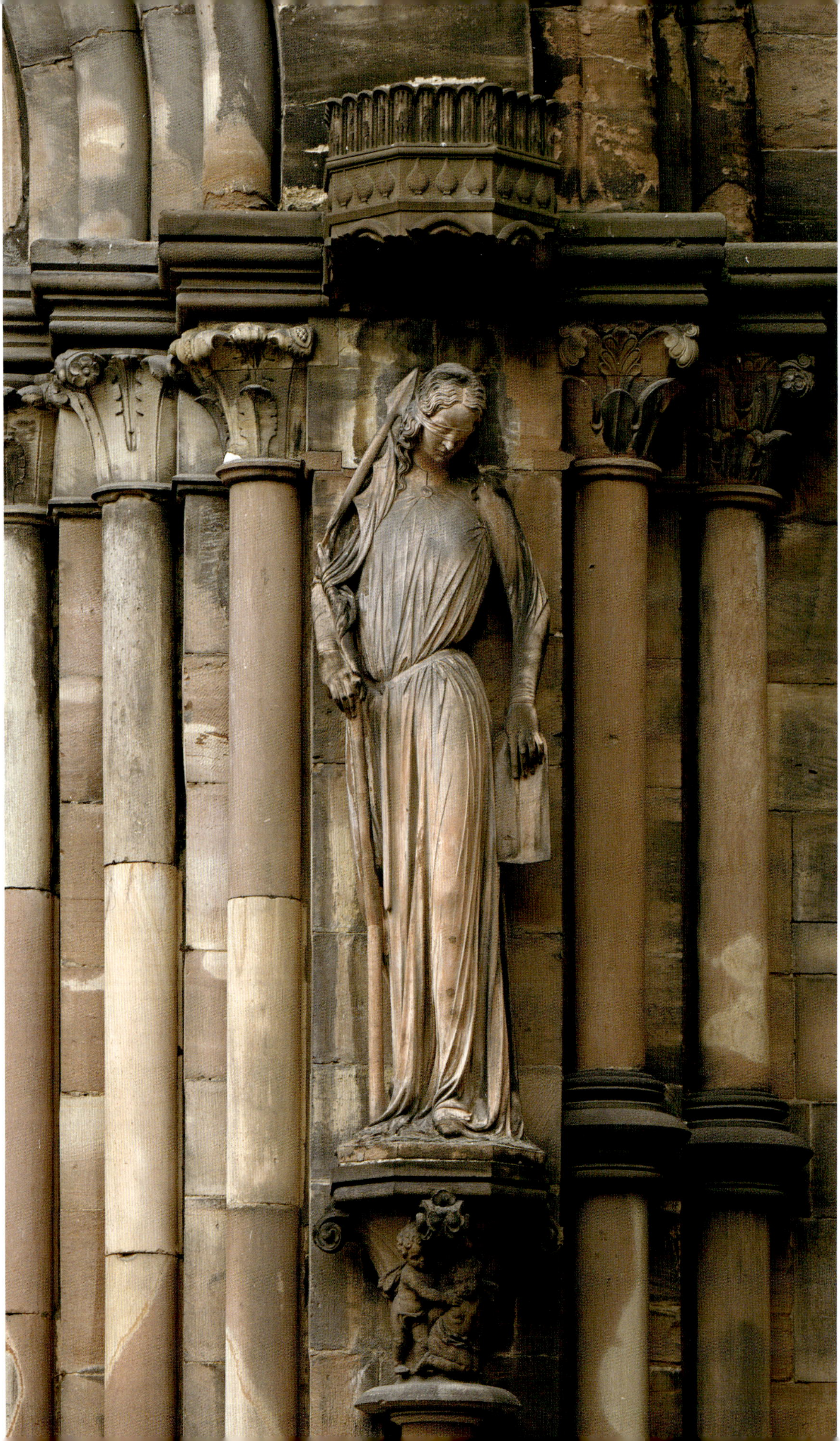

might also vary because the affects were themselves understood to be inherently mixed and in flux, which is partly why figuring them out is contextual and estimative, as I have already suggested.[93] Some of the most odd yet gripping later medieval images such as the 'joyful' *Pietà* (examples from St Walburg, Eichstätt, and St Martin, Bamberg) are complex paradoxes, for tears are not identified with specific inward or psychological states: they can accompany joy as the sweet accompanies the bitter.[94] The image does not hustle us into primitive sentimental identification; rather, it poses a problem. Each one of us, in Julian of Norwich's words, is 'a mevelous medelur both of wele and of woo'.[95] In such paradox lies theological wisdom.

The same sort of objection applies to moral readings of portal figures. We understand from John of Garland that a moralised, and therefore ethical-mimetic reading of portal figures was absolutely authentic to the times. But this understanding does not entail that specific virtuous, or for that matter vicious, states were fully and aesthetically incorporated into these figures and so naturally inferable from them.[96] It is one thing to infer a generally virtuous disposition from a sculpted figure, another to infer specific virtuous attributes distinguishing, say, temperance from humility. The view that this inference is possible places such images under great pressure, and runs the risk of falling into the so-called 'naturalistic fallacy' whereby virtuous states (or emotions) are regarded as having self-evident or natural physical outer forms which themselves automatically imply certain (moral, social, psychological) norms: we unjustifiably derive what ought to be the case from what we take to be the facts of the case. The facts of the case are usually more complex, and certainly more relative. Shakespeare nailed this problem in *Macbeth* (Act 1 scene 4) when Duncan says ruefully 'There's no art to find the mind's construction in the face'. I have argued elsewhere that even the apparently innocent action of laughter, as convincingly depicted in Gothic sculptures of the mid-thirteenth century, does not necessarily point to a humorous inner state or a happy radiance of soul, but to the possibility (to put it no more strongly, since there were many forms of laughter) of something more ambivalent and to our modern eyes less pleasant, namely the 'superiority' theory of laughter.[97] This Aristotelian-derived theory maintained that laughter, though natural to humans, was not a sign of joy or humour but of supercilious scorn and derision, expressing not benevolence but lack of pity at the ridiculous, unfortunate or indecorous. This is certainly inconsistent with a simplistic or altruistic notion of empathy because it reveals the acculturated and artificial nature of what we now call expressivity. A moment ago I cited an instance of this, the public mocking by laughter of Synagoga. The fact is that the surface of a face is a mask, that humans are skilled dissemblers, and that our modern emotions are not necessarily occasioned in the same way as were theirs. Medieval rhetorical practices as set out in the *ars poetriae* noted that words may have misleading faces, for (to cite Geoffrey of Vinsauf's *Poetria Nova* of about 1210) words, like

36 Strasbourg Cathedral (Alsace), south transept, Synagoga
(a modern copy; original in the Musée de l'Oeuvre, Notre-Dame, Strasbourg, about 1230)

faces, may be fictions, merely hypocritical whitewashed walls.[98] It is at this obstacle that the behaviourist reading falters.

In regard to the Foolish Virgins' deportment at Magdeburg, Jacqueline Jung catches the sense of this when she states that the Virgins are engaged in 'demonstrative acts of public communication meant to highlight the seriousness of a situation', a different issue to my mind from personal empathetic or mimetic engagement as it is often described.[99] Earlier I remarked on the presence of law courts before portals such as that at Strasbourg. In her study of the imagery of Ecclesia and Synagoga on such portals, Nina Rowe draws attention not to the seductions of affect or empathy, but to the punitive and so social role of imagery of the ethical-typological sort. At Erfurt the Wise and Foolish Virgins are aligned respectively with Ecclesia and Synagoga in order to sharpen the point. At Bamberg accused criminals were bound to the post beneath its image of Synagoga: such things were 'an index of the larger spiritual developments of the late thirteenth and fourteenth centuries', the disciplinary pastoral culture of penitence and repentance.[100]

I maintain, then, that *figurae* were demonstrative guides, ways of indicating which deliberately stirred affects in their audience by inclining or bending the audience's intentions. They were lures as well as means of emphasising and pointing in publicly verifiable fashion.[101] That which is striking, attractive or human-seeming was deployed as a technique to produce and guide thinking and felt responses according to a path, a narrative of understanding in the light of *evidentia* (I use the word 'narrative' to underline the developing rather than knee-jerk character of understanding). Because the responses are felt, they are far from dispassionate. However, the purpose of this creation of sensation was not a calculated and cold-blooded arousal of personal feelings, or emotional diktat: emotions are activities on the way, not outcomes, and they are experienced and constituted socially.[102] Rather, they direct the audience's inclinations, beliefs and judgements. One possible outcome of such direction is change of mind: *metanoia*, or repentance. And from that follows action: again, affect-effect.

Yet, as I have said, it has become common to consider responses to portal sculptures more in terms of the natural, personal and private than the conventional, cognitive and social. That the key period of the twelfth and thirteenth centuries – my main concern – suffers from a dearth of objective evidence for response of any type has not detained the trend towards emotivist discussion, from which the 'affective turn' in medieval studies – a turn towards the study of the relation of emotion and culture – has not been free. The medieval notion of affect exposes a further issue about that false friend in any historical engagement, familiarity. We value most and understand best, or so we think, that which is familiar to us. What is often held explicitly or implicitly to be a broad historical transition in the arts of the period from symbolic to aesthetic or expressive modes, I submit, is based on a privileging of the familiar which is implicitly grounded in modern veristic or indexical notions of realism and which underplays the essentially artificial or technical character of art and affect. This outlook is typical of the 'affective turn'.

THE AFFECTIVE TURN: SOME ISSUES

I shall postpone to a later chapter any thoughts about sculpture and the issue of 'presence'. Instead, I focus next on the formulation of a now long-familiar narrative in the religious and cultural history of Europe in the high and late Middle Ages which has underwritten the 'affective turn' in medieval studies – a preoccupation with emotion and changes of emphasis in theology on the humanity as well as the divinity of Christ, the rise of more individual, inward or personal devotional or other religious responses and increased lay participation. This issue matters because it has coloured our understanding not just of sculpture but of medieval art more generally.

My aim here is not to sideline the emotions from within what James Elkins calls the 'Ivory Tower of Tearlessness'.[103] In regard to later medieval devotional and mystical piety that would be an uphill task. It is rather to try to place emotion in a historically appropriate way, and to question what explanatory force affectivity may have in the formation of indexical imitation, the imitation of actual appearances, in the period before 1350 or so. As is well known (in anglophone scholarship), the leading figures in this grand narrative of the 'new emotionalism' are often recognised as St Anselm, St Bernard and St Francis together with a significant input from religious women; the historians of this turn extend from Emile Mâle, Frederic Raby and Richard Southern to writers of the present day.[104] Raby's 1953 formulation is still current: the new age of Gothic pathos, the new emotionalism (pl. 37), replaced 'the old calm theological symbolism' with 'a terrible and sorrowful realism of detail'.[105] Southern's *The Making of the Middle Ages* (also published in 1953) subscribed to this idea and lent it authority and a wide audience.[106] In that year too appeared Otto von Simson's celebrated paper on *compassio* which argued along the same lines.[107] Eric Auerbach's influential thoughts about the anti-Stoical character of medieval glorying in suffering, *gloria passionis*, followed in 1958.[108] This narrative still holds, though significantly extended in recent decades by the study of gender.[109] Stated as such it has obvious implications for art and the way affective religion and piety were represented. John Arnold says, 'The development of "affective piety" in the late middle ages brings with it . . . a rich vocabulary of love, fear, desire and the pull and sway of transcendent feelings'.[110] In his studies of Gothic sculpture, Bruno Boerner has concluded that 'les activités sensorielles et les émotions jouent un rôle essentiel'.[111]

One underrated and perceptive exception is to be found in a book published in 1966 by a textual philologist, F. P. Pickering.[112] Pickering's exploration of the origins of what

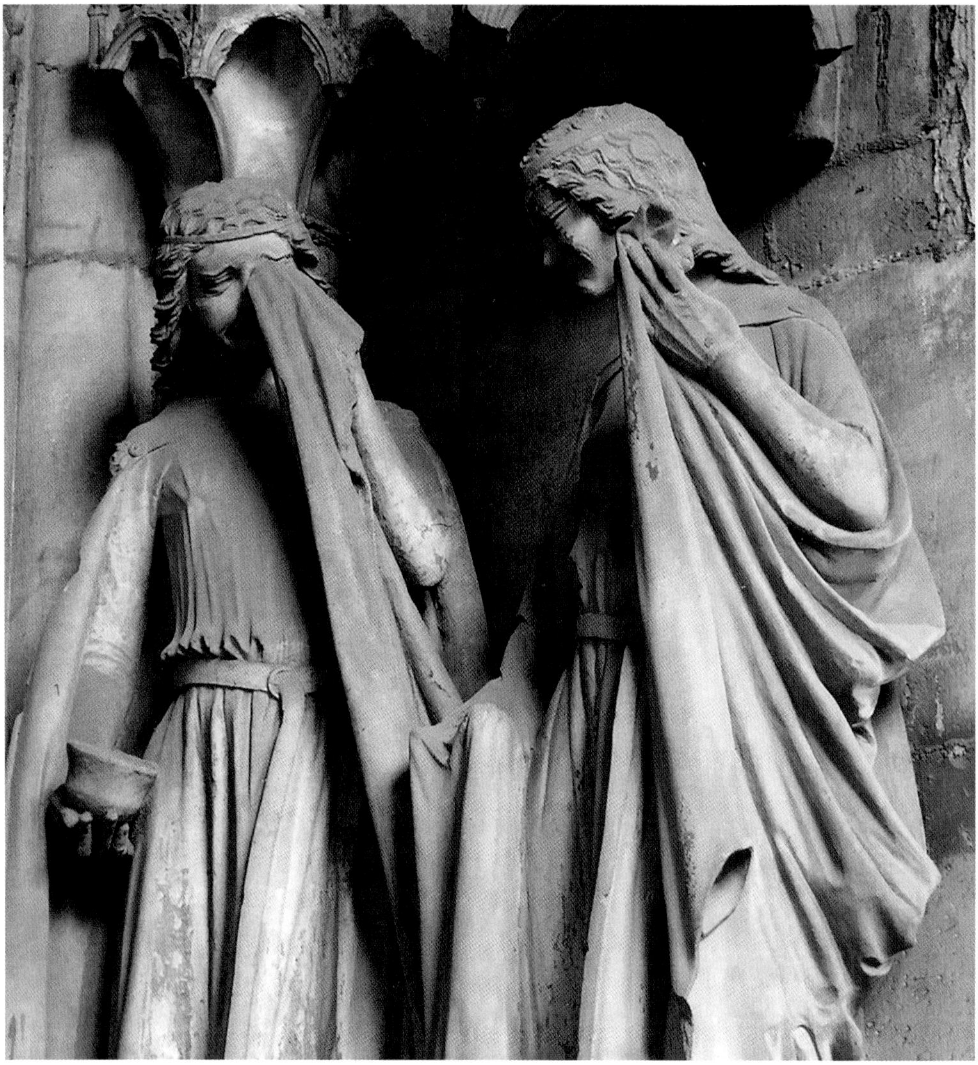

37 Magdeburg Cathedral, north transept, Foolish Virgins, detail, 1240s

he called 'late medieval realism' proceeded from the premise that the religious art of the Middle Ages was primarily theological and textual, though he was not unsympathetic to images. His critique was based on the idea that the conviction purpose of medieval art was primarily discursive or intellectual, and that even the most seemingly original visionary experiences owed their imagery to prior textual or visual sources.[113] In the light of my emphasis on the coupling of emotion and reason – in such a way that emotions can themselves be reasonable – Pickering's account seems reductive and one-sided because in it the affective and sensory dimension of conviction is downplayed. According to Pickering, 'What characterises the Crucifixion story is . . . its capacity to convince rather than to move'.[114] On the spectrum of medieval opinion, Pickering is perhaps closer to Lydgate than to St Anselm: here indeed is the ivory tower of tearlessness. Conviction surely entails a movement of the passions as well as of the mind, and objects and affects unquestionably play a part as much as reasoning. Still, Pickering makes two telling general points. The first is that 'realism' is not readily separable from text and textual artifice and convention: the 'realism' of the Crucifixion was first and foremost a textual not an artistic event, because it had to convince and conform doctrinally, and when that event became artistic its discursive basis was inescapable.[115] The second is that to argue that the changes implicit in the new Gothic pathos were caused by some antecedent adjustment in sensibility, identified by Southern as a 'general change of attitude which found expression in many different ways', is, according to Pickering, to argue impressionistically and in circular fashion, seeking, as he puts it 'an explanation of the art of the Gothic in a *sentiment religieux*, and then finding the same sentiment reflected in art': the history of feeling cannot be both a cause and an effect of the changes apparent in art.[116] What Pickering spotted was that naturalistic theories about the 'new emotionalism' were causally vague, inherently expressionistic and confused about the nature of naturalism itself.

As a critique of even comparatively recent art-historical practice, some at least of Pickering's charges stick. Art historians have tended to tiptoe round causal issues, preferring – as Pickering points out – to displace major changes onto the history of spirituality, the rise of secularism, drama and so on, as if art itself did not present particular conventional and technical problems that demand corresponding, if hard to locate, explanations. An instance of this causal deferral is Peter Kidson's admirably succinct 1987 essay on the extraordinary sculpted rood and Passion images on the *lettner* (sculpted choir screen) of Naumburg Cathedral (see pl. 12).[117] In assessing their 'realism', Kidson distinguishes between two 'modes of empathy', one pre-mimetic and one frankly and explicitly mimetic; he avows that artistic change is 'not something to be explained in terms of superficial causes' but maintains nevertheless that change can come from 'impetus', from the 'different mood and purpose of much Gothic religious art', which found it 'expedient' to shift emphasis from Christology to 'what it may have been like' to have witnessed events in the Gospels, thereby launching a 'sustained onslaught on the emotions of the devout'.[118] This is indeed the typical narrative of the 'new emotionalism' in which 'mood' works both as cause and effect.

In my judgement, this pervasive style of argument deserves interrogation precisely in order to be able to understand affectivity and its roles in regard to the criticism of artefacts. So anchored is this argument to modern ideas of indexicality that, at first sight, it appears intuitively obvious that because an image does not 'look' affective, historically it did not have an affective role. But intuitions mislead. Let me suggest an analogy from another medium, music. Harmonically, medieval music was based on a system of 'modes' derived from the ancient world, which pre-dated the system of major and minor keys familiar to us from the early modern period when the doctrine of affect in music was made explicit.[119] The old modes were associated with different affects much as were the later major and minor keys, though those affects differed. But we could not assume from the fact that because the modes lack major and minor formations (associated now with positive and negative affects), they were not affective. Their registration of affect was culturally different from what we now naturally expect of music – a natural expectation based on key-sounds that are as artificial as the earlier modes. This is why experiencing the affects of medieval music (or music from outside our own cultural traditions) can be confusing or obscure: the aesthetic experience of it has a strongly acculturated and situational dimension. Why should images have differed?

Intention and expectation are vital to overcoming the illusion that familiarity helps. There is no necessary causal connection between any one set of representational conventions and their affectivity, precisely because the notion of affect as an intentional attitude towards something requires agency on the part both of object and of viewing subject. Object and subject are both participative and historically situated. The notion of subject agency is useful because it helps to account for the vivid role in medieval acts of viewing and contemplation of, to us, apparently bland, uninformative images which were functionally affective and which possessed great imaginative power. Indeed, the less specific the agency of the object or representation in regard to detail, the deeper and more vivid was the corresponding beholding subject's supplementative imagination, or 'beholder's share' in response.[120] An instance of this 'seeing in' would be the type of devotional attention to Christ's face, envisaged as a portal to higher religious understanding, assisted by Matthew Paris's bland mid-thirteenth-century drawings of three faces of Christ, one with His mother (pl. 38), which originally opened the first volume of his great chronicle or *Chronica Majora* drawn up at St Albans, contemporary with the veristic triumphs of Reims and Naumburg (see pls 41 and 47).[121] In such a case the issue is not whether the beholder sees the face of Christ as Christ, but whether the beholder can bring to the representation a sense of a state of affairs, a narrative, symbolic possibilities or other qualities which are seen in the face and which enrich it as a representation in the beholder's mind. The objective or formal properties of the representation are fictional, but the properties steer or guide the imaginative and intentional possibilities. Such images' relative blankness, as a form of surface property, provokes the beholder's engagement. In these cases attention is formed by monastic disciplines of meditation and contemplation; it was itself a sort of skill, a technique. A monk could not think just anything when face to face with Christ: this was not a fantasy relation but was guided by memory, habit and imagination understood as a faculty of composing. Meditation is served by images – even talismans – that possess quietness or lack of interference from surface detail extraneous to a

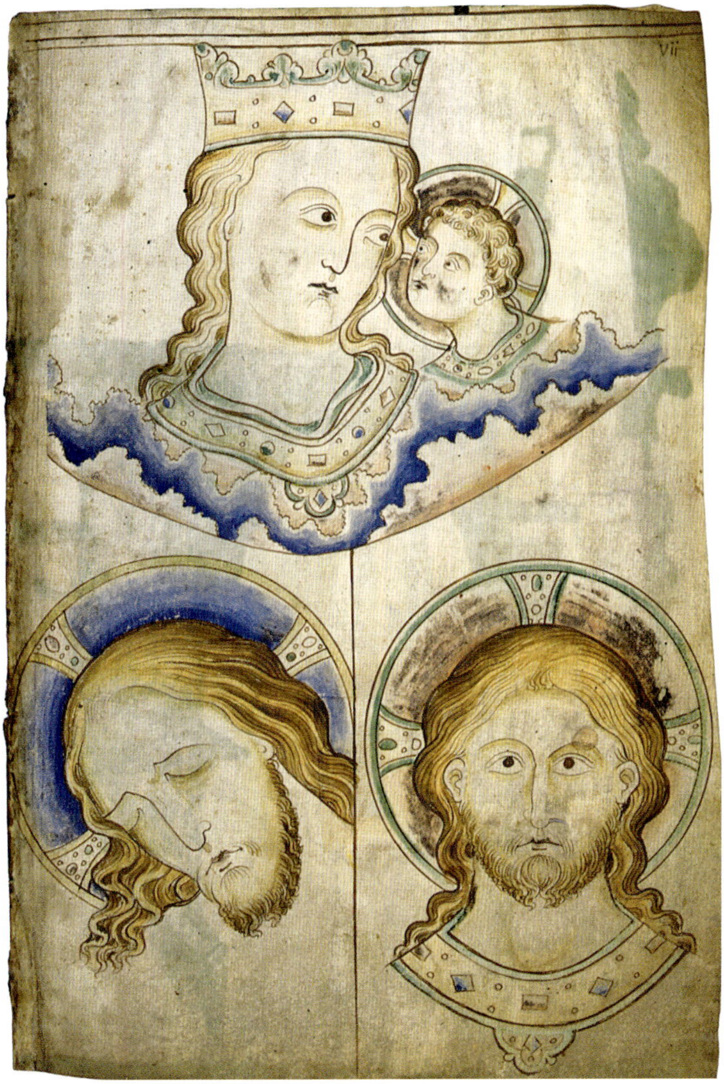

38 Matthew Paris, the Faces of Christ, *Chronica Majora*, 1240s (Cambridge, Corpus Christi College MS 26, fol. vii, formerly p. 283). An image probably intended for monastic contemplation

core message. This is their 'mode'. Things do not have to be spelt out, because they are maps or guides for imaginative compositorial elaboration in which discipline, habit, recollective and heuristic function are paramount, not formal mimesis.[122]

This example is admittedly specialised because it pertains to a class of people, monks, whose contemplative skills were deliberately honed as if they were athletes. But devotion is inherently practical, not speculative or intellectual in character, and because it is practical it can be communicated, crafted and understood socially. Anyone could and can do it to a degree. For people at large it contains a truth, too: people of a certain age still say that 'the pictures are better on radio', since the effect of realism can be amplified precisely by limiting the amount of sensory information pouring in. Literalism hedges the imagination. This recognises that object agency is not diktat but, as in any thoughtful and intentional process, just a starting-point in a reciprocal and imaginative subject–object relationship. It also points forward to another issue, namely change: indexical mimesis of the thirteenth-century sort could be said to have tipped the balance of subject–object agency in favour of the object. A truly affective attitude to images, a truly imaginative response, was not widened by indexicality but limited and controlled by it. As more was rendered explicit and everything spelt out, so much the less was left to the compositorial imagination. Suitably excerpted, the tremendous image of Christ on the cross from S. Maria im Kapitol in Cologne of around 1304 is that of a snarling criminal on a gibbet (pl. 39, see also pl. 108), quite other than the delicate version deliberately excerpted by Matthew Paris (see pl. 38). But this problem has always been hard to admit in turn because of the connection of the idea of indexical mimesis to the rise of human freedom, emotional consciousness and the modern centred subject. Southern refers, for instance, to the 'emergence of the individual' and to the 'impulse towards individual expression' in the romance sensibility as if these ideas were uncontentious.[123] For that we can take the Renaissance and its apologists to task – consider Panofsky's great account of the rise of autonomy and self-possession and 'intrinsic' classicism as a sign of true Gothic sculpture.[124]

My point is that whatever virtue the affective turn may have as a framework for discussing religious art of the time, it is itself implicated in an unacknowledged meta-narrative of realist and individualist thinking. We are expecting medieval images to sound like modern keys when in fact they sounded like modes. One of the affective turn's own rhetorical features is a ready appeal to art as evidence, and especially to images of the Crucifixion and Virgin Mary of the period between the eleventh and thirteenth centuries. These are summoned in order to corroborate or flesh out the affective narrative, without making it clear which was cause and which effect. The appeal to the supposedly self-evident data of images starts with Mâle's vision of the guileless emotional sincerity of Gothic art moving from doctrine to sentiment: 'Jesus no longer taught; he suffered'.[125] The word 'expression' looms constantly. In her seminal study of English religious lyric, Rosemary Woolf refers to a 'change in religious temper' and to a 'new spirit' which was even 'expressed in art before it was formalised in doctrine'.[126] Richard Southern writes of an antecedent 'intensity of human feeling' the expression of which 'artists of the late eleventh century were beginning to achieve'.[127] Writing in 1995 about a deepening and passionate devotion to Christ's humanity in the eleventh century, Giles Constable saw this 'shift in spirituality' as corresponding to

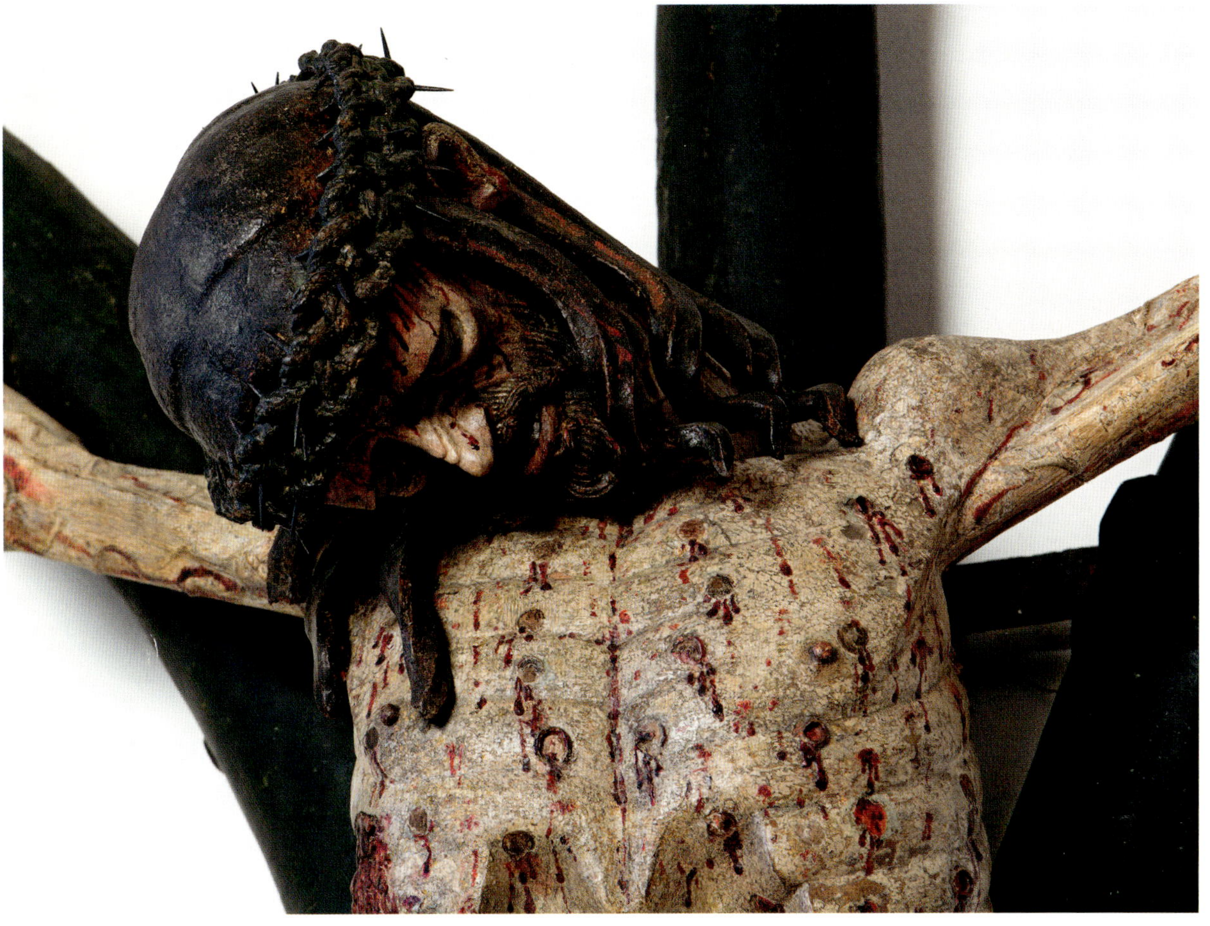

39 Cross, painted wood, S. Maria im Kapitol, Cologne, detail of Christ, about 1304

changes in visual representations of Christ.[128] Art found 'new emotional content', becoming 'explicit' in representing grief and tenderness.[129] In his (far from isolated) view, by the time of the Gothic age images had an even greater constitutive role in fostering affective piety, to the point where nothing was 'left to the imagination of the beholder'.[130] Indeed verism was not solely a Renaissance attainment but reflected the essence of late medieval spirituality.[131]

While the eloquence of these accounts is not to be doubted, nor should be the fact that their thinking is not just incidentally but actively art-historical in character: they are driven and justified by an unstated prior theory about representation itself. The governing concept of the representation of the emotions is essentially expressionistic and tied to post-Romantic assumptions about emotion, representation and indexicality. It requires that we agree about emotion as something beyond question, and that we agree too about what its 'natural' representation might consist of. The art of Giotto by this reading is just obviously more affective than that of the Anglo-Saxons or Ottonians. This may not undermine the affective turn's general descriptive value, its capacity to illuminate and its (justified) recognition that images are constitutive as well as reflective of experience. After all, as Woolf's discussion of the English religious lyric shows amply, images and affective responses to them are directly implicated in the late medieval lyrical sensibility itself, for all its didacticism.[132] The point is that in its tendency to generalise about temper, feeling and spirituality, in its commonsense view of expression, and in its essentialism and tendency to circularity (as Pickering noted), it raises questions about cause and effect. First, in its pursuit of the natural it sets aside the truth that the representation of affect is necessarily artificial and so contextual or occasional. As noted earlier, this is the central objection to expressive realism, of which the affective turn often seems like a version.[133] And second, it tends to overlook the origins of Christian affectivity itself. It is increasingly recognised that the 'new emotionalism' of the high Middle Ages was founded in large measure on the writings of late antique Christian rhetoricians: the new 'realism' was in effect patristic in origin, and benefited from what Pickering calls 'the accumulated formulae of a thousand years of study'.[134] In other words, affectivity long predated what, since the mid-twentieth century, we have been encouraged to think of as affective and realist practices in the visual arts proper to the high and late Middle Ages.

Overlooking this tends in effect to rob pre-Gothic art of its affectivity. Something, in short, may well be awry with our understanding of the emotional and rhetorical chronology. This recognition has a significant consequence for any progressive, naturalistic or teleological view of Christian representation in the twelfth and thirteenth centuries because it causally detaches discourse from visual practice. As noted, vividness, realism, could be true of widely different representational traditions (as in some Byzantine art) or of representations whose appearance does not immediately conform to what we ourselves now might expect of the eloquent image. The obvious instance is the surviving painted Crucifix at S. Damiano that spoke to St Francis, according to his legend; Matthew Paris's *Chronica Majora* faces of Christ are another instance.[135] This insight about intentionality and will destabilises the implicit view that pre-Gothic images are dumb cult objects unresponsive to the viewer, because it maintains that acts of perception are affective and so relative.[136] As noted, they are fully imaginative acts, in the medieval sense of imagination as that which deliberates and composes.[137] For this reason it is just as well that some commentators on the anthropology of medieval gazing and visuality stress the issue of active intention rather than passive reception.[138]

This in turn raises two issues. The first is that the notion of a master discourse of theology or religious practice described by the affective turn may have a weaker or more unstable causal connection to what I have called 'indexical' mimesis than has been claimed. Gothic verism was not a necessary outcome of a 'new emotionalism', and such emotionalism was not a product of Gothic. The theology of affect was objectively or indexically mimetic long before the images were. Images may therefore have been changing for other reasons.

The second point concerns means and ends in the public and private domains. Emotions, as willed affects operative in private or in public, are both educable and educative: they can be trained, crafted or, in Sarah McNamer's word, 'scripted'.[139] As we have seen, affects are to be understood instrumentally. In classic Gregorian terms, a portal's 'arc of address' included what Pope Gregory fatefully called the *populi imperiti*, that is to say the mass of ignorant 'everyman' in whom images provoke the 'ardour of compunction' – affectively driven understanding.[140] The 'poor man's Bible' was undoubtedly possessed of feeling. The belief that affect formed part of the function of works of art or *ornamenta* is closely and extensively documented in the Gothic era, and earlier. Images actual or mental were central to devotional practice throughout the Middle Ages and increasingly so: the Crucifixion, Virgin and Child and innovative image complexes such as the *Arma Christi* were concentrated on, even kissed and fondled as occasions for personal engagement.[141]

But these practical activities were still rooted in public experience, general argument and habit. Affective imagining of the sort proposed by Edmund of Abingdon, noted earlier, was a commonplace of liturgical regulation for the laity.[142] That affective methods were encouraged by such devotional images (*Andachtsbilder*) as the *Pietà* (see pl. 88), Christ with St John and the Man of Sorrows, coming into currency in the fourteenth century in northern Europe, is established.[143] These images played roles in both the public and private domains. Their origins as themes were essentially monastic and so communal, cenobitic rather than egoistic. Inner stillness comes to prevail in what Giles Constable beautifully calls the 'hermitage of the heart': action is supplanted by contemplation, and image is removed from the continuum of narrative.[144] That these images were practical in nature – that they implied spiritual skills, a kind of craft of religion, and prompted an affect or stance towards them as a matter of method – is beyond dispute. Their calculated rhetorical quietness does not distract from their complexity and bitter-sweet nature: on the contrary, it allows it to be explored and savoured. We have already noted the 'joyful' or smiling *Pietà*, a complex paradox or visual oxymoron. Devotional images of this type appear at first sight utterly absorbed, unlike the theatricality or ostentation (to use a noted insight of Michael Fried[145]) of the portals. But a dynamic is still implicit in them for all their slowing of time. 'Movement' of mind, of emotion, is transferred to the devotional act as itself affective, dynamic, questioning, affirming. Experiences, emotions, may provoke and direct us. But they are not the end to which that direction leads. Their ends are also our actions, and it is this purpose that prevents affect ending merely in self-indulgence or infantilisation.[146] Any rhetorical analysis necessarily connects the personal and the public because, as said earlier, the audience of an artwork requires adjustment of personal subjectivity to the social whole. Individuals 'fit in': 'we' come before 'I'.

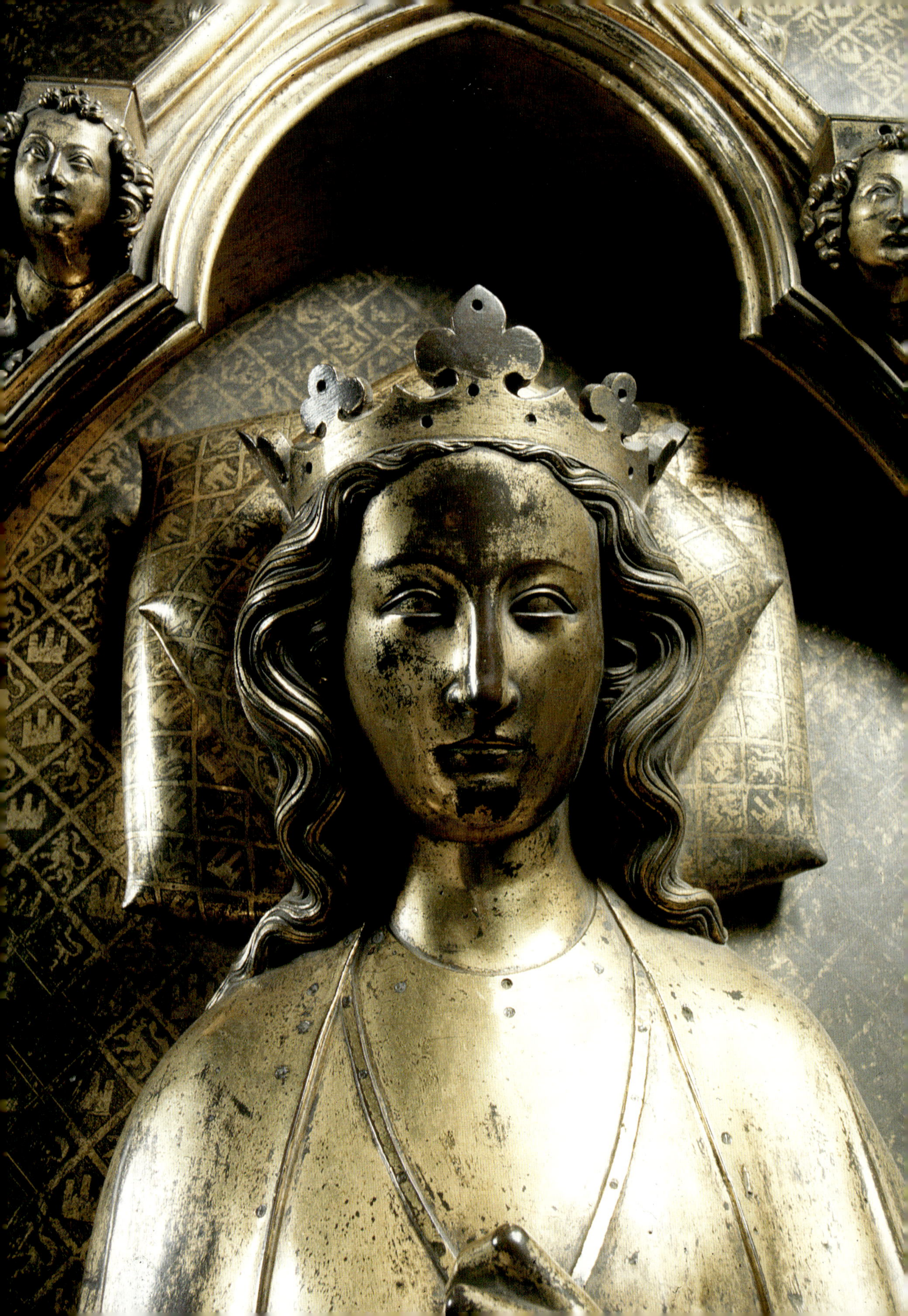

3

EULOGY AND TECHNIQUE

The fluid meaning of such images as the Naumburg founder-figures of the mid-thirteenth century (see pl. 41) does not, to my mind, necessarily entitle us to extend to the monumental public sphere affective regimes suited to specific image types of later medieval genesis. For the most part, portal sculptures seem not to have been objects of devotional attention before the fourteenth century, though cases are certainly known where sculptures were placed in portals for pilgrimage and donation, as in the case of the rood set near the door of the north transept of old St Paul's Cathedral in London, and there is at least one instance, associated with the Abbey of Déols in France in 1187, of a portal image of the Virgin and Child miraculously bleeding and exposing its breast when damaged.[1] We can never determine absolutely how people respond or responded to things and nor should we wish to. The methods of *Rezeptionsgeschichte* (the history of reception) have long underlined the vulnerability of sculpture as an object of outright misinterpretation in the public domain, not least during the Renaissance.[2] Indeed, the history of popular, apocryphal misreadings (or alternative readings) of medieval public sculpture, particularly of the formalised ecclesiastical portals, needs far more attention than it has received. For instance, in his study of the great Apocalypse portal at Moissac (see pl. 16), Meyer Schapiro noted a local tradition, perhaps of no great antiquity, that its central commanding figure of Christ was actually Clovis, the mythical founder of the abbey, or 'Reclobis' in local parlance.[3] How many more such instances of this were there? There is astonishingly little medieval evidence for the extent

40 Westminster Abbey, gilt bronze effigy of Eleanor of Castile (detail of pl. 54)

or nature of public comprehension of the most complex sculpted monuments; when, in his fifteenth-century itinerary of England, William of Worcester encountered the west front of Wells Cathedral (see pl. 9), his reading of it was, to say the least, inexact.[4] The giant church facades of the twelfth and thirteenth centuries were obvious challenges to ordinary public understanding in view of their scale and complexity, and the ambivalences of effigial tombs also created an apocrypha.[5]

This difficulty, this absence, is addressed in part by the theory of the simulacrum, a theory attracted not to religious monuments in the public domain whose significances were circumscribed (at least in common parlance) by doctrine and convention, but rather to secular or quasi-secular images such as the Naumburg choir founder-figures, the Bamberg and Magdeburg Riders, the sculptures of the cathedral in Vienna and other urban sculpted presences such as the Roland or giant figures found in German cities like Bremen, none of which readily submits to ordinary art-historical analysis, and many of which were right at the heart of urban milieux.[6] One can see from the presence of images at the heart of the city as well as of the church how this notion of the simulacrum might have developed from Schapiro's secularised free externality discussed earlier (pp. 36–7). In the face of these ambivalent and sometimes amusing and strange works, the conventional methods of art-historical analysis are held to be little more than modernist, fixed, intentionalist fictions.[7] Any question of an intending author or patron is cast out, leaving behind the thing and its audience. Simulacrum theory suggests that such artefacts, often impressively naturalistic or striking and typically wrought in sculpture, were in effect telling but empty likenesses which encouraged viewers to adopt and project their own emotional and interpretative stances onto them.[8] The currency of the simulacrum arises from the post-modern concept of the real and the hyper-real, an idea owed ultimately to Plato's suspicion of representation expressed in the *Sophist*, a text (incidentally) unknown in the Middle Ages. In its modern iteration, the boundaries between reality and fiction, human subject and art object are blurred seamlessly. The simulacrum is a form of sophistry which sets its own terms of reference and reality, in effect killing the 'real'. It is a plausible likeness which is all surface, no heart, an empty vessel; in setting its own terms it permits all terms. Top-down fixed intellectualist, iconographic and hegemonic readings of the sort favoured by old-fashioned art historians (so to speak) give way entirely to a polar opposite, a beholder's share ungoverned by authority and its intentions. The theory of the simulacrum simultaneously asserts the free agency both of objects and of subjects, and the capacity of images of this sort to attract variant narratives.

In the light of my emphasis so far on the directive, but not conclusive, power of imagery it is difficult not to have some initial sympathy with this line of argument. It is both a strength and a weakness of this theory that its idea of the widely variant reading and competing narrative is something that we cannot strictly refute, even if we wished to do so. The limits of the excessive image are, and always have been, boundless.[9] All images are caught in networks of agency regardless of their exact mimetic standing, including those set within the sort of constrained milieu, such as religious liturgy, that Schapiro posited in contrast to free externality.

Yet it is precisely because of this that it is unclear where the simulacrum ends and other forms of representation start. The whole notion tends in practice to be tied to images with a high level of indexical verism. However, the Christian critique of the simulacrum is necessarily a critique of the fallen character of all likenesses as human fabrications, and not necessarily veristic images.[10] To argue that 'naturalistic' later Gothic images of the sort found in Germany are more obviously simulacra than, say, the sculptures of the west portal of Chartres is rather like implying that the art of Giotto is just obviously more affective than that of the Anglo-Saxons. This raises the question of whether images on cathedral portals, such as the undoubtedly veristic images at Reims, are not also simulacra. Logically they should be. The simulacrum is in effect held to be a general model for a form of experience which is principally intuitive, immediate, asocial and sensual, rather than mindful and socially negotiated.[11]

Simulacrum theory is energised in particular by such works as the famously ambivalent founder-figures circling the choir at Naumburg (pl. 41) around which many opinions have gathered: image ambivalence becomes the occasion for, indeed attracts, post-modern theoretical leverage. This concentration acknowledges a truth, that there is something both fascinating and ambivalent about such highly coloured veristic images. They exalt the 'trivial and contingent' while at the same time being 'bland and banal'.[12] They must fight against a clean-living, abstracted modernist value system wary of verisimilitude, of the glibness and vulgarity of the waxwork.[13] But it is well said that hard cases – and the Naumburg instances are a hard case – make bad law. It remains unclear that simulacrum theory can address all the questions posed by medieval public sculpture. That post-modern theory is well adapted to exploiting points of irresolution in medieval art is evident. It is perfectly true that an encounter with the founder-figures surrounding the choir at Naumburg may be slightly disconcerting, and has certainly tested art-historical opinion.[14] Because they are secular not religious figures, they are not subject to a clear-cut controlling narrative. It is not wrong to see something brilliant, elusive, evanescent and even slightly disturbing in the Naumburg ensemble which, perhaps because of its enclosed but strong-willed jocularity, had few immediate successors, barring the figures in the choirs at Meissen and Nordhausen.[15] A little art-historical paranoia in response to it is excusable. Coming into their presence for the first time we may feel like the innocent entrant into a party full of laughing, joking people who, when the room suddenly falls silent at their arrival, is understandably thrown: something is clearly going on, possibly at the entrant's expense, but what that is, is at first unclear.

The point, however, is that this uncertainty does not rule out the possibility that in such cases something really was going on, and was intended. An initial sense of dislocation

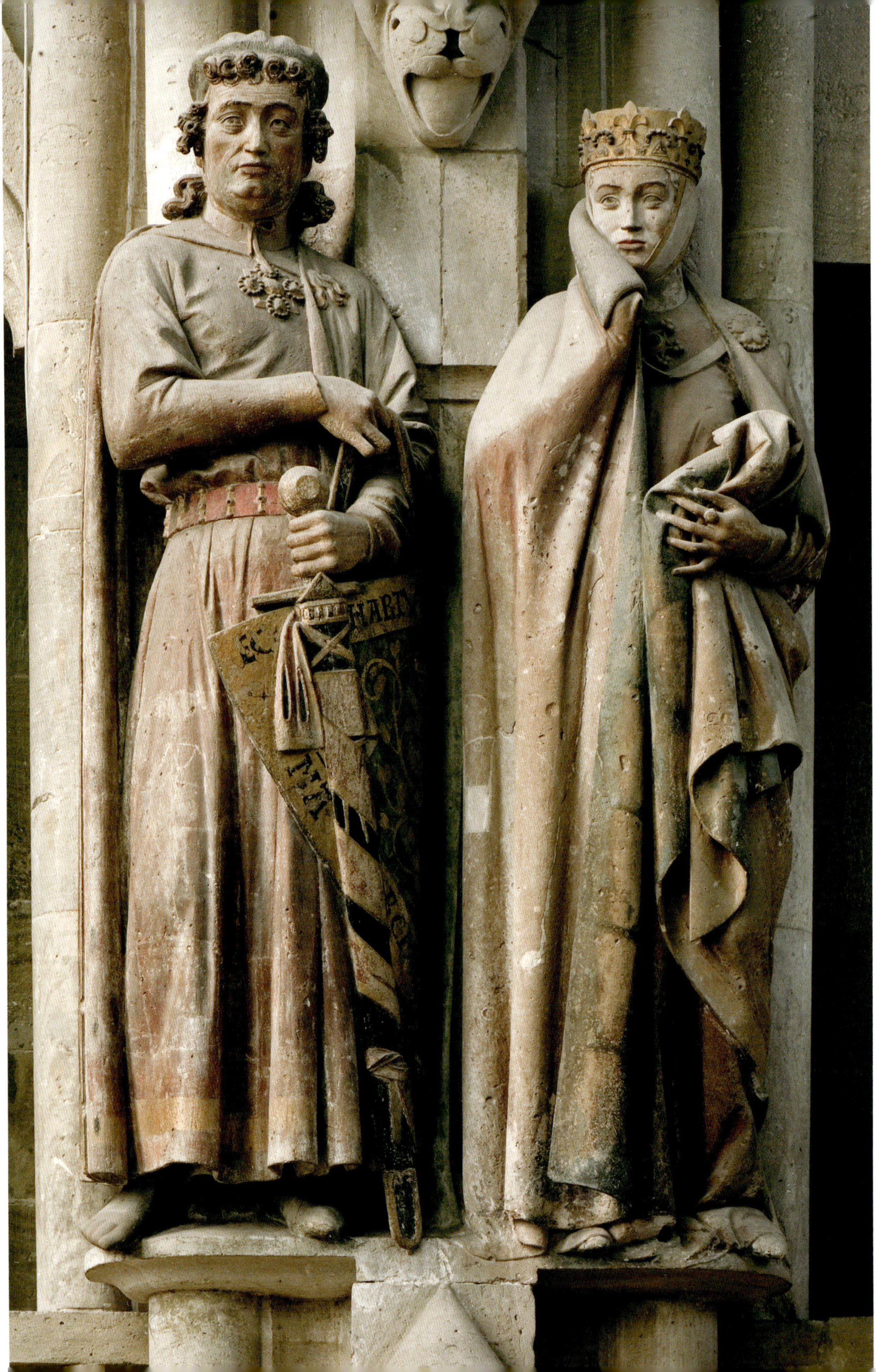

(as I noted earlier) is common to many encounters with impressively scaled or assertively complex artworks. This sensation, in later centuries called *inquiétude*, is the trigger for legitimate speculation, wonder: many images work like this, because they are attractive yet dynamic starting-points, in relation to which the spectator actively probes forward.[16] By entering the Naumburg choir and by trying to engage with its *dramatis personae*, we ourselves enact an entrance to a make-believe court where the immediate disclosure of exact relationships or codes is not necessarily appropriate, and into which we may remain uninitiated. The joke really is on us. Such 'courts' of images were sociable creations which guided, directed, questioned, created a ludic space without generally available rules, yet which were not obviously subjective.[17] German art and architecture of the later Middle Ages is full of *ludus*, whether it consists of veristic sculptures such as the imperial images of Charles IV and his entourage acting out an *acclamatio* on the south gallery of the Marienkirche in Mühlhausen, or the amusing professional jokes about nature and artistic incompetence cooked up by architects which are now left stranded and vulnerable because the framing jocular discourse has fallen away.[18] The point is that a joke requires some shared basis in convention.

Here the key issue concerns purpose, commissioning and social understanding. While sociability and gamesmanship create space for questioning, they do not for that reason set aside intent. In showing the way through and guiding (but not, as I have argued, dictating), artworks operate within a social and public world whose perceptions are formed and energised by convention and memory.[19] Medieval practice made room for inventive viewing and for the operation, within reasonable limits or horizons, of *voluntas*, desire or choice. But invention had persuasion as its end, its arguments working *ad usum*, that is, according to more or less shared socially based assumptions and the task to hand. We think again of Jauss's 'horizon of expectation' or of Fish's 'interpretative community'.[20] Purpose is key to this, not least pragmatically. Why would the commissioners of such works as those in Naumburg and Bamberg, to say nothing of Reims Cathedral (see pl. 46), go to the trouble and sheer expense of commissioning and paying for huge and complex public monuments whose terms of reference might be open to serious misconstrual or, worse, even ridicule? That they did not plan in this way is demonstrable from the fact that displays of human affect in artworks were carefully specified by commissioners. Strikingly, among the early explicit references to the facial or bodily expressions of carved or painted images from medieval Western Europe are mandates issued by Henry III in the period from 1240, when the first evidence for migration of ideas precisely from the Reims workshops to the English court is provable, shortly before the execution of the works in Naumburg.[21] In January 1240 Henry ordered that a figure of Winter should be painted on the chimney of the queen's chamber at Westminster to be depicted (*protrahi*) in such a way that by its sad look and miserable 'portrayals'

41 Naumburg Cathedral (Saxony-Anhalt), west choir, the founders Ekkehard II and Uta, mid-thirteenth century

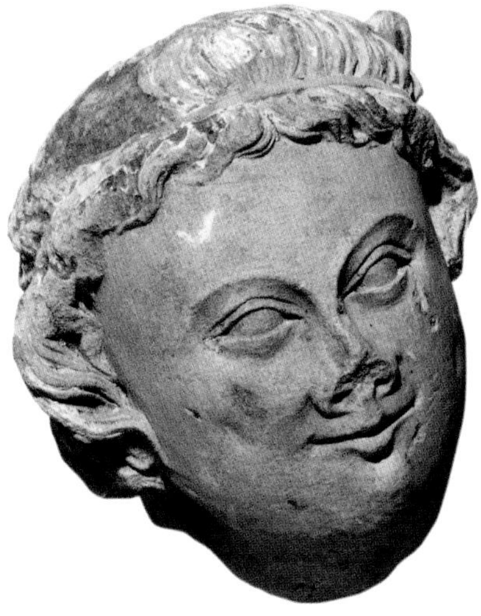

42 Westminster Abbey, head, probably of an angel from wall arcading at east end, late 1240s

(*protractionibus*) of the body it might justly be likened (*assimilari*) to winter.[22] That this turn affected the face as well as the body is shown by a writ of December that year for two sculpted cherubim to be placed in the church of St Peter ad Vincula in the Tower of London carved with 'cheerful and joyous countenances' (*hyllari vultu et jocoso*).[23] Two years later, as noted earlier, Henry commissioned images of the Wise and Foolish Virgins for the queen's chapel at Windsor, also an 'affective' topic. The existence of such mandates shows that it is far from fanciful to claim that bodily dispositions were matters of active interest to patrons specifiable in contracts.[24] Figures with smiling features survive from Henry's works at Westminster Abbey (pl. 42). It is hard to see how a commissioner could be more explicit or purposive. The fact that the audience might have made this or that of the result is secondary.

In short, we need better evidence than we have been provided with that 'official' attitudes, and with them the intention of the artefact, can readily be set aside or contrasted with an opposing contrasted zone of *laissez-faire* subjectivity in which the artefact acts out of bounds. Assaf Pinkus, in his stimulating study of the simulacrum, has called this latter freedom 'Tristanism', alluding to the modern Romantic-nationalist agenda which focused particularly on the great sculptures at Naumburg and Bamberg.[25] By this reading such medieval simulacra are inherently fantasy objects subject to all desires, and the reception of such sculptures in the modern era, with all their unfortunate nationalist associations, stands as proof of this. But the implications of this are several. To understand them, let me set one anachronism against another, by comparing fantasy with imaginative regard.[26] This restates a distinction I made earlier between contrivance and thoughtful, imaginative engagement. In fantasy relations of the sort advanced, in effect, by simulacrum theory, thought and imaginative regard play no role between subject and object. Reality and the simulation of reality become indistinguishable; true reflection becomes impossible; and nothing is left to the imagination, as in the places of true simulacra, namely pornography, cinema or waxworks. Not surprisingly, an interest in the fantasy relation is also an interest in voyeurism.[27] Objects of fantasy are not representations but substitutions, and it is for this reason that we may find them both strangely attractive and repellent. Fantasy is literal and invasive, excludes thought and entails the objectification of that which is subject to fantasy: persons submitted to the needs of fantasy are 'objectified'. Things and persons can easily be exchanged. Simulacra are ideal sites of objectification and mystification, not thought: no wonder medieval critics of idolatry were suspicious of anything realistic. The fantasy object, the surrogate, is an unreal object of actual desires, yet its appearance of reality is fundamental to the fantasist. The surrogate object of emotion must be as real as possible. True representation, in contrast, entails thought about an object or a person in a compositorial process of imaginative thoughtful reflection. Representation entails distance, not substitution, imaginative regard and not assimilation or sheer will. Imaginative regard does not necessarily produce real emotion – for 'real' emotion is the topic of fantasy and desire – but rather 'entertained' emotion. As I suggested earlier in relation to quasi-emotion, we might say of an image that it looks arousing, without actually being aroused; we may instead represent arousal to ourselves.[28]

I do not, in short, believe that medieval sculptures in general were intended to be objects of fantasy, and it is unclear what other aspects of medieval thought and practice might sustain this notion. As said, we cannot refute the idea that all manner of notions and desires were (and always will be) brought to bear on such images. Hyper-veristic works such as those at Naumburg form a difficult case, subject to special needs and special hostilities. But the risks of framing debate about medieval imitation as a whole in terms of the simulacrum are, I think, akin to the emotivist insistence on empathetic relation. These risks arise because the relation of subject to artwork is more like an imaginative than a fantasy relation: will, intention, thought, affect and judgement are integral. Rhetorical analysis provides a historically verifiable framework for the belief, grounded in social negotiation, that the audience is not simply seduced but arbitrates meaning. Out and out iconographic rigidity and its mirror image, out and out licence, are both illusions which produce and deserve each another.

A moment ago I raised the vital issue of the compositorial nature of the beholding imagination. This returns us to the question whether imitation of the veristic type is automatically tied to greater subjective freedom. As the 'simulacrum' case indicates, it is tempting to see the wonderfully informative sculpted bodies and faces at Reims or Naumburg as signs of a new liberty, offering dramatically new subjective possibilities to audiences.[29] However, accepting this also raises the possibility of a radical neutralisation of the power-intention of such projects. If I am right about the nature of imagination as opposed to fantasy, about reason and conviction and the public and social role of the sculpted monument, then it follows that these new wonders were less about freedom and more about constraint as a necessary companion of will and skill. They embodied a form of literalism. In the world of emotional make-believe, the artists – and so ultimately the patrons, not the audiences – were gaining control. This understanding seems to me consistent not only with the generic character and occasion of much public sculpture but also with the declared objectives of power, religious or secular, in this period.

To explore this claim, we need to consider constraint of persons and things, and so the broader issue of form or disposition. I disagreed earlier with the view that the goal of the more 'expressive' sculpted portal images of the Gothic era was to take expression of, or reflection on, emotion as their object and purpose. While the role of emotion was important to the attainment of the goals of medieval art, their aim was not simply or solely attaining an emotional attitude but rather a state of persuasion that was both emotional and rational. To think otherwise, I suggest, runs the risk of emotivist fallacy, that is to say, emotion-justified individualistic perception.[30] Emotivism tends unhelpfully to dissolve the boundary between persuasion and manipulation: thus the outcome of our portals would not be a persuasive experience but a more fundamentally manipulative, emotion-driven and unusual, irrational, even charismatic experience. It will be clear from the general tenor of this chapter that I find such emphasis unhelpful. The aesthetics of charisma discount habit, even *ennui*. For most people, locals especially, the decorations on the exterior of the neighbourhood church were perceived habitually, not as one-off dazzling events intended for unsuspecting innocents on eternal pilgrimage. It seems questionable to transfer to medieval experiences of 'slow' looking the models of instant gratification and overwhelming effect familiar to modernity. To my mind a less inauthentic approach to these doorways as public monuments derives from the admittedly cooler stance that they were instances of religious and moral artifice operating within the (creative) constraints of occasion and style.

That my line of argument as a historian is not totally sympathetic to the grand narrative of the rise of human freedom, emotional consciousness and the centred subject will be evident. In pursuing it I am not alone.[31] What I take to be an extraordinarily pervasive and basically modernist vision of a nuanced psychological, later medieval art sits ill with much medieval artistic and textual practice which is social and disciplinary (that is, formulaic, artificial and traditional) rather than natural, individual and personal. Alasdair MacIntyre's critique of emotivism asks us to explore an analogy from drama, that of character:

> There is a type of dramatic tradition – Japanese Noh plays and English medieval morality plays are examples – which possesses a set of stock characters immediately recognizable to the audience. Such characters partially define the possibilities of plot and action. To understand them is to be provided with a means of interpreting the behavior of the actors who play them, just because a similar understanding informs the intentions of the actors themselves; and other actors may define their parts with special reference to these central characters. So it is also with certain kinds of social role specific to certain particular cultures. They furnish recognizable characters and the ability to recognize them is socially crucial because a knowledge of the character provides an interpretation of the actions of those individuals who have assumed the character. It does so precisely because those individuals have used the very same knowledge to guide and to structure their behavior . . . they are a very special type of social role which places *a certain kind of moral constraint* [my italics] on the personality of those who inhabit them in a way in which many other social roles do not. I choose the word 'character' for them precisely because of the way it links dramatic and moral associations.[32]

MacIntyre's citation of medieval morality plays as exemplifications of character that embody not psychological or emotional essence, but cultural and artificial constraint working with specific situations, seems to me extremely astute.[33] To see moralising images on portals not as objects of empathetic identification but as publicly recognised role-players is to understand that character in MacIntyre's sense works socially, consensually. Artifice becomes an antidote to the special place accorded to subjective individualism. John Benton, for example, writes that in the modern world, the idea of 'finding ourselves' means stripping away layers of conformity and contrivance to expose an authentically essential self, whereas in medieval sensibility the *persona* was not inner, but outer: a *persona* was a mask.[34] Our Gothic figures are *personae*, masks, not personalities. Crafted *figurae* become the demonstrative vehicles of artificial character types whose ethics are a product of the discipline of moral and political culture itself.

Shedding modern psychological notions of the self is the first step in this book I will take towards critiquing notions of authenticity. I shall return to another instance in discussing materiality, and so crafting. The key note here is artifice. So far, I have agreed that representation, far from being a form of substitution, entails thought which both describes and explores a topic. This is what separates fantasy and objectification from morally alert imaginative regard to character. Ordinary day-to-day experience is fundamental to such regard and, I think, to the role of artifice in representation. Under the pressure of Romantic and post-Romantic thinking about 'higher' and 'lower' categories of activity and outcome, however, art tended to be split off and ring-fenced from ordinary experience within a special charmed world, the nature of which is now under challenge.[35] Rhetorical analysis is one of the discourses which helps to overcome this unhelpful divide because it insists on the importance of what Mary Carruthers calls 'ordinary beauty', and realises the daily craft-based concern with getting things right in everyday life, rather than exceptional experience.[36] Because that sensation of rightness involves reasonable judgement and a sense of decorum, it connects artifice of the self, self-regulation in ethics, to the artifice or crafting of things, regulation by art. The connection will always tend to have a reasonable and, as MacIntyre's discussion of character shows, publicly verifiable and understandable dimension. This needs stressing because sculpture, of all media, is the most prone to irrationalist, animist and fetishistic readings which the 'simulacrum' perspective particularly acknowledges.

PUBLIC DOMAIN AND THE HIGH MIMETIC MODE

We return to public monumentality and the question of social and rhetorical engagement. The veristic glamour of some French, Anglo-French, German and Iberian sculpture of the thirteenth century, of the 'canonical' monuments of verism, has always tended to capture the imagination of art historians. The key monuments from the 1180s onwards include the Pórtico de la Gloria at Compostela (not always sufficiently stressed; see pl. 10), the sculptures of the south transept of Strasbourg Cathedral of about 1230 (see pl. 36), much of the exterior imagery of Reims post-dating the north transept portals (see pl. 47), the Sainte-Chapelle in Paris of the 1240s, the works at Bamberg, Mainz, Meissen, Naumburg and Magdeburg cathedrals (see pls 31 and 41) and, in the English and Castilian domains, the sculpted foliage of the late thirteenth-century chapter house at Southwell Minster (pls 43 and 44) and the cloister at Burgos.[37] In the case of Paris, Reims, Westminster, Naumburg, Meissen and Burgos, the commonalities of approach seem to have arisen within supranational political or dynastic connections and aspirations: these ensembles had social cachet and mutual recognition.[38] Not unsurprisingly, the whole development towards high-flown verism has attracted ambitious explanatory or interpretative theories. Some are derived from science – Aristotelianism in particular but also the later techniques of physiognomy; some from within the classical tradition such as Panofsky's account of 'intrinsic classicism'; those of the civilising process and the history of ethics; those which see in naturalism an ideologically motivated strategy of displacement; and a thoroughly mixed agenda of affectivity and ease-of-access arguments concerning low style or vernacularity.[39] The last owe much to the exponent of the *sermo humilis* or 'low style' in Christian realism as a whole, Eric Auerbach.[40] In all their ways – science, classicism, civilising process and accessibility – these positions are progressive in tone and intent: the story of mimesis is, ultimately, a forward-looking human good. They would have delighted the Renaissance, and indeed owe something to it, though some of them are even more indebted to Romanticism. All contain a grain, in some cases a significant grain, of truth and it is not exactly my objective to topple them.

I do, however, want to explore further the position which stems from the work of Auerbach on *sermo humilis*, because it is germane to the issue of public attention and has proved influential. Auerbach, moved by St Augustine, argued that the classical hierarchy of style and subject matter which produced the so-called *genera dicendi* (high, middle and low speech) was set aside by the Judaeo-Christian 'realist' dispensation and by medieval literature, in such a way as to favour the lowest, ordinary, form of speech, *sermo* or *sermo humilis*.[41] Thus the humble or daily, as in the Gospels, could be rendered sublime. Following Mâle's emphasis on religious drama, Auerbach invoked the 'plastic art of the medieval churches', 'the most perfect sculptures in Chartres, Reims, Paris or Amiens' as evidence of the way that this accessible idiom 'opens its arms invitingly to receive the simple and untutored and to lead them from the concrete, the everyday, to the hidden and the true'.[42] In retrospect, much in Auerbach's extraordinarily broad comparative vision of the treatment of realism in literature is political, class-based. Realism as he defines it is a matter for the ordinary people, a form of vernacular, a plebeian rejection of the exclusive thinking of a hierarchical ancient world.[43]

43 Southwell Minster (Nottinghamshire), chapter house vestibule and entrance, about 1288–94

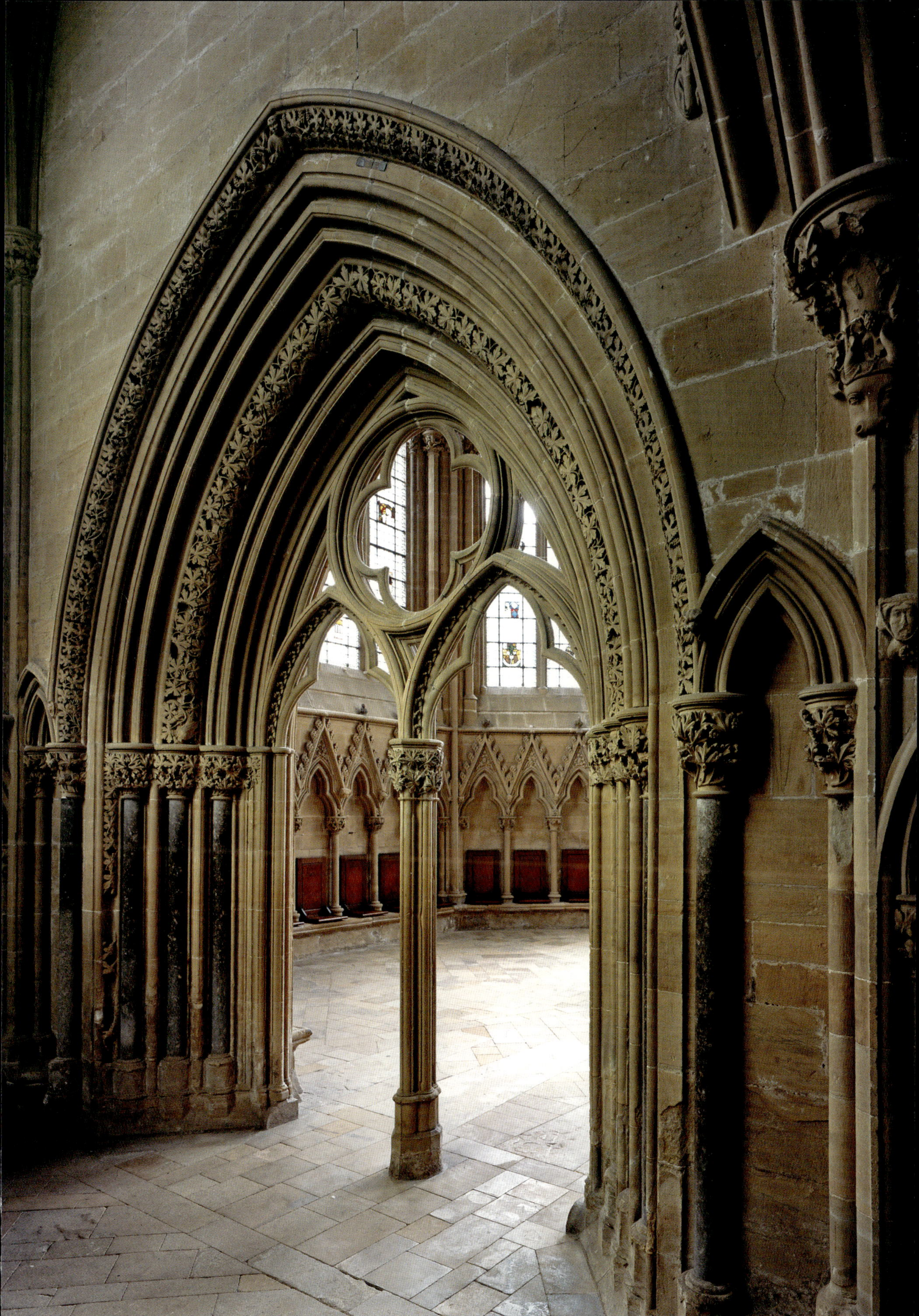

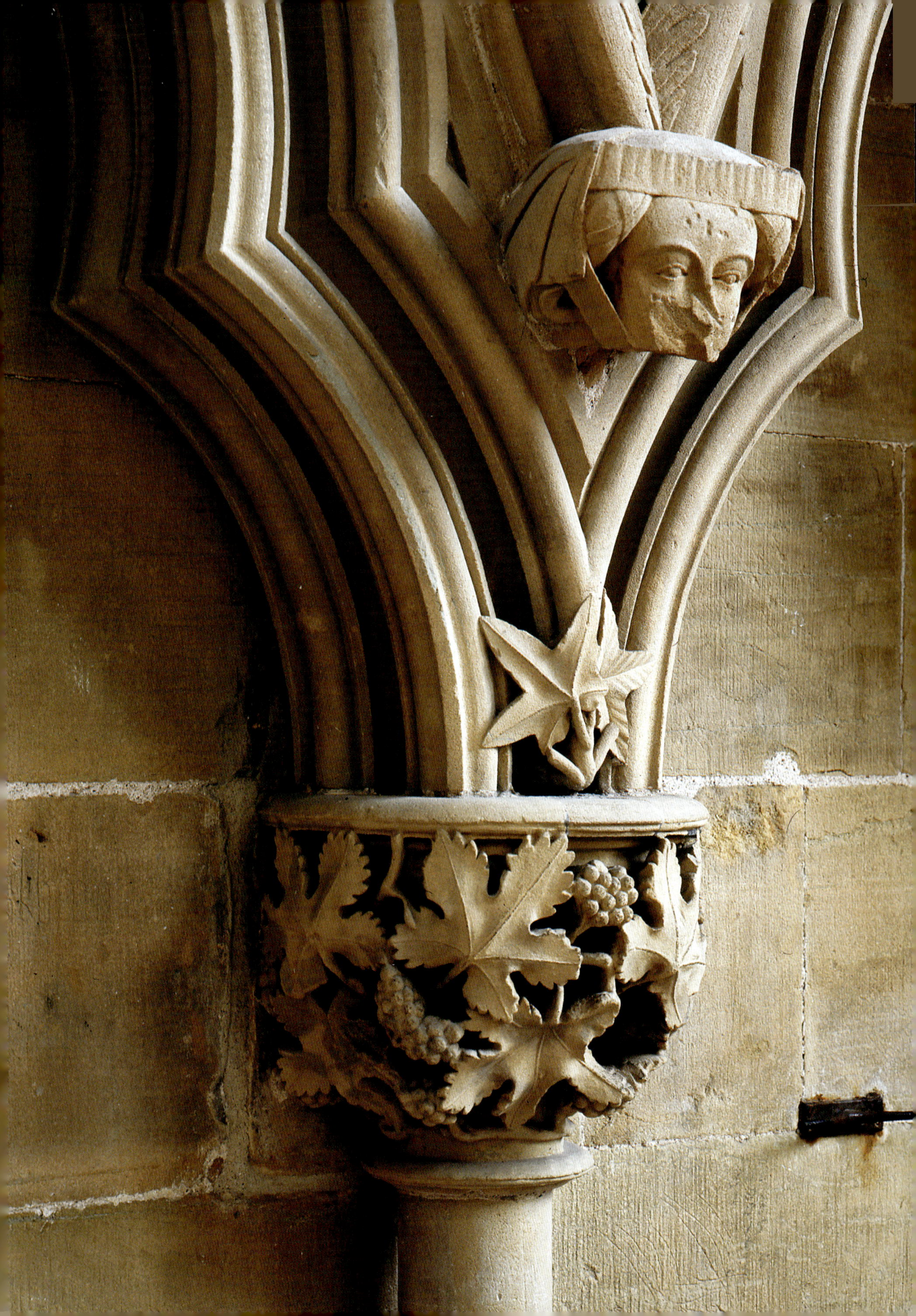

Stemming from Auerbach's case regarding *sermo humilis* has been an assumption or near-assumption that Gothic art too set aside rhetorical hierarchy, that it was possessed of humility but not *magniloquentia*. Auerbach's discussion is in some ways well suited to late medieval northern European devotional art with its frank and paradoxical truths and tendency to align literary and social style.[44] Its wider impact in regard to visual culture, however, may have been reductive, for it has tended to hypostasise the idea of Gothic art, especially later Gothic art, as essentially a form of low-style vernacular celebrating the scandalous and primarily theological Christian mixture of the ordinary and the sublime in a way that undermined classical *dignitas*.[45] Some difficulties with the theory were raised in the first reception of Auerbach's study: levels of literary style were not absolute but were governed by function and occasion, and they could co-exist within a hierarchy.[46] Complex artworks, almost by their nature and internal dynamic, embody mixed, even competing rhetorical styles, a point recognised by Rocío Sánchez Ameijeiras in her study of the mixture of elocutionary styles on Gothic portals such as that at León, with its amusing smaller-scale sculpture in the naturalistic mode (pl. 45).[47] Sánchez Ameijeiras has suggested that changes in the theory of rhetoric in the thirteenth century, the era of the development of the *ars praedicandi*, could, in her words, 'help define one of the major differences' between Romanesque and Gothic imagery conventionally defined.[48] I agree but also note that any suggestion that Gothic artworks, especially great churches, were locked into the *stilus humilis* might overlook the extent to which they also magnified and amplified their subjects pretty much in accordance with old ideas of hierarchy and dignity.[49] The emphasis on the lowest style of rhetoric may have tended to distract modern criticism from the continuity between the ancient and medieval worlds in regard to public speech: not the *genera dicendi* but the types of rhetoric we noted earlier – judicial, deliberative and demonstrative rhetoric, which themselves could mix and compete. Medieval literature shows that this antique system was still accessed in the works of Cicero, Seneca and Quintilian and that, of the three modes, the demonstrative or epideictic was still the most influential not least in regard to medieval poetry.[50] As John Burrow has shown in his work on medieval poetry of praise, it is exactly this mode that has fallen out of fashion and been systematically disregarded by modern ironists and class-based analysis.[51] It needs restoring because without it we may not fully understand portal talk and related conversations.

Display oratory, the rhetoric of praise and blame, *laus* and *vituperatio*, was a mode that took pleasure in the art of eloquence itself. In a sense it put on display that which was beyond argument, that which was self-evident. Gothic art never loses sight of its practical ends. But nor was it blind to appetite, the yearning for beauty and virtue as moral, spiritual and aesthetic goods. To enlarge on the importance of display rhetoric, eulogy or praise, let us first recall that in classical understanding (in Aristotle's *Rhetoric*) display oratory was geared as

44 Southwell Minster (Nottinghamshire), chapter house wall arcading, capital with vine leaves and grapes, about 1288–94

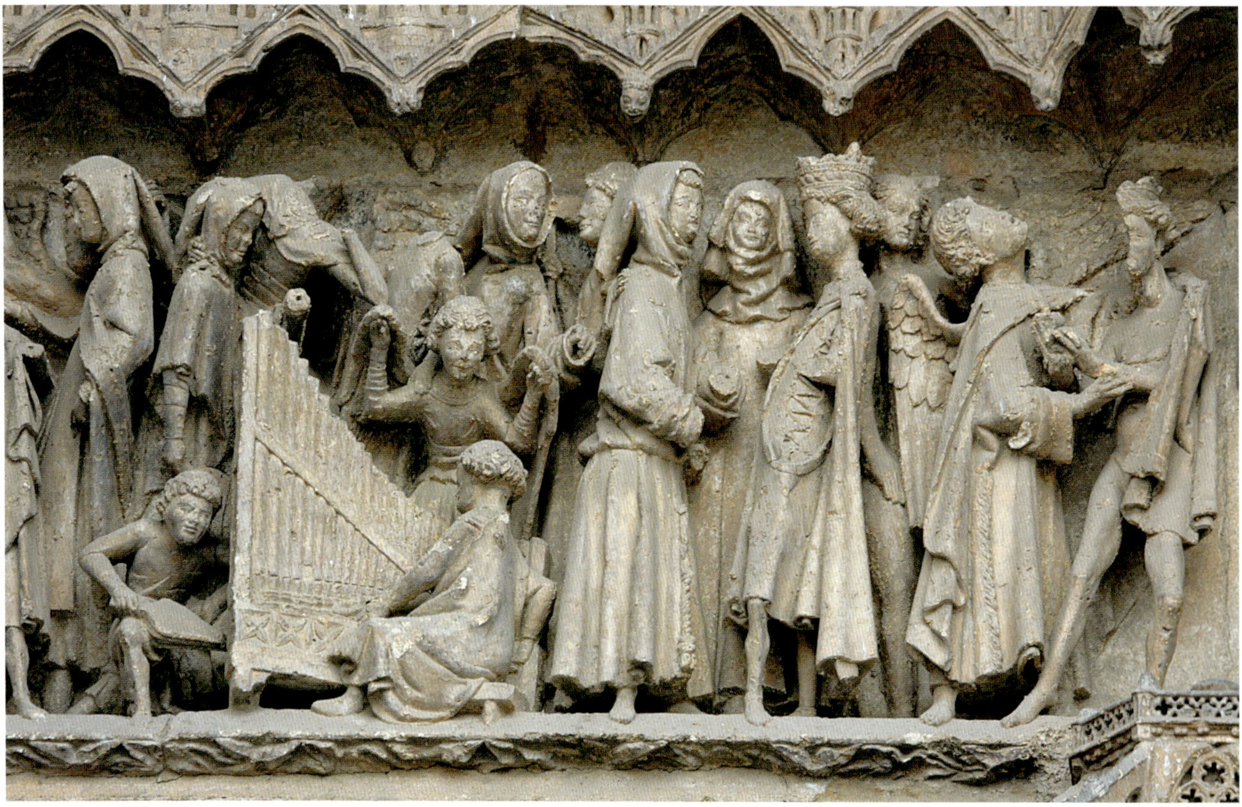

45 Léon Cathedral, west facade, central portal of Last Judgement showing delights of the Blessed including a merry organ conducted by an angel, third quarter thirteenth century

much to appetite as mind or passion: so praise which embodies longing or desire has as its object that which is beautiful.[52] This is also essentially true of medieval eulogy: the Christian liturgical, hagiographical, lyrical and salvific dispensation has at its heart a lofty, complex and moving language of eulogy, of praise, and this language was widespread. What has obscured the importance of this for medieval representation is the artificial divide, encouraged by Panofsky, between a 'retrospective' ancient sensibility and Christian super-individual prospection or eschatology.[53] The heritage of medieval letters, however, reminds us forcefully that Panofsky (who knew better) was himself prudent to observe that this change was neither universal nor unequivocal.[54]

Eulogy is above all a form of speech whose aim is to celebrate greatness, of things and people. Ernst Curtius states: 'Of the oratorical genres, the epideictic oration had by far the strongest influence upon medieval poetry'.[55] Subjects of eulogy could include (in Curtius's discussion of *topoi* or commonplaces) gods, human beings, countries, cities, animals, plants, seasons, virtues, arts and professions. Curtius also draws attention to a demand throughout the Middle Ages for poems 'glorifying secular and spiritual magnates'.[56] The range and purpose of eulogy seems to me helpful both critically and historically. First, the urban cathedral or great church was itself a recognised occasion for the public praise (*praeconia*) of place: the saints of the city and its cathedral are the subject of a form of glorification used for countries and cities which was given, in Curtius's words, 'an ecclesiastical turn'.[57] As I have suggested elsewhere, the period of greatest pace, daring and accomplishment in Gothic art was accompanied by eulogistic literature which celebrated and connected human greatness and human artefacts in a 'heroic mode'.[58] Two instances can be given swiftly which connect architecture and human excellence. The first is hagiographical: the *Metrical Life of St Hugh of Lincoln* composed *c.*1220 to celebrate both a saint and his architectural works, amplified into a surprising and complex account of the new cathedral choir that St Hugh himself began in the 1190s.[59] The second is entirely in the tradition of the classical city eulogy: Jean de Jandun's encomium of Paris composed in 1323, which effortlessly associates the great human achievements of Paris, its university especially, with its dazzling new Gothic buildings, Notre-Dame and the Sainte-Chapelle.[60] In Jandun's case the claim is larger still: it is a claim about French cultural supremacy as a whole, for the French are the new Greeks, and of this Paris and its people are evidence. This context of political and cultural attainment seems to me to matter because it signals the extraordinary level of cultural confidence of the French and Anglo-French accomplishment in the key centuries we are discussing.

That the greatest cathedrals – to say nothing of their saints, patrons and builders – should attract eulogy simply recognises what contemporaries such as Jean de Jandun themselves recognised: that there was a connection between the heroic mode and the exercise and discourse of power. Henry III explicitly acknowledged the accomplishment of one of the buildings mentioned by Jandun, the Sainte-Chapelle, when he instructed his own masons to borrow motifs from it for Westminster Abbey around 1245. The *dispositio* of Westminster is based too on the French coronation church, Reims Cathedral.[61] Reims's art is not a monument to Auerbachian *sermo humilis* but to *magnificentia*, the enlargement by praise of the deeds of the saints and, in turn, the magnification of the capacities of monarchy and archdiocese. Consider Reims's portals (pl. 46). By 1200, as is well known, the largest Gothic portal ensembles were not simply Christological in form but hagiographic: the doctrine of the intercession of saints, the cult of relics and the pastoral emphasis on the deeds, virtues and beauties of the saints was bearing fruit. Christ the Judge is accompanied from the mid-twelfth century onwards by intercessory saints who mollify and persuade the Redeemer. In major portal ensembles, entire gateways are phalanxes dedicated to local saints – St Calixte at Reims, St Firmin at Amiens (see pl. 19, left portal), for instance – or to the mother of all saints, Mary, whose coronation begins to figure as the main topic of Gothic portals in

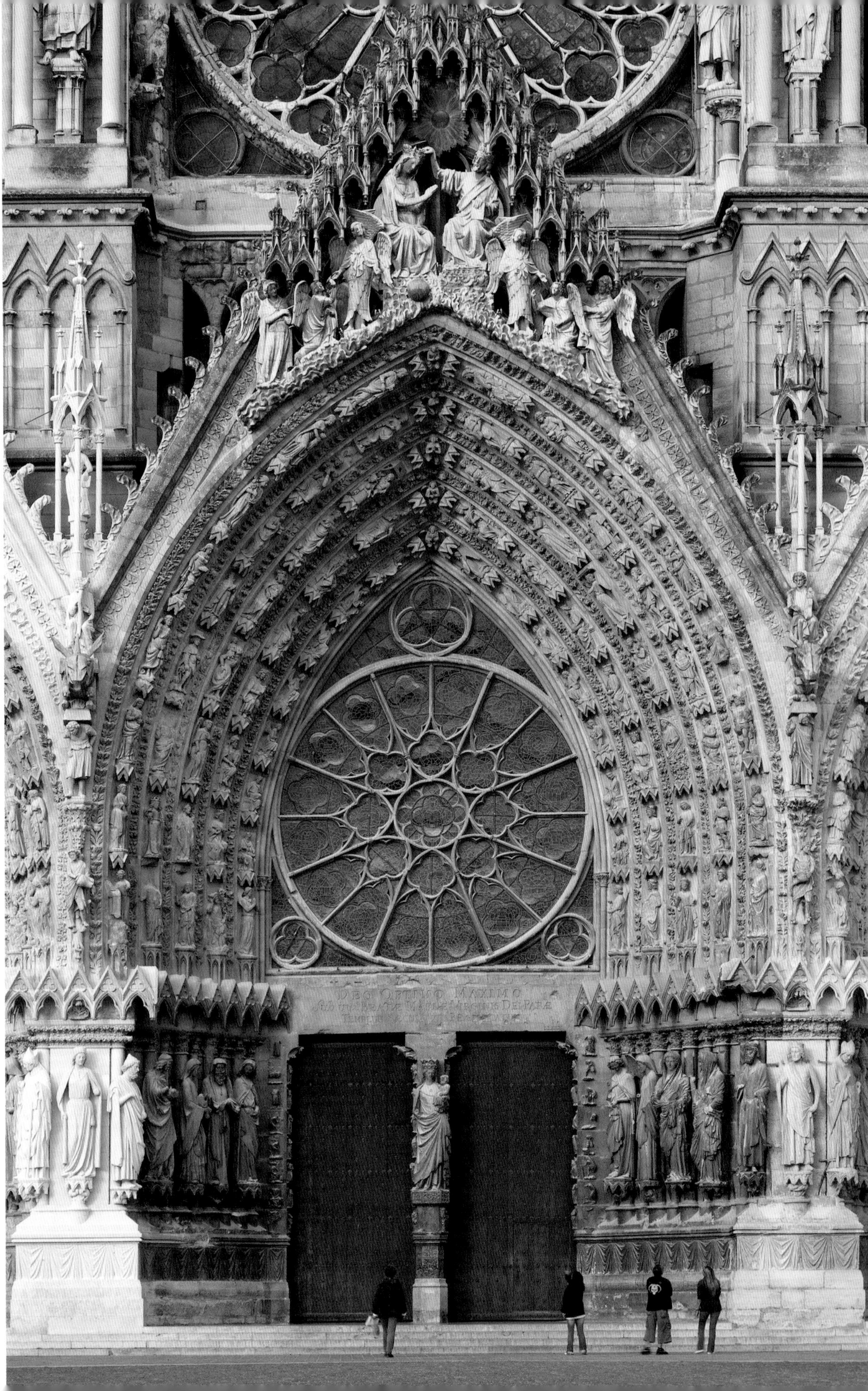
DEO OPTIMO MAXIMO

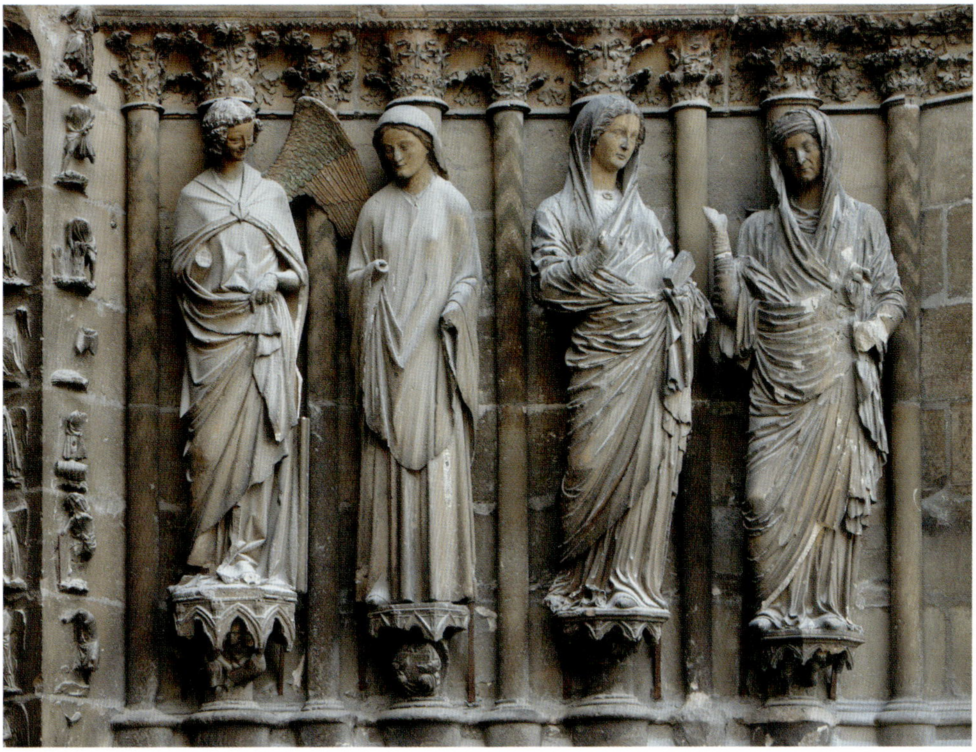

facing page 46 Reims Cathedral (Marne), west front central portal, mid-thirteenth century

this page 47 Reims Cathedral, Annunciation and Visitation groups, second quarter to mid-thirteenth century

France from the 1170s or so (Senlis).[62] Their altars, the true sites of devotion, lay beyond. We would expect the imagery of eulogy of such exemplary people, the 'very special dead' in Peter Brown's unforgettable phrase, to be a form of conferral.[63] The saints were their churches. As the Virgin Mary comes into prominence in the course of the twelfth century, she has the crown of heaven conferred on her (see top of pl. 46). Christ is now shown in merciful Judgement with his trophies, his wounds and instruments of suffering as emblems of triumph. The angels become, to an extent far greater than in the twelfth century, the agents of conferral – of crowns, of radiant or benificent looks of smiling grace. On the Pórtico de la Gloria at Compostela a benign angel distributes armloads of crowns to the blessed; the two shining angels framing St Nicaise on the west front of Reims positively beam at him, like the great Gabriel from the Annunciation nearby (pl. 47).[64] These conferrals, these wreathings, are eulogistic; and, as with the genre as a whole, praise accompanies blame (or invective), as apparent in the Wise and Foolish Virgin portals.[65]

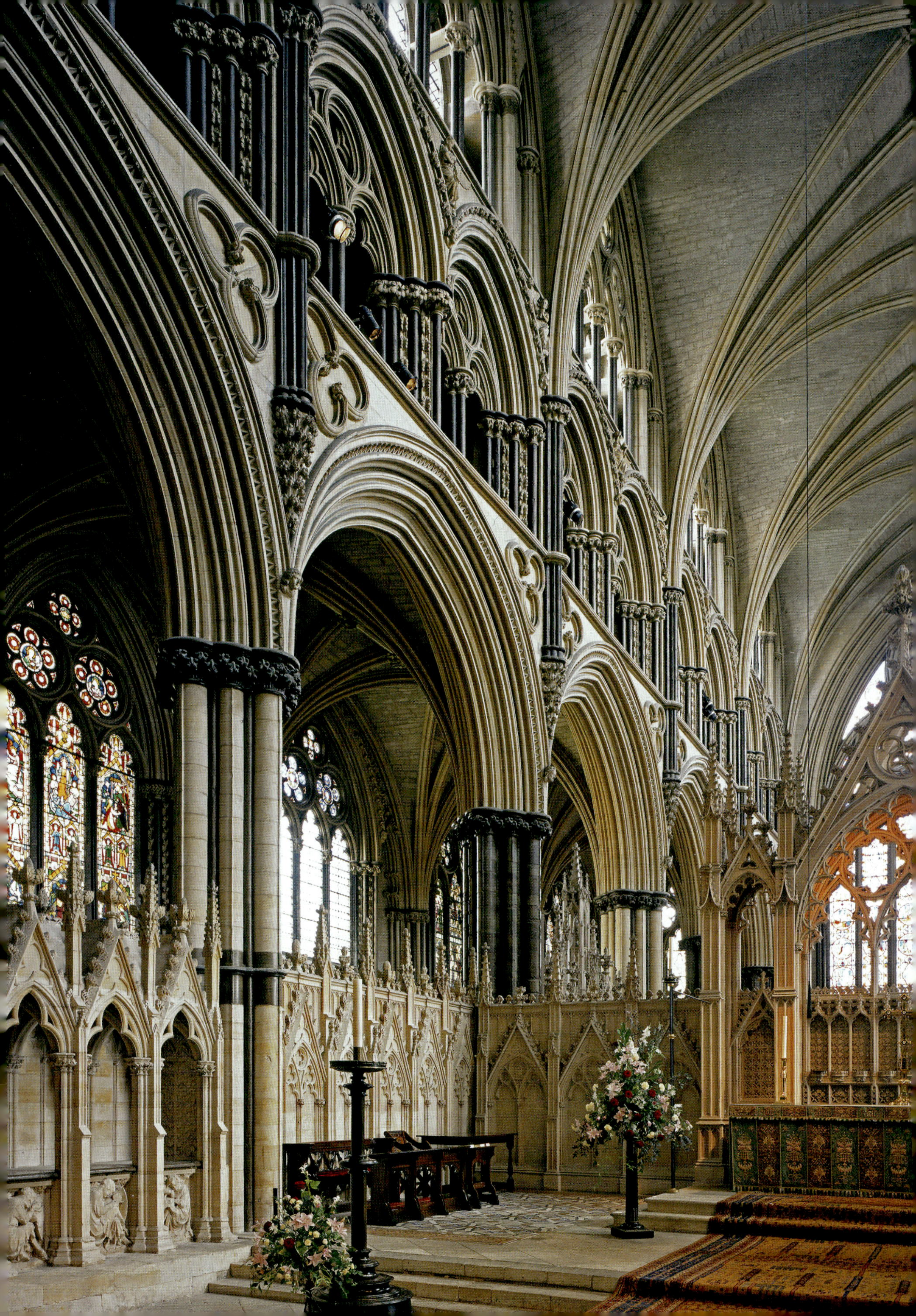

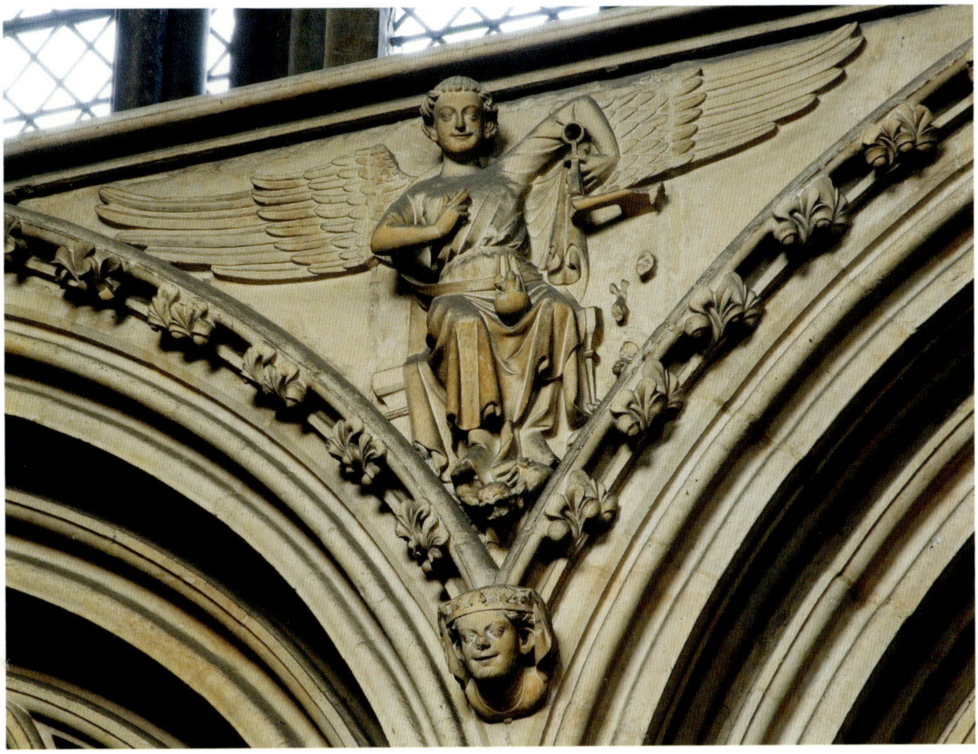

facing page 48 Lincoln Cathedral, Angel Choir, looking north-east, 1256–80

this page 49 Lincoln Cathedral, Angel Choir north side, a beaming St Michael with his scales (contrast pl. 24), and matching female head, about 1270. The group is visible at the top of pl. 48.

As something is conferred on these figures, something too is conferred on us. Although the Last Judgement remains a vivid incentivising theme on Gothic portals, the abandonment of the prominent threatening inscriptions of the sort encountered on Romanesque Last Judgements with their language of horror and terror is striking. Fear still matters, but it seems much more exact to think not of outright terror but of *timor Domini*, awe or reverence serving a beneficial or pastoral end as the beginning of wisdom.[66] The spectator is not diminished but enlarged by such sentiments. And to beneficial fear are added other passions and looks, looks embodied metaphorically in the very architecture itself. This poetry of uplift, wonder, strikes me as characteristic of the domain of architecture and the sculpted arts at Lincoln, the Angel Choir of which is a fruitful-looking masterpiece of cheerfulness and zest furnished throughout with smiling angels and corbel heads (pls 48 and 49).[67] At Lincoln the liturgical intention was laudatory. On the tympana of the west portals at Reims (see pl. 46), a building in the artistic background to Lincoln, the pains of Hell were removed

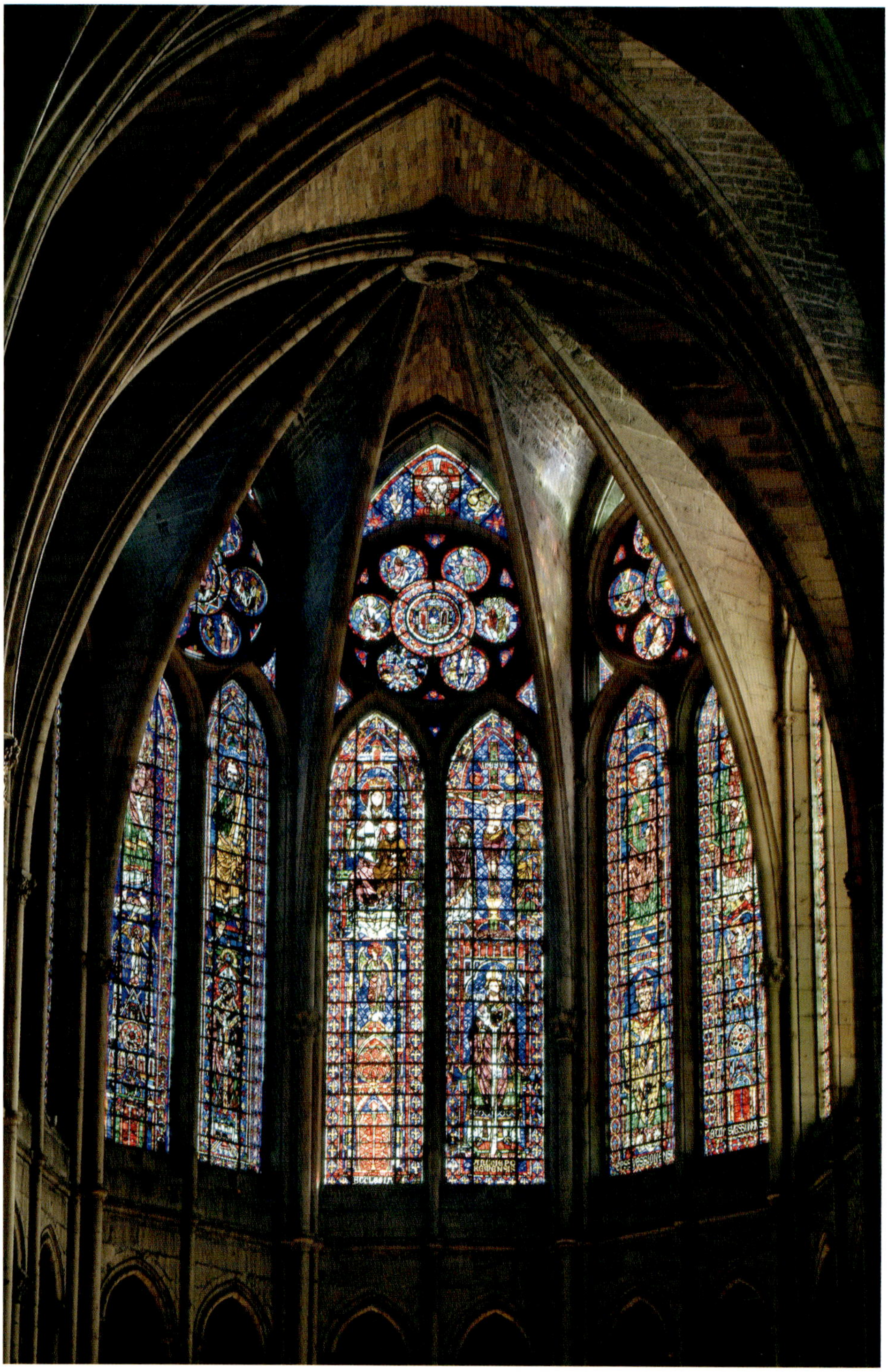

50 Reims Cathedral (Marne), apse and clearstory, complete with stained glass by 1241

entirely and replaced with joyful stained glass, the language of clarity, joy and delight (*claritas, laetitia, jucunditas*) coalescing, so to speak, in a building which, like its figures, radiantly 'smiles' at us both within and without, not least through its huge lofty glazed clearstories (pl. 50).[68] This transference may remind us that the Latin *miror*, to wonder 'at', is derived ultimately from an Indo-European word for 'smile'.[69] Topics previously accorded to tympana are elevated at Reims high onto the major portal gables, where we find the adoration of the Cross, the Coronation of the Virgin and a Christ in Judgement; and these uplifting themes are manifested with a jocularity unparalleled on any other monument of the time. Curtius saw the celebrated tropes of inexpressibility, outdoing and wonder as developments of eulogy.[70] Magnification of scale and elevation of position, as we see in the case of the huge figures on the west front at Reims, are forms of *auxesis* or 'increase', which in Latin was called *amplificatio*.[71] The tremendous heightening of the interiors of such great structures is itself arguably an aspect of the amplificatory mode: the term *sublimitas* in the Vulgate commonly means stature or loftiness in the poetic sense.[72] It is for this reason that, to repeat, the experience of Gothic sculpture is an experience of its occasion as a whole: and that occasion effected not only personal but also social and pastoral uplift.

The changing balance of affects is one thing, but what of surface? Classical and medieval language of praise was preoccupied with outer manifestations of beauty and strength. Latin handbooks showed interest both in beauty and external circumstances, epitomised in the widely consulted *Ad Herennium* (3.6.10) thus: *Laus igitur potest esse rerum externarum, corporis, animi* ('The following, then, can be subject to praise: external circumstances, physical attributes, qualities of character').[73] The eulogy had a method of elaborating on such explicit qualities of externality, namely *expolitio*, a way of stating and restating a familiar case by amplifying, repeating and extending its details or metaphors. Surfaces, as the term *expolitio* or 'refining' suggests (*Ad Herennium* 4.42), must be polished, exact, for praise has specificity as well as generality, is always evidential.[74] Geoffrey of Vinsauf in the *Poetria Nova* states of *expolitio* that while maintaining a thought we amplify it by changing its 'raiment', ensuring sameness and yet variety.[75] *Expolitio*, to revert to a point made earlier, is a way of managing the rhetorical colours, *figurae* and externalities included, by extending them so that the persons or personifications represented are given greater force. So, as in imagined dialogue, we refine and extend the idea of the Annunciation by 'polishing' the figures of Mary and Gabriel (see pl. 47) to show not just the basic effects but what also might be vividly imagined about them, since the Gospel itself says little – their speech, their expressions, their body-language – and so too with St John at the foot of the Cross (see pl. 12). By this means the figures now appear to participate more richly in a narrative. An exact instance of such formalised and thorough poetic description of top-to-toe female beauty (a *descriptio pulchritudinis*) is given in Vinsauf's *Poetria Nova*, starting with physical beauty and then the beauty of attire. Vinsauf begins:

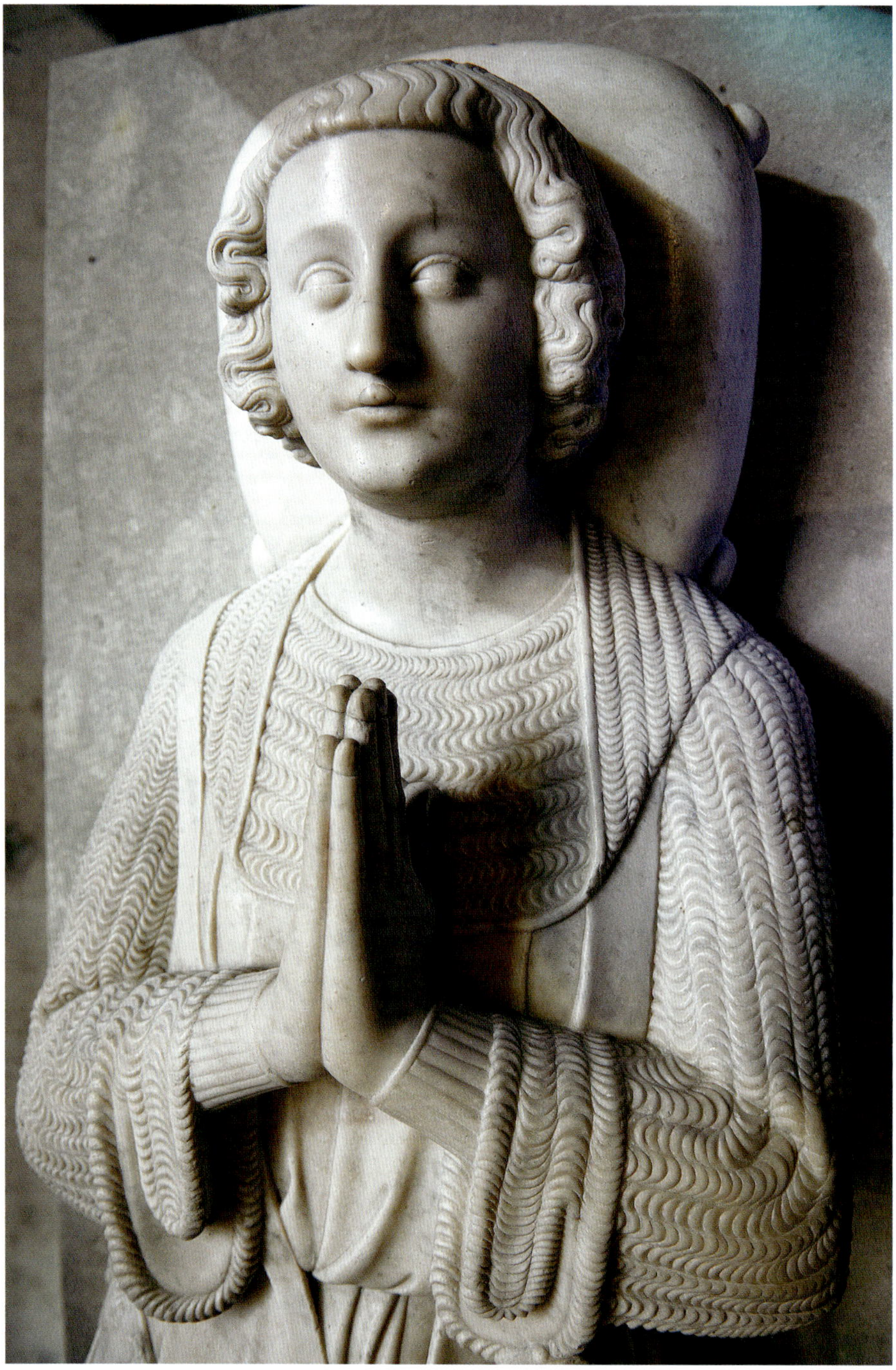

51 Effigy of Robert II (d. 1302), Count of Artois, now at Saint-Denis, formerly in the church of the Cordeliers in Paris, early fourteenth century

facing page 52 Toledo Cathedral, *Virgen Blanca*, painted marble or alabaster, third quarter thirteenth century

Let the compass of Nature first fashion a sphere for her head; let the colour of gold give a glow to her hair . . . Let her eyebrows resemble in dark beauty the blackberry, and a lovely and milk-white path separate their twin arches. Let her nose be straight, of moderate length, not too long nor too short for perfection . . . Let her mouth be bright, small in shape – as it were, a half-circle. Let her lips be rounded and full, but moderately so. Smoother than polished marble let Nature fashion her chin . . .'[76]

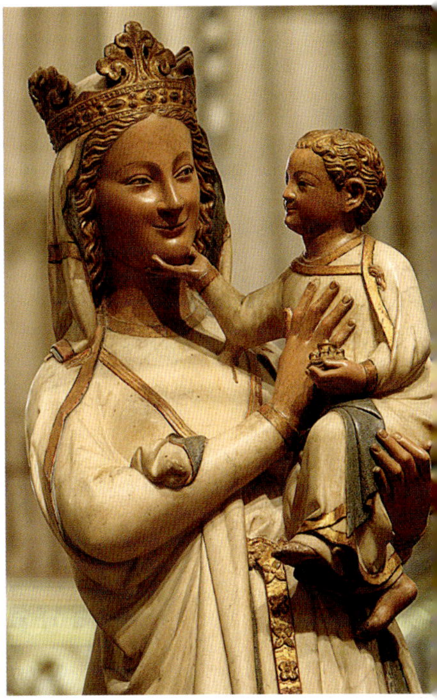

Note the reference to polished marble: done well, these refinements run through the face–body union and its surfaces, and have affective agency. The notion of specifically aristocratic beauty, the beauty of *hauteur*, may assist here. Consider for example the exquisite soft features of the tomb effigy of Jeanne de Toulouse (d. 1271), formerly in the Abbey of Gercy (Essone), smiling almost imperceptibly, but manifestly both fetching and warm; or the delicacy of the effigy of Robert II, Count of Artois (d. 1302) now at Saint-Denis, apparently a model of chivalric restraint despite the fact that Robert himself hugely enjoyed practical jokes at others' expense (pl. 51).[77] Faces and bodies work together in this regard: we might say of the angels at Reims that their smile is an aspect of their total disposition (Bartholomaeus Anglicus states amusingly, but truly as we all know, that a dog smiles by wagging its tail).[78] The greatest of all smiling images were those of the Virgin and Child, such as the magnetic *Virgen Blanca* supposedly donated by Louis IX to Toledo Cathedral in the 1260s (pl. 52; compare also pl. 63); Mary's sweetness of disposition, happiness and beauty were self-evident agents of consolation for the authors of the great illustrated songs of praise, *Las Cantigas*, dedicated to her at this time.[79] No less a figure than St Thomas of Canterbury donated an ivory image of the Virgin Mary to St Edward at Westminster Abbey which was both 'extremely beautiful' (*nimis pulchra*) and also 'very dear' to him.[80]

In regard to mimesis and beauty, such things are undeniably *opinable*, as Roland Barthes notes in his account of the 'reality effect'.[81] They were not necessarily tied to specific representational conventions, norms or styles, and we can disagree about them. But we can also see that the techniques of epideisis might open the way to an alternative account of pictorial verism to that provided by *sermo humilis*, or (as art historians tend to define it) ordinary speech. Cicero, and following him Geoffrey of Vinsauf and John of Garland, thought of hyperbole (Latin *superlatio*) as the 'appropriate exaggeration of truth'.[82] It served the out of the ordinary, socially or metaphysically: Becket's beloved ivory Virgin Mary was not just beautiful but *extremely* beautiful.

There may also be some value in considering the commonality of approach between rhetorical amplification and the influential body of Christian apocryphal writing and imagery in this period. As Pickering and others noted long ago, a thorough filling-out of narrative and other material is a classic feature of apocryphal writing of the sort which dilated especially on the events of the Passion of Christ in the thirteenth century.[83] Such writing shares with the epideictic tradition a detailed, meticulous approach to amplification or 'troping' (the extension of the existing material to hand by the finding of new material): amplification, the lengthening or spreading process, was the task of the *trouvère*, giving work 'fullness and magnitude' in William Ryding's words.[84] Sánchez Ameijeiras is quite right to my mind in emphasising the role of rhetorical amplification in the development of the full, lucid and eloquent programmes of Gothic sculpture, on the lines of the *artes praedicandi*.[85] Pickering too was alert to the connection between Christian verism and this amplificatory process. That which the Church regarded as canonical was true, *vera*; that which was believable was *credenda*; that which was apocryphal was *non vera, sed credenda*: untrue but believable.[86] The apocryphal trope is that which enhances the believability of a subject, its 'reality effect'. This is an effect produced by the accumulation of extension of veristic detail additional to the main case being made. In the ancient ekphrastic rhetoric of such 'beautiful' description, Barthes argued, lay the ultimate basis of the reality claims of modern realist fiction.[87] In contrast to deliberative or forensic rhetoric, display rhetoric was graphic, detailed. The aggregative mode of this form of mimesis cannot be doubted, which is why the amplification of detail matters in refinement: facial expression, the carriage of a head, the nuance of a gesture, clothing, ornament, precisely the things celebrated in the most veristic Gothic statuary from Reims to Claus Sluter, to say nothing of the 'nominalist' triumphs of Netherlandish painting.[88] These amplifications or accumulations are persuasive luxuries which remind us of the images and methods used in ekphrasis or conventionalised evocations of works of art (discussed later in this book, pp. 173–8). They point to their most specialised outcome in the simulacrum. It is not essential to these mimetic effects that they live, though 'live' they do: *enargeia*, as said, is not primarily mimetic. As in Graeco-Roman image-making, the notion of the living image needs to satisfy several criteria: it should appear to breathe, or see, or feel, move and express itself, even speak – not all, but some of these things.[89] The notion that a sculpture or a painting might live is one of the ancient and Christian tropes of art.[90]

Constraint and control all mattered to this artificial Gothic order of demonstration and praise. Conviction requires a doctrine of self-possession and also, artistically, tremendous technique and resources. But the control was not just within. Aesthetic verisimilitude in representation entailed authority, for as images amplified, refined and extended their meanings, as they gained in explicitness, so much the less was left to the imagination: subject agency gave way to the agency of the object. Whether or not it was successful, we can turn the tables on the normative modern account to suggest that Gothic verism was not so much a means of opening access to images, as of foreclosing and channelling debate. This was the price of literalism. Again I sense here a working hypothesis concerning the relation of amplification and *expolitio* in the visual arts and an official nailing-down of an uncontrollable apocrypha, a chaos of readings, by the reformist pastoral Church. The 'reality effect' was a method of bringing one (official) realism to bear on, and repudiate, the possibility of multiple (unofficial) realisms. Paradoxically, the powers of invention brought about a narrowing of the options, a deliberate constriction of signification. For this reason I restate my view that the mimetic artworks of this period were not necessarily simulacra provoking open-ended fantasy. Their role was social, constitutive and political. In these arts, I suggest, lay a certain ethical authoritarianism apparent both in their *figurae* and also in the increasingly conventional programmaticism of the portals themselves. As the inscriptions disappeared and as the responsibility to lay audiences grew, so much the more did the surfaces of the works alone need to hold and illuminate signification. Perhaps, by the key years of the mid-thirteenth century, a common account of such portals, then in existence for the better part of two centuries, held that they were a little too open to interpretation and the beholder's share, for therein lay the risk of interpretative anarchy, a kind of beholder's apocrypha – the plight of the simulacrum as presently formulated. The humanist reading of these arts as arts of individual psychological and emotional liberation, an account borrowed from the German Romantic concept of the autonomy of the gods themselves, tends not to acknowledge the price of foreclosure that, to me, they entailed.

In the apt words of one recent commentator, these Gothic animating syntheses 'were designed for consumption as rhetoric, clever constructs produced by gifted human agents'.[91] And there is one telling further development of this period that suggests that attention to eulogy, not as an all-embracing explanatory principle of change but as an important aspect of the changing tone of representation, its context and interpretation, might be justified. Earlier I mentioned Isidore of Seville's remarks about the nature of the monumental as that which admonishes the mind, an idea intended first for the tomb but also, it seems to me, to that which stirs us in the public domain. What I have in mind is the far from fortuitous rise, at exactly the same time as the spread of Gothic portal statuary, of the sculpted effigial tomb, in the twelfth and especially the thirteenth century.[92] To be sure, this well-known consonance arose in part simply through the circumstances of Gothic art production: the same sculptors probably produced both genres with the same skills. For the most part, thirteenth-century effigial tombs raised at the same time as the great cathedral portals have affective intents whose nature is conventionalised, as in the case of the displays of 'weepers' or ritual mourners gathered around the tomb-chests of French and English royal monuments, such as the dignified processional figures on the tomb chest at Saint-Denis of Louis IX's son Louis of France (d. 1260), formerly at Royaumont, or the examples in Westminster Abbey.[93] The mid-thirteenth-century cenotaph of the founder Dagobert at Saint-Denis is,

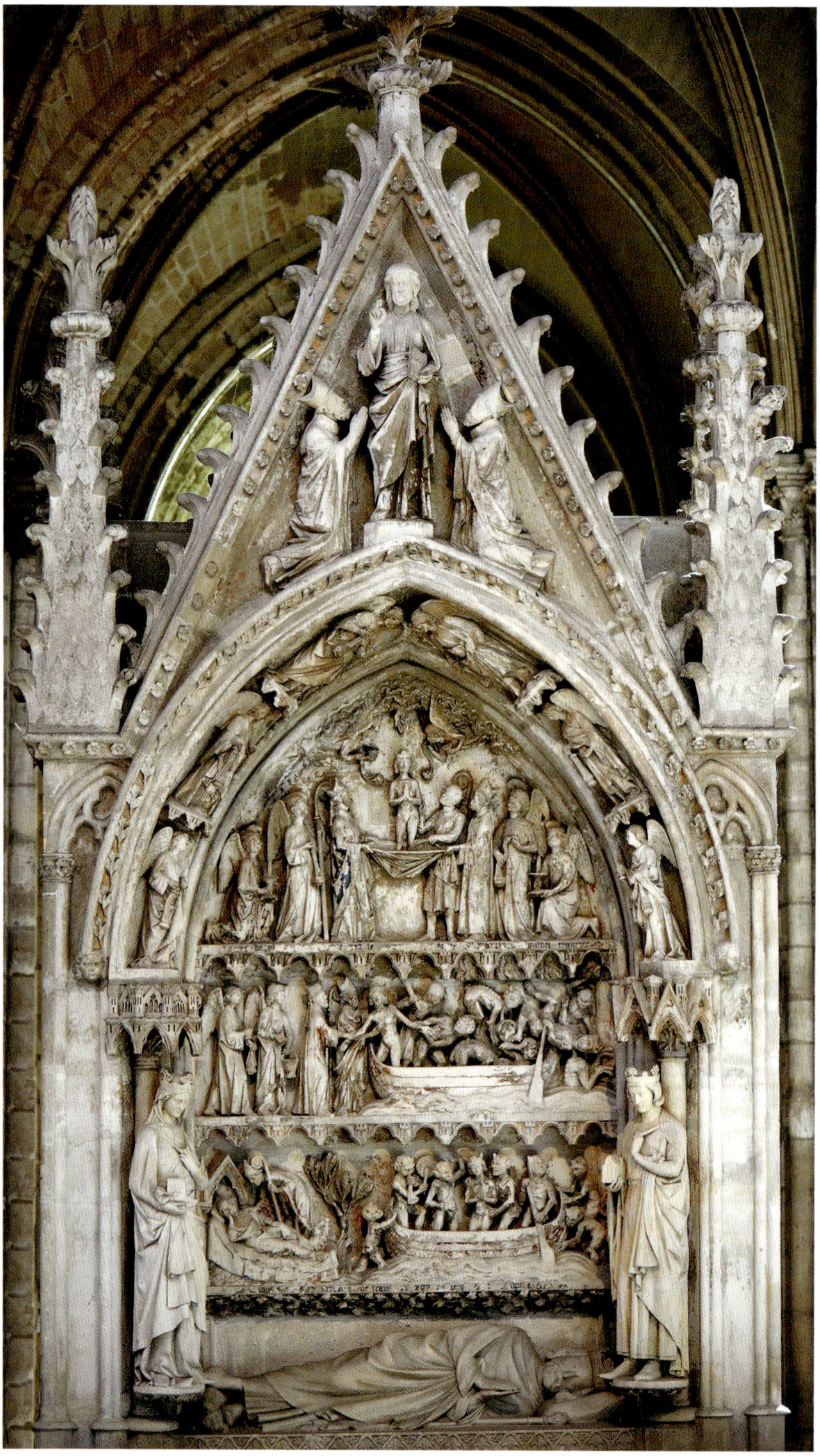

53 Saint-Denis Abbey, choir, cenotaph of Dagobert I, 1260s with nineteenth-century restorations

to all intents and purposes, an indoor portal with arch, gable, pinnacles, column figures and French-style narrative tympanum with registers (pl. 53).[94] Tomb art, in other words, participated in the same mixture of scales and figurative composition as that typical of portals.

But the central point, to my mind underplayed by many studies of sculpture, is that the 'tomb beautiful' had a fundamental sympathy with the portals that was rhetorical and aesthetic as well as technical, a sympathy which was mutually illuminating. It is easy to think of tombs as being the natural 'home' of panegyric, less so of the lowest style of rhetoric, *sermo humilis*. The emphases apparent at the royal mausolea of Saint-Denis and Westminster on courtly restraint, dignified tone, on grief apparent but reined in, on virtue and beauty, are consistent with the moral and rhetorical purposes of the portals.[95] Convention aside, the evidence suggests that the depiction of kingliness or aristocratic virtue as a thing embodied and worthy of panegyric was a counterpart to the idea that the sculpted portal could depict *moralitas*. In the course of the thirteenth century, effulgent, intractable and costly materials such as bronze and marble came to dominate the material culture of Anglo-French royal tombs; the imagery of polish, shine, long associated with virtue and improvement, came to reflect anew the ethical emphasis on sovereign probity as well as magnificence.[96]

A passage in the panegyric of Edward I (d. 1307) known as the *Commendatio lamentabilis* makes a striking connection, fully in keeping with the notion of charity towards the dead cultivated along with the doctrine of Purgatory, between Edward's magnificence in charity and the execution of carefully carved monuments for his dearest ones.[97] At Westminster Abbey the refined bronze images of Henry III (d. 1272) and Eleanor of Castile (d. 1290; pl. 54) executed in the 1290s are praiseworthy in just this sense.[98] The roadside crosses erected for Queen Eleanor in the course of 1290s, probably based on the similar crosses erected for Louis IX (d. 1270), the *Montjoies*, are also acknowledged masterpieces of English small-scale inventiveness.[99] Eleanor's standing image is raised up and repeated on all sides of these spire-like polygonal structures, commanding the landscape panoptically (pl. 55). The crosses were directed by Edward I to be placed in prominent urban centres, as at Cheapside and Charing in London: theirs was a 'political', possessive gesture, founded in charity and reciprocal giving but also a keen sense of territory. Other tombs executed in the same vein at Westminster, such as that of the Earl of Lancaster (d. 1296), sublimate an image of the deceased by raising it up to the tomb gable in a way consistent with the spread of images on the facade at Reims, which was undoubtedly familiar to the Westminster masons.[100] But it is the beauty, grace and saint-like ambivalence of the images that captivates, that serves the conviction purpose of charity and so salvation.

The Eleanor Crosses help underline one further point: such memorials and effigies were understood not just as objects of affective attention but also as demonstrative assertions of family and tenurial rights which might actually be cited in law in a way that fits exactly into the picture of rehearsed demonstration or scripting.[101] In matters of law and possession

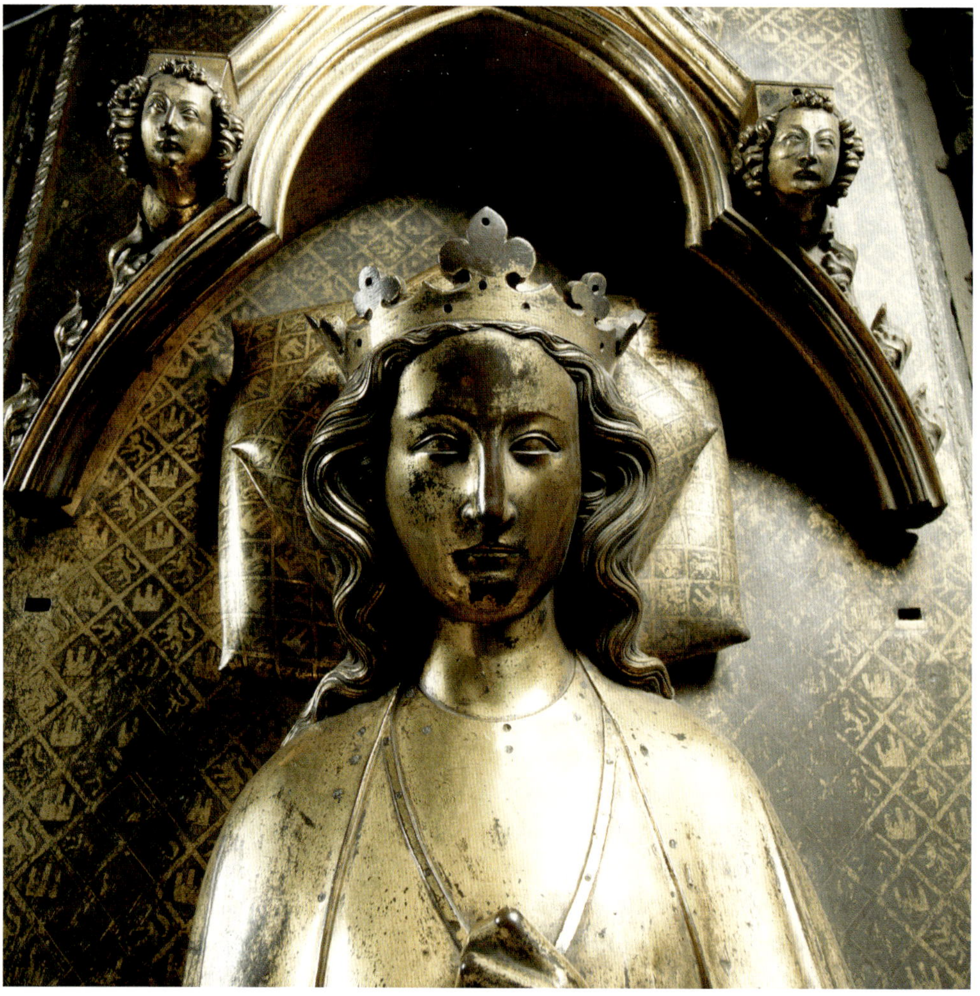

54 Westminster Abbey, gilt bronze effigy of Eleanor of Castile, 1291–2

too, conviction purpose mattered, had material outcome. The Eleanor Crosses addressed a 'public' but also the interests of certain groups. Eulogy was itself above all a formal mode of funerary oration, the beauty of those commemorated mattering. It is also characteristic of this mode of panegyric, of virtue and technique displayed, that portraiture as we understand it should first have arisen convincingly within the sphere of monumental sculpture both in portals and tombs.[102] Portraiture actual or idealised is that 'making present' of the individual, time-bound dead which is a key aim of panegyric, of the eulogy, as a form of eloquence.[103]

In drawing attention to the process of amplification and polishing serving the appetitive will, the desire for inner and outer beauty and ultimately charity towards the dead, I am

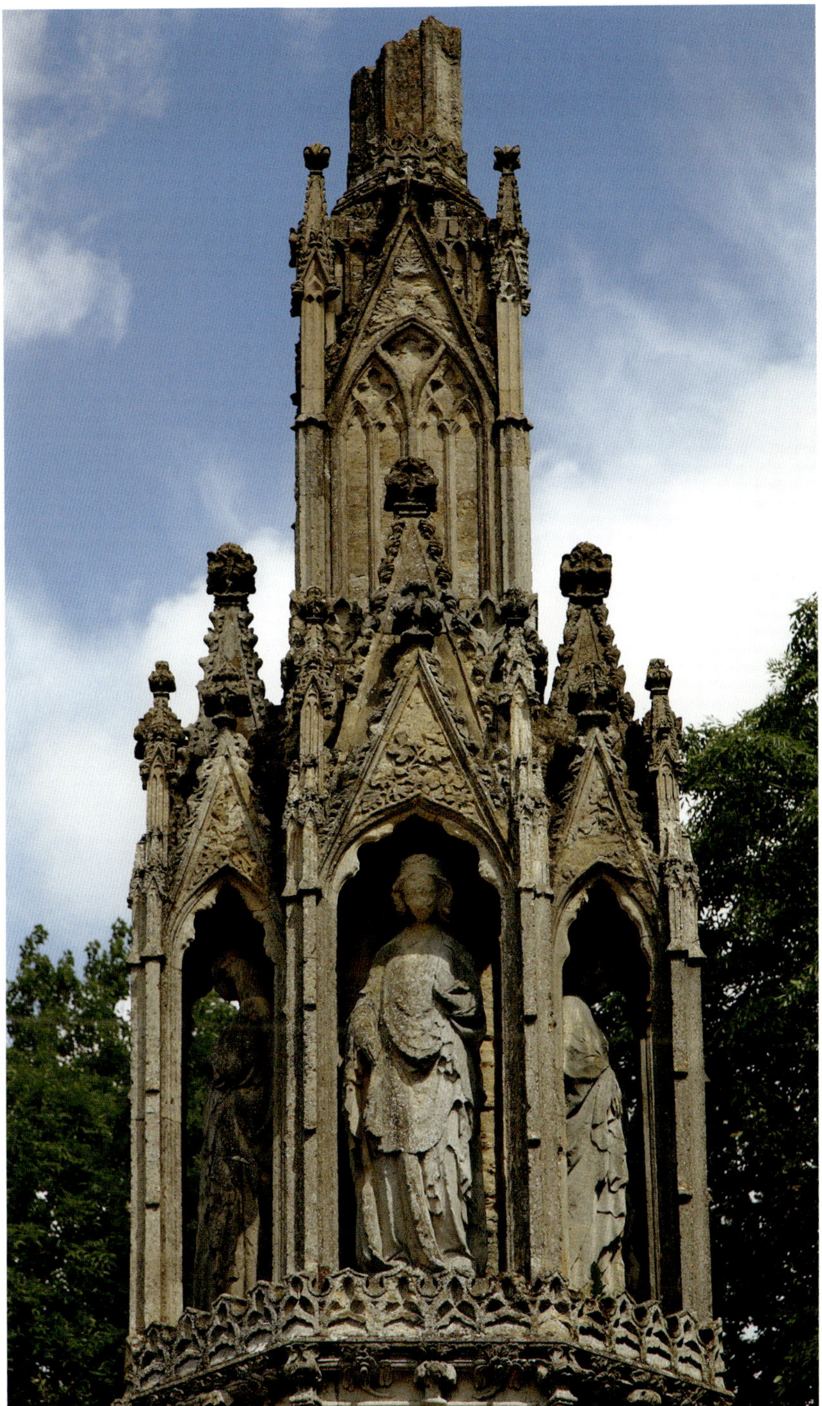

55 Hardingstone Eleanor Cross, top tier, 1290s

really emphasising the issue of genre: eulogy was as appropriate a vehicle for confident aesthetic activity, for the dazzling integument of verism, as *sermo humilis*. Levels of style, whether lofty and panegyrical or humble and everyday, follow from genre and occasion and do not precede them. By stressing one style level or another we have decided in advance within which generic context style operates. A genre choice is implicitly a political choice. Yet we know that portals were too complex to be reduced solely to one generic rhetorical mode, and to do so is not my aim. The keynote was always mixture, appropriateness. In stressing the yearning for beauty, virtue, exemplarity, happiness, amplification, strong and instructive typological contrast and the physical act of wreathing – all fully comprehensible within the mode of eulogy as it was understood in the Middle Ages – I seek to draw attention to those things that are absent from discussion of the low mimetic mode of Gothic representation. My supposition is that much of the actual practice and occasion of sculpture in the twelfth and thirteenth centuries operated within the genre of lofty speech, *magniloquentia*, rather than the everyday or vernacular, and that it was in serving this genre that a 'realist' mode could be appropriate. But the heights of such realism in the thirteenth century were reached very rarely, and when they were attained they fell quite as much into the category of the marvellous as the ordinary.

Here too we must admit the fugitive character of explanation of style *tout court*. What I have omitted is one factor which may be as fundamental to the matter of explanation as it is inseparable from the circumstances just mentioned, and particularly the operation of power: know-how.

KNOW-HOW

Technique matters as much as genre, for one serves the other in the manufacture of the 'clever construct', and it is the clever construct which creates the experience. Production and reception need to be balanced. Since the nineteenth century, however, a divide has opened between the imperatives of technique, skill, craft (*Können*) and artistic will (*Kunstwollen*).[104] As I have suggested, *Können* has tended to suffer at the expense of artistic will, because philosophical romanticism regards will as 'higher' than craft. Craft and process have fallen victim to culture and idea, production to reception, and it is only recently that the rhetoricians in particular have reminded us of the importance of balancing these factors in the non-verbal and verbal arts.[105] A particular taboo has been the association of knowledge, craft, with progress. No one would now dare to argue that medieval art looks the way it does because of 'primitivism', lack of knowledge or even incompetence *vis-à-vis* the heights of later Western European art generally. I have tried to respect this taboo. Yet the sense in which the great cathedral workshops of the Romanesque and Gothic era produced exceptional outcomes which may, after the event, have validated later art-historical notions of the real, still seems to me apparent. This is not the same as arguing for a progressive history of representation. It is to suggest that within that style of argument lie truths about technique and artistic capacity which relate to particular circumstances of production linking will and skill dialectically. Here the connection between what appear, after the event, to be realist projects and the technological ascent of Gothic architecture itself, becomes notable.

The development of Gothic architecture in northern France between 1150 and 1250 or so represents one of the most astonishing and rapid accomplishments of Western visual culture. In 1150, prior to the erection of the choir of Notre-Dame in Paris, Gothic remained a nascent building event with no certain future in the history of a hitherto architecturally conservative region of Europe.[106] By 1240 or so entirely new technologies of buttressing, stone vaulting and large-scale stained-glass manufacture had produced an idiom known to us as High Gothic, which also quickly became a recognised and exportable type, a 'product' (see pl. 50). The building boom across north-western Europe between the eleventh and thirteenth centuries which underwrote both Romanesque and Gothic had produced large numbers of church buildings with carved doorways. At first these doorways were of extraordinary diversity. They gained in scale, complexity but also homogeneity: they too became a 'product'. Because the configurations of Gothic portals with ranks of jamb figures, archivolts and tympana were by common recognition architectonic in nature, their scale and ambition had in effect grown *pari passu* with their framing buildings. From the 1230s throughout much of northern Europe, Parisian Rayonnant architecture then consolidated these features in the face of increasingly unfavourable economic circumstances. The 'product', still French-derived, was adjusting but also gaining even wider international recognition in Germany and to a lesser extent in England and Iberia. Yet, just as by 1240 or so the technologies of Gothic were established, by the last quarter of the century so too had the central aesthetic tenets of Gothic as a style become more or less fixed. Gothic had ceased to be a nascent building event and had become a self-aware idiom. These developments were more or less in place by roughly 1260 or 1270 when the major French cathedral *chantiers* (workshops) such as that at Reims (see pl. 46) were winding down or fragmenting.[107] Portals, like towers, were luxuries, and if a cathedral church in Continental Europe was not begun before about 1225 the possibility that these add-ons might never be completed, or would be completed late, was increased.[108] The veristic project, in other words, was connected to the period of maximum extent and vitality of the great *chantiers* between the late twelfth century and 1260 or so. These *chantiers*, I suggest, were participants in a form of heroic and panegyrical discourse, beneficiaries of tremendous and surprisingly sustained economic support, and composed of relatively large teams of artificers. The long-term coherence of this 'project' was far from certain, but its self-assurance and its momentum is not in doubt.

This heroic mode was a socio-cultural phenomenon which manifested itself in at least three ways. One was the recognition accorded to architects and their products in thirteenth-century discourse about the professions in France especially.[109] Another was the coordination of architecture with heavy technologies, including metalworking, which contributed to the 'great speech' of the cathedrals in religion – bells, organs and clocks, all actually or potentially understood as wonders.[110] These churches were laboratories of the big effect. The third way was a self-conscious recognition that this mode was a success to be emulated, that it had started to confer advantages. That cathedrals such as Reims, indeed Reims especially, were perceived as resources of invention early in the course of their erection is evident, but it is also striking that Chartres, Reims and Paris were regarded as canonical exemplars of portal design towards the end of the Middle Ages when economic recovery eventually brought about the completion of projects long set aside in the century or more of building recession from the late thirteenth century. This is clinched by the remarkable report in the documents for Troyes Cathedral in 1455 that its master, Bleuet of Reims, when asked how the portals of Troyes might be undertaken, replied that it would be good to visit several churches, such as Reims, Amiens and Notre-Dame (*qu'il seroit bon de visiter plusiers eglises comme Rains, Amiens et Nostre Dame de Paris*) on which basis he would give his opinion.[111] After the trip a drawing was duly made for the Troyes scheme.[112]

That the cachet of Reims especially had been apparent more than two hundred years earlier is well recognised, and the evidence for its study at Westminster Abbey (where the first master mason was also called *de Reyns* or *Reins*), León (like Westminster, a coronation church), Bayonne, Tournai, Trier, Marburg and Bamberg, to say nothing of the portfolio connected with Villard de Honnecourt and so Cambrai, is extensive.[113] No other Gothic building, with the possible exception of the Sainte-Chapelle in Paris, was so rapidly and widely cited in the mid-century years before the building boom tailed off. Here speed of reference and creative momentum mattered in a form of 'snowballing'. The re-entry onto the stage of artistic deliberation of something like a canon of great buildings was a medieval restaging of the heroic mode of the ancient Wonders.[114] We note especially the political weight of the institutions involved. The fact is that Reims innovated simultaneously in more than one medium. Its introduction of bar tracery (see pl. 50) was revolutionary and widely cited. This citation provably involved not just the *parti* of Reims's plan, elevations and tracery but also the unfolding sculptural decoration on the church's exterior, its monumental north transept portals and the smaller-scale masks (pl. 56), figures and angels on the upper parts of the chevet and transepts, probably being installed by the 1220s, and certainly in place by the opening of the choir in 1241.[115] In contrasting the somewhat summary but efficient sculpture of Amiens with the sculpted lavishness of Reims, it has been argued that what characterised the two projects were fundamental differences in economic provision and city–cathedral relations, Reims proceeding more lavishly without compromise

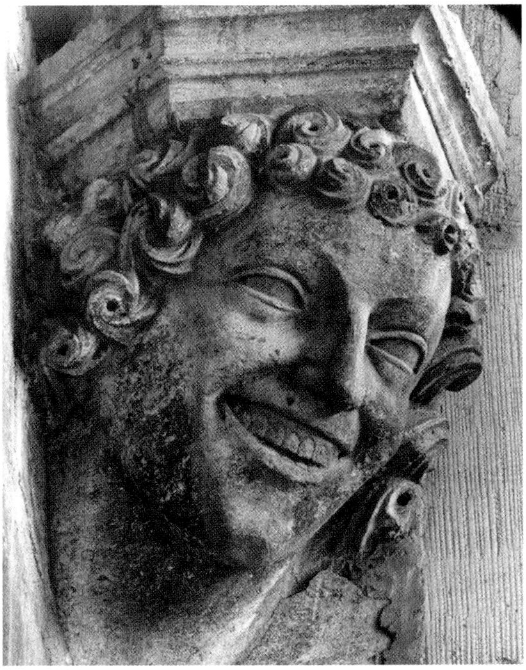

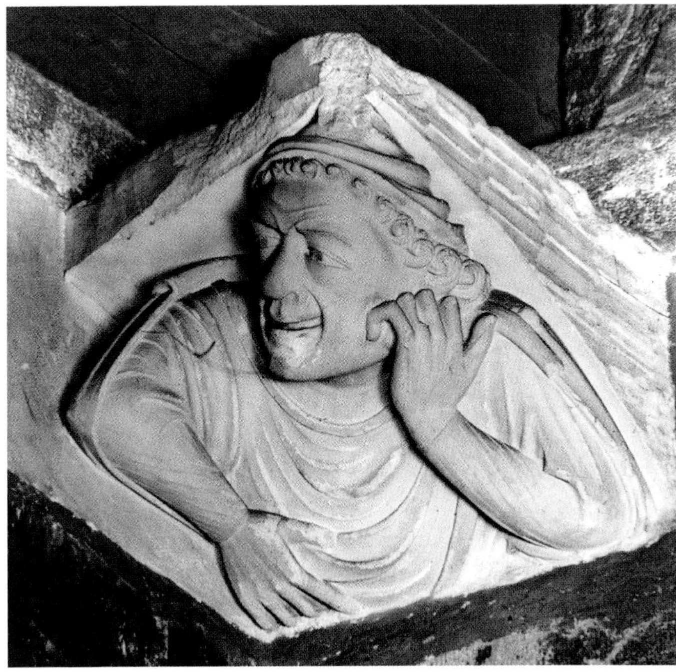

56 Reims Cathedral (Marne), laughing mask from exterior of chevet, before 1241

57 Westminster Abbey, corbel in tribune at east end, about 1250

and without regard to insolvency.[116] Its sculpture was finished to qualitatively superior and more labour-intensive standards than Amiens, with higher finish of detail and variation of facial type. Reims's carved flora, unusually prevalent both within and without the building, resemble modelled clay.[117] And this extraordinary technical accomplishment was true of the approximately 2300 carved images which originally decorated the church, many of which were destroyed outright in the First World War.[118] This prodigious project provided, in effect, a large and sustained laboratory for what we must assume were not only fast-working but extensive teams of highly organised, capable and well-funded sculptors. Efficiency of production may be one factor in the spread of the broad-fold style from the Reims and Paris workshops from the 1230s and 1240s, because it enabled a kind of selective intensification of attention on the eloquent parts of figures such as heads and hands, which become even more finely considered and wrought.[119] The resources were clearly such that spare capacity existed for experiment and risk. This capacity, I suggest, is what separates the sober 'classicising' work of the north transept portals at Reims from the astounding grinning, frowning and gurning masks on the upper parts of the chevet and transepts, images which mark a kind of paradigm shift in Gothic verism. These masks are not the products of some furtive marginal sensibility, but arguably the by-products of a hot-housing culture of competition and inventive play, *ludus*.[120] We recall that works of art of this sort, viewed collectively, can emulate, outdo and even subvert themselves.

The same culture, I suggest, is apparent in the portfolio connected with Villard de Honnecourt; but the key point is that the great laboratory of Reims, to pursue my 'scientific' image a little further, was directly connected to the workshop practices of Reims's artistic dependents, at Westminster (pl. 57 and see pl. 42) and at Bamberg and Naumburg. Earlier I noted that it is within the Reims–Westminster sphere that explicit contractual statements emerged around 1240 regarding the affective disposition of *figurae*. In understanding the progress of works at Reims we are indebted to Peter Kurmann's extensive studies of the way its artists and models circulated between the canonical projects – Amiens, Paris, then Strasbourg and Bamberg.[121] Reims gave, but it also took. And this circulation was preoccupied with exactly the conceits or tricks of verism, the reality effect, itself: the same head-types recycle between these projects, as also between Naumburg and Meissen, suggesting the circulation of small models in clay or wood, or moulds.[122] By combining and recombining heads, hands and bodies, much as a clay modeller or woodcarver might do, an eloquent world emerged as if by magic from a box of tricks, a shared and sharable toolkit. Too little, as yet, is known about the cunning methods of reproduction required, for example the extent to which the obvious reproduction of Flavian and Augustan head types at Reims in the 1220s established methods of copying and derivation which almost immediately mutated into a decidedly non-classical, yet still modular and permutational, facial aesthetic higher up on the chevet and transepts within a few years.[123] And if the documented processes at Troyes in the early sixteenth century were continuing earlier practices, painters too might have been drafted into the process of designing portals, and their expensive skills were provably deployed to finish off and render surfaces.[124] Such linked and mutually dependent projects permitted the growth of a kind of extended, concealed network of multi-medial exchange, a spreading artistic mycelium which created, connected and facilitated competing yet collaborating great church projects, in which pooled talent was proving exceptionally adept at problem-solving.[125] The implications of this for our understanding of mastership and authorial control – which seem to me to have been parts of this environment – are considerable.[126] Again, older, nationalistic, ways of studying the relationships between the great French and German cathedrals and their sculptures obscured the possibility that these projects formed a technical network, with shared and developing production techniques aimed at clever effects. In passing, I simply suggest that similar conditions arose in central Italy between the mid-thirteenth and early fourteenth centuries to produce the 'Giottesque' revolution in painting associated geographically with Rome, Florence and Pisa. But that is another story.

In this way knowledge realised itself systemically, in production. In attempting to understand this phenomenon and its by-products we may have been looking in the wrong places, too much at will, and too little at skill. The veristic project of Gothic – if it was that – was a masquerade, a make-believe, of artifice which grew not from some shifting philosophical base (as was argued often in the intellectualist twentieth century) or indeed from some external impetus, but actually from within a particular privileged regime of production sustainable only until the end of the thirteenth century when the key requirement, momentum, stalled.

That is why we opened, from on high, with the image of a diverse Romanesque visual culture ceding ground to a much more homogeneous Gothic one. It is difficult to posit for the eleventh and twelfth centuries the same levels of resourcing and network exchange, distributed yet interconnected projects of invention, as those emerging by 1250, though this is not to suggest that Romanesque artworks were never interconnected. Romanesque art was both international and regional, yet its dialects were particular and its interdependencies less marked than at the economic and technical highpoint of French Gothic.[127] In the course of the thirteenth century, architects and masons not only promoted their professional images more aggressively and more sharply than had been true in the Romanesque era, but encouraged the use of graphic means of transmitting their ideas, notably architectural drawings, which served further to encourage interdependence, and hence a kind of brilliant conformity. Only complex, cunning and highly organised processes could arrive at such visual outcomes. At the outset I considered the play on narrowness of entry, yet amazing freedom and tangle of display, on the Scandinavian stave church portals; in Gothic France, by the time of Reims, the portals are capacious, the layout lucid, yet the emotional life foreclosed for all the illusions of affect. To arrive at this paradox requires a shift in the value of artifice. Motives must always be realised in some crafted form. Process and facture, seen within the framing political, religious or rhetorical culture of the times, was key. The history of Gothic realism and its attendant rhetorical and affective orders, was in reality a history not just of an imaginary but of technique itself.

Part II

Wood, Flesh and Bone

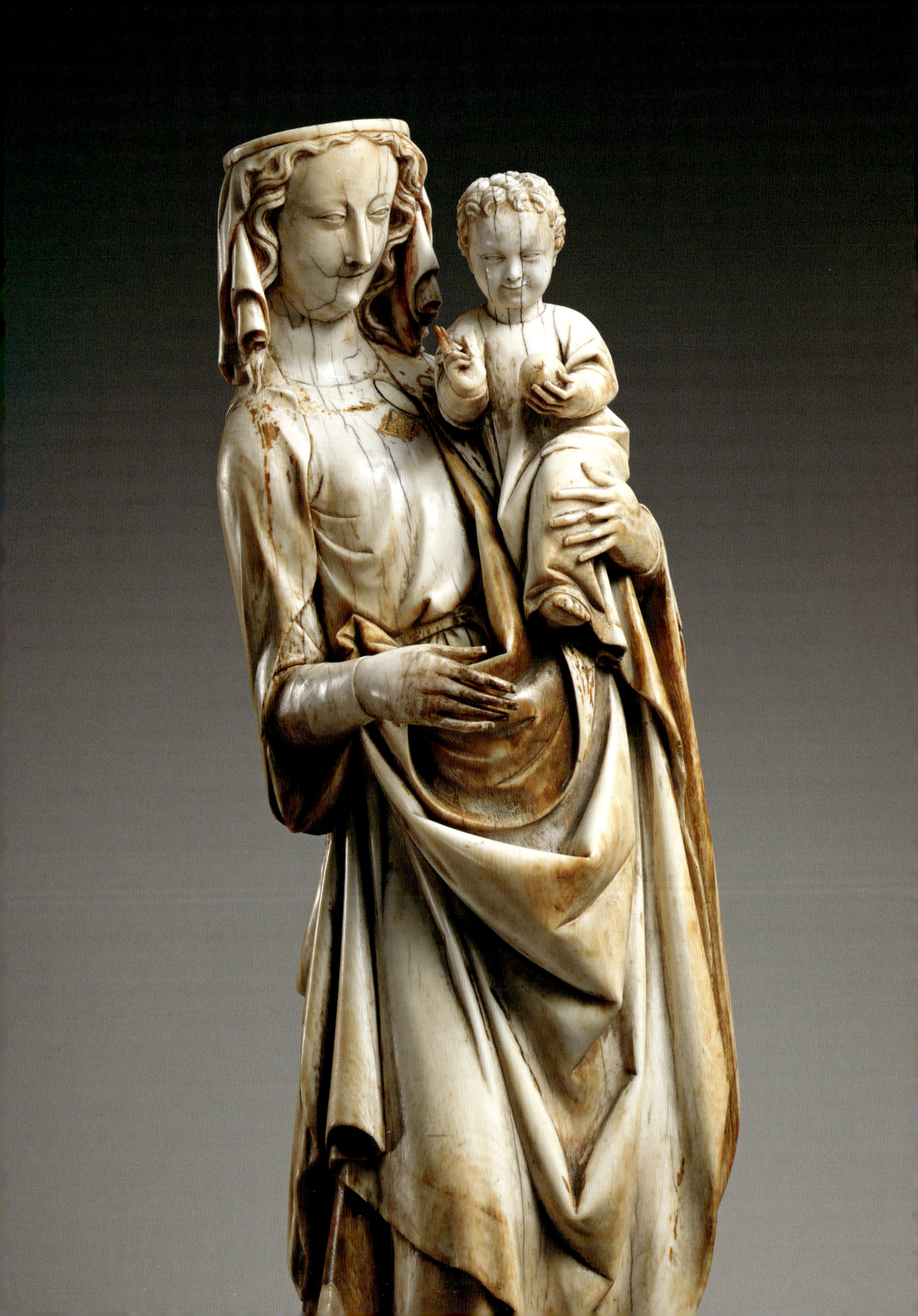

4

MATERIAL, STYLE, REPRESENTATION

A wit, on hearing an earnest report of an apparition of the Virgin Mary, enquired mock-innocently, 'Really? I wonder which Period?' A living vision the Virgin might indeed have been but she was still perceived in whichever guise came to mind, Gothic (pl. 59), Renaissance, Baroque, Pre-Raphaelite, 'Chris Ofili' and so on. This quip expresses in a nutshell some of the thoughts which follow here: imagination and convention, *visio* and *revelatio*, are mediated by human art. Arthur C. Danto, reviewing a well-known study of the power of images, made a trenchant intervention about the tendency of art historians to dig holes for themselves: he said of the book that it is as if '*either* you relate to images claimed to possess such powers as lacrimation and lactation, *or* you are some kind of formalist, numb to the magical power of art'. He went on to observe, I think rightly, that 'almost everything interesting about art lies somewhere between these disjuncts'.[1] Danto was not hostile to the power of images: 'an altarpiece is literally a trap for saints', he remarks in the same place. Neither am I. Yet he was rightly suspicious of efforts to corral imagery either into an animist camp in which images are not just lively but alive (two things not always adequately distinguished), or into a reactionary and embarrassingly empty formalism. In the Introduction I wrote of the unhelpful antithesis of two modern idols of thought, Kantian aesthetic detachment on the one hand and the 'excessive' image possessed of life and presence on the other. Danto has a point: what is of interest often lies between the two.

Danto illuminated this issue by considering the distinction between 'immanence' and 'transeunce'.[2] Put simply, immanence is 'cause from within' the thing, transeunce is 'cause

58 Virgin and Child, northern French (detail of pl. 63)

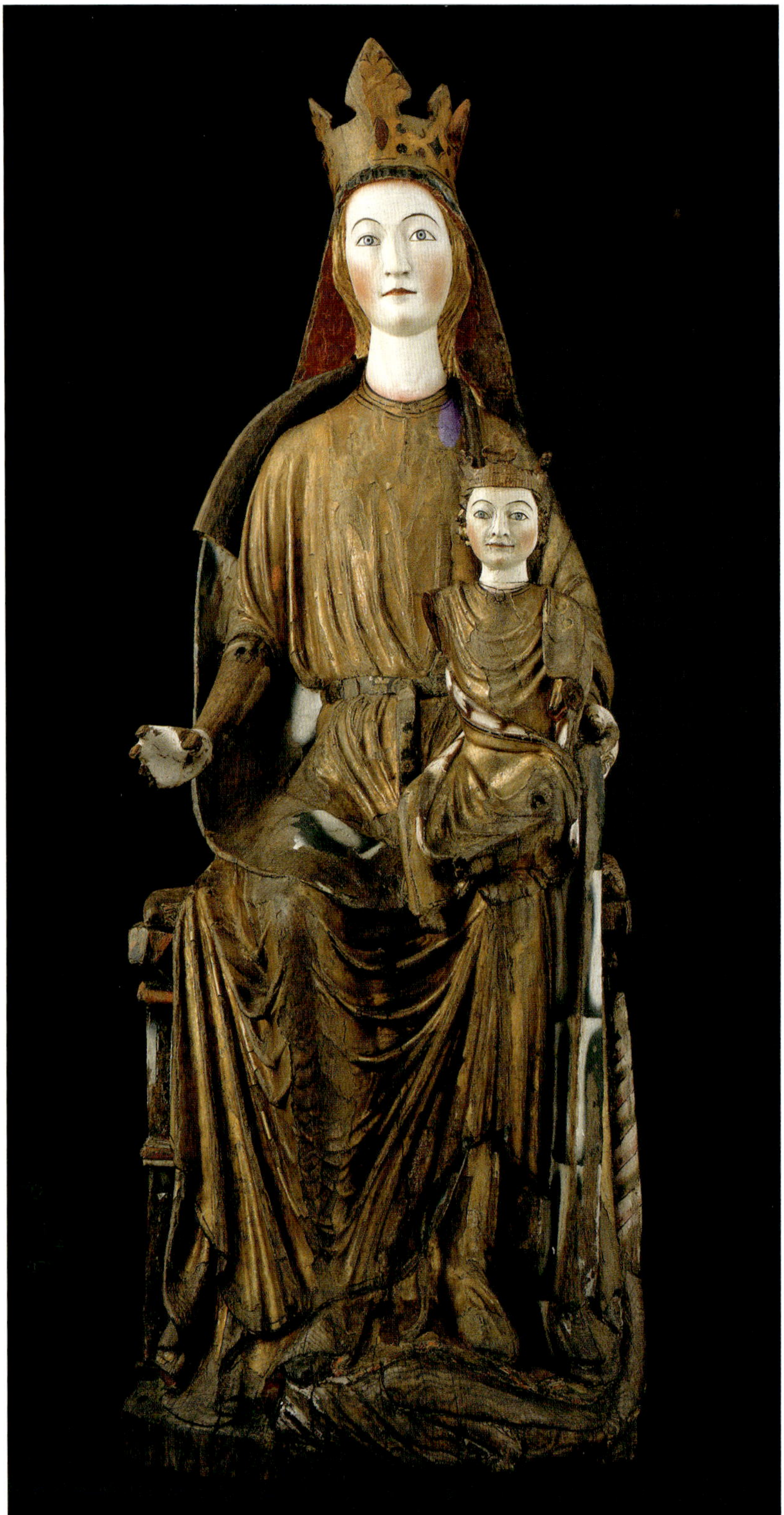

from outside' the thing. Each might be religious in implication (the belief that God created the world from without is transeunt; the belief that a statue of the Virgin Mary in some sense 'is' the Virgin Mary is immanent). The philosophical distinction between immanent and transeunt causality is not always clear-cut. But while an immanent view of an artwork will necessarily be connected to the belief that it contains within itself some sort of self-moving 'life', however defined, a transeunt experience of that artwork need not necessarily do so. The first conflates sign and signified, the second separates them.

Despite this separation, the transeunt modality is not an empty experience: it is not necessary to a full sensory and intellectual encounter with an artefact that we should believe it actually to be alive or self-moving. In the last chapter, for instance, we saw that the wonderful smiling angels at Reims were lively, but it is far from clear that to have this perception of them we need to see them as actually alive. Were this the case, we could not give an aesthetic account – by which I mean far more than a formalist account – of the experience of architecture, or of a text. This is one reason why theories of medieval (or indeed any) art which focus solely on the figurative arts may mislead. An artwork may or may not be alive; but either way it possesses agency as an artefact.

One starting-point for all such discussion, Aby Warburg's *Denkraumverlust* (identified by Gombrich as the 'tendency of the human mind to confuse the sign with the thing signified'), is the richness of metaphor itself.[3] There is no need to dismiss the idea that some or many 'medieval people' believed that images had presence; many 'modern people' still do.[4] To deny the powers of images to move or apparently perform the miraculous would be pointless, for they were acknowledged throughout the Middle Ages.[5] Immanent and transeunt notions of the image probably co-existed historically, much as they do now. Were this not so it would not have been necessary for an orthodox poet and thinker like Thomas Hoccleve (d. 1426), probably defending images in the face of Lollard critiques of idolatry, to insist that the images of saints were precisely *not* saints.[6] The standard defence of images in the Latin Church for the most part rejected the ideas of immanence, presence or inherence. As Donal Cooper puts it in a study of the monumental Cross in medieval Italy, 'Images directed and channelled devotion towards eternal figures and mysteries, but were not ontologically elided with them'.[7] What Michael Baxandall called the 'decent and rational theory of images recommended to the people' regarding the dangers of idolatry was also probably conformed to by many before and after the Reformation which, in England, did much to destroy the medieval landscape of images bar rare survivals such as the Langham Virgin and Child (pl. 60).[8]

It is emphatically not my role here to argue against the excessive or 'out of bounds' object: we can and should allow our images to live and even exceed because here we are asking

59 Virgin and Child, oak with chalk primer, original paint and gilding, from Hedalen (Oppland), Norway, mid-thirteenth century (Universitetets, Oldsaksamling, Oslo). In style and technique the image is close to contemporary English work.

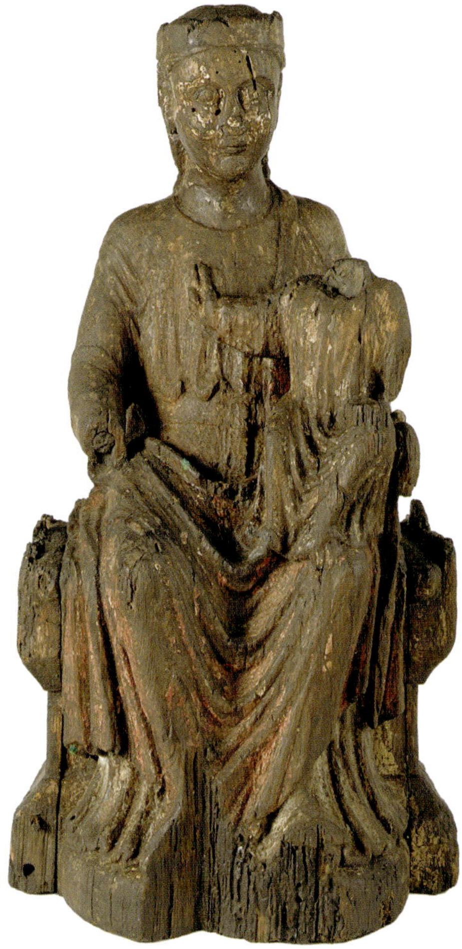

60 Virgin and Child, oak with traces of paint, from Langham parish church (Essex), early thirteenth century (London, Victoria and Albert Museum, no. A. 79-1925)

different things of them.[9] We do not have to choose. But in setting aside these categories and choice, we still encounter our two idols. Anthropological modes have offered particular challenges to Western aesthesis and the concept of art, by endeavouring to breathe life into old things, to see them instrumentally, magically or performatively, but precisely not aesthetically.[10] The taboo here derives from an insistence on the link of aesthetic experience and Western-style aesthetic discrimination as an elitist and Eurocentric pathology: in distancing the discussion from the latter, aesthesis itself is rejected. This rejection, I suggest, in turn robs our objects of study of one aspect of their agency, namely that they are representations as well as presences. The roots of this unhelpful slippage run deep in modern Western thinking. Goethe and Hegel noted that religious power and devotion generally attach to poor not great works of art, thereby validating a long and perhaps troubling association of certain forms of Christian art with 'low' cultural or social form.[11] It was only a short step from this to the belief that the 'being' of an image might be more powerful, and so more interesting to us, than its art, or that the power of art might actually detract from the power of the image, its presence. Medieval sources occasionally appear to lend weight to this privileging of image over art. The celebrated dialogue on miracles written by the thirteenth-century Cistercian Caesarius of Heisterbach mentions the powers of an old, unskilfully formed yet virtuous image of the Virgin Mary of which a woman remarked tactlessly: 'Why does this old rubbish stand here?'; the Virgin punitively deprived the woman of all good fortune.[12]

In its modern form, as Danto noted, this mindset implicitly considers aesthetic experience itself as a form of idolatry, the worship of things empty of life. Characteristic of it is a preoccupation with the function (in the sense of use-function) of artefacts, rather than with their purpose or their experience: indeed, purpose and function, ends and means become one, and a new idol is lifted up. In his study *The Gothic Idol*, Michael Camille, approvingly citing the anthropologist Clifford Geertz, stated: 'The aesthetic anesthetizes. It annihilates function, taking the object of interest out of the realm of necessity into the disinterested contemplation of the subjective viewer's consciousness'.[13] Alfred Gell also stresses the agency of art in bringing about changed social behaviour, yet he also strips out aesthetic experience from that agency.[14] In doing so, such writers set up a false dichotomy between a basically post-Kantian notion of aesthetics and 'depth' of meaning which bears no relation to medieval notions of *aesthesis* as sense-based, surface-bound experience and knowledge, which precisely constitute rather than mask ordinary experience. Agency occurs within the experience of an artefact and its surfaces and is not independent of it.[15]

Such methods are therefore constitutionally disinclined to engage in close reading of the actual appearance of works of art, and so to explore the particularity of experience and what emerges from it, because close reading is regarded as a compromised vehicle of distinterestedness. Any image might be substituted for any other, provided such images act adequately as illustrative or demonstrative signs of an instrumental role or use-function. The flattening effect of this way of thinking should be noted. Clearly, a rich account of experience is not readily reducible to, or ascertainable from, function in this sense. I can easily ascertain the function of a piano by trying its keys. I can pretend that the function of the piano 'explains' the music of Bach or Beethoven. But not for long: without having any sense of the music a piano produces, something of an entirely different order is missing, namely what it is to experience music, let alone the difference between Bach and Beethoven. Difference disappears but the use-function is the same. So the objection to such reductive instrumentality runs deep. Artefacts are enmeshed in complex patterns of intentionality that require not just a function but also intending objects and intending subjects, in other words a specific experience that is grounded in historical and social context. They possess agency through their *intentio* or inclination, manifest in their purposive formal organisation and stylistic aspect. This in turn is shaped by the intentions of those experiencing them. The mixed agency of artworks entails a prior imaginative concept, an Idea or representation: the apparition of the Virgin Mary belongs to a 'Period' of art.[16]

Social-rhetorical analysis, rooted in medieval theories of mind and emotion, clarifies some of these questions by restoring aesthetic experience to its proper place (that is, as something workaday, not an object of idolatry) and also, more specifically, by providing a practical historically based critical language to evaluate that experience. It understands that imaging and imagination are connected, and that they are social, engaged, participative but also purposive. Transeunt analysis is transactional. Important to it is a shared and sharable body of human experience, method and judgement typical of the working of material into art, textual or visual. Ovid's famous, and throughout the Middle Ages widely cited, dictum *materiam superabat opus* (*Metamorphoses* 2:5), 'the workmanship surpassed the materials', suggests the priority of artifice without demoting materiality: if you think the materials are great, consider the workmanship![17] Yet, as we shall see, some current versions of the materiality immanence theory explicitly or implicitly demote human agency. We might well ask of them why Ovid's dictum in praise of artifice was popular in the first place. Surely artefacts have both material and formal causes? They are made of stuff, and they work towards an end: but they are made.[18] By sidestepping this we run the risk of disregarding the processual character of artefacts: that objects are not in fact just stuff but are formed deliberately by human intent and process, and that their perception, too, is crafted, artificial and so involves rational calculation and judgement.

Indeed, we may find ourselves tip-toeing towards a second kind of fundamentalism, not functionalist but materialist. W. J. T. Mitchell spots this danger when he remarks of the 'Romanticist' interest in materials that 'We are in danger of supposing that somehow the turn to the physical is a tough-minded and realistic gesture, a politically progressive act of getting down to the concrete, hard facts, the obdurate stuff of things in themselves'. Regarding this turn to the physical as illusory, he observes that the physical 'is a thoroughly metaphysical concept' and that 'objects only make sense in relation to thinking, speaking subjects'.[19] Materials are necessary but not sufficient conditions for the creation of complex artefacts. We need to acknowledge the power of human intent and affect and the capacity to think sideways, through simile, metaphor, allegory and the other devices of style that operate beyond physical presence, and which must be crafted into an artefact or text. The 'materiality' of images is held – I think questionably – to be a fact, not a process, to be ontological not processual. But process – the process of making and realising, and also the process of experiencing – is as inescapable as work done by thinking, feeling subjects. It is in this way that we can avoid the materialist trap of essentialising the qualities of stuff and losing sight of the fact that aesthetic experiences are just that, experiences within subjects, not things or beings within objects.[20]

So, to consider these points further, let us turn to another material and another sort of situation.

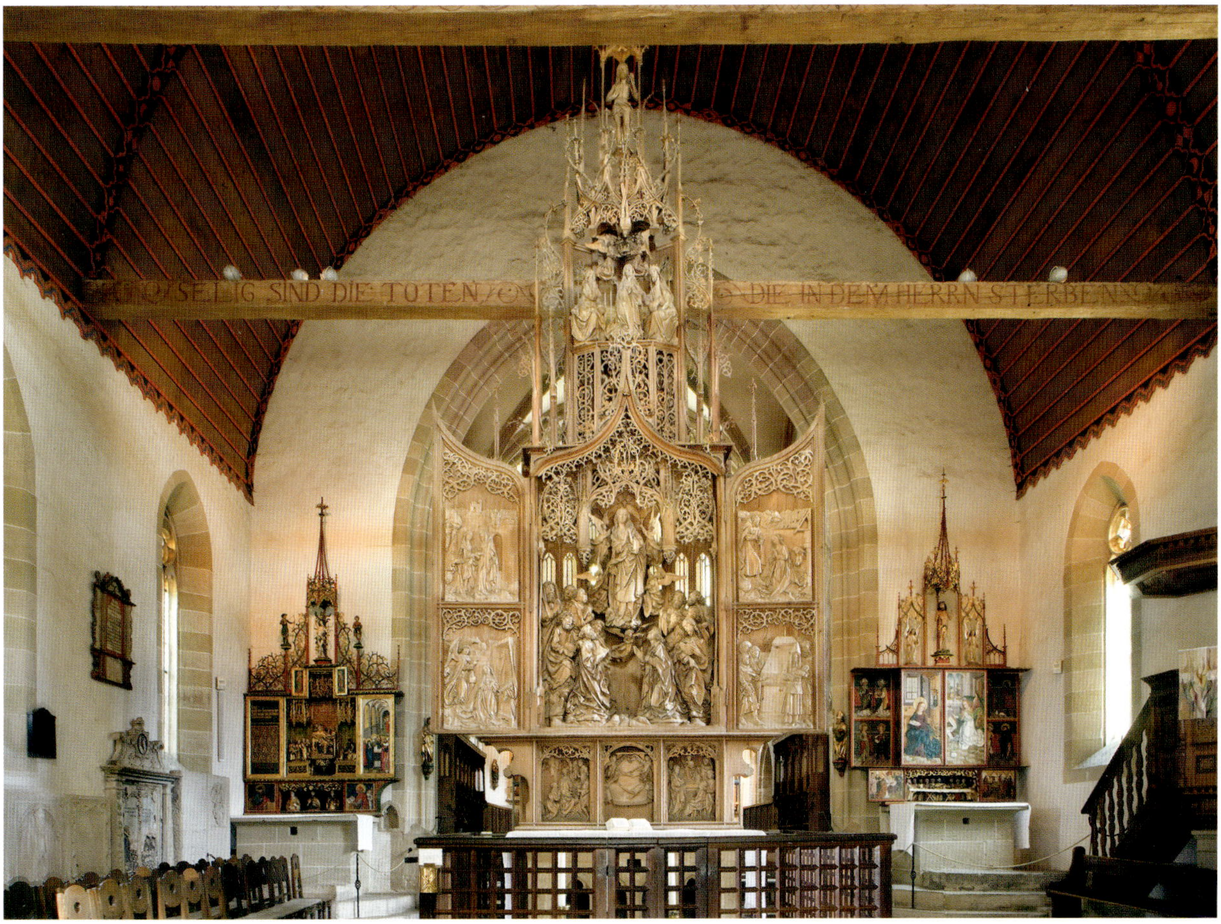

61 Creglingen (Baden-Württemberg), Herrgottskirche, interior east end ensemble with central Marian altarpiece by Tilman Riemenschneider, about 1505–10

WOOD, IRON AND CRAFT

Passing through our great portals and their tremendous sense of occasion, we enter the inner world of the sanctuary and a different zone of material experience. We start to encounter a material that, precisely because it grows, changes and decays, can be thought of as living and immanent – wood, the material of church furnishings and images as carved and painted by medieval artists. Such images were most commonly of the Virgin Mary, the Cross and the saints. Many hundreds of greater and smaller churches throughout Italy and north-western Europe, as at Creglingen (pl. 61), still bear witness to the experiential power of the medieval installation, whether a wooden or stone screen, a great painted

Cross with figures, a sacrament house or font cover with a bravura canopy, or a glittering altarpiece. Carved and painted wooden artefacts survive in sufficient numbers in Scandinavia, Germany and Spain – spectacular later losses aside – to indicate that the affective and demonstrative powers, the aesthetic experience, of the church interior was just as eloquent, just as marked by a sense of occasion, as the great doorways on the cathedral and abbey churches. Earlier in this study I discussed occasion as if it were relevant to starting-points, scene-setting; but, as stated earlier, occasion is always a process, leading on. In those churches that possessed both, the interior installation was a development, or amplification, of the exterior frontispiece. Interior display punctuated, excited (in the medieval sense) and celebrated the progress of the audience through the various stations of liturgy and devotion. Artefacts, furnishings and images laid out a cognitive map of this interior world.[21] Colour, tincture or metal, was as much a feature of the exterior stonework as of the interior carved wooden surface, and current conservation work on Europe's sculpted facades is revealing the original extent of such colour and gilding.[22] Carved surfaces, through their very working and shaping, bore *colores*, effects and techniques of style directing experience which included literal colouration with pigments. These *colores* or vestitures, both drawn over and worked into surfaces, included more subtle or complex verbal matter such as allegory and metaphor, matter which might run the risk of obscuring meaning and effect but which, used clearly, also greatly enriched it. Christian doctrine at an everyday level allowed for spiritual ideas to have a material or carnal basis, a basis in stuff but also in method, habit, practice.

It was precisely for this reason that many of the most fundamental decisions regarding the choice of materials for an artefact were practical. The data for art technology in well-researched regions such as medieval Scandinavia charts a number of factors and developments in the making of sculpture and panel paintings. Woodcarvers might choose to make sculptures from a range of soft and hard woods, but during the Gothic period oak, a hardwood, became more common throughout not only Scandinavia but also north Germany.[23] This may have arisen partly from considerations of trade, cost and availability, given normal ecological variation in the distribution of wood species. Woods could combine in a single artefact. The many fine, carved and painted crucifixes remaining in Norway from the thirteenth and fourteenth centuries show, for example, that while oak tended to be used for the crucifix figure, pine was used for the actual cross (pl. 62).[24] Why? It is hard to point to a specific symbolism for such woods, but it is easier if not easy to give a practical account of their character. All carvers will know that stones work differently under the chisel and are suited to different ends: marbles and freestones have different qualities and uses. So too with woods. The various hard and soft woods handle differently, a dense wood such as oak requiring different tooling from softer woods but producing finer, shinier finish. Woods such as poplar or limewood, characterised in a fourteenth-century English text as useless for building but

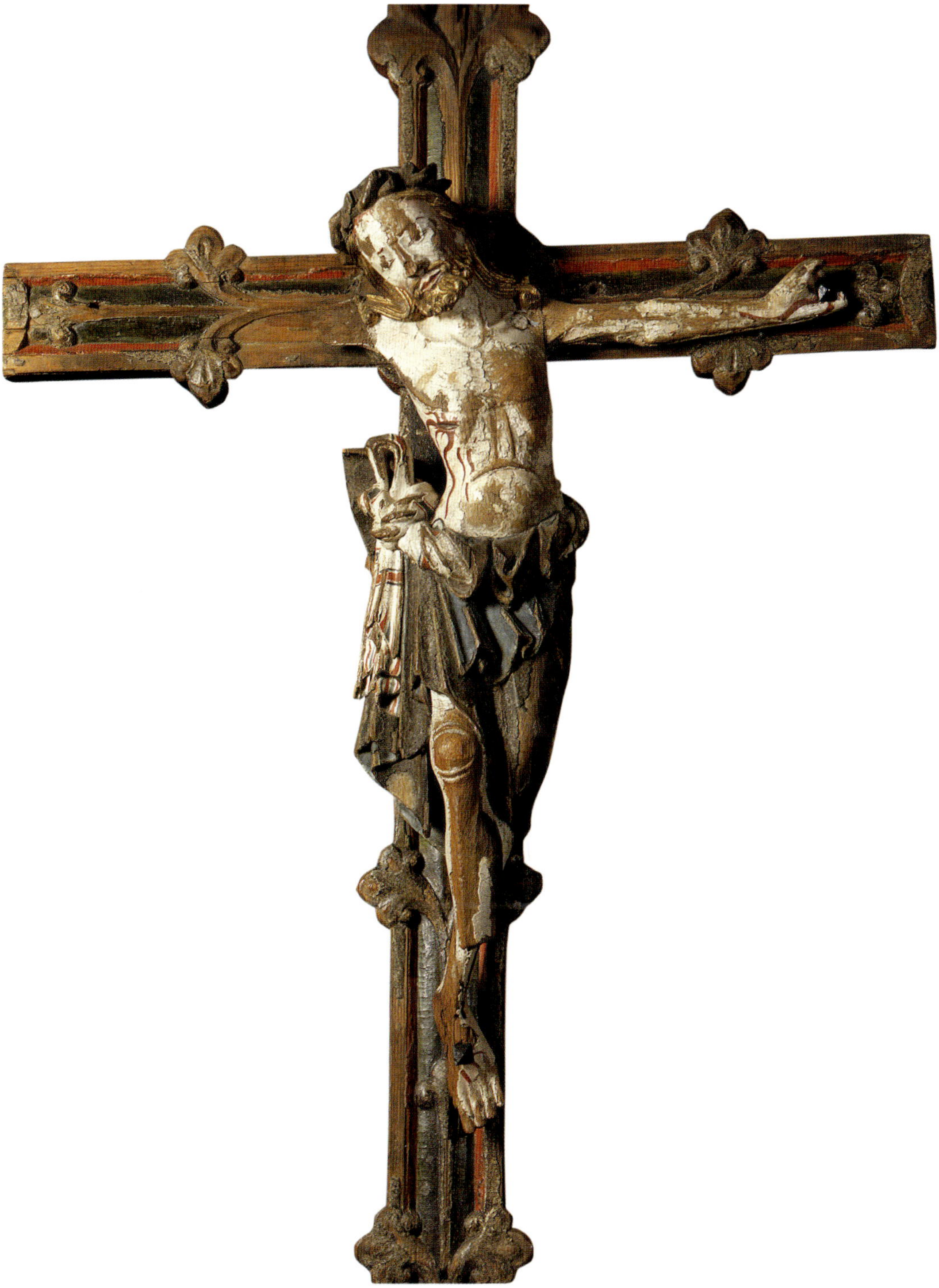

62 Crucifix, oak (figure) and pine (cross) with original paintwork, from Øren, Gudbrandsdalen (Oppland), Norway, third quarter thirteenth century (Universitetets, Oldsaksamling, Oslo)

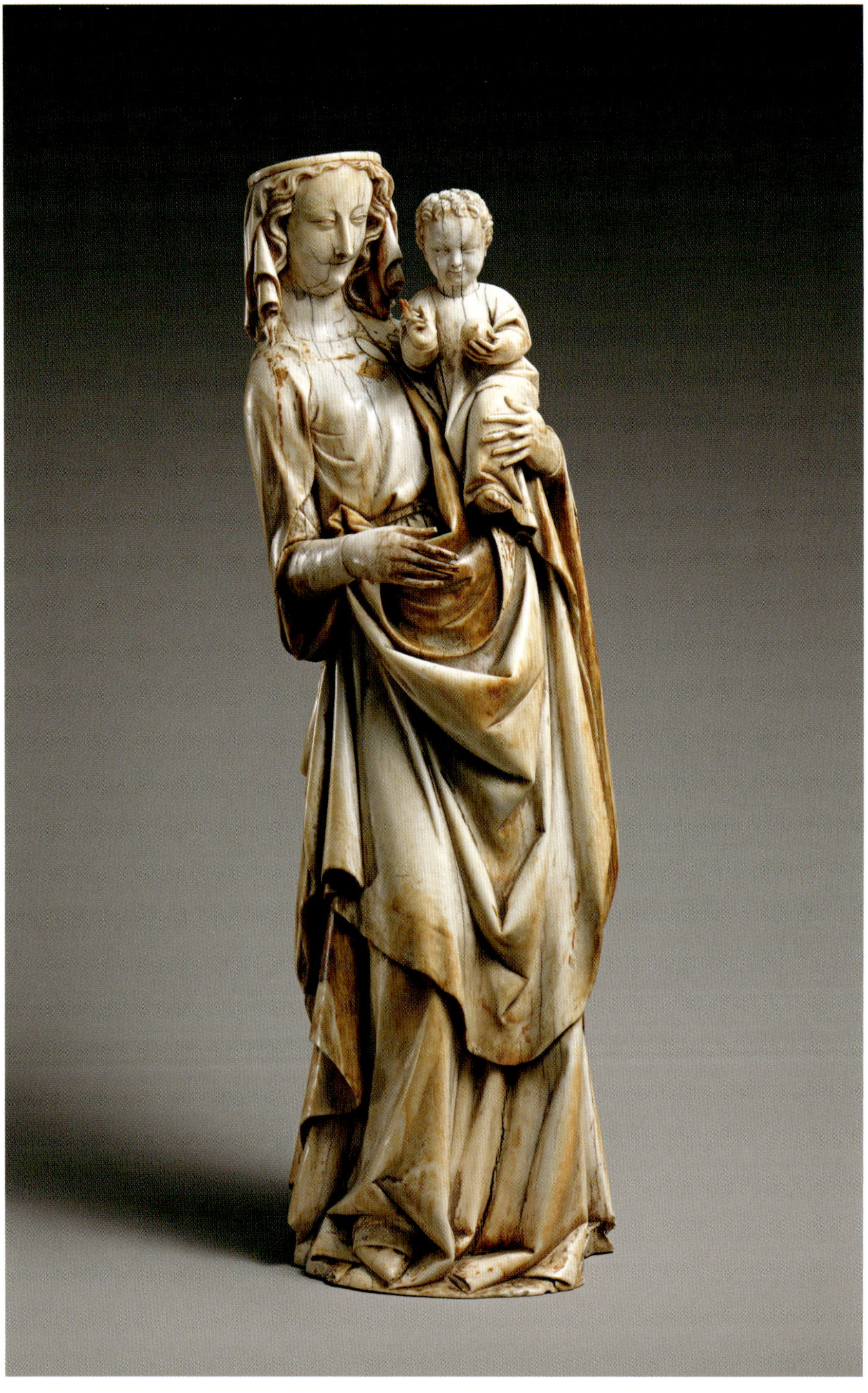

63 Virgin and Child, elephant ivory with traces of colour and gilding, northern French, late thirteenth or early fourteenth century (New York, Metropolitan Museum, Theodore M. Davis Collection, no. 30.95.114a)

excellent for carving, had their own roles.[25] Oak is durable and takes finer detail than pine, and was probably thought more suitable for nuanced detailing of a figure such as Christ or Mary. Pine can take the vigorous ornamental carving proper to a cross and, per cubic metre, is a significantly lighter material than dense oak, so its use for the main structural element reduced the weight of an object that had to be raised or suspended.[26] These issues were matters for methodical technical understanding, experience; reading and then going with, not against, the grain. Finally, the crosses – like many medieval images of Christ and the saints – were painted and gilded, so masking their underlying material character.

The first lesson in the study of any material is to begin with its sourcing, its handling in a workshop, and its masking and manipulation by tradition and experience. For instance, polychromy gives the lie to simplistic theories about the pure 'virtue' of materials: it cannot always have been clear whether a painted sculpture was made of wood or stone. It was nineteenth-century writers such as John Ruskin who, as a matter of ideology, gave us the concept of the truth, the sincerity of materials and the honest display of structure.[27] To understand why this moralising artsy-craftsy loftiness is objectionable to an understanding of the Middle Ages, and why practicalities are foremost and not ancillary, we have to get our hands dirty and understand that medieval materiality is relational, not essential. Materials do not and cannot assert by themselves: they are good for some things, useless for others; they are part of a field, a network, which involves many factors, craft, practical wisdom and signification included, but also recollection, inherited cultural practice or tradition, and the poetics of things.

Experience and method aside, then, all materials form part of a prior representational or imaginative order of relationships which craft negotiates and judges. Wood's particular power as a medium in which to push non-structural yet architectural form to its most *outré* extent, as in late medieval English choir stalls or German altarpiece and sacrament house-carving (see pls 61, 94 and 95), needs little comment.[28] Woodworking of this virtuosic type challenged the primacy of stone as an inventive medium and in some ways surpassed it. Stone spoke and speaks of the permanent, the monumental, that which, like a statue, 'stands'. Stone, precious stones especially, possessed *virtus* or power.[29] Wood is a growing and mutating thing, immanent in its growth, 'tending' (from *intentio*) in certain directions through its grains and knots and curves; wood is 'anisotropic' or directionally dependent. It also decays and rots. In all this it has much in common with other organic materials such as ivory, often retaining the curved form of the tusk from which it is extracted, and possessing the inner and sometimes intractable grain of a life-form.[30] When used in the thirteenth century for delicate swaying images of the standing Virgin and Child, ivory's tendency lends an inherent eloquence and charm to the group (pl. 63). This tending was useful because it pointed to and affirmed a representational and metaphorical ordering that started in, but went beyond, a material's inherent character that skilled crafters could read and respect.[31] Manifestly, wood and ivory handle significantly differently, display technique in different ways and cannot operate at the same scale.[32] Crafting an image is something done in the medium not with it – in fact, the word 'medium', implying something which is merely a transparent vehicle that is not itself a force possessing agency, misleads us.[33] We think 'in' wood as we talk or sing 'in' music. This is not a translation, because content and material become part of one phenomenon which, well handled, speaks in unison.[34]

Wood commonly formed those liturgical images placed on or close to the altar, such as statues of the Virgin and Child, often seated and later standing, and the Cross. Both were drawn into ontological and functional arguments about 'real presence', Mary as the symbol of the Incarnation, the Cross as the major sign of the Eucharist, to be present before the priest at every Mass as a memorial.[35] In the dialogue on miracles composed by Caesarius of Heisterbach we find a number of reports of images, typically on or near altars, which were certainly carved and painted, some described as being of wood and some of which are active – images of Christ on the Cross bowing his head or bleeding, a wooden Madonna with a lively Christ Child, an image of St Catherine which turns round, Madonnas which sweat or utter responses, and so on.[36] But in Cistercian writing the interest is not simply in the 'living' potential of wood, but also in its ethic. St Augustine had asked of Christ, 'But why was he crucified? Because the wood of his humility [*lignum humilitatis ejus*] was necessary for you'.[37] It was after all the rubbishy but virtuous (because humble) statue of the Virgin mentioned by Caesarius that led to the persecution by the Virgin herself of the woman that abused it.

This complex discourse lies at the heart of the notion of the Christian Cross as a polyvalent sign, partly because it was receptive to the kind of thought apparent in Augustine's question, partly because wood and trees were attractive to the mythopoetic imagination of narrative and symbol.[38] At all levels of thinking, 'popular' or 'high', the Cross was *the* Tree, the English word 'rood' connecting to such words as 'rod' (German *rute*). This thought was both practical and theological. The core texts and ideas were few and not absolutely consistent: the two trees, the Tree of Life and the Tree of the Knowledge of Good and Evil (Genesis 2:9, 3:3–4, 22) – which Genesis conflates; the Tree of Life in Revelation 22:1–2; the text *Regnavit a ligno Deus* from the Old Latin of Psalm 95:10; and the text *Ascendam in palmam* in Canticles 7:8.[39] Bound up with the Cross were thoughts about labour, death, rebirth and growth, thoughts constantly in play, never resolved, always in process. There was no trajectory through them to some point of resolution or ontological stability. The Cross required work to understand it, and the work was unceasing. Central to it was not just antithesis, beloved of Christian aesthetics, but paradox, that which is contrary to ordinary belief but which nevertheless affirms it. Paradox was consciously part of Christian doctrine from the start – the Incarnation, the glory of the Cross: it is to be believed because it is absurd, Tertullian claimed famously of the Cross.[40]

Such precious paradoxes were part of everyday experience, not just as unfathomable mysteries but as challenges. Nor were they typical only of the late Middle Ages: behold the *Dream of the Rood*, the Anglo-Saxon poem on the paradox of the Cross which is itself a dream-invention.[41] In it the Cross is apprehended as a vision of a thing covered in gold and gems, with five gems on its crossbeam for Christ's wounds. That some mystery or sense of otherness is involved is clear from the description of the Cross as *syllic*, 'unearthly'. What engages us is the revelation of the tree beyond the precious vestment, for through [*þurh*] the gold is discerned the narrative of the Cross's earlier aggression, as set forth by means of the imagined voice, *prosopopoeia*: the eloquent tree has a biography, is felled, raised. Then 'they drove me through with dark nails' creating wounds like 'wide-mouthed hate-dents'.[42] The journey and reversal of fortune, or *peripeteia*, is not only between reliquary and wood but also wood and flesh. Soaked in blood, like a corpse the tree is buried; then it too is raised up and adorned with gold and silver. Human discernment, like a nail, punctures the apparent glorified surface to yet another greater glory, but this puncturing is unstable, like a vibration to and fro, between a humble gnarled relic and a resplendent reliquary, settling on neither. In this dual consciousness lies the beginning and also the very character of our experience, which, though it starts within and is part of the encounter, does not stop there but, as with paradox itself, thrills and challenges in its strangeness like some Anglo-Saxon riddle.[43]

Some of the complexity of experiences of this sort lies within sensory experience and the fruitful ambivalences of language itself. An instance relevant to the experience of the *crux gemmata* of the earlier Christian centuries is the semantic range of the word *gemma*, not just a precious stone or gem but a bud on a plant, one hard, one delicate, one immutable, one transitory.[44] The most graceful crucifixes of the thirteenth century, whether in manuscript illuminations or carved and painted wood (see pl. 62), have formalised displays of budding foliage in simultaneous allusion to the rough-hewn or sprouting Cross and to the *crux gemmata*.[45] Such references entered the vernacular tradition, as in the account of the way the Cross flourished marvellously after the Crucifixion, between midday until night, until the time of Christ's burial, in the Middle English poem *Cursor Mundi*.[46] Grasping the (not difficult) paradoxes and theology involved creates for us an intellectual and spiritual dynamic. But the end of this dynamic is not some 'final impression' of 'stuffness'; it is the attainment of conviction, confident belief which paradox at once challenges yet brilliantly affirms.[47]

The energising character of paradox serves as a preliminary warning to us about literalism. Doctrines of materiality that do not consider where materials come from, why they and not other materials are chosen (for function or purpose or cost), and what their prior reputation might be, may be reductive. To my mind, on the contrary, the 'materiality' of an artefact is relational and hence differential, for materials do not simply possess their own eloquence. Their eloquence is occasional, contingent: we do not have to choose between objects and

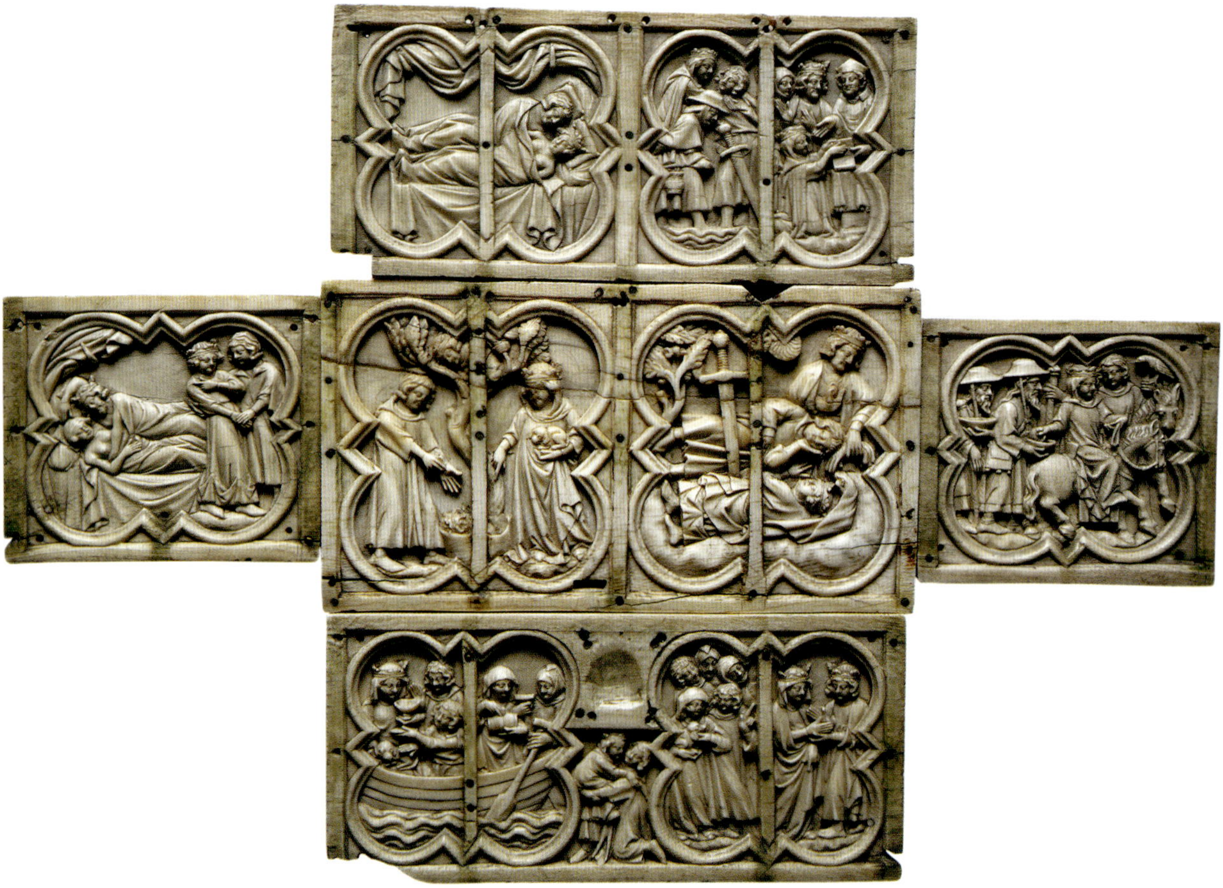

64 Casket, elephant ivory with scenes from story of Tristan and Isolde, Paris, second quarter fourteenth century with nineteenth-century lid (St Petersburg, State Hermitage Museum, no. F.60)

contexts. A systematic iconology of medieval materials will for this reason never satisfactorily account for their actual uses, because that which is occasional is always pragmatic.[48] This point is well made by a material to which, in the thirteenth century at least, were attributed specific properties – ivory. In his *Postilla* the Parisian Dominican Hugh of St Cher (d. 1263) includes a remark about the biblical symbolism of ivory: the ivory houses or perfume containers in Psalm 44:9–10 are complex metaphors whereby cold ivory (*ebur frigidum*) symbolises the chastity of the saints (*castitas sanctorum*).[49] But as Sarah Guérin also notes, it is precisely this traditional poetic of chastity that lends savour to the frequent use of ivory for small caskets depicting romance and erotic encounters such as the adultery of Tristan and Isolde (pl. 64), the coolness of ivory being that which needs to be warmed up and softened, like wax, to reveal the sweetness within.[50] As with alabaster (which I discuss later), *castitas* and *luxuria* go hand in hand in a sophisticated, knowing game typical of the courtly and urban elites who alone could commission such precious and slightly edgy objects. Even Gothic micro-architecture, supposedly a sign of the sacred and so typical of devotional ivories, is drawn into this culture of secular *ludus*.[51] Such cases tell us as much about attitudes to devotion within specific market conditions as about the poetics of materials.

For all our modern desire for stability and sincerity, the significance and power of things is resistant and non-normative. Materials are mixed in themselves as well as joined together in elective affinities by human agency; indeed, it is in crafted and pragmatic mixture itself that sense-based knowledge finds pleasure and power. The earliest Christian rhetoricians understood this well. When, in the great Good Friday hymn to the Cross *Pange lingua* ('Sing, tongue, the glorious battle'), Venantius Fortunatus says of the Cross that 'no other wood brings forth such excellent flower, leaf or shoot – sweet [*dulce*] the wood, sweet the nail sustaining the sweet weight', he was, in Mary Carruthers's words, exploiting 'the terrible paradoxes inherent in the aesthetic quality of *dulcis/suavis*', that whether for good or ill we taste the sweet with the bitter.[52] That an entire Christian heuristic could be based on the imagery of the tree and the sweet medicine of the Cross cannot be surprising, as for example when the genius of the Tree of Jesse as an expression of spiritual blood-line and a statement of doctrine was morphed onto and into the Cross in the form of the *Tree of Life* of the Franciscan St Bonaventure (d. 1274).[53] The step from paradox to Christian understanding set out in the ramified, multicursal form of the Tree of Knowledge sustaining a dolorous Christ Crucified, as revealed to us in the fourteenth-century example in St James's church in Toruń in Poland (pl. 65), was typical of the sustained intellectual powers of the Gothic era not because of its smoothness, but because of its difficult and antithetical character, its artificial yet profound contrast of punishment and sublime knowledge. In his *Poetria Nova* Vinsauf says of ordering things that 'the order of art is more elegant than natural order', for artificial order may be many branched and difficult, even labyrinthine.[54] Of us it requires work. Aristotle, in his *Metaphysics* (9.1048b1–5), likens the unwrought and the wrought to the blind and the sighted.[55] Ovid's *ars superabat materiam* is an image of overcoming, for it was seldom if ever admitted by poets that the material or 'matter to hand' might actually surpass the craft, though this was and remains an obvious peril of all artistry. An artist of any pretension who cannot control their chosen medium is in trouble.

The victory of the Cross was itself work, coloured by ideas of craft, but craft of a peculiarly dystopian kind. The Cross involved narratives of wood and iron. Even its confection, apparent to us first in the Bible's narrative of the fulfilment of prophecy which in effect creates the 'back-story' of the Crucifixion, is a cruel thing. Its timber is struck hard into obedient form by blows from sharp metal implements, for, as Esther Cohen has said, pain was invoked not because it was pleasurable but because it was useful.[56] It is an implement which, as it itself reminds us in the *Dream of the Rood*, bears the crimes of its makers.

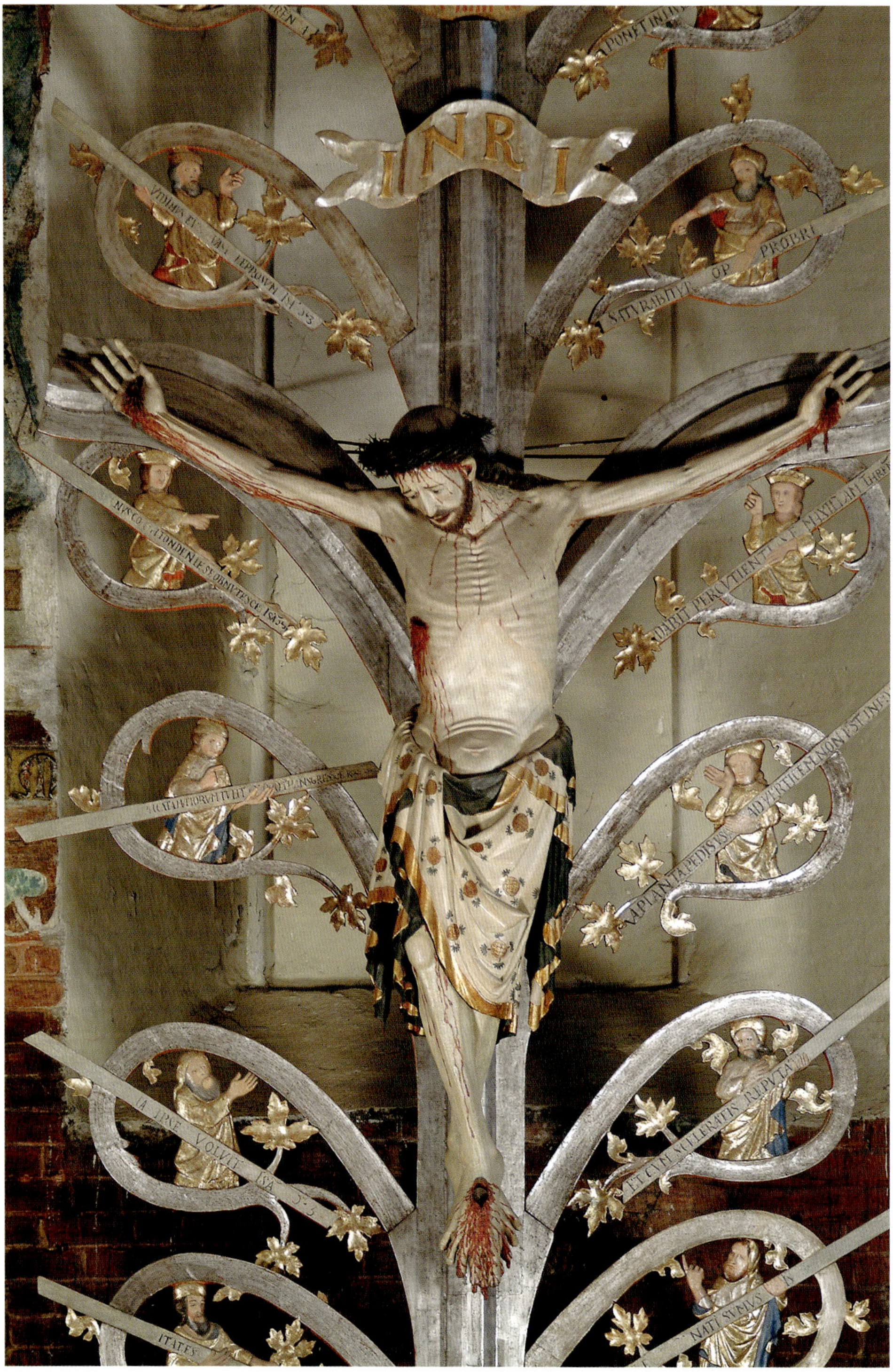

65 Toruń, St James's Church, Tree of Life, painted wood, fourteenth century

Christ's body becomes an inventory of the labours of sin: *supra dorsum meum fabricabantur peccatores*, 'The wicked have wrought upon my back' (Psalm 128:3), understood patristically as ploughers, with their ploughs drawing deep furrows on Christ's back.[57] Those who made the Cross had not even bothered to plane it smooth, so that following the Scourging, Christ was dragged to and fro on the Cross, grated by the splintered stumps of wood and then horribly stretched to fit nail holes drilled too far apart. The irony of the son of a carpenter tortured in this way on a timber instrument was not lost on late medieval Passion imagery, which likened the Cross itself to a carpenter's or mason's square.[58] In writing of the believer as artisan and as artefact, Lisa Cooper has shown how the carpenter's square represented a complex symbol of Christ's nature as the son of an artisan and himself a *faber* (Mark 6:3).[59]

Iron is involved too, for Christ is a smith as well as a carpenter, who through his sacred art warns all crafts of the danger of prideful ambition.[60] Tools as well as stuff did spiritual work, and every believer was in effect 'the artisan of the *opus* of his or her own soul'.[61] Tools and tooling pointed up the nature of cruelty and vice as well as virtue. Tools might represent vice, starting with Pride, and the abuse of everyday norms. This idea was depicted literally in the late medieval image of the so-called 'Sunday Christ' or 'Christ of the Trades' in which Christ, terribly wounded, is hemmed in by the various tools and implements of everyday work whose use on the Sabbath so damages Him.[62] The moral ugliness of those who cut the timber and forged the nails of the Cross is not spared in the Holkham Bible Picture Book (London, BL Add. Ms 47682) of the 1330s (pl. 66).[63] But tooling produced moral beauty as well. In his comments on ivory noted a moment ago, Hugh of St Cher goes on to state that ivory as a natural thing is at first dull: it is only by being cut and filed and polished that it comes to stand for those processes, those tribulations, by which the saints gained their virtue. Meditation on the Passion of Christ required a gathering together or *collatio* of little images of the implements or things used in the Passion called the *Arma Christi*, a sort of mental toolkit.[64] The idea of crafting the soul produces a striking image of the Passion in the late thirteenth-century poem *Le Rossignos*, attributed to John of Howden, which celebrates the power of the Heart carved and painted by the blood of the spotless Lamb of God: *De son sanc le paint et l'entaille*.[65] Holy Church was herself born in the 'labour' of the Cross from Christ's side-wound.[66] Whether its imagery concerned carving, planing or casting (as with wax), the idea of the inner and outer person as things to be formed and reformed from the heart outwards was a commonplace of much religious and ethical imagery throughout the Middle Ages.

Indeed, sacramental theology has at its own heart the notion of crafting. The sacrament of Mass is a confection, from the Latin verb *conficio*, a putting together or making, prior to that sacrament's reception. Eucharistic bread is a crafted thing, artisanal work like the Resurrection itself.[67] The body and blood of Christ are artefacts formed in co-operation with

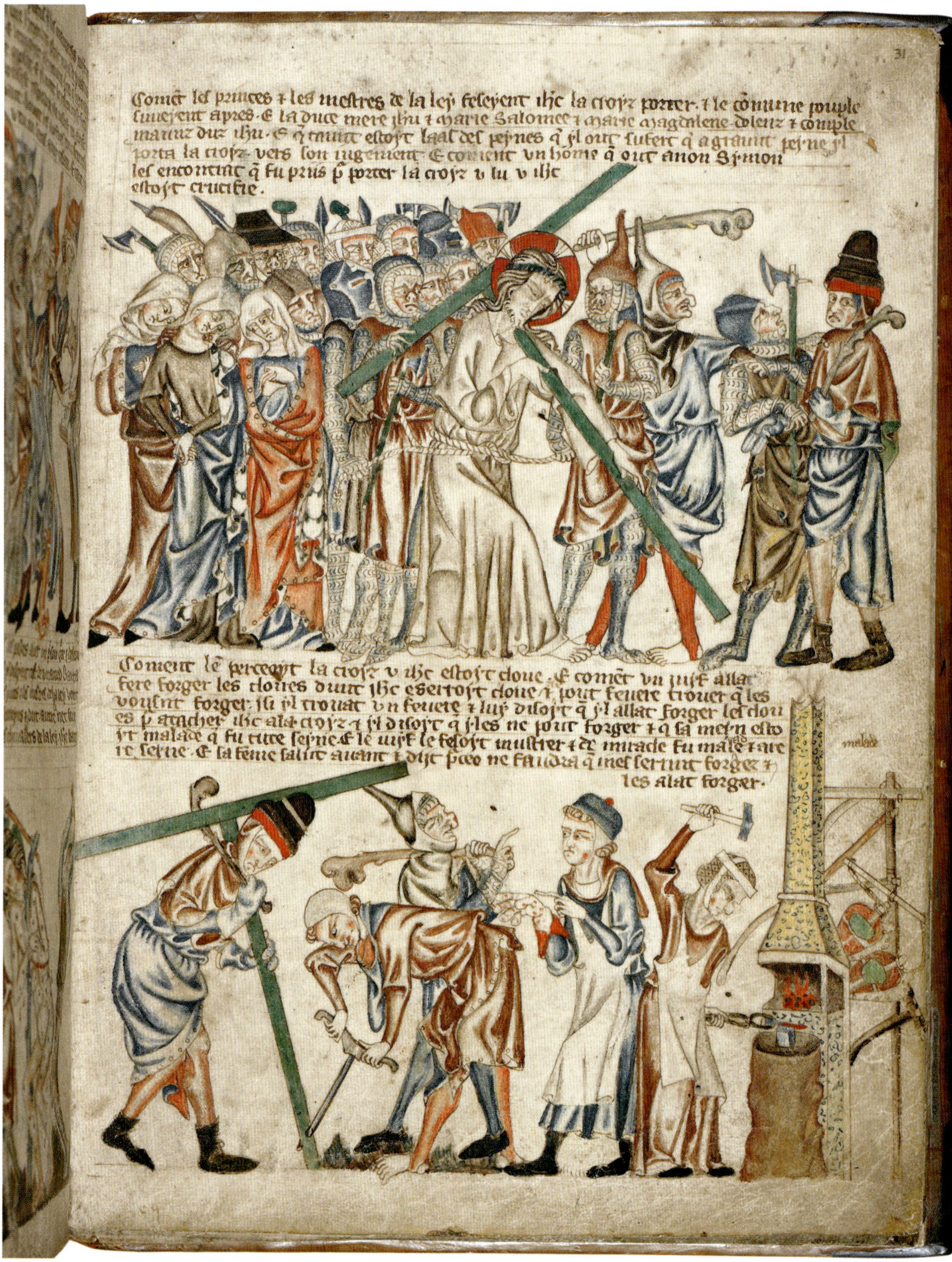

66 The Carrying of the Cross (top) and the Drilling of the Cross and Forging of the Nails (bottom), Holkham Bible Picture Book, 1330s (London, BL Add. Ms 47682, fol. 31)

God and the people, who are sweetened, healed, by their administration. Crafting is the very image of Creation and Incarnation in which delight is taken: 'I was with him forming all things: and was delighted every day, playing [*ludens*] before him at all times' (Proverbs 8:30–31).[68] In this delight the products of nature consorted with the deftness of the hand. The two are not separable, and it is because of this that artefacts possess aesthetic, and so significatory, ideological and theological power.

THE RUDE ROOD: *OPPOSITIO* IN STYLE

This ideological and theological power was worked, crafted, into the appearance of things such as the Cross, an excellent instance of aesthetic negotiation precisely in virtue of its contrarian character as a sign, a thing signifying both death and spectacular triumph over it. Since the Carolingian era, and by about 1200, the form both of the Crucified Christ and of the Cross itself had changed in such a way as to establish not one but several versions of the image, in which Christ was either shown erect and alive or dead or dying and suspended painfully from the Cross by either four or, more frequently, three nails; the Cross itself rang the changes from a planed wooden instrument, to a lopped and gnarled object cruel to the eye yet full of potential, to a beautifully controlled sprouting and burgeoning thing of soft buds and foliage in the process of healthful realisation.[69] These versions could co-exist in single works of art and as a rule were probably not regarded as contesting truths about the representation of the Crucifixion. That some of the outcomes were controlled and harmonious is shown by the Scandinavian instances of painted wooden crosses such as those from Øren (see pl. 62), Borre and Tretten in Norway from the thirteenth century.[70]

The crucial issue is the range of finishes that artists sought in wood, because the finishes varied with the intention of the object. A key innovation was the emergence by about 1300 in Germany, Italy and Scandinavia of the so-called *Crucifixus Dolorosus*, so to speak the agonised Crucifix, the origins of which were explored in the 1930s by Géza de Francovich.[71] The *Crucifixus Dolorosus* was a deliberate intensification of the Gothic form of the Crucifix, apparent from around 1260, in which Christ's feet were pinned high up beneath his thighs while his torso and head hung markedly downwards and forwards, so stretching the arms into a Y shape. With the change in profile arose a deliberate selection of alarming carved effects of theological import: Christ's grotesquely stretched and sinuous arms and bursting emaciated ribcage answered to the passage *dinumeraverunt omnia ossa mea ipsi vero consideraverunt et inspexerunt me*, 'they have numbered all my bones. And they have looked and stared upon me', in the so-called Passion Psalm 21:18.[72] Christ's face becomes the discomposed snarling visage of a criminal on a gibbet (see pl. 39), following Isaiah 53:2 *non est species ei neque decor*, 'There is no beauty in him, or comeliness'. Importantly, all things concerning

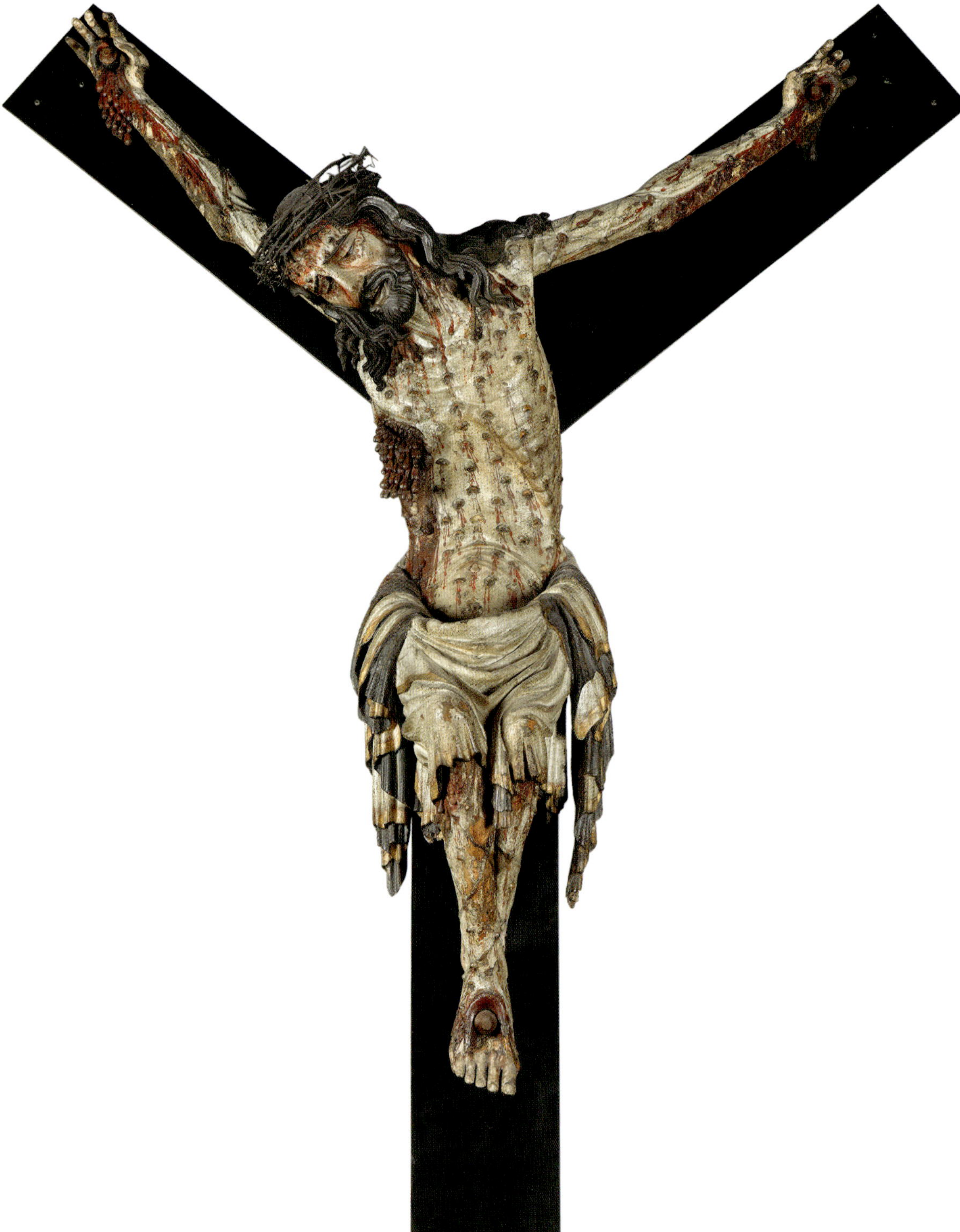

67 *Crucifixus Dolorosus*, from Wrocław, Corpus Christi church, wood with original paintwork and gilding, 1370s (Muzeum Narodowe, Warsaw)

Christ and his abjection are worked into and onto his flayed skin, since, although up to the late thirteenth century Christ's skin is generally fair, even delicate, and the wounds marked yet circumscribed, in the *Crucifixus Dolorosus* his entire body is leprous, pocked and peppered gunshot-like with the bleeding holes of flagellation, the side-wound bursting outwards in great protruding gouts of congealing blood rendered in lovingly painted wood or plaster, as in the example from the church of Corpus Christi, Wrocław (now in Warsaw; pl. 67).[73] A series of crosses surviving in Cologne alone from the first half of the fourteenth century do just this work – those from S. Maria im Kapitol (see pls 39 and 108), S. Severin and the Allerheiligenkapelle (All Saints Chapel).[74] In them image and reality seem to become one: the belief, however illusory, of ghastly suffering, butchery, becomes convincing. We think again of Thomas Bradwardine's mnemonic use of things of 'great dignity or vileness, or wounded with greatly opened wounds with a remarkably lively flowing of blood, or in another way made extremely ugly'.[75] For a moment our 'looking and staring', to allude again to Psalm 21, transcends the 'materiality' of the image, for flesh has been rendered as flesh and is felt and understood as such. The association of such crosses with the emergent cult of Corpus Christi is probable.

This craft exploration of the interdependent terms 'beauty' and 'ugliness', as suggested, can have theological content, and exactly how these crosses were looked and stared at is not clear. This must have depended on the occasion. In 1305 a Cross of this type, made by a German probably from Cologne, was first displayed on Good Friday at a London chapel not far from the Cologne Guildhall, later associated with Corpus Christi devotion:

> In that year, on April 15th, a certain horrible cross [*crux horribilis*] was taken to the chapel of Conyhope, and on the following day called Good Friday was adored by many; on account of which Geoffrey of Wycombe, the rector of that church, incurred considerable harm at the instigation of the canons of St Paul's cathedral. On May 1st of that year, the aforesaid cross was taken away by night to the canons of Holy Trinity (Aldgate).

Evidently the poor rector was beaten up for daring to show off such a cross near London's cathedral. Its banishment by night is especially striking. Perhaps it subsequently found its way back to Cologne as one of the surviving horror-crosses there.[76] Accounts of this episode have at least two notable features for our story. The first is the term *crux horribilis* used by the London Annals. We have already encountered the term *horror* in the great inscription in the Last Judgement at Autun (see pl. 24). The semantic range of this word in later Latin is notable. In giving an account of his translation of the Psalms, St Jerome states that *horror* commonly means despicable or sordid but also something worse, which he conveys by alluding to the *Aeneid*, at 3.29–30 when Aeneas while making a sacrifice breaks branches from bushes which then stream with blood: at this Aeneas is himself frozen and shaking with horror, *mihi frigidus horror / membra quatit*.[77] We encounter the same association of bone-shaking *tremor* and goose bumps in Job 4:14–15 where Job recalls a spirit passing before his face in the deep of the night. The sensation of horror is fully embodied, fully aesthetic; indeed, as Carruthers explains in her admirable discussion of the problem, the word *horribilis* derives from the verb *horreo*, 'to bristle'. So we might reasonably suggest that a *crux horribilis* was at the very least 'hair-raising'.

The second, and I think more social, issue is the connotative power of finish, the ostensive power of wrought surfaces sublimated from wood into texture, plaster and paint. Apprehension of the fairness of the flesh of Christ is an apprehension of beauty which is both theological and aesthetic: but the illusion of beautiful flesh can also be the illusion of deformity. *Horror* pointed to that which was wild, rough or shaggy in regard to verbal style, that which was unpolished or lacked the finish of craft. It was the domain of the ugly or alien, differentiated from beauty, yet standing in relation to it.[78] Such strong, connected contrast was fundamental to much Christian thinking and experience, including the liturgy. When, as in the case of the London *crux horribilis*, the Cross was unveiled according to tradition on Good Friday to the amazement of those gathered, it would have been coupled liturgically with the chanting of the *Improperia* or Reproaches supposedly addressed by Christ from the Cross to the Jews. The Reproaches, actually antiphons and responses, consist, in Rosemary Woolf's words, of 'a series of ingenious antitheses' which developed into a more or less frank discourse of shaming.[79] These are developed in the Dominican *Summa Praedicantium* which contrasts Christ's Crown of Thorns with the spectator's wreath of flowers, Christ's nailed hands with his nice gloves, the dainty use of feet in dancing while Christ labours (*laboravi*) on the Cross, the genteel slitted sides of fashionable fourteenth-century dress and the wound in Christ's side, and so on.[80] Such contrasts are related to contemporary social satire. Those who wear gloves and have white and clean hands (for instance, the higher artificers, such as architects) were contrasted with those who, like Christ, do the actual labour; the dandyish fastidiousness of contemporary dress, its polish and vanity, is set against the terrible asperity of naked suffering.[81] Such ironic and satirical language permeated the arts and religious patronage more generally.[82] In this complex and subtle ethical discourse, ugliness is the attribute both of the supreme good and of the wicked, a complex sign of the *evidentia* of the Passion. Those who bring about the Crucifixion, such as the vigorous bonnetted woman in the Holkham Bible Picture Book – a biblical Lady Macbeth – who does the dirty work of bluntly forging the dark nails of the Crucifixion because her smith husband has a diseased hand, are physically hideous (see pl. 66).[83] Perhaps by calculated antithesis, Nicholas Love's early fifteenth-century *Mirour* says that at the Crucifixion, Joseph of Arimathea and Nicodemus sheltered the Virgin Mary from the sight of the nails, acting as anodynes to those who ploughed upon Christ.[84]

From one point of view the *Crucifixus Dolorosus* troubles the idea of mimesis: such ghastly representations appear deliberately strange, archaic even in their vividness before the eyes.[85]

Yet in the light of the foregoing it is clear that their intention and appearance might well be understood dialectically, relationally. They could be experienced against something else, for their nature – their aesthetic and ideological nature – is contrarian. Their contrary, it could be argued, was the courtly visual language of Gothic as established as an elegant *lingua franca* in the second half of the thirteenth century: to this new refinement of royal, aristocratic and clerical patronage, the horrible crosses, far from being merely crude, might well have been a skilled rebuke. As the Cologne and London instances show, their performative space, so to speak, was the contested urban milieu, the milieu that could at once produce the horrors of the extant cross at S. Maria im Kapitol and in the same years the elegant, swaying and beaming polychrome stone statuary installed round the choir of the cathedral church of Cologne.[86] By style, the lack in such beautiful complacency could be exposed. The ugliness, deformity, falling-away of the dolorous crosses embodied a skilled askesis, a calculated rhetoric of contrast and not a deficiency of ability, taste or patronage: being 'uncrafted' was itself an aspect of style. These antithetical categories were long familiar in the aesthetic language of the Cistercians and Mendicant Orders, but their debt to yet older rhetorical strategy was evident. Earlier I argued that the ethos that produced the great portals of France and Germany especially from the mid-thirteenth century onwards had its own rhetorical character, one suited to panegyric, the lofty uplifting display of the most beautiful. That this rhetorical mode should simultaneously issue in its own dialectical contrast, its own *Kulturkampf*, rings true, much as the aesthetics of the natural were issuing in the aesthetics of Death. To the mode of praise, the mode of blame was a companion. Perhaps to the clerical classes whose attitude to such images may well have been – and in London provably were – distinctly ambivalent, such timber horrors hinted dangerously at the myth of Wotan hanging from the boughs of Yggdrasil as much as the Passion of Christ.

But in the contrast of the rough and the smooth, the humble and the proud, the criminal and the fastidious, lay a fundamental and ancient difference (a form of rhetorical *oppositio*) in the register of speech – between roughness, rusticity or barbarity, *sermo rusticus*, and smooth urbanity, *sermo urbanus*.[87] This distinction runs through the history of style in Western Europe. Geoffrey of Vinsauf, a widely cited authority on style known to Chaucer, characterises eloquence in terms of cookery and barbering, raw or overcooked, shaggy or combed, rough or polished.[88] *Oppositio* did not need to have moral, religious or ideological content: it could be playful or it could be serious. Strong contrasts of the plain and the complex were important to later Gothic art, not least in architecture. The point is that such contrasts were registered not primarily in the stuff of which things were made – granted that humble wood was a good vehicle for certain sorts of reproach – but rather in the workbench toolbox of eloquence and understanding, in style. They were a matter of etiquette, grooming, of subtle understanding, for the rough and the smooth are, after all, points on a linked scale, understood relationally and as much in contact with each other as the two sides of a page of vellum.

That painted wooden or stone surfaces produced effects that were intended to be ugly or beautiful, and through that ugliness and beauty both creating sensations and conveying ideas *ad usum*, according to need, is indisputable. The *Crucifixus Dolorosus* could be represented in stone or wood, but wood, in its roughness and ability to take paint, was the more typical material. It is interesting to note how the precious media of silver-gilt metalwork or ivory dealt with the theme of the dolorous Cross from the late thirteenth century onwards. Here scale mattered: the drama of full-scale, even over life-size, liturgical crosses was not relevant to the radical intensification of effect apparent in the micro-arts in the Gothic period. In the precious micro-arts we tend not to find the awful integument of bursting plaster and paint wounds and weals whose nature was essentially coloured. An instance would be the refined silver-gilt Crucifix from the now shattered shrine of St Gertrude at Nivelles made in the last decades of the thirteenth century, whose skin surfaces were once glowing and unblemished, now tarnished not by fleshly decay but by war (it was a victim of the Second World War).[89] As with many ivory crucifixes, the image of the lopped or sprouting cross at Nivelles is the only thing which connects it to the dolorous crosses, aside from the corpus's general attitude on the Cross. We do find the terrible surfaces in fourteenth-century manuscript illuminations such as the Holkham Bible Picture Book, and in panel paintings of the same era such as the Norwegian frontals from Røldal and Årdal.[90] The distinction is clearly between painted and non-painted media, including those cases common in ivory or alabaster where added pigment lifts the material into a pictorial domain. Materiality is no more vital to this lifting than representational imperative.

That quite sophisticated ethical and visual calculation was involved in the making of artefacts in ideologically sensitive contexts – such as churches belonging to the Cistercian order – is apparent in the case of objects in the halfway house between fully formed sculpture and paint. The method in such cases was to create a subtle low-relief image in wood, whose soft half-protruding surfaces were then tinted, creating a delicate aesthetic of projection. In the case of the 'legislative' aesthetics of the Cistercians, clear prohibitions were repeatedly issued concerning sculpture and colours other than white, while allowing wooden images of the Cross.[91] The preoccupation had always been far more with relationships of tone (white, grey) than hue. As the 1231 Cistercian statutes put it, such superfluities 'deform the ancient honesty of the Order' (*deformant antiquam Ordinis honestatem*).[92] This form of prohibition created delicate powers of discrimination, a sort of collective visual sensitivity. A fine and uncharacteristically large (5.56 metres tall) example is from the Cistercian abbey church of Sorø in Zealand, Denmark, dating to the mid-thirteenth century (pl. 68).[93] It is executed not in full sculpture but in bas-relief with a pleasing play of tone and surface – pleasing at least to those familiar with the sculpture of, say, Eric Gill: as with many ivories or limewood

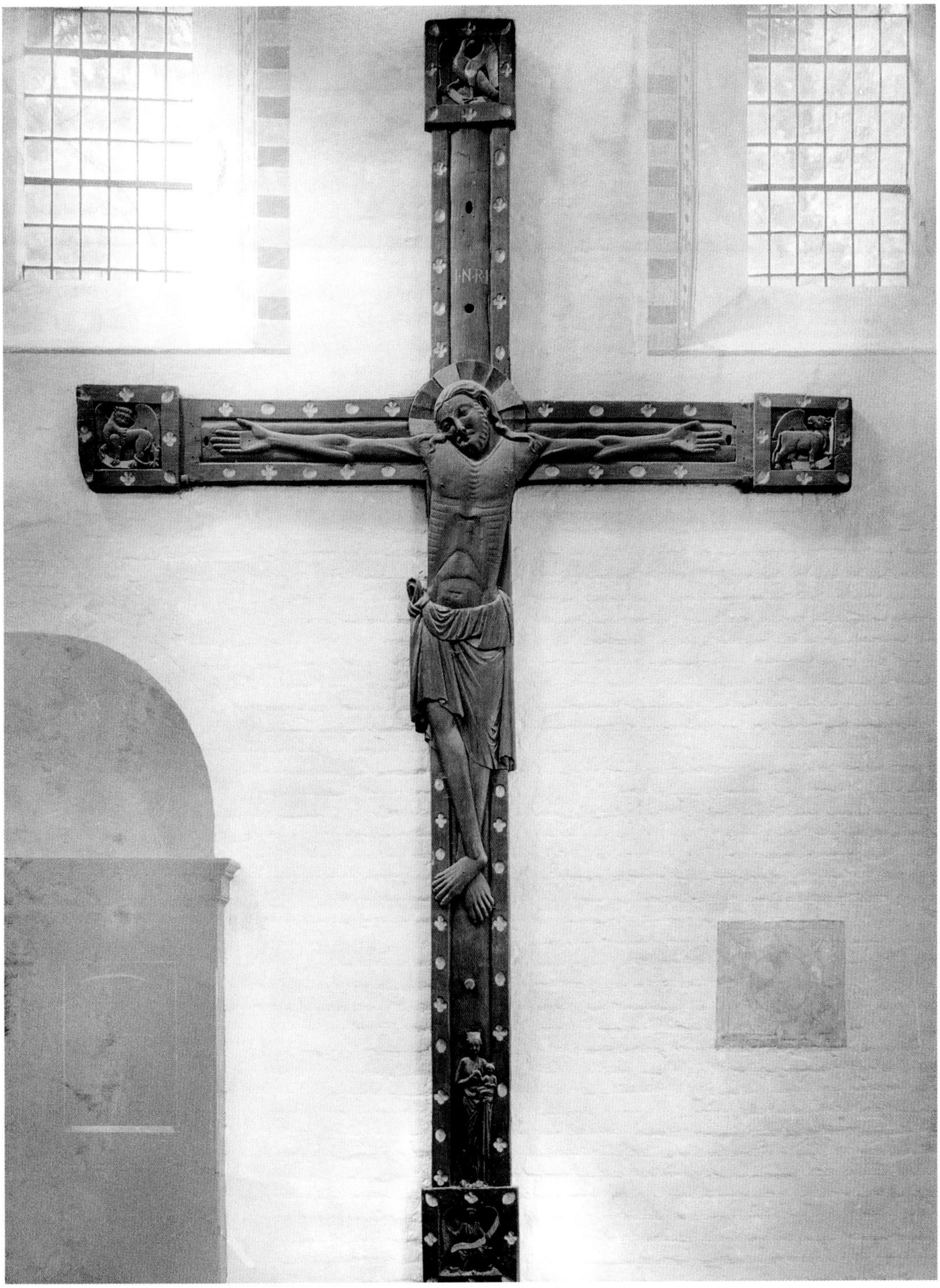

68 Crucifix, polychromed oak, from Cistercian church at Sorø, Zealand, Denmark, *c.*1260
(National Museum of Denmark, Copenhagen)

carvings, polychromy is not essential to its effect, though discreetly coloured it originally was. The work hovers gracefully and slightly hauntingly between media, not least because reference beyond the Cross to anything precious is markedly restrained, limited only to the sunk quatrefoils and ovals which run along the edges. In this regard the Sorø carving differs from the spectacularly 'Mosan' giant bas-relief cross from the Cistercian church at Oplinter in modern Belgium, dating from the 1260s or so, whose aesthetic is much closer to *repoussé* and enamelled metalwork, or ivory.[94]

A moment ago I used the word 'pleasing' of such effects – as one might of the low-relief limewood work of Riemenschneider – fully in the knowledge that in their social context of ascetic religious observation such effects were not always intended to be so. The relation of high to low relief and the role within relief of painting and gilding, and of the discriminations involved in such decorum, remain to be more fully explored.

The subtle surfaces of the fragments from the *jubé* of Chartres (pl. 69), a work in a non-monastic context, indicate how much attention was given to variegation of low relief and tactful colouration in Gothic art generally, much as in ivory work.[95] The 'less is more' aesthetic of withdrawal was the mark both of religious askesis and of courtly understatement: historically, the emergence of the two is not unrelated.[96] In one case the manufacture of a fourteenth-century carved cross, referred to at the Cistercian abbey of Meaux in northern England, was accompanied by the woodcarver's ascetic practices, only working on Fridays and only eating bread and water.[97] With subtlety of surface and colour there is always ambivalence, a possibility of brinkmanship which implies a set of rules. Persuasion and seduction differ but are near neighbours. The term *subtilitas* is especially useful in relation to the fine effects of Cistercian restraint, since it also carried with it the sense of 'plain speaking' in private matters, being contrasted with a more public style that was *ornatior* or fancy.[98] One can see how such effects as those on the Sorø cross were appropriate to familial, household or private communication proper to an enclosed monastic choir, social, yet restrained and practical. The key point in such instances was to strike a balance between flat, blank abstraction and the provision of just enough engaging detail to sustain the role of the image in providing *evidentia*. Later, the history of carved and painted Veronica images (see pl. 78) shows how this delicate play with projecting, floating pictorial surface was actually a form of *enargeia*, a making evident to both the eyes and the eyes of the mind.[99] Carved relief was deployed to create just the right balance, and balance of that sort is always relational.

This aspect of relation is usefully explored by means of those things which worked together on an artefact to create its style. In the first part of this study I broached the fundamental issue of the *colores*, effects of language or artefact which, as aspects of style, give them power.[100] The *colores* in the visual arts included far more than literal colour, but colour as such mattered. It gives pleasure, creates mood, it signals difference – as in the case of the Cistercian artworks which deny colour or plasticity – and, like a gloss, it is a form of interpre-

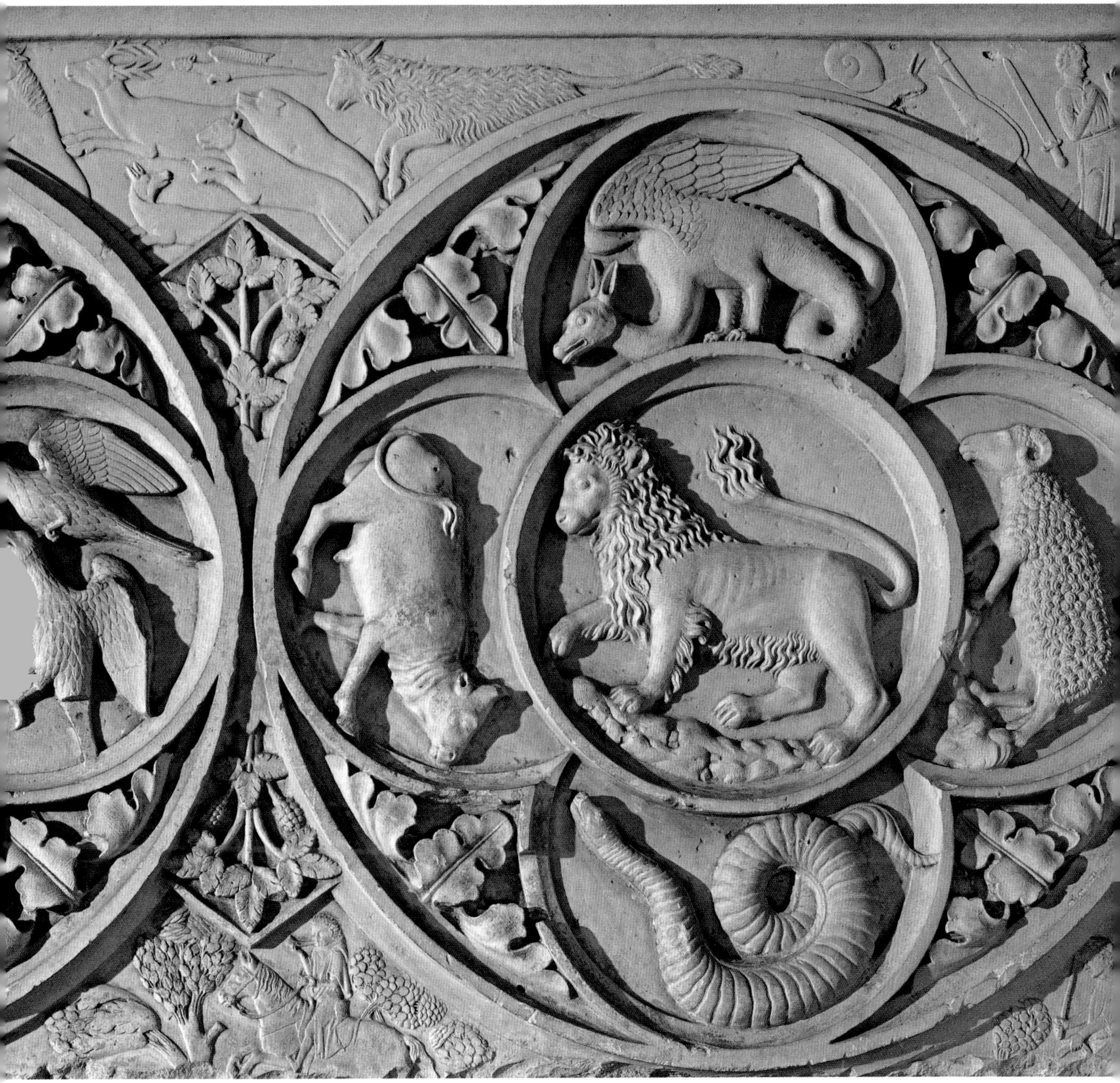

69 Low relief panel with beasts and hunting scenes, detail from former *jubé* of Chartres Cathedral, limestone, second quarter thirteenth century

tation representing thoughts about a subject, 'realising' the latent forms of sculpture. Colour is central to representation because it 'picks out' things, hence its relation to the notion of selection from the best and so elegance, as I noted in the first part of this study (p. 57). When eyes, eyelashes and brows, blood, veins, hair or fingernails are picked out in tempera or oil paint laid over a suitable plaster or gesso ground on a sculpture (whether wood or stone), they become *evidentia*.[101] Earlier we also read of the *colores* being likened to fragrant flowers (p. 55). The figure of Rhetoric in the frescoes of the Spanish Chapel or chapter house of S. Maria Novella in Florence, painted in about 1366 by Andrea Bonaiuti, holds a scroll saying *Mulceo, dum loquor, varios induta colores*, 'Arrayed in various colours, I soothe while I speak'; the term *mulceo*, to soothe or stroke, or sweeten, takes us to the 'tactile' senses of touch and taste important to the middle, the sweetest and most persuasive, of the three levels of style familiar to rhetoric.[102] Rhetoric equally had a strong sense of the opposite sensation of roughness, *asperitas*, a quality of rural style, one to be smoothed out.[103]

Colour is an aspect of that warming up which is persuasion. For that reason, in a more limited spectrum of medieval as well as Reformation opinion whose origins lay in Stoic or Platonic suspicion of the senses, colour as a sensory vehicle was ethically dangerous. Asceticism enjoys a noble lineage, from the asperities of ancient philosophy, via the medieval monastic and religious orders, to the moral utopianism of modernist thinkers and gurus of taste and judgement. In origin and application it was a socio-aesthetic conviction wrapped up with a totalising or idealising view of human behaviour, the 'habitus', which emphasised constraint. The true heir of this position was Le Corbusier. Yet, as I noted earlier, the 'Lamp of Truth', to cite an influential chapter from Ruskin's *The Seven Lamps of Architecture*, was only truly lit in the nineteenth century. Only then did truth to materials (natural materials especially) and truth to structure become symbols of a Romantic preoccupation with authenticity or sincerity (that which is 'unwaxed'), the same sincerity whose implications for the understanding of emotional expression I critiqued in the previous part of this book.

We should try to distinguish this individualistic Romantic notion of freedom, authenticity and sincerity from medieval collective, social notions of the ethical. The two perspectives need distinguishing precisely because some medieval thinking persisted with the ancient view that colour could mislead, and especially that complex, mottled or shiny surfaces could signal cunning, danger or quaintness. Quintilian, in challenging the basically Ciceronian idea that rhetoric was essentially persuasive, made the point (*Institutio Oratoria* 2.15.11) that persuasiveness had a dubious aspect: money, the 'mere look of a man', courtesans, flatterers and corrupters are all persuasive.[104] This made persuasion a larger issue than speech alone. It is an easy matter to trace suspicion of such sensuous things as colour all the way from rhetorical thought through to monastic critiques of the eleventh and twelfth centuries and later Lollard and anti-fraternal literature such as *Pierce the Ploughman's Crede*.[105] The point, however, is that while truth or honesty might have pertained to decent, traditional and restrained human arrangements in the Middle Ages, honesty was not an aspect of some essentialising or authentic notion of the inner life of stuff. It was a matter of ethical style, of utility, what was morally fit for purpose – as painted wood might be for the asperity of the Crucifixion – rather than of an overarching, and I think essentially modern, even psychological, conception of authenticity to self or to nature.[106]

Honesty, not surprisingly, was a matter for the marketplace, of ascertaining commodity value and thereby moral value. The evidence of the Parisian so-called *Livre des métiers* (Book of Trades) compiled around 1268 points up the numerous forms of sharp practice by statue-makers and those who sold *fausses oeuvres*, that is, passed base things off as precious.[107] There were trade regulations for image-makers from other parts of Europe, such as the Norwegian regulations for *likneskjusmider* or 'image-smiths'.[108] In Paris the regulations were certainly harder on the sculptors than on the painters, those two related branches of imaging. Carvers were limited to one apprentice each, might not work at night and could not produce images speculatively for fear that they might be purchased for mischief. Painters could have as many apprentices as they wanted and could (and did) work by night.[109] Perhaps those who made things, three-dimensional images, susceptible to idolatry needed closer watching. There again, neither a painter nor a sculptor could claim that a work was gilded unless its gold was laid over silver rather than tin.[110]

The point is this: medieval social regulation of this type indicates the extent to which the work of painters and sculptors was not honest in the naive sense, the extent to which it could puzzle, even cheat, as well as give pleasure by producing brilliant and unexpected effects. Some of the finest surviving artefacts we have from the court circles of Paris and London from the time of the *Livre des métiers*, such as the great high altarpiece or retable made for Westminster Abbey at the end of the reign of Henry III and executed to the most exacting standards of the day, are miracles of the alchemical skill of craft celebrating serious sacramental purpose (pl. 70). With plaster of Paris, paste, several different forms of gilding, stained glass, silver foil, linseed oil paint and varnishes, they converted finely worked oak, carved to tolerances of a millimetre or two, into a dazzling liturgical object which, for normal public scrutiny, looked like a blend of panel painting and metalwork.[111] The paintwork alone consists of pigment combinations (orange shaded with ultramarine, for example) which entirely defeat any notion of authenticity to materials.[112] If this is not illusion what is? As the *Livre des métiers* shows, it takes a trained eye, the eye of a connoisseur, a player who 'knows', to tell the real from the fake.[113] And those who know, the experts, are unlikely to have been the general public. The notion of sincerity, of the frank speech of materials in the many hundreds of similar instances which survive from the Middle Ages, fails us totally in regard to such confections, such pleasurable and admirable triumphs of artful play. It is only the new forensic expertise of modern art history, after all, that has allowed us to know for certain what many artworks are made of at all.

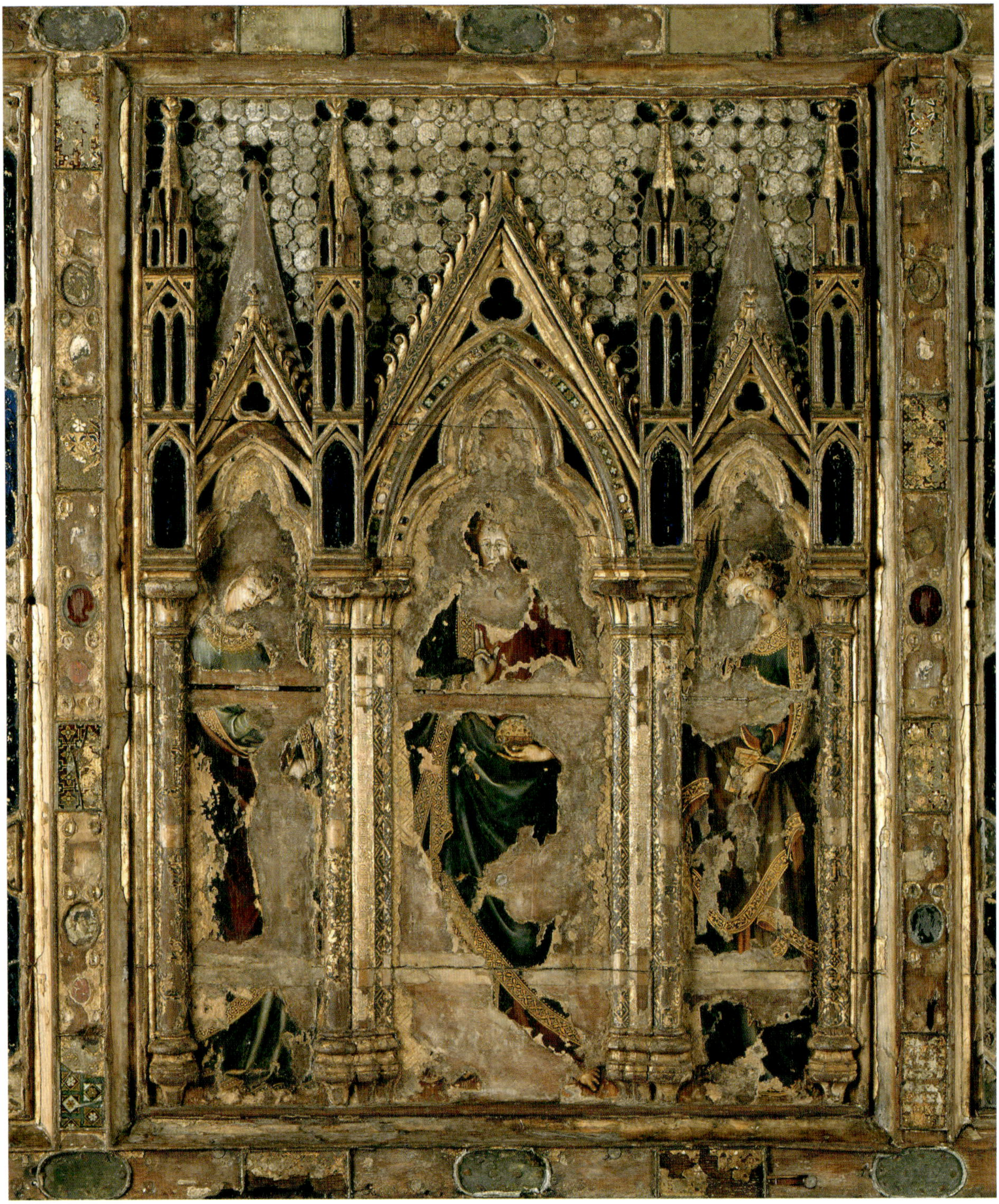

70 Westminster Abbey, high altar retable, central section with Christ, Mary and John, oak with gesso ground, linseed oil paint, gilding, painted decoration and inset glassware, 1259–69

At the heart of the last paragraph was the word 'illusion'. Illusion is artful contrivance understood as such, a pleasurable product of sensation. Its basis lies in the Latin noun for 'play', *ludus*, and its character as an experience of artefacts involves regard for fine, subtle and appealing workmanship, the 'play' of artificial effects.[114] It is a form of undeceived depiction. Instances are so common in medieval art that it is difficult to avoid them. I have already cited the brilliant play of technical effect, essentially illusionistic, on the Retable at Westminster. This is but one instance of a vast surviving European-wide inventory of medieval ludic effects, often summoning up a distant, heroic and authoritative visual language: consider the marvellous painted faux marbling of the western French Romanesque basilicas of St Hilaire in Poitiers (pl. 71) or St Savin sur Gartempe, imitating the swirling revetments of Byzantine or Roman churches, giving the churches in question that *venustas* (beauty but also blush-

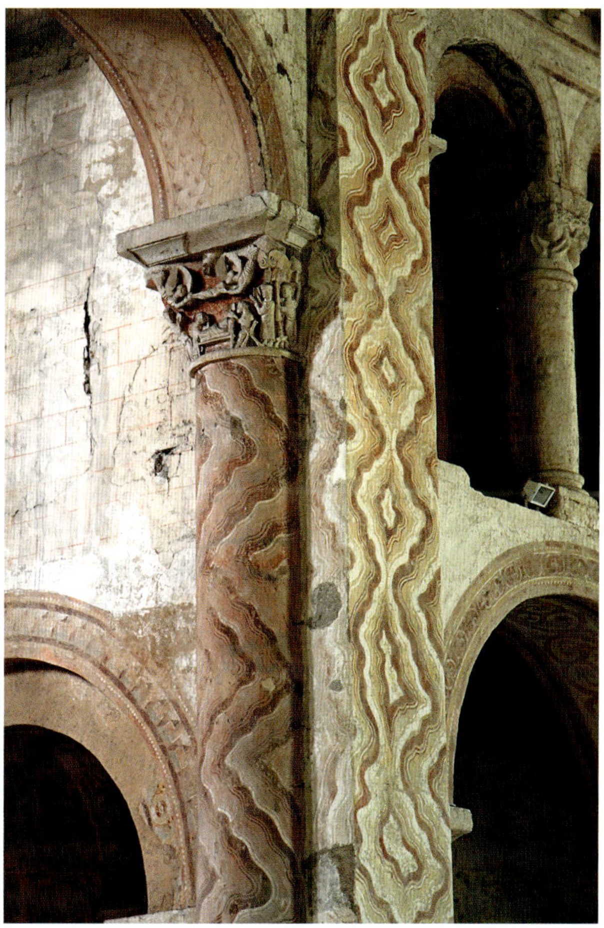

71 Poitiers (Vienne), basilica of St Hilaire, faux marble painting, eleventh century

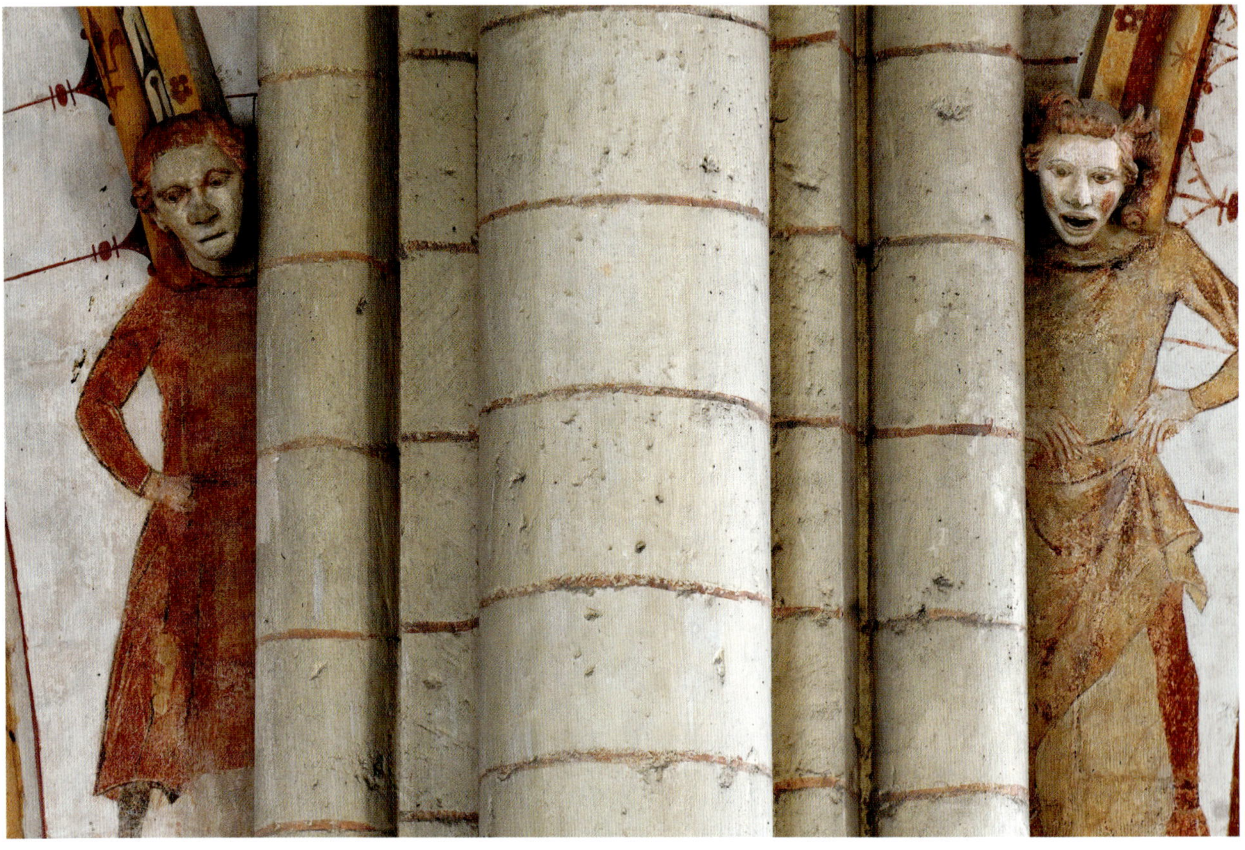

72 Poitiers Cathedral (Vienne), vault at west end of nave, sculpted heads with painted bodies, second half thirteenth century

ing suffusion) of which Isidore of Seville writes in talking about the elegant cladding of churches.[115] It may take the form of somewhat obvious (but no less compelling for that) tricks of the eye such as the sculpted corbels of the vaulting at the west end of the Gothic nave of Poitiers Cathedral (pl. 72), consisting of heads later extended in paint with bodies, to create the eerie effect of a face emerging from within the stonework like a ghost peering through a wall – a trope turned to moral purpose by Durandus, as we saw earlier (p. 53).

However, we need to note a body of modern opinion which states that medieval art was not given to illusion or mimesis at all. According to it, illusion and mimesis were the preserve of Renaissance art that deliberately tried to trick the senses, while medieval artists stressed instead the objective or material character of art. In her discussion of 'Christian materiality' Caroline Bynum states: 'medieval devotional art is the opposite pole from the art of the southern or northern renaissances that followed it. Renaissance artists aimed for mimetic, illusionistic modes of representation that deliberately try to trick the senses . . . In contrast, medieval artists expected viewers to notice and admire the stuff they employed *as stuff*'.[116] Her concern that late medieval art should not be assimilated to a Renaissance mindset – for instance, perspective as a 'symbolic form' – is at first sight understandable and certainly represents, or appears to represent, a rejection of Erwin Panofsky's opinion regarding the liberating power of Italian ideas for the Gothic north (that is, late medieval art) in the fourteenth and fifteenth centuries. According to Panofsky, symbolic Gothic art was eventually freed and elevated aesthetically by contact with the pictorial rationalism of perspectival Italian painting.[117] Yet the underlying polarities and narratives deployed by Bynum remain pretty much those of Panofsky, even Burckhardt. And her alternative idea – that medieval art as a whole should be separated from the concept of illusion and returned to its material base – also has implications. It runs against the extensive evidence that enjoyable illusion, a play with subtlety, craft and visual appearances, was a concern of medieval art *tout court*. So we are left in effect with the choice of accepting and imposing a Renaissance model of illusion or none at all. It also has the effect – to be considered shortly – of pushing medieval art into a materialist corner by applying to it a limited theory of representation. Finally, it underplays the obvious materiality of post-Renaissance art.[118] Its body of beliefs is founded on an anthropology of medieval images, described by Hans Belting, which sees them as 'images' (defined functionally) before the era of 'art' (defined aesthetically, in Renaissance terms).[119] The ultimate charge against it is that it is reductive, and that in emphasising the speech of materials it demotes human facture, human response and the human imaginative and discursive faculty.

In my view this outlook is unhelpful. My critique will consider next three issues: the nature of medieval representation, the nature of medieval materiality and the implications of this for the senses, which I shall consider under the heading 'tact', pointing not just to touch but to the delicacy of all interpretative action.

Let us begin with the fundamental question of representation, already opened out here with reference to sculptures of the Crucifixion. As I argued in discussing sculpted stone portals, mimesis in medieval art was not always central. Still, it mattered, partly because the notion of mimesis involved not just the imitation of nature but the imitation of other artworks. In his influential *De Memoria*, Aristotle drew a distinction between a configuration or thing in itself and its perception as an image of someone, as a representation: we might 'recognise' a portrait of Coriscus even if we have never seen him, once the portrait is declared as such.[120] Portraiture is acknowledged as the outcome of a specific representational act. It becomes an idea 'emergent' from a set of merely physical properties. This distinction was noted in the later Thomist argument that we render reverence to images of agents just as we do to agents themselves, because the apprehension of images is 'double' (*duppliciter*), since images are seen as things (that is, just as configurations, shapes) or as persons (that is, the person 'emerges').[121] One can see immediately how this distinction would clarify the question of idolatry, because it separates a thing from a person, the mind moving towards each in a different way. In the standard Latin defence of images, reverence was only due in the case of a person. So in considering a carved wooden crucifix, we should venerate Him and not the wood – *Et lui dovendo adorare et non questo ligno*, as is said in a short written prayer actually inserted into a crucifix made by the Sienese carver Lando di Piero (d. 1340).[122] Once we have the concept of a likeness of something that is not necessarily present, that concept may stand separately, as a memory or as a copy, from its material incarnation as an image. It should have rememorative power, and in that sense its mimetic character matters. But the material, efficient and formal causes of a work of art, as set out by Aristotle (*Physics* 2.3 and *Metaphysics* 5.2), while ideally working together towards a *telos* or end in the way that a skilled orator uses the matters to hand, are also understandable separately.[123] Indeed, the force of *enargeia* showed that images did not need to be material at all to have power: a *pictura* was not necessarily something made literally of paint, but a mind-image.

Another way of putting this is that medieval images did not create a representational order through their materiality but, rather, presupposed a representational order, a referent, or put more classically, an Idea rooted in pictorial imagination or *Bildvorstellung*.[124] The object did not sanctify the image: the image sanctified the object.[125] Demonstrations of this are several. One is the way that images of the Virgin Mary were periodically repainted or reshaped to suit changing canons of beauty. The reworking of the face of the Virgin Mary, as occurred quite frequently in medieval Italian panel painting and in northern Gothic wood sculpture, can be viewed functionally as a reverential or devotional activity; but this explanation cannot account for the evident emphasis on updating the looks of the Virgin as a mimetically convincing model of bodily beauty or garb, *pulchritudo* and *munditia*.[126] Whether picking out and changing the beauty of Mary or the deformity of her Son on the Cross, colour and the illusion of flesh mattered directly to the conviction, purpose and even the theology of such art.[127] If an image attracts, it works better. (Interestingly, it did not necessarily follow that if an image repelled, it worked worse, as the aesthetics of the macabre indicate: purpose is all.)

A further demonstration is that familiar images such as that of the Virgin Mary or the *Pietà* might be rendered in a huge range of materials, from silver gilt to alabaster, to painted wood, ivory or stone. The use of the materials could be explained as much by pragmatic or aesthetic reasons (cost, supply, personal taste, context) as by theological or significatory ones. In all such cases the choice of materials matters because of the intertwined relation of material and image: no one would argue that the choice of painted wood or alabaster for a *Pietà* would be without consequence for the image. Yet materials could be exchanged without fundamentally undermining the function or purpose of an image: their material cause could be exchanged in a way that their formal and final causes could not. That –

conservative critics aside – was the lesson of Chris Ofili's sensational and in its way orthodox commentary on the Incarnation, his *Holy Virgin Mary* first exhibited in 1999 and adorned with elephant dung.[128] What, after all, in virtue of *mere* materiality, separates Ofili's representation from any medieval gilded Madonna? Either makes the same theological point: yet theology could never of itself get to grips with the singularity of the images. As with the use-function in anthropological method, theology risks flattening experience, overriding difference because it has no critical method as such. In contrast, to learn that a gorgeously fashioned image of Mary is, in fact, an image of Venus, would surely be radically to reframe any rememorative, symbolic (to say nothing of metaphysical) character the image and its materials might have. I choose the instance of Mary and Venus because it was itself chosen by Theodulf of Orleans to illustrate the priority of concepts and texts over images.[129] Recognition, prior belief and imagination – human faculties exercised in the face of representations – cannot readily be displaced, for it is they that lend coherence to the experience of an image as much as its actual stuff. This is why materials do not work abstractly or essentially, but relationally. An expensive blue pigment used on the gown of the Virgin Mary, a rare red marble celebrating the martyrdom of saints (see pl. 84), an aloof white ivory signalling the purity of virginity (see pl. 63), all serve the purposes of images in virtue of what those images (or other signs) represent, what symbolic traditions they belong to, what religious or other metaphors are at work and so on.

The tendency to de-aestheticise representation, characteristic of the imperatives of some (not all) forms of anthropology, has had a significant outcome for what we imagine representation to be. Materialist arguments tend to elide representation with substitution. What things look like formally is therefore of less, or at least no greater, consequence than the stuff from which they are made.[130] So instead of representing brocade, or gold, medieval artists just made brocade or gold, forging becoming depiction. This argument is problematical because it is founded precisely on the type of Renaissance value system that the medieval materialist argument itself seeks to clear away: it restates what L. B. Alberti has to say at the end of Book 2 of *Della Pittura*, namely that we do not add real gold to pictures, we imitate its effect.[131] 'Real' art does not substitute, and medieval art is fundamentally substitutive. But from what has been argued so far throughout the present study, this cannot be so. It is not necessary to downplay the many devious methods medieval artists used to create effects, indeed illusions, in order to see that the dislocation of what are often held to be 'Medieval' and 'Renaissance' attitudes to art and representation is misleading, and that representation is not exactly the same as substitution. If that were so, as indicated, we could not exchange the materials of an image without destroying the image itself. One would have become the other. Materialist theories tend, in effect, to be immanent in character because to them, material itself has a kind of vitality or eloquence. But representation, on the contrary, is intentional and artefactual: it entails thought about a distanced subject, and so is a form of deliberation and exploration in the light of other beliefs, concepts and percepts. It is an act of imagination and separation. Were it not, and were the representation to become one with the thing depicted, it would cease to be a representation. And because such deliberation and exploration is conducted in the light of other beliefs and ideas, it necessarily has a history external or transeunt to the object as such.

HAIR AND TORQUE

In a memorable phrase which encapsulates my objection to the corralling of medieval art into a reductively materialist position, Umberto Eco wrote of 'shaggy medievalism', capturing an earthy mindset of savagery, barbarity, pain and stupidity.[132] So let us consider the representation of something that tests all artists, and yet which is (in theory) easily substitutable and certainly shaggy: hair. Hair is as much a concern for sculptors as painters, perhaps more so, since of all relief surfaces it is probably the most demanding and time-consuming to execute well, with the possible exception of foliage. Between 1100 and 1300 the sculpted depiction of hair went through changes as marked as any other representational feature. Romanesque carving was especially alert to hair's eloquence: in the twelfth century, hair often looks like the weird result of electrocution: it participates in that initial sense of dislocation on encountering such works I described in the first part of this study. The image of Medusa was not forgotten either. Beside the great main early twelfth-century Apocalypse entrance at Moissac the personification of *Luxuria* bears lank clotted tresses not unlike the snakes which suckle at her dugs (pl. 73 and see pl. 23).[133] The conventions used to depict the tresses with small fine parallel lines are essentially the same as those used for the flames which gnaw at the Three Hebrews in the Fiery Furnace in a capital in Moissac's nearby cloister. In the cloister, hair can be shown as a neat compacted sub-classical collection of little coils (Sts Peter, Simon and Matthew), while the visionary prophets on the trumeau have long, alien-looking and fantastic beards and moustaches, as does the astounding figure of Isaiah at Souillac (pl. 74 and see pl. 15) whose hair and body seem equally dynamic, as if their counterpoint indicated metaphysical powers.[134] At Autun, Eve floats strangely, almost sub-aquatically through thickets of strange foliage, her neck and shoulders covered in finely combed hair.[135] That hair signifies is beyond doubt. The Romanising curls that pile up over the chubby sensual face of the so-called 'woman with the skull' on the south transept of the cathedral at Santiago de Compostela connect hair with death and sin, as do *Luxuria*'s locks at Moissac.[136] Some sense of the association of hair with transience and death is conveyed by the depiction of ranks of mourners, all clutching at their long locks of hair in a threnodic 'gesture of despair', on a panel from the tomb of Don Sancho Saiz de Carillo at Mahamud (Burgos) of about 1300 (Museu Nacional d'Art de Catalunya, Barcelona).[137]

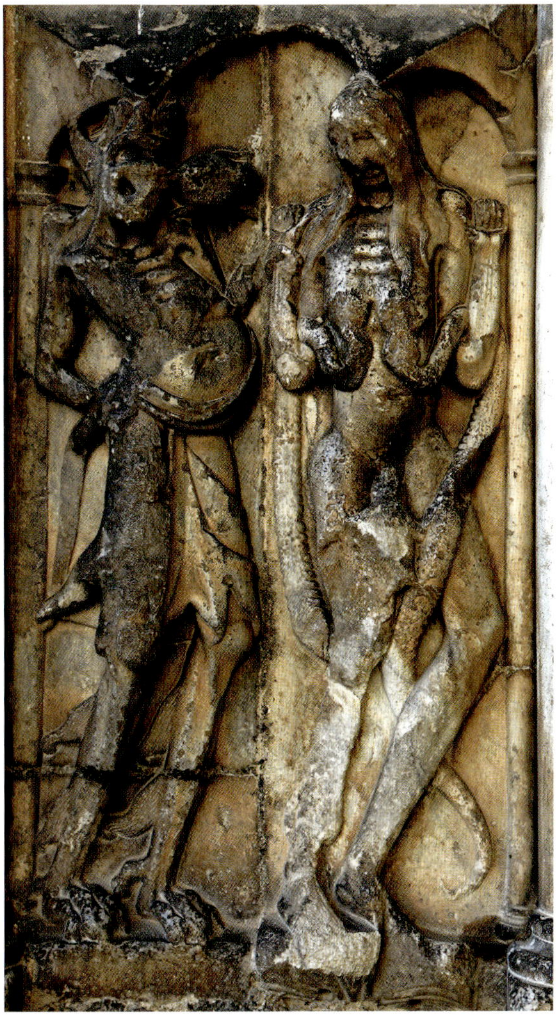

73 Moissac Abbey (Tarn-et-Garonne), south-west portal, left flank panel of *Luxuria* tormented by a demon

The classicising practices of Gothic art around 1200 had tended to rein in the earlier dramatic effects as sculptors began to scrutinise and deploy the methods, such as drilling, that Roman sculptors had used to produce heads of tight short curled hair (see pl. 56).[138] A return to hair as a bravura expressive vehicle, long, waving and gratifyingly sensual, began in the second half of the thirteenth century along with the other changes in figure style at this time, as at Reims and the Sainte-Chapelle. As in Romanesque art, Gothic hair from 1250 or so onwards became part of a total order of mimesis, indeed gained in importance and visibility as the surface simplification of garments, in the so-called 'broad-fold' style initiated in France by the 1230s, threw into high relief more highly wrought hands and heads as instruments of *actio*, eloquent conduct. Concentrations of bravura curling, coiling, winding

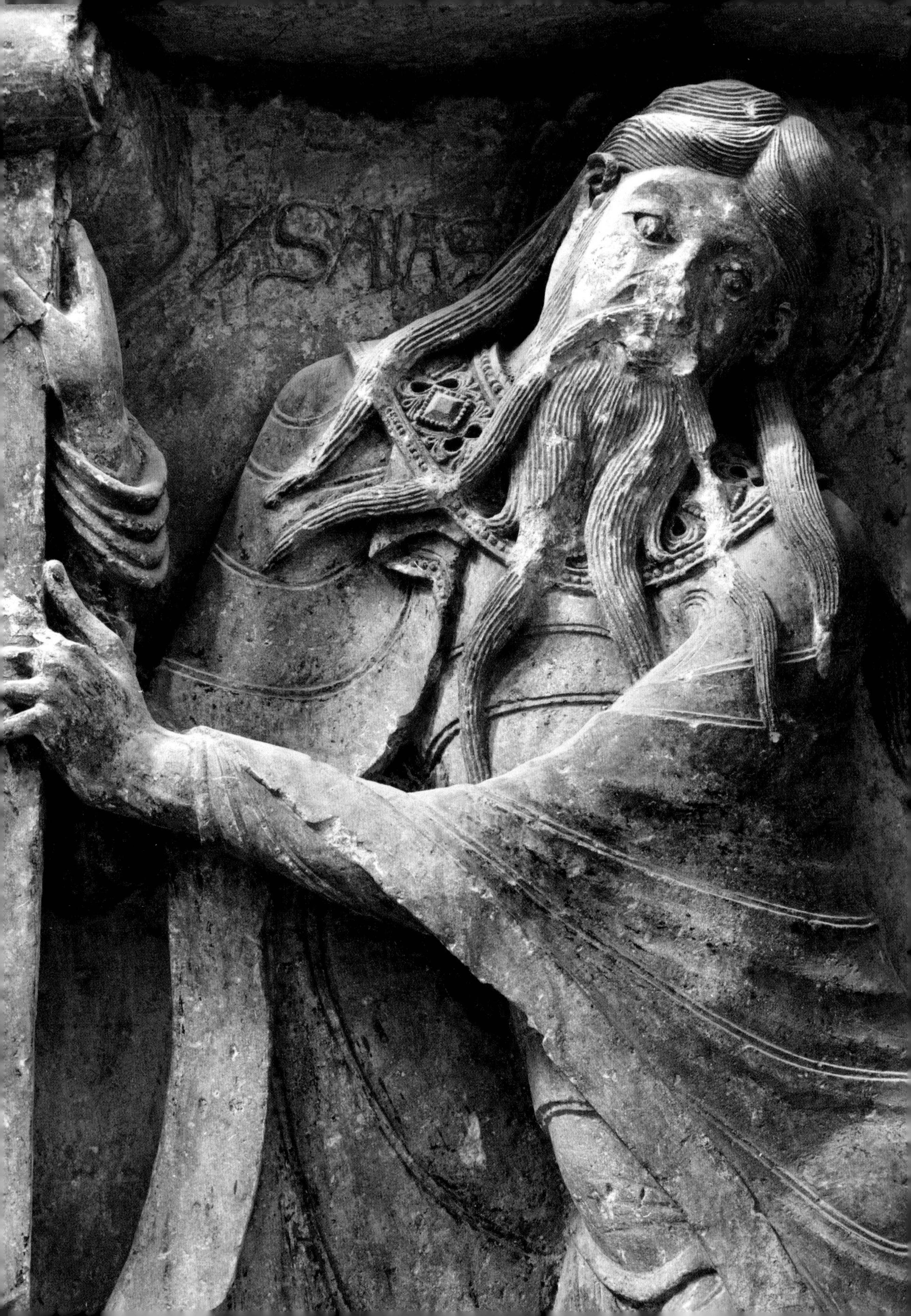
YSAIAS

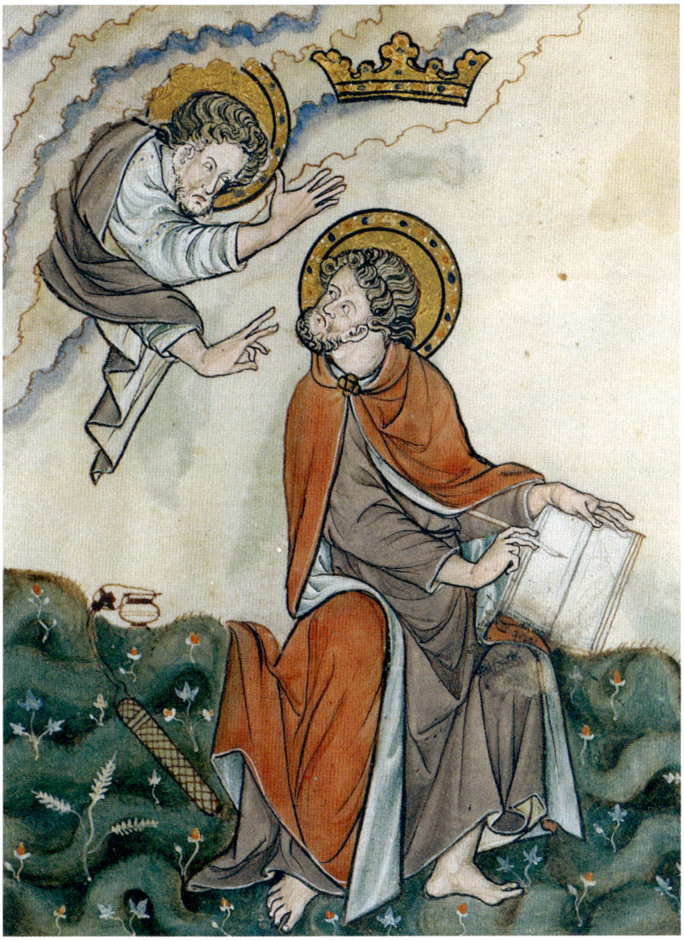

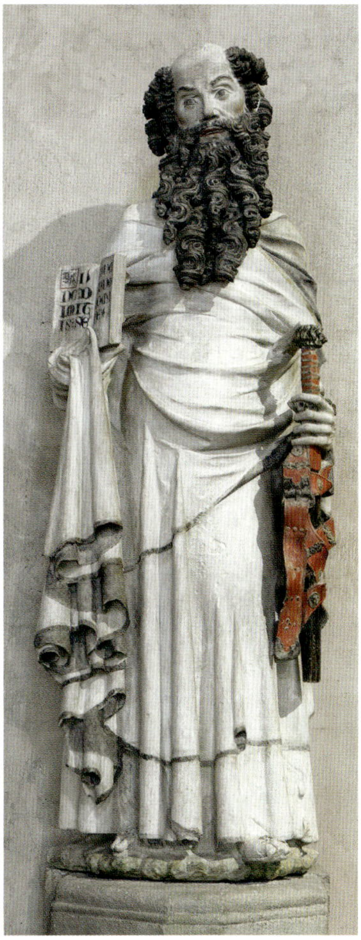

facing page 74 Souillac Abbey (Lot), inner west portal, Isaiah, about 1120

this page 75 St John writes to the Church at Smyrna, Douce Apocalypse, about 1265–70 (Oxford, Bodleian Library Ms Douce 180, p. 5)

76 St Paul, from the church of the Cordeliers in Toulouse (Haut-Garonne), limestone with original paint, 1330s or 1340s (Toulouse, Musée des Augustins, no. RA 555 C)

and waving hair are found in the English courtly Douce Apocalypse of the 1260s (pl. 75), on the Apostles on the west front of Strasbourg and on the prodigiously bearded figure of St Paul from the Cordeliers at Toulouse of the second quarter of the fourteenth century (pl. 76).[139] The mid-thirteenth-century image of Eve on the west front at Bourges already has the full undulating hair of this phase, as do many of the smaller images at Reims, and from Bourges it spread via the 'laboratory' of great Gothic projects to León.[140]

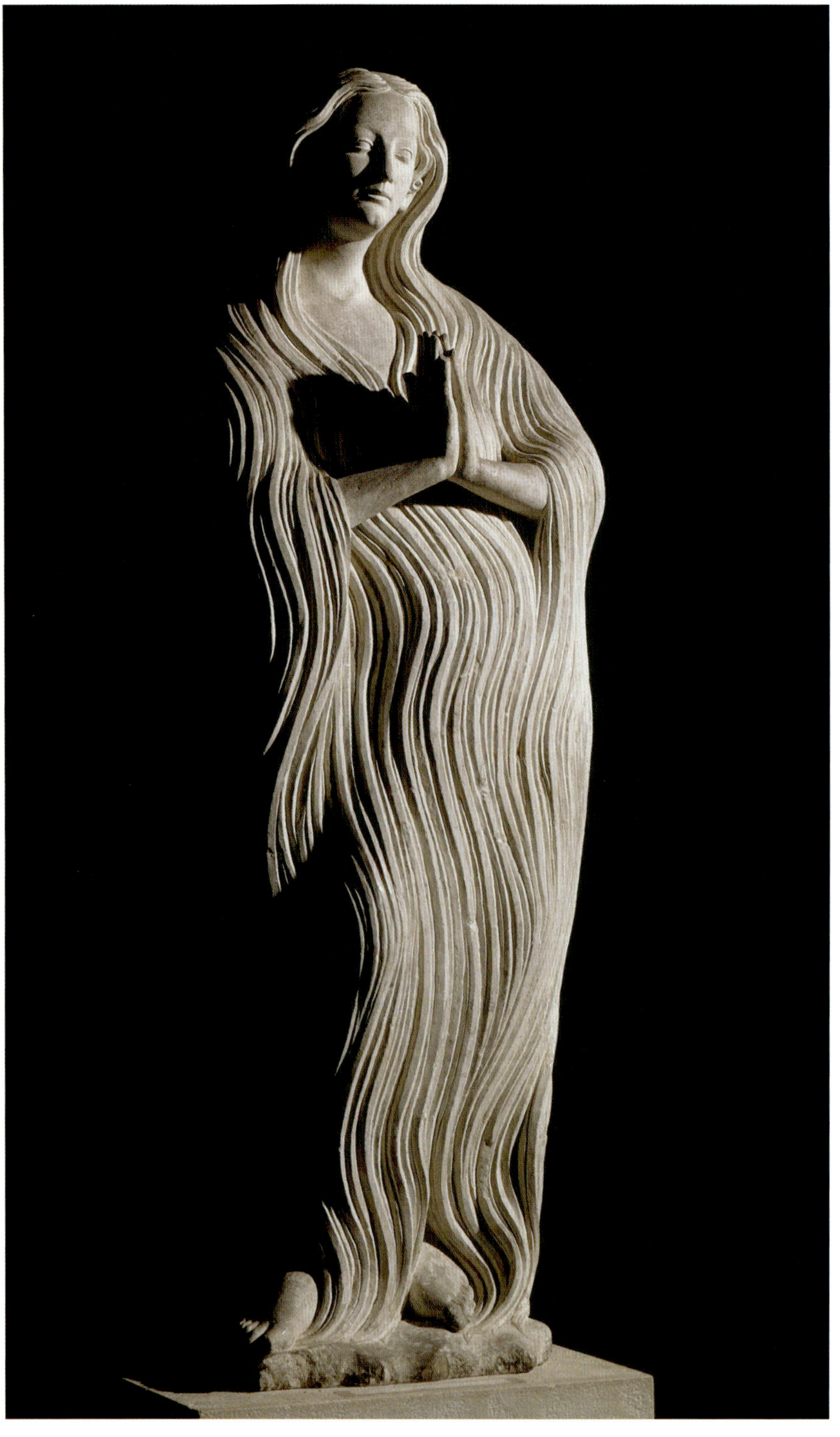

77 St Mary Magdalen, from the collegiate church at Écouis (Eure), limestone, about 1313

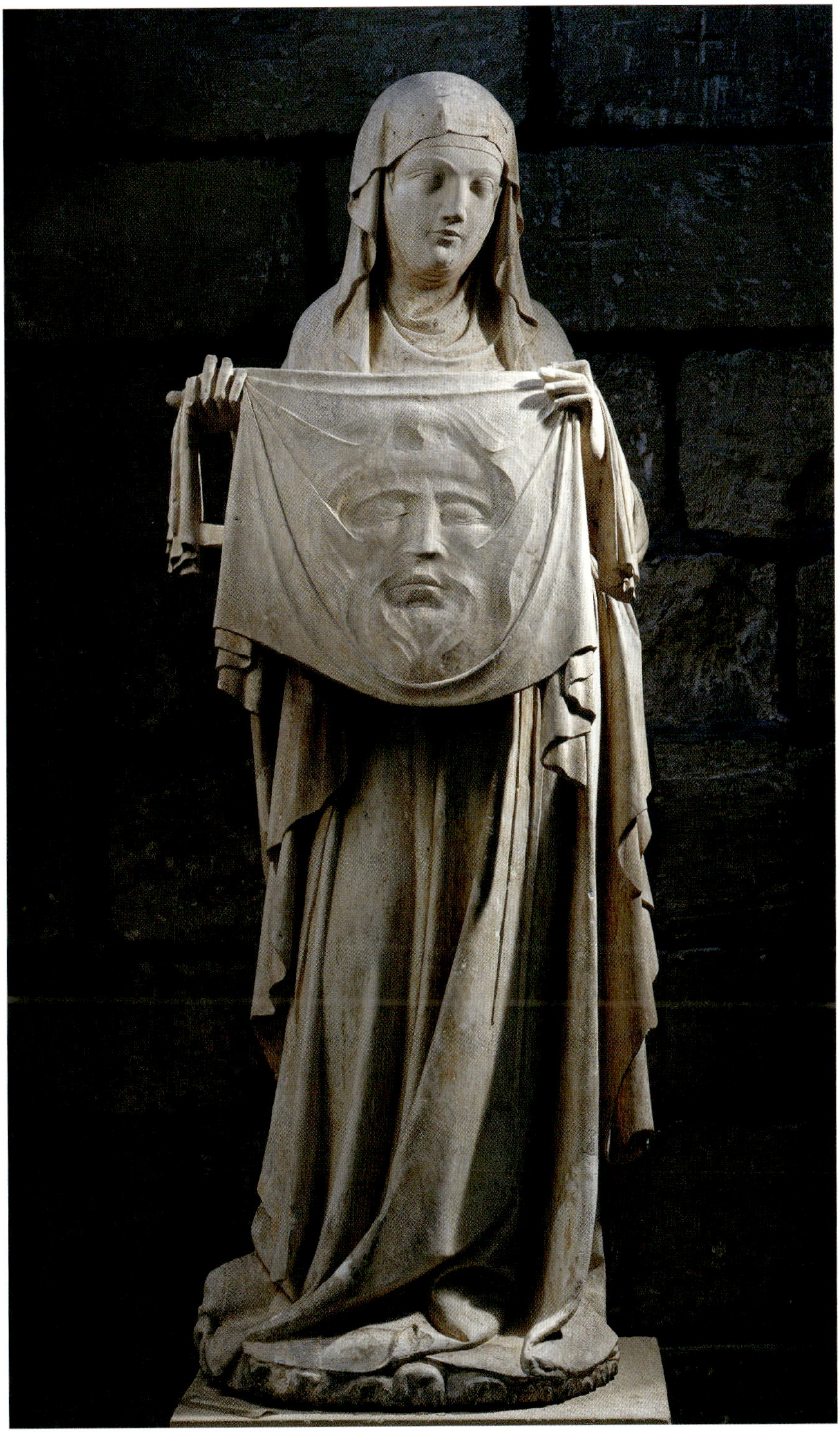

78 St Veronica, from the collegiate church at Écouis (Eure), limestone, about 1313

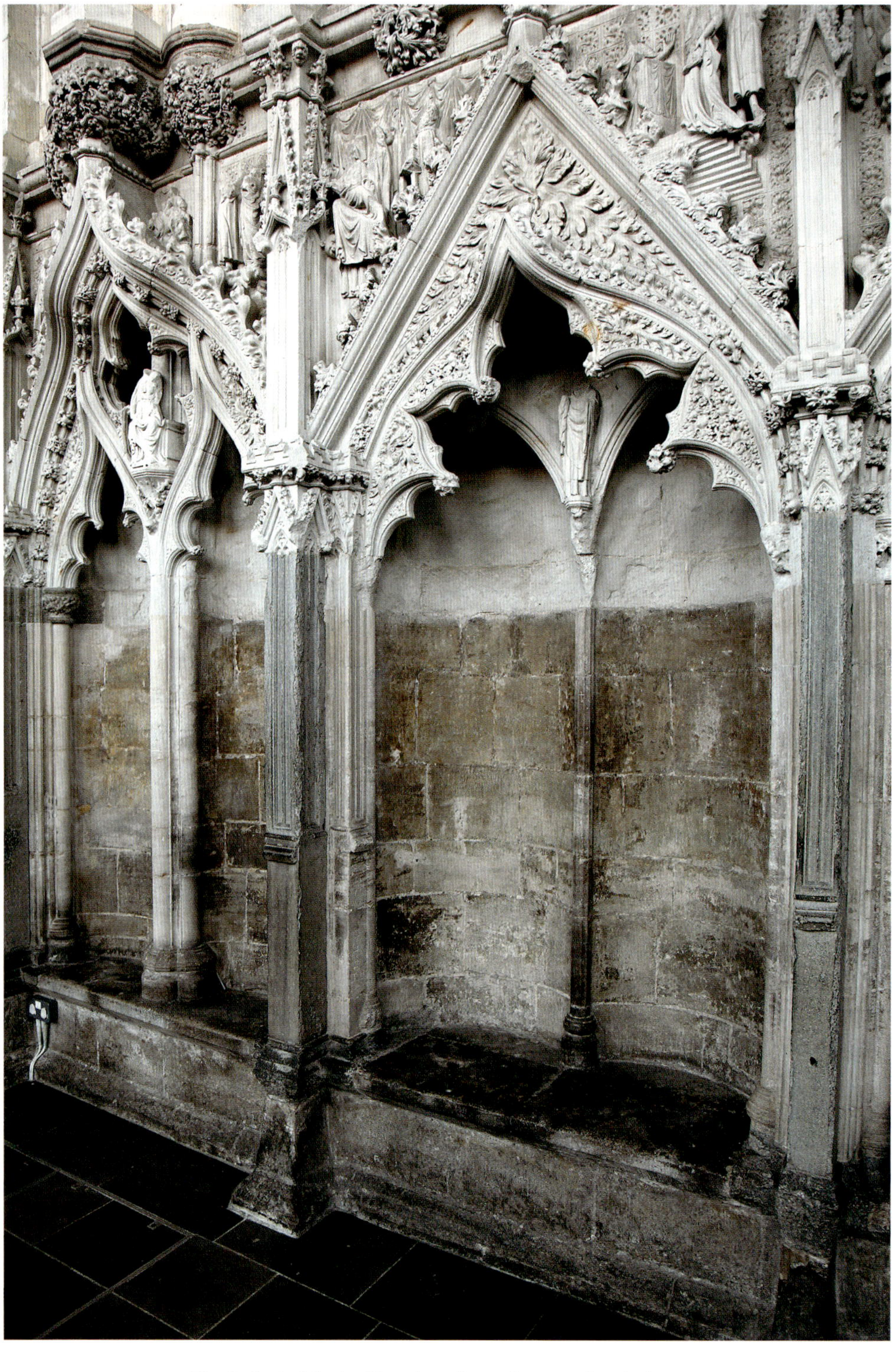

79 Ely Cathedral, Lady Chapel, wall arcading, south side, begun 1321

bending the intention and affect of the receiver. The artefact operates through its formal properties or style to intend and so affect its beholders – movement towards the attractive and away from the unpleasant. In medieval theory of the affects these were known as the powers of concupiscence and repulsion, important agents in the working of emotional experience as cognitive and active, rather than passive.[155] Poets such as Dante, Petrarch and Boccaccio wrote of *vaghezza*, 'loveliness', 'delight', 'longing', inexact tone words which capture the 'bending' power of love as a soft power.[156] The dispositive topic of the wave or Gothic S-curve has become a surface colour. Hair – represented, not substituted – conveys value in a particularly vivid way. Mary Magdalen's hair is undoubtedly an attribute, a sign by which she might be spotted, or least quickly grouped with St Mary of Egypt or St Agnes as a type of penitent sinner. But it is more than an attribute, because in its crafted and artificial state it in itself gains calculated metaphorical power. To represent is to think, guide, control and distance; to guide a thing is to prune it for greater productivity.

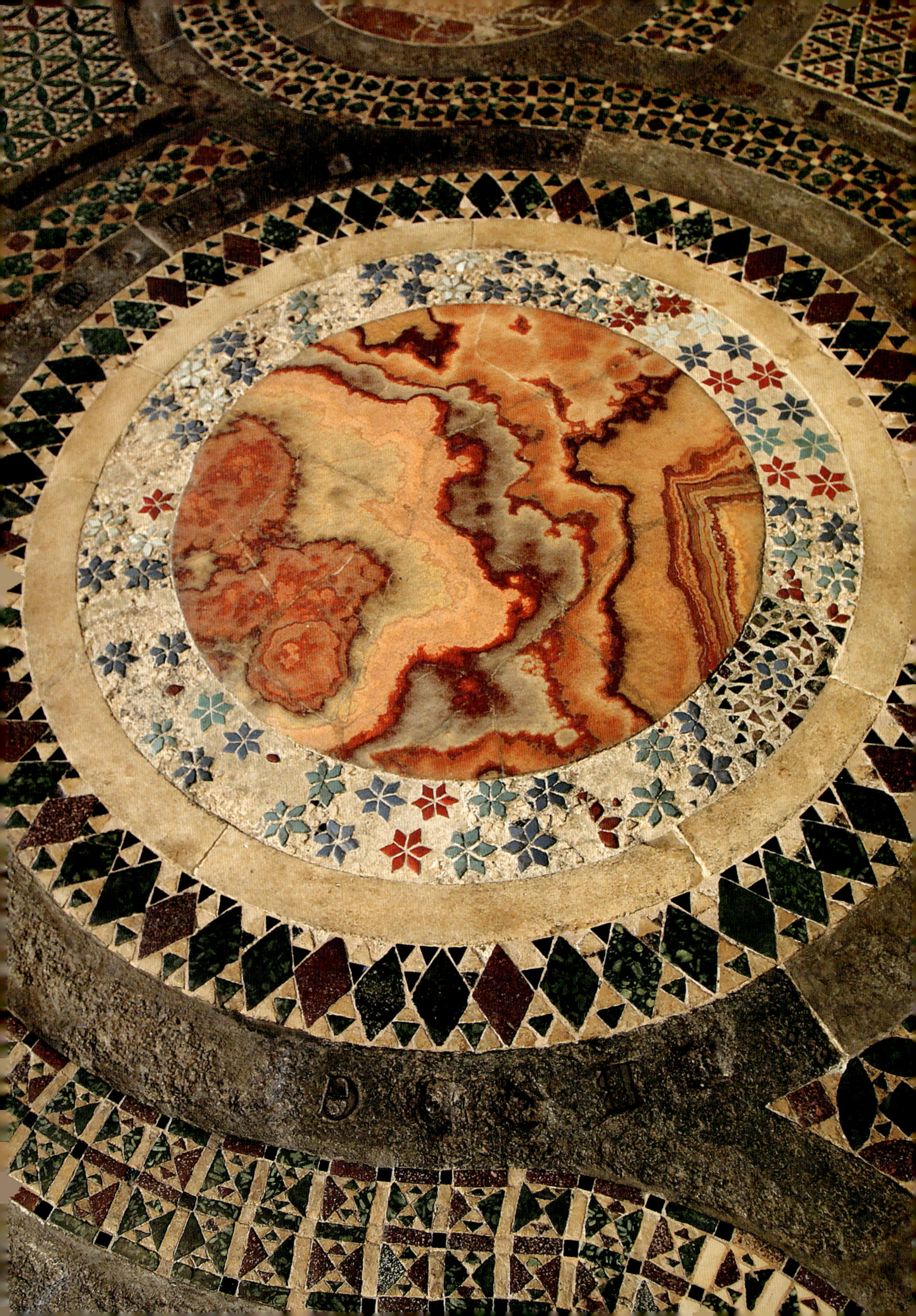

5

THE POETICS OF MATERIALS

The point of the previous discussion was to get the materiality of medieval objects into some sort of perspective by pointing up issues of representation and belief: that images are not sanctified by their 'stuff' but by what they show. Indeed, it is not philosophically or empirically obvious how the vibrancy of stuff transfers to human artefacts without either unacceptably anthropomorphising natural things or simply dissolving human agency.[1] Materiality studies risk a well-intentioned form of normativity or literalism. In Chapter 4, I stated that colours are never exactly rule-bound but discretionary, calculated. Colours are materials: materials do not simply possess their own eloquence, because the significance and power of things is traditional, occasional and rhetorical. One pointer to the difficulties I have in mind is provided by the eminent historian of religion Caroline Bynum, who has provided a bravura negotiation of idea and material, word and flesh, in regard to the Christian doctrine of Incarnation.[2] Materiality is, so to speak, the flesh and bones of the matter. It is frank, honest, vigorous or in her words 'overt', 'pregnant with significance', 'per se living', unavoidable in the encounter with the thing to hand; art in contrast is a deception, sophisticated, dead, illusory – if it exists at all in the Middle Ages.[3] This view is not without animist sympathy: 'By the fifteenth and sixteenth centuries', Bynum suggests, 'there was a growing sense that material objects were not merely labile but alive'.[4] The practical lesson of conventional art history has always been that the materials and media involved are inescapable. But a more or less explicit tenet of this school of thought, strongly influenced by Hans Belting's anthropology of images, is that art is not a medieval category

80 Westminster Abbey, Cosmati pavement (detail of pl. 83)

at all, but a post-Renaissance one: hence the common rhetorical ploy of using the words 'objects' and 'images' in lieu of 'works of art'. Earlier in this study (pp. 18, 157) I objected to this point of view, partly because its central theses about artefacts and representation seem to me questionable, and partly because it is not clear whether an exacting critical method could ever emerge from a highly generalised and inclusive incarnational analogy, by its own admission riven by contradiction and change precisely because of its materiality. Nevertheless, as noted earlier, theology has advanced as a master-narrative: in virtue of their very materiality, medieval artefacts become objectifications of all the issues inherent in the doctrine of the Incarnation itself.

The roots of this whole idea lie in a seminal text of the study of materiality as cultural history, Michael Baxandall's *The Limewood Sculptors of Renaissance Germany* (1980).[5] As Robert Scribner put it in reflecting on Baxandall's work, 'the very materiality of the image encouraged the viewer to see it as pure object, as mere material'.[6] Baxandall's careful account has two features of note. The first is that he insisted on the inseparability of material and skill: in observing rightly that 'Noticeable art draws attention to itself quite as much as noticeable material', Baxandall drew attention to 'a contradiction between the religious image and the most accomplished art that was difficult to evade'.[7] Second, Baxandall's account gathered together skill and material under the heading of what he called 'secular satisfactions'.[8] On this basis art was susceptible to ascetic religious critique. The notion of Christian materiality replies to this by regarding materiality as bearing theological import, and so value: to think of 'mere' materiality is to miss the point. Materiality is licit because it is doctrinally not just acceptable but eloquent.

This in turn raises two issues. First, as Baxandall's theory recognised, not all medieval art was explicitly or implicitly religious. It is just that secular art is often less well-preserved than religious art. Critical theories with any claim to general application cannot be developed on the basis of an essentially privileged (because well-preserved and valued) body of evidence which is by nature and intent essentially religious: theology is not a universal explanatory device.

Second, arising from this is a question about what Baxandall called the 'character to be respected' of materials.[9] Crafting is profoundly material in that it requires strength, dexterity and knowledge of the way materials behave when worked and used. In both the verbal and non-verbal arts, the craft involved entails a preliminary understanding, practical in nature, of the character of the materials that form the basis of invention; this understanding in turn entails judgement and experience. 'Character', the essential imprint of a material, seems preferable to the anthropomorphising and emergent notion of 'personality'. Material needs first to be sniffed out, tasted, touched, 'read', and its manipulation has to be thought through, pre-measured, as in the craft of poetry. To repeat, to craft an image, like talking or singing, is something done *in* the media concerned, not *with* them. As I have already suggested, the image is thought directly into the stuff, not translated into it. Medieval poetry and rhetoric made use of the idea that materials have a 'character' or intrinsic power. In discussing *abbreviatio*, for example, Vinsauf in the *Poetria Nova* likened the distillation of a thought to a concentration on nouns, not verbs, nouns being the material which, like iron, is wrought on the anvil by the hammer of the intellect.[10] Materials duly push back, and the task of forming them is not without honourable difficulty. So iron 'honours' itself in its contentious working and forging – an image drawn from the account of Lady Dialectic's metalworking in Alan of Lille's *Anticlaudianus*, which speaks of the artisan's weapons, her conquest of informed material, her compelling of stubborn matter to obey her.[11] Materials are resistant, argumentative, wilful, but they are ultimately overcome by human agency, for workmanship surpasses them: *materiam superabat opus*. This resistance and its understanding and overcoming are fundamental to the appreciation of difficulty and attainment in the medieval arts with their admiration for 'difficulty, complexity, ornateness, circuitousness, artificiality', as Penelope Doob puts it.[12]

The human imaginary is inescapable. Materials come ready-freighted with signification because their usages are old, often traditional, and it is hard to see how their valencies, no matter how various, could ever be separated from cultural understanding and so context. In this sense 'natural' meaning – unless it is to be reified into something normative – always has to contend with the complexities of cultural superimposition unless it is to become a form of literalism. This was undoubtedly true of some of the most important language of materials in the Middle Ages, as in the ancient world. Materials were not necessarily seen as themselves but as things subjected to artifice. They were not seen 'as' something but something was seen 'in' them (to borrow Richard Wollheim's terms), namely a fiction which acknowledged the difference between object and medium – the basis of *trompe l'oeil* effects more generally. Medieval art is full of such play on substance and reality, the basis of which lay in the verbal and visual conjurations of classical and post-classical ekphrasis.[13] Theology, however, was not central to it, for ekphrastic practice predated Christian belief. What was central to it was what John Mitchell calls 'the expenditure of imagination', that compositorial activity on the part of the beholder which enacted ways of seeing common to images and stuff.[14]

Ekphrasis was itself a mode of representation, of rhetorical play with words in praise of great buildings and artefacts, which brought them vividly before the eye of the mind and which automatically assumed the far from innocent nature of natural things and their materiality.[15] To bring out their beauty, as in a 'gloss', much as an oily polish might reveal the deep sheen of a marble, enriching words for materials always hunt out other natural things and develop them in a narrative of understanding which is, again, relational. All this mind work lacks is the sense of physical contention, of combat, involved in physical crafting. An excellent instance of visual and sensory promiscuity is Paulus Silentarius's sixth-century

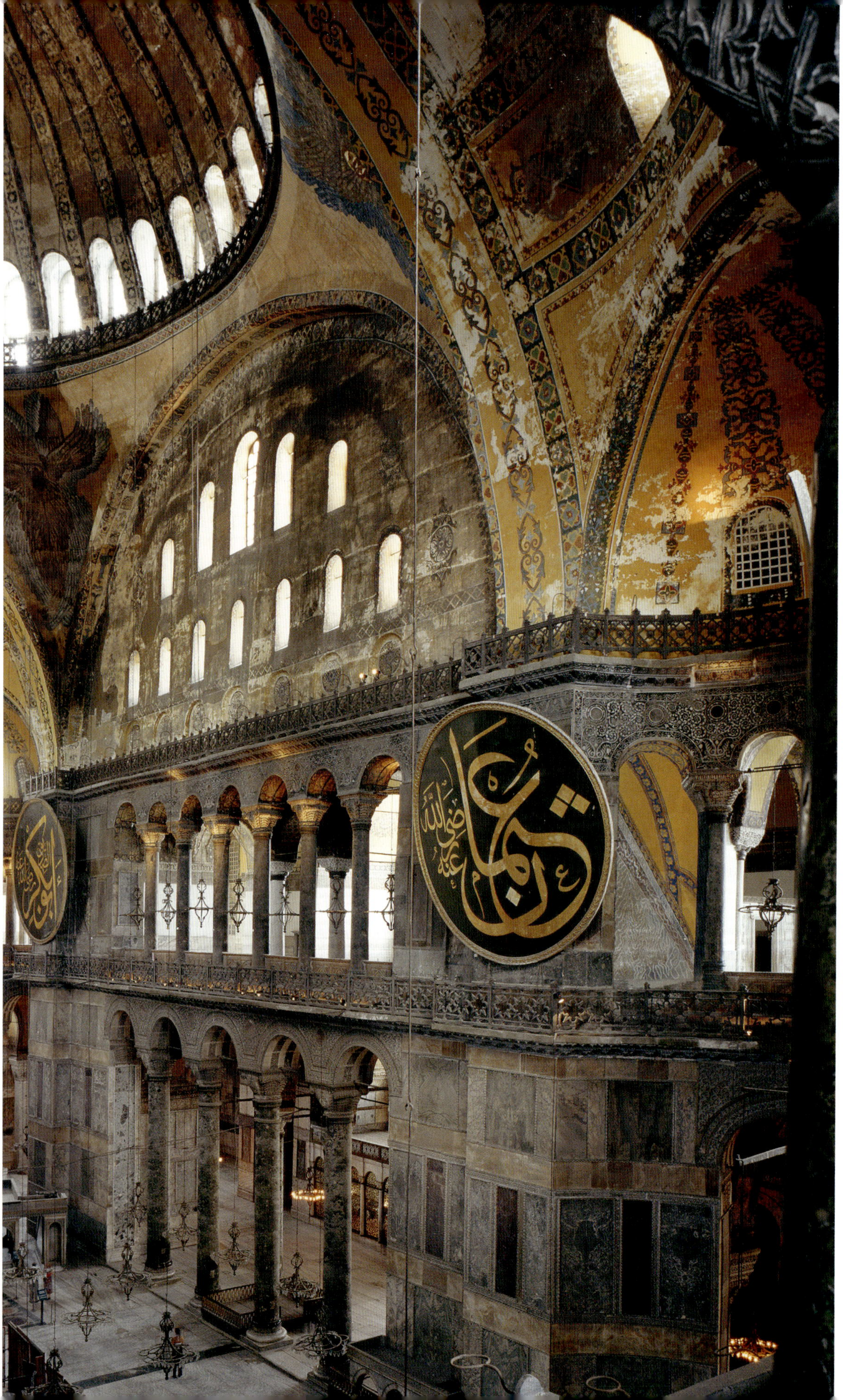

description of the ambo and interior of Hagia Sophia in Constantinople (pl. 81).[16] Each object in the church, such as the elaborate marbled ambo or pulpit, becomes the rhetorical occasion for a kind of associative venture, in which the polychromy of materials is likened to eddying water, or boxwood, or beeswax; or is seen to bloom like the flowers of the field, the white lilies mingling with roses, or anemone: we hear and then see by *enargeia* 'a rose bloom mingled with pallor', the stones having 'the fair brightness of human fingernails', being 'rosy with a tinge of white', or 'white with a tinge of fiery red', stones with 'veins' which together flush 'with purple, like the blood of the Laconian shell'. In their veined redness and whiteness these stones embody *venustas*, that eloquent and sensuous, living and full-blooded property or colour of surfaces.[17] Whatever the agency of such materials there is also a supreme and cunning agent, Nature, who not only competes with art but also compares and competes with itself.[18] When Paulus Silentarius uses ekphrasis in order to 'paint', materials are made to look like other things: they are a lively, winning masquerade. Their appreciation involves a conjuration of other images, other materials.

But there is no question here of false belief: the beauty of the fiction lies not in using language to change the identity of stuff, but to reveal under what aspect stuff can be seen. Overlooking the distinction between the sense in which something can be seen 'in' an artefact, as opposed to seeing the artefact 'as' something else, is at the heart of the confusion in reductive materiality theories. Once an image of a saint is seen not as a representation but as the saint in question, or as the material of which the image is made, the artefact has vanished and we are no longer dealing with a representation but with a person, or just stuff.[19]

I am hardly the first to note that ekphrastic techniques, with all their clever conjuration, persist through the medieval period. What matters is the way this rhetoric is enjoyably illusionistic: there is no question of deceit, but rather of the pleasure taken in being teased and mistaken by an admirable contrivance which allows a sort of two-fold seeing. In such accounts materials are not egotistical: they provoke doubt and certainty, praise and blame; they enrich, clarify, point to other things, they participate in masquerade: they mystify and insinuate. Above all they participate openly in the creation of fictions. Artists, like the practitioners of ekphrasis, transformed and sublimated these qualities. Experience did not stop at materials; it started with them.

ALABASTER: FLESH, FAT AND BLOOD

Take the one art material the English were famous for in the Middle Ages: alabaster. From the middle of the fourteenth century English-made alabaster products, including devotional images, altarpiece panels (pl. 82) and tomb effigies, proliferated, in part – in the early years at least – with royal encouragement, and there was a significant export industry.[20] But the

81 Istanbul, Hagia Sophia, interior, 530s

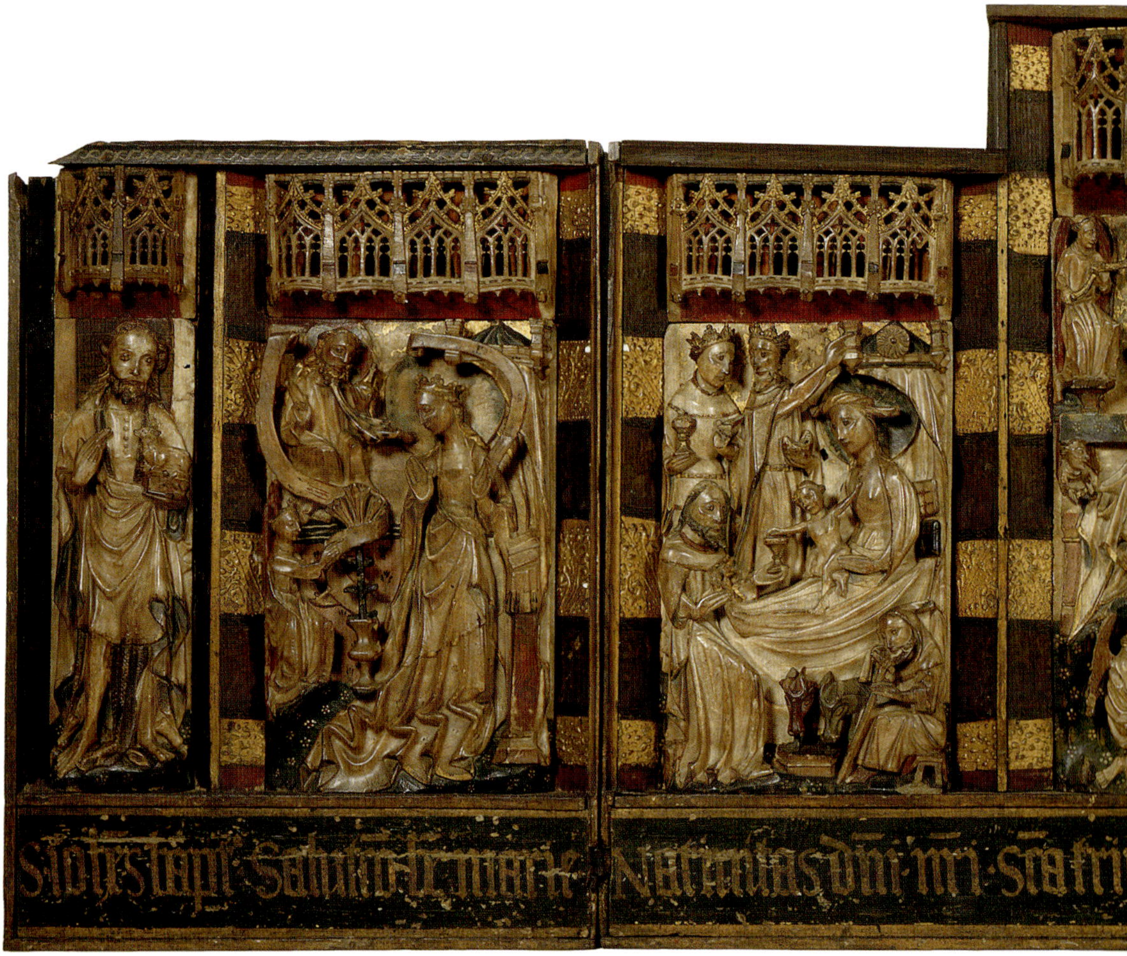

82 The Swansea Altarpiece showing the Joys of the Virgin, alabaster in original oak frame, original paintwork, second half fifteenth century. A number of such altarpieces were exported to Continental Europe (London, Victoria and Albert Museum, no. A. 89:1-8, 10 to 15-1919)

story of alabaster is far older and weightier. Within the medieval Christian dispensation, the backstory of alabaster begins in the Gospels with a small *alabastrum* or receptacle produced by Mary Magdalen and broken (*fractum*) over the head and feet of Christ to release its precious oil or scent (Matthew 26:7, Mark 14:3, Luke 7:37 and John 12:3). In Luke and John's Gospels, Mary, the sister of Martha and Lazarus, anoints Christ's feet with her hair. The moment is one of extraordinary sensory and spiritual intensification: the events in the house at Bethany frame the raising of Lazarus (in John's Gospel) and point forward to the Passion and Resurrection of Christ himself. Luke and John intermingle Mary's gestures with her hair, her tears of penance in the act of washing. In John 12:3 the house is filled with the

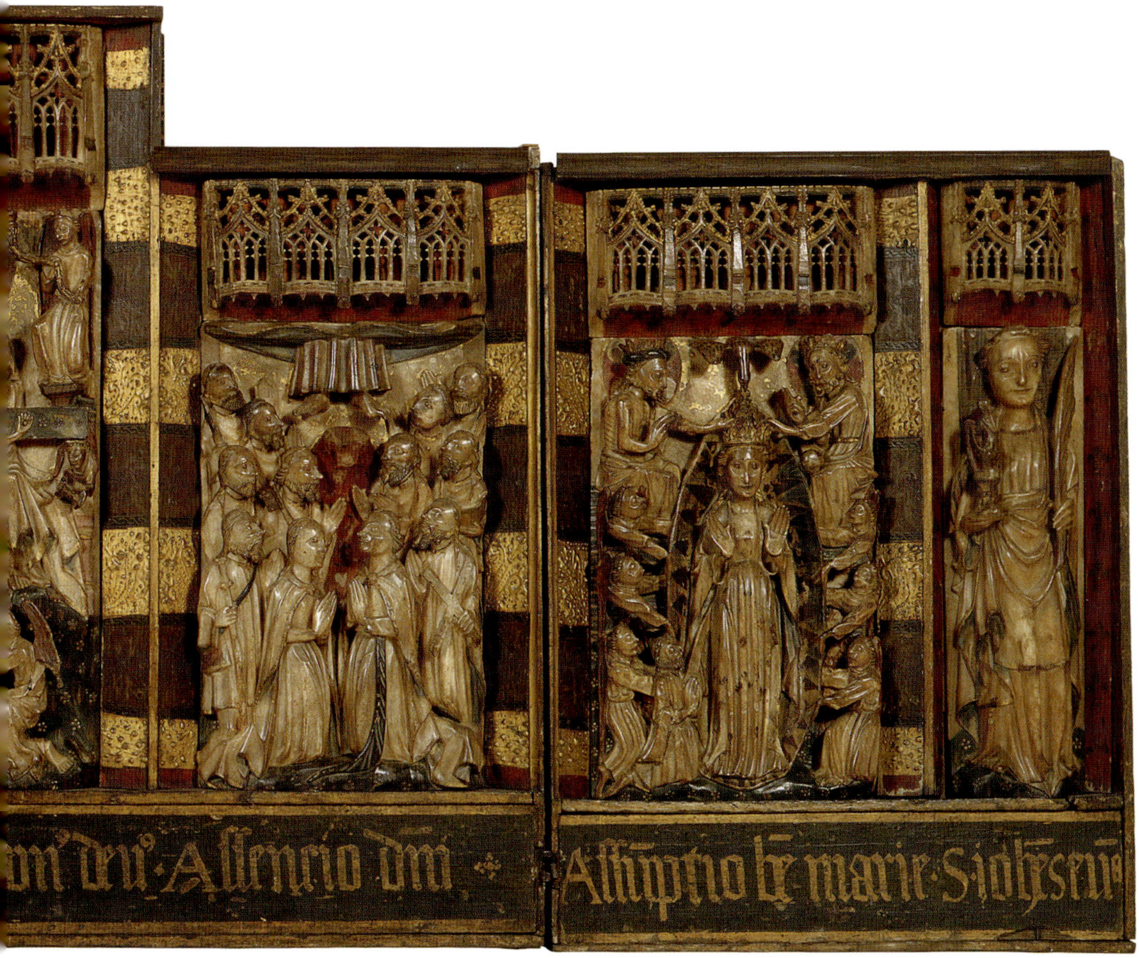

sensuous perfume of the ointment, *et domus impleta est ex odore unguenti*. And the disciples, including Judas Iscariot, object to the display of waste and luxury, only to be reproached by Christ: 'for the poor you always have with you; but me you have not always'. Mary is among those who come to the tomb with sweet spices to anoint Christ (Mark 16:1). And so one might say that *eros* and *thanatos*, the erotic and death, are linked. The luxurious thing is the oil, but alabaster enjoys guilt by association. The mixed character of these events is key because it reminds us that the affective frame of materials is often complex; it is mixture and complexity that create both pleasure and that sense of danger, of transgression, in this Gospel event, picked up on by the disciples who object to the display.

Pliny in his *Historia Naturalis* (13.3) reminds us with Roman practicality that unguents commonly keep better in alabaster and, of such scents mixed with oil, he simply says 'the fatter the better', for the perfumes improve with age.[21] That the harder alabasters of the ancient world were used in funerary rights must have been known in the first century CE.[22] Indeed Graeco-Roman rhetoric and aesthetics, rather than theology, established those links between pleasurable complexity, variety and even enjoyable danger – a sense carried by the Greek *poikilia* – that came to serve the medieval world comprehensively.[23] Rationally, alabaster was classified with other marbles in the pre-medieval worlds.[24] Along with onyx and multi-coloured white marbles, it was drawn into the sophisticated game of ekphrasis.

It is not therefore surprising to find skilled Latin versificators and rhetoricians echoing the methods of Graeco-Roman and Byzantine ekphrasis and its powers of conjuration. Their occasion was not so much the celebration of great patrons as great saints. An instance is the Latin *Metrical Life* written, it is thought, by Henry of Avranches around the time of the canonisation (1220) of Hugh, Bishop of Lincoln.[25] The *Life*, written for the cathedral canons, is in the heroic mode: it is composed in dactylic hexameters, a traditional epic metre, and opens by citing the start of Virgil's *Aeneid*: *Arma virumque cano*, 'I sing of arms and the man'. About a tenth of the poem is devoted to the construction of the new cathedral at Lincoln under St Hugh's tutelage. The cathedral is an animated thing not of art but of nature (*non esse videtur ab arte/ Quin a natura*). It has its own will, and can express ambition: not content with being of just one colour, it uses black stonework (*lapidum nigrorum*) as well as white. This marble flashes with glint upon glint presenting a starry brilliance, for nature has painted it (*pinxit*) with great variety. The onlooker's mind is held in suspense with fascination as to the nature of this material. Perhaps Paulus Silentarius himself is echoed in the idea that the marbles are 'more polished than a fresh-grown finger-nail'; and again, while the exterior is like wax (*quasi cera*) the interior is like honeycomb (*intus est favus*), revealing its sweetness through beeswax.[26] There are many competitions at work here: the contest of art and art, of art and nature, of art, nature and the rhetorician. And there is also that key quality of wonder, starting with hesitation of mind as to the true nature of things. Materials are not egotistical: to repeat, they provoke doubt and certainty, praise and blame; they enrich, clarify – but they also mystify and insinuate, are moving.

This quality of complex enrichment is experienced first, and arguably best, within the occasion of liturgy and sainthood. Alabaster was used but rarely in English architecture, as on a portal of about 1160–70 at Tutbury Priory; around this time onyx-like columns were used in the cloister at Canterbury Cathedral.[27] The liturgical associations of flesh-like stones, as much as of 'power' materials like porphyry, survived. By 1268 a large onyx rota of highly variegated appearance had been installed at the centre of the cosmati pavement before the high altar of Westminster Abbey (pl. 83), explained shortly afterwards by an inscription as being the archetypal macrocosm, a kind of unformed chaotic *silva*.[28] Henry III had requested that white stone, probably alabaster, be used in this pavement, but none is now to be found.[29] It was here, at the centre of the cosmic progress, that the kings of England were anointed at their coronations: once again, flesh-stone and oil.

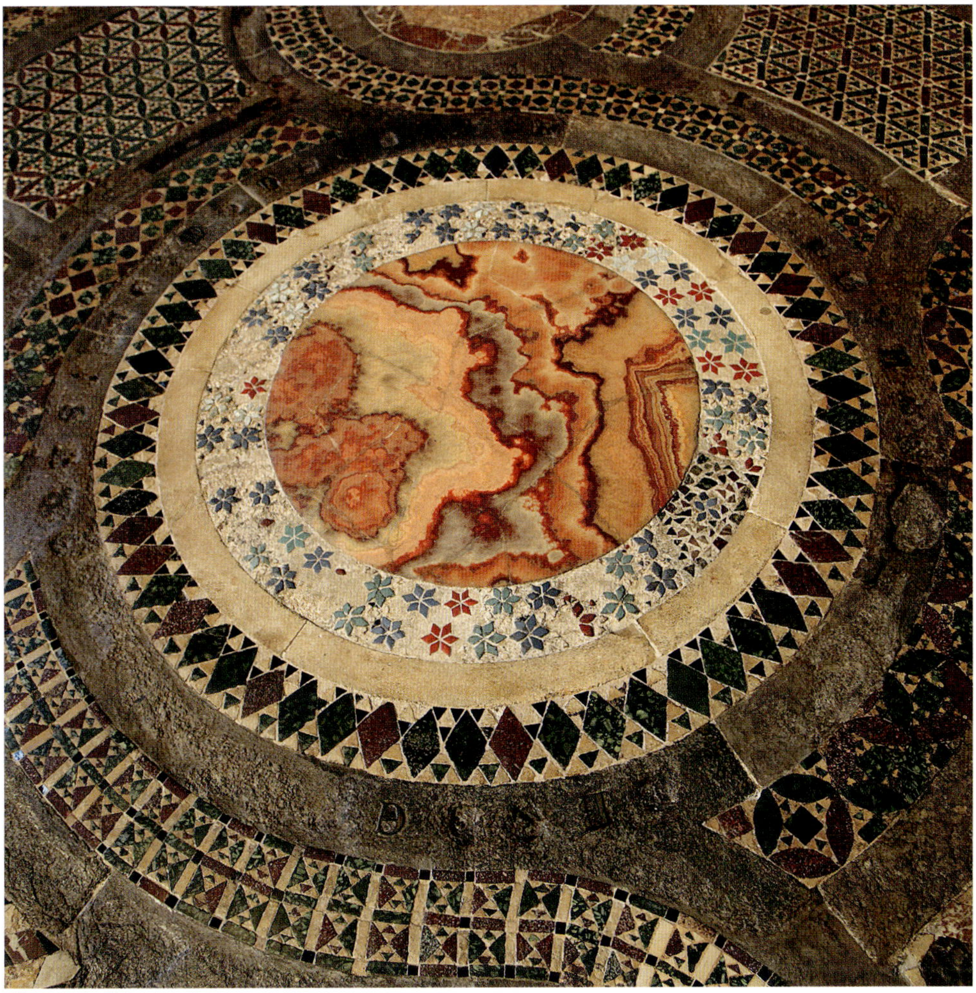

83 Westminster Abbey, Cosmati pavement in sanctuary showing central onyx roundel, blue glass inlays and fragments of inscriptions, the site of royal anointing and coronation, executed 1266–8

By far the most dignified instance, however, of the way materials are illuminated by a backstory provided (as in the Gospels) by the lives and deaths of charismatic people, is yielded by the Trinity Chapel at Canterbury, as rebuilt after 1174 to house the shrine of St Thomas (pl. 84). Canterbury enjoyed no ekphrastic reception at the level of Silentarius or Henry of Avranches. Had it done, what might have emerged would have been not simply the partnership of art, nature and rhetoric but all of these working with theology, exegesis. I have already noted the importance of red and white imagery in the ekphrasis of the ambo and its surroundings in Hagia Sophia: this *venustas*, this emphasis on the beauty and vigour

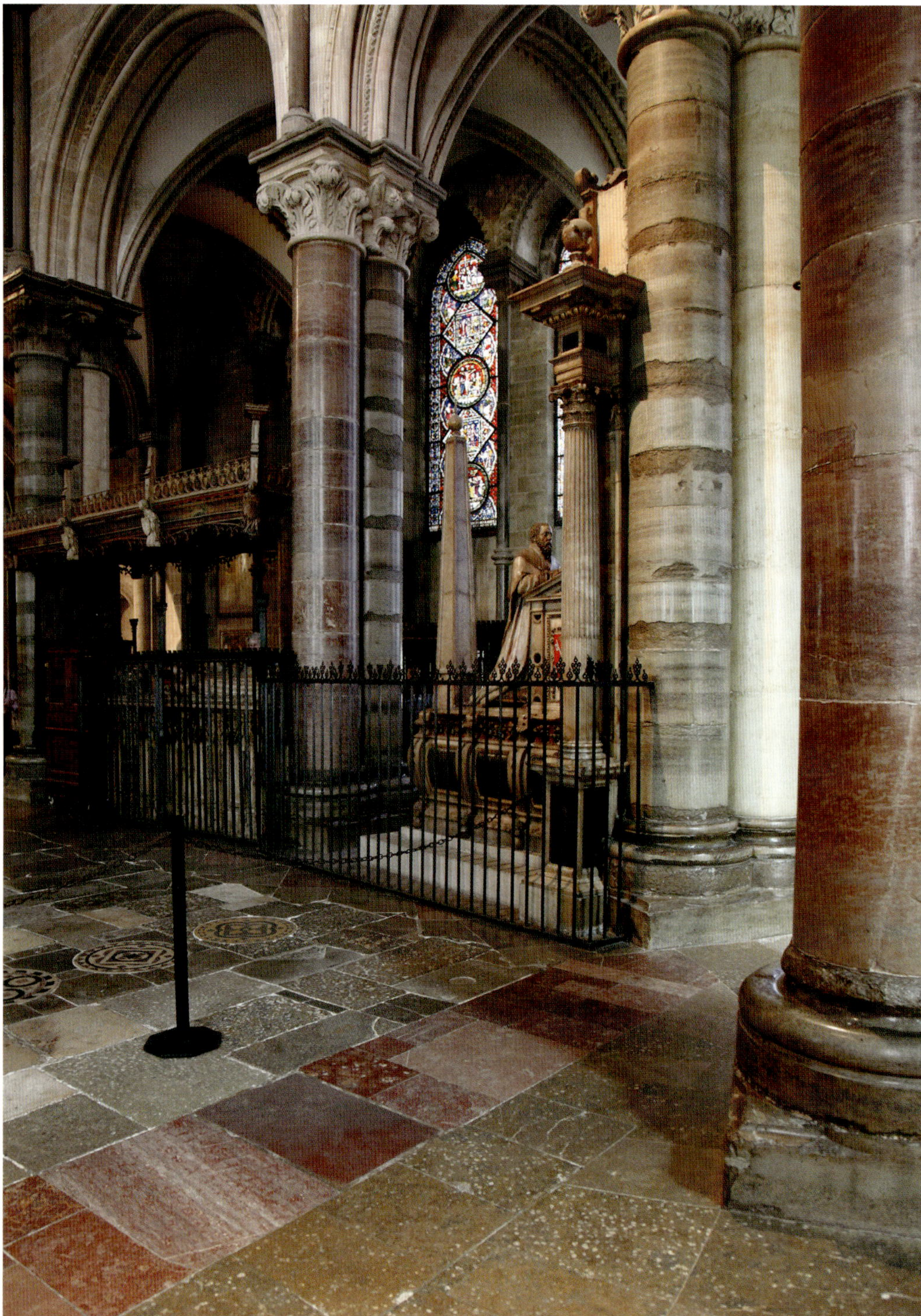

84 Canterbury Cathedral, Trinity Chapel, showing Purbeck, white limestone and pink Belgian marble columns and flooring around the shrine of St Thomas, completed by 1220

of flesh and blood, is a trope of medieval perceptions of images and buildings.[30] When in the 1170s and early 1180s William of Sens or his successor William the Englishman (probably the former) established the supply lines for the marbles used for the flooring and columns of the Trinity Chapel at the Gothic east end, raised up over its vaulted crypt, they turned to English and Continental sources.[31] The coupled columns at the east end are coloured, various, but within that variety lies order. A hard but cloudy, variegated rose-pink marble from what is now modern Belgium covers the pavement area round the site of the shrine of St Thomas. The columns rising from it have a regular scheme of polished stones, using the same rose marble, a smooth creamy-white pelletal limestone and a grey-green Purbeck from Dorset. They are paired differently: to the west are limestone and Purbeck; either side of the shrine Purbeck greets rose marble with the rose on the inside facing the shrine; Purbeck and limestone are repeated, and then the two easternmost piers couple limestone and rose, white and pink-red. Such coloured marble columns remind us more of Apostolic Rome than the new Gothic churches of northern France. Indeed, the thinking here is strikingly independent, but coherent, for actual style is (literally) immaterial. At this spot the white–red coupling is theological, because it incorporates the beautiful sponsorial sentiment in the Song of Songs 5:10: *dilectus meus candidus et rubicundus electus ex milibus*, 'my beloved is white and ruddy, chosen out of thousands'. The elect is St Thomas, and as his hagiographers show in alluding frequently to this image in their accounts of the martyrdom, the red and the white, and the mixing of the two (as in the ekphrasis of Silentarius) signifies his martyrdom and virginity, but more exactly the terrible spilling of his red blood and his white brains in the cathedral in December 1170. The levels of crafting here, material, intellectual, verbal, are astonishing, and while we might think the shift from marble to blood and brains unpleasant, shameless even, we see that mixture and virtuosity of this type are, again, products of moments of intensification. Canterbury actually held a relic of the *alabastrum* of the Magdalen.[32]

At Canterbury, allegory and hagiography together provide a revealing aetiology for the stones in the cathedral, how they came to look like that; but allegory too, as the hagiographers show, is a means of assimilating the horror of martyrdom, rendering significant the arbitrary and disastrous. Through sanctified multi-coloured material, given direction by a great narrative, we celebrate, memorialise and mourn at same time. Alabaster, often mixed aesthetically in colour and surface effect, brings to mind the analogy with skin and especially what lies beneath it, blood and fat, as much as flesh: it can have a waxen soapy look, or be adipose, fatty. Bartholomeus Anglicus notes its veins, its streaked *venustas*.[33] Its sympathy with human remains, with death, is understandable. Because its colours and effects vary, so too do its temperaments. Alabaster, like flesh, has 'complexion', and in this regard differs subtly but significantly from the more homogeneous white marbles used for French royal tomb effigies from the thirteenth century, which are sometimes thought to have provoked

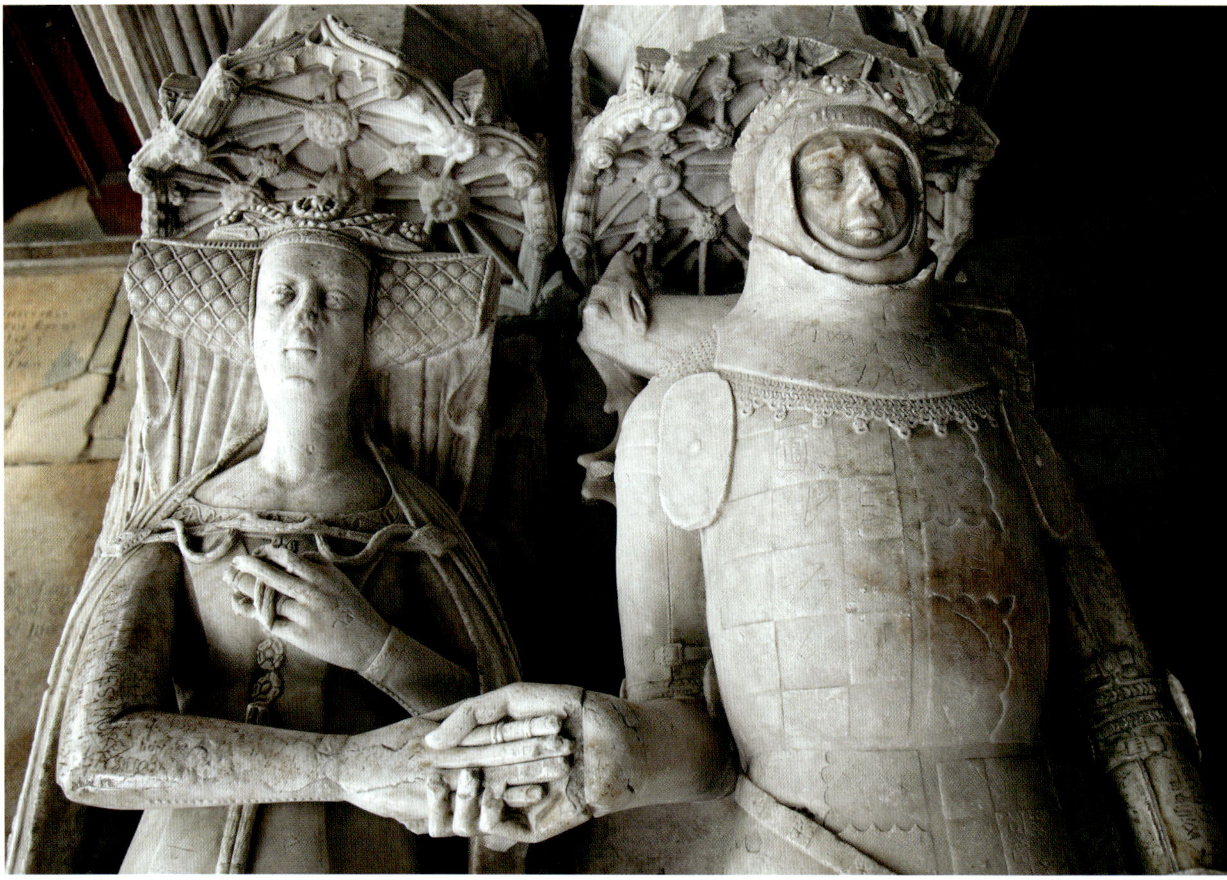

85 Lowick parish church (Northamptonshire), alabaster effigies of Ralph and Katherine Green, 1419, showing variegation of colour

the memorial use of alabaster in England.[34] It is not difficult to see why alabaster was thought superior. Consider the gentle colour variegation of the alabaster effigies made in 1419 of Ralph Green and his wife at Lowick (Northamptonshire). The extant contract for the tomb, to be made by Thomas Prentice and Robert Sutton of Chellaston, specifies that it was to be made of 'the stone called alabaster, good, fine and pure'.[35] In fact, while the effigy of Katherine Green, who commissioned the work, is rendered in carefully chosen, clean white alabaster, her facial features courtly and fresh, that of the armoured Sir Henry, perhaps no less thoughtfully, is made of alabaster flushed with red around his chest and face (pl. 85). He may be the embodiment of choleric Mars, a commonplace of astrology and medicine.

In England as on the Continent, 'white virgins' made of alabaster (pl. 86; see also pl. 52) or marble enjoyed particular popularity in the fourteenth century possibly because, as

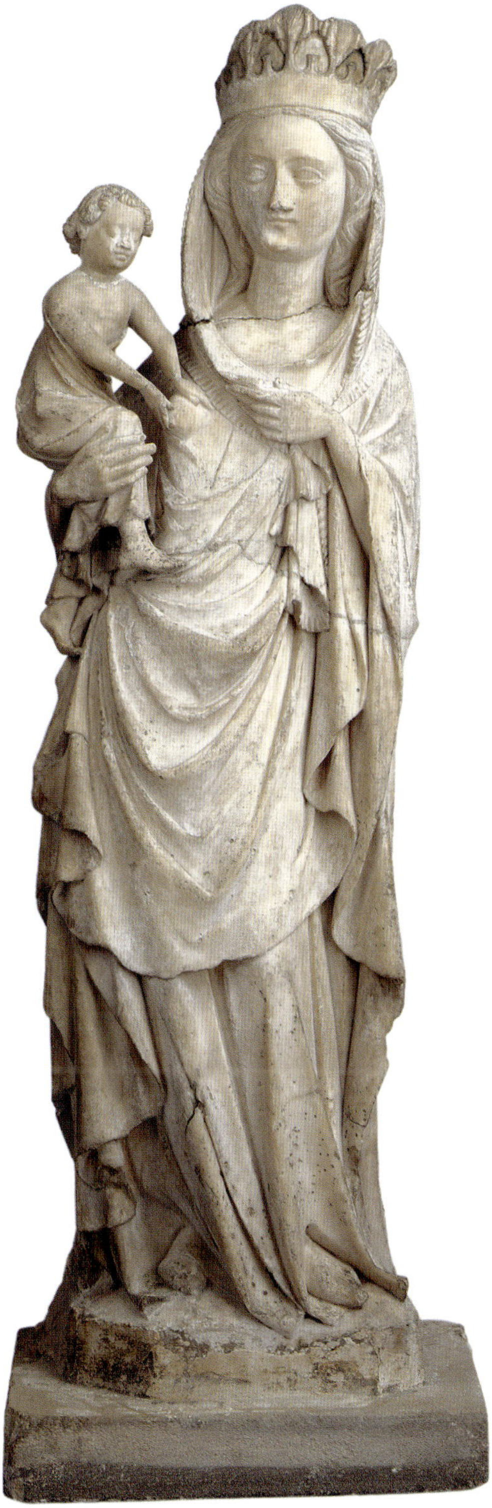

86 Virgin and Child from Flawford parish church (Nottinghamshire), alabaster, third quarter fourteenth century (Nottingham Castle Museum, no. 08-146)

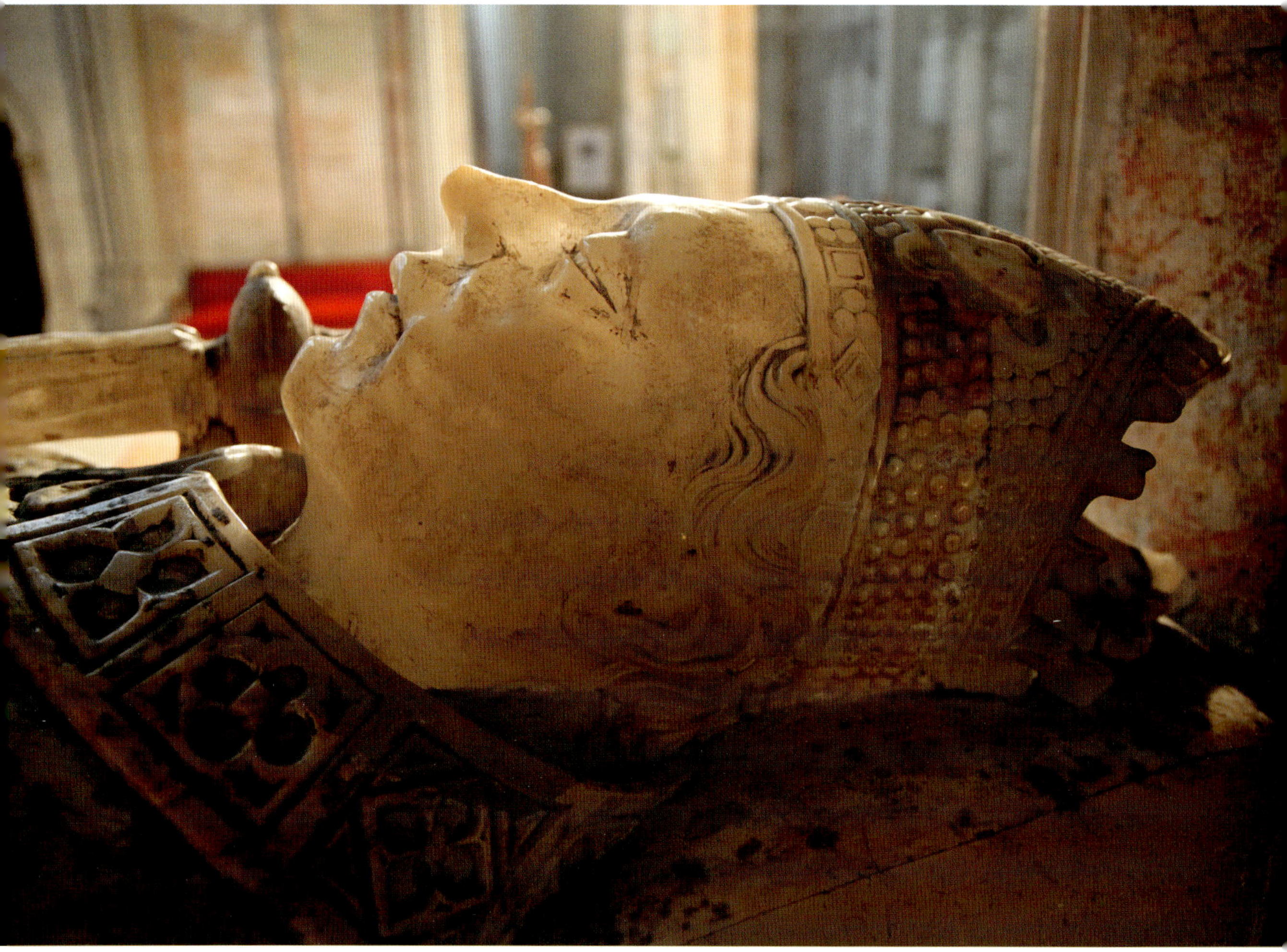

87 Carcassonne, church of St Nazaire (Aude), backlit alabaster effigy of Géraud du Puy, Bishop of Carcassonne (d. 1420)

Richard Marks suggests, they contrasted with the brilliant polychromy of wood or stone statues then in vogue: 'complexion' became a form of *oppositio*, or enjoyable contrast.[36] Alabaster is not necessarily a cheering material: it also possesses a certain melancholy, pure yet sullied, perfect yet imperfect, a metaphor for flesh and the Incarnation itself.[37] It exemplifies the aesthetic of purity and 'cleanness' (itself complex) celebrated in later medieval English writing, as in the *Pearl* manuscript.[38] Alabaster sets a mood and its inability to take sharp detail establishes a certain distance. Its translucency, like a hand held up to a bright light, can be seen in the glowing effigy of Géraud du Puy, Bishop of Carcassonne (d. 1420; pl. 87), for alabaster has a history in France as well as England. Wherever it is to be found, alabaster exemplifies soft, not hard, power; the power of suggestion, not hard unarguable dominance or identity. By association its poetics are those of loss, delicacy and vulnerability, withdrawal rather than domination. The point is that mood always shifts; it is an attribute, because what sanctifies alabaster is not just its powers of contrast with other materials but its backstory, what it represents. There are no innocent materials, for they all point backwards (temporally) and beyond (metaphysically), and their agency is always layered, complex, resistant and compromised.

In short, the notion that medieval materiality is 'overt', 'pregnant with significance', 'per se living' and that materials signify without audiences, as it were on their own behalf, is open to the charges of materialist essentialism, blurring or conflating person, relic and image and overlooking the different significatory and relational powers and histories of actual materials, their differing poetics. In the domain of human artifice, in contrast, there has seldom if ever been a domain of innocent or sincere materiality, an idea owed more, as I have already suggested, to nineteenth-century than medieval aesthetics. It was embedded in later twentieth-century art history by the imperatives of some forms of anthropology which in effect opened a divide between a pre-rationalist, pre-modern 'savage' mindset – Eco's 'shaggy' Middle Ages – and a modern rationalist mindset. This divide is uncharacteristic of the rhetorical basis of medieval art, which always tended to connect *ars* and *materia*, the formal and the material causes, not divide them.

TACT

Materiality studies necessarily entail a view of the senses because different materials are experienced in different ways, so our discussion seems at first sight to involve some sort of *paragone* or debate about their relative importance. The dominant theoretical preoccupation of the last generation of study has undoubtedly concerned sight and visuality, including such distancing mechanisms as the 'gaze'.[39] The relatively new interest in the oral senses and especially touch goes hand in hand with the direct experientiality implicit in materiality study, a getting to grips (at least in theory) with the reality of stuff, not abstraction.[40] Sight as the master sense, the sense of rationality, is being challenged by means of a greater emphasis on the totality of bodily perception. Eco-criticism is also lending weight to this recalibration by advancing the view that materials, natural materials that is, possess agency, a sort of vitality in themselves.[41]

But, as recent discussions of the role of the senses have tended to stress, the senses are not just in debate but in co-operation: for everything perceived by sight, something is also touched, heard, tasted and smelled. The *paragone* or contest of the senses and their related

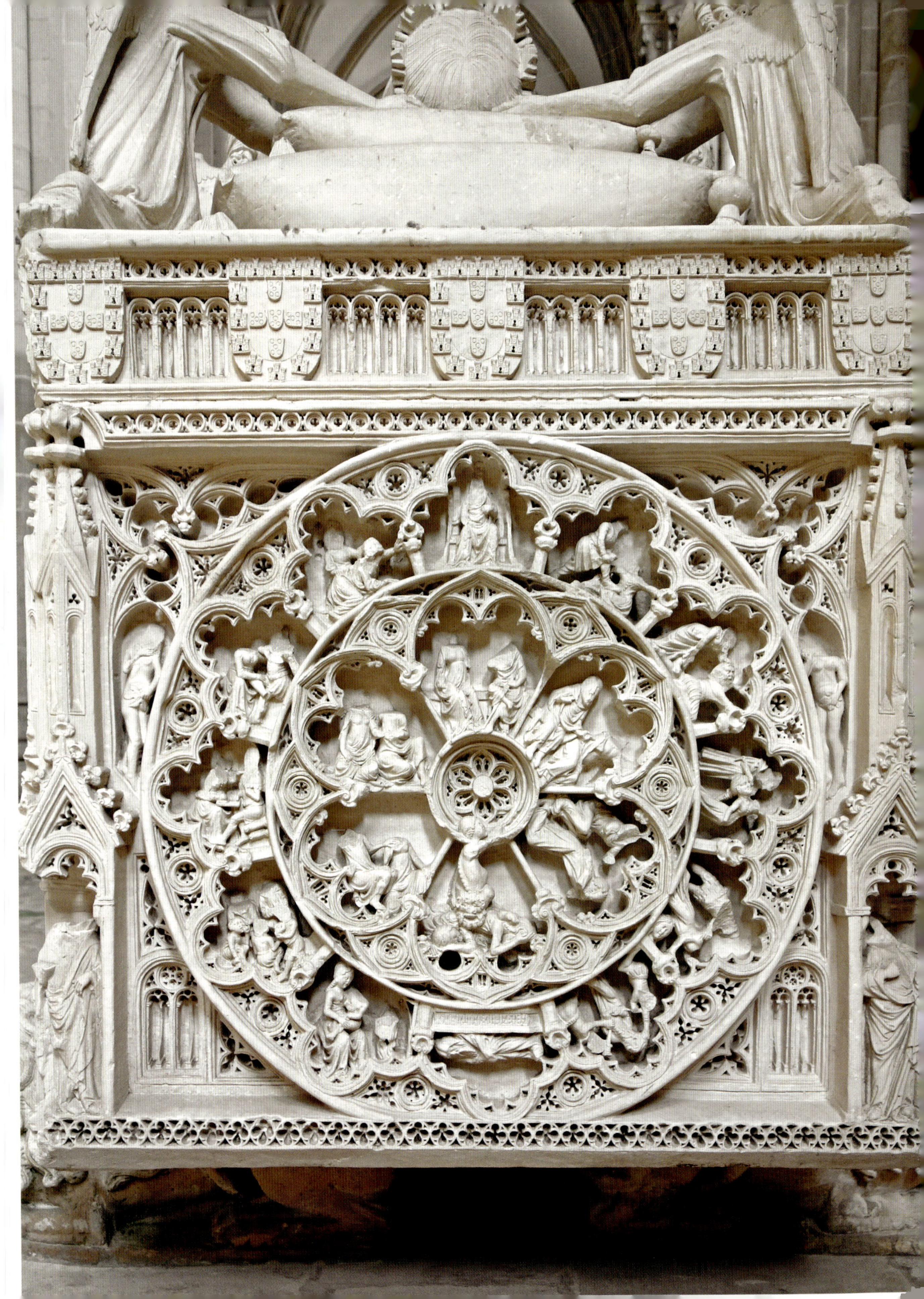

6

THE WILD AND THE DEAD

In the first part of this study I made a case for understanding the role of stone portal sculpture primarily in the public domain of monumentality, rather than in the domain of personal response. In this section, I have pondered sculpture in media more often seen as the domain of the interior both physically and psychologically, in order to understand the proper place of materiality within the forces of calculated restraint and balance which were as central to medieval art-making as they were to medieval health and ethics. Here the importance of human agency via craft seems to me inescapable. The term 'craft', which I understand in the light of poetic reasoning, imagination and physical art production and self-management in all its forms, lies at the centre of my aim of understanding such arts in their human perspective. My final keyword, which I use to encapsulate notions of self-management, is the Greek *askesis*, literally 'exercise', a word signalling self-discipline, self-control, exercise, from which we derive the term 'ascetic'. We generally connect asceticism with off-puttingly severe, inimitable, religious practices, body and spiritual. There have always been those who stand outside public life: they might be the outlandish religious hermit in the woods or the Romantic artist in his garret occupying and controlling the territory of Art. I am not concerned with these special zones of egocentrism. My preoccupation is with the idea that artefactual invention involves limitation as the basis of realisation of the self, or of things; askesis, I suggest, is a generally distributed principle of life public and private, a thing to be admired and feared, but also something fundamental to making.[1] I propose finally to consider this idea in terms of the works of Nature and of Death.

89 Cistercian monastery of Alcobaça (Portugal), tomb of King Pedro I (detail of pl. 113)

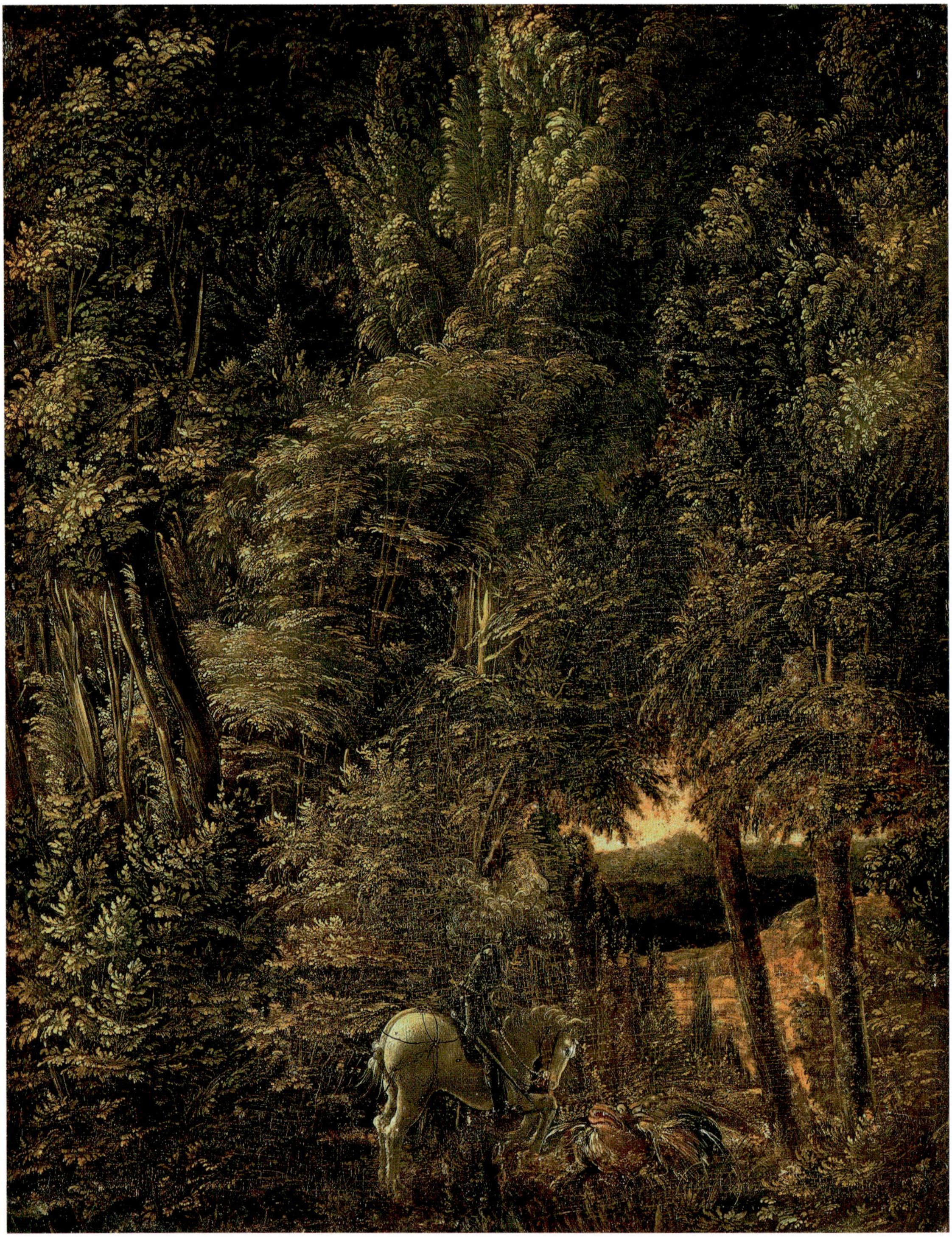

90 Albrecht Altdorfer, *St George and the Dragon*, 1510 (Munich, Alte Pinakothek)

At the heart of one of the most powerful Romantic concepts of Gothic art and architecture is the idea that Gothic is a style of 'becoming' rather than 'being'; that rather than being a style of perfected, unalterable and unaltering beauty like Classicism, it is a style if not exactly of beauty, then at least of action, of dynamic change, like a natural thing urging towards self-realisation. This concept is often attributed to the great Swiss formalist art historian Heinrich Wölfflin.[2] But its roots extend even beyond the sublime of the poet Goethe, who when writing on German architecture in 1772 saw in Gothic architecture the urge to 'build toward heaven ... like a sublimely towering, wide-spreading tree of God which, with its thousand branches, millions of twigs and leaves more numerous than the sands of the sea, proclaims to the surrounding country the glory of its master, the Lord'.[3] The forest had for some time been an image for the inner imperative of Gothic architecture (pl. 90). In thought, the basis of all such notions of becoming lies in the distinction drawn in Plato's *Timaeus* between being and becoming, intelligible firm knowledge and shifting opinion; it was God who implanted intelligence into the created world and who as maker, father and builder coaxed order out of chaos.[4] The *Timaeus* was the only work of Plato known directly in the Middle Ages.

It was not lost on ancient and medieval conceptions of nature that creation itself was in a constant state of becoming, always at risk of reversion into primordial imbalance, disorder and decay. The whole thing was like some marvellous balancing act, held delicately together in equilibrium, always at risk, its mixtures and components poised in everlasting but perilous suspense. That system's microcosm, the human body as envisaged by Plato, Aristotle, the Stoics, Galen and medieval physicians, was also a shifting unstable compound, tensive in nature, viscous and humoural, needing balance.[5] The humoural character of medieval aesthetics allows us to understand what style and ornament are – not superficial things but ways in which outward appearances, surfaces, were suffused connectedly from within, their style, elegance, colour and working all indicative of inner ordering.[6] This is why surfaces are eloquent things and why medieval, and especially Gothic, art could use the natural imagery of growth, secretion and change persuasively, becoming, as Michael Camille put it, part of 'an integrated myth of meaning in the elaboration of its structure'.[7] Vigour, the natural vigour of stuff and of human experience, is a keynote. The medieval imaginary accepted that such things as stones possessed *virtus*, power, and that natural things could morph and shape-shift, a truth as apparent in the understanding of the lability of late medieval Gothic architecture as of the Green Man (pl. 91).[8] This too the crafter had to cope with and put to good use, for materials, as noted, have (metaphorically speaking) a 'character': they urge, tend and fight – and the artisan duly urges, tends and fights back. If they lost, the Wild could easily become the Dead. Natural science, art and ethics all acknowledged

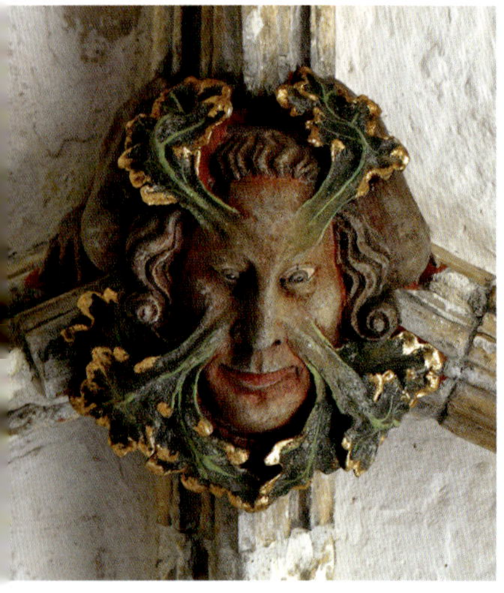

91 Norwich Cathedral, east walk cloister boss with Green Man, paintwork modern, 1297–1325

that the world urges and pushes, strains towards flourishing, pleasure and death, risking excess and vice: and it was through restraint and discipline – through askesis – that rebalancing was sought and found. These necessary and health-giving constraints entailed effort, willed mastery (*enkrasia*) and inevitably difficulty – an uplifting, even heroic, concept in the verbal and non-verbal arts. The 'ascetic imperative', as Geoffrey Galt Harpham argued, may be understood as a generalised principle in this dynamic.[9]

We can understand this kind of tempering of stuff involved in these processes by thinking of tending and turning, in the sense of turning on a lathe. For Aristotle, as for Aquinas, the virtue of temperance, *temperantia* – the regulation of appetite, pleasure – governs the sense of touch, for touch, along with taste and smell, is the sense nearest the pleasures of animals and thus most needing to be regulated: what makes humans human is the tempering of such appetite by reason.[10] Temperance had wide practical and ethical purchase. It required getting things back to a balanced state, back into proportion – *proporcioun* and *mesure* as understood in the previous chapter. The notion of a medium, that which stands mid-way between things in a combination or blend – and which is also a thing in itself – is useful here. In the visual crafts, we encounter a substance that blends and binds together pigments into a productive and correctly balanced state, namely tempera. We speak of the tempering of steel, and indeed of temperament in the tuning of a musical instrument, producing a satisfying concord – the 'well-tempered clavier'. That we encounter ill-tempered human beings goes without saying. The purpose of tempering is harmony and therefore an experience, sensory and rational, of rightness and well-being – that practical everyday rightness which makes life livable and which is the objective of craft as much as of medicine. In regard to this objective, crafting and tempering are essentially social or cenobitic in nature, aimed at attaining that which is generally agreeable and imitable, as in an organised monastic community.[11] The greater extremes of asceticism are eremitical, asocial and hermit-like, admirable but not agreeable or so readily imitable or imitated.

To tend to something is, so to speak, to encourage through care, even 'tough love'. It is the proper direction of the will or desire of someone or something (the term 'tend' is related to the group of words also including 'intention'). It carries with it the idea of tempering and controlling the desire or natural inward movement of a thing, as perhaps with the inherent tendencies or 'character' of ivory or wood that need cutting or carving.[12] The Romans understood that while we end in a tomb, we pass pleasurable life in gardens real or imaginary: cultivation – itself a powerful metaphor – provided the ancient and medieval world with a useful body of concepts for shaping and directing things, as did the image of building and architecture. Through their skills and methods, the gardener, woodsman or farmer allied utility with beauty. They understood the *virtus* of the natural world and that things were divided, approximately, into the wild and the tamed. In his *Historia Naturalis* (16.78) Pliny the Elder classified two kinds of trees – wild ones, *silvestres*, and kindly or civilised ones, *urbani*.[13] For Cicero the difference between the rustic, *sermo rusticus*, and the urbane, *sermo urbanus*, was as much a register of differences of speech, of social cultivation.[14] Roughness or *asperitas* was a quality of style to be smoothed out unless it served a purpose, as it does in the case of some carved imagery.[15] Our term 'rude' still signifies both impoliteness and something unworked. These terms of civility, language or style are relational. They are also processual, embodying a narrative, because tending and tempering change this into that.

Quintilian, the rhetorician who vividly bridges the art–language divide, writes of the difficulties of writing itself, but in terms of the analogy with cultivation. In composition he says that we can, if we wish, imprudently rush a text out, so creating a mass of unformed 'raw material': for this he uses the term *silva*, alluding to abundant thickets of woodland, that which is always becoming but is not fully realised. But a better way is to plan things with due care (*cura*) and to carve them into shape (his word is *caelandum*) only in a finishing or polishing process.[16] Beauty and good order have utility, the expression of which is the orderly planting of fruit trees in straight lines according to a formal *dispositio*, as well as their vigorous but judicious cutting back to prevent them running off or bolting.[17] The point is that we discipline, prune, things in order not simply that they may display but that they will flourish better and so be useful. The Latin verb *putare* includes the senses of pruning, cleansing, reckoning and thinking. So things should be correct, and that correctness turns frequently on nature's management and self-management. For instance, in Book Three of his influential work on the nature of learning, *De Nuptiis Philologiae et Mercurii* (3.224), Martianus Capella in the fifth century presents the figure of Grammar taking her pruning knife out of a toolbox to excise faults of pronunciation in the young.[18]

Central to this preoccupation, carried over into the Middle Ages, was the belief that artifice is akin to Nature not so much in regard to similitude, mimesis, but processually, in regard to the actual operations of Nature 'naturing', *natura naturans*.[19] Natural and crafted things are both fashioned from primary matter, the matter of the cosmos which Aristotle identified by using a word for wood, *hyle*.[20] *Hyle* is that out of which things are 'realised' either in nature (*physis*) or art (*techne*). Primary 'stuff' is conceivable as a forest prior to its ordering and tending. According to Cicero's *De Inventione* (1.2.2–3) the process of ordering and tending, of cultivating and civilising, is essentially *eloquent*: originally, humans were persuaded or coaxed into a state of cultivation.[21] In the fourth-century commentary on the *Timaeus* by Calcidius, which he also translated into Latin – the version usually known in the high Middle Ages – *hyle*, now called by the Latin word for trees, foliage or forest, *silva*, is the same thing as primordial chaos. This *silva* is a complex composite which could be differentiated, coaxed out, into figures (*figurae*) and modes, which are likened to branches and twigs.[22] It needed form; but equally, form needed it.

Calcidius's notion of *silva* as something which, as Cicero's earlier thinking seems to suggest, could be realised in the arts as in nature, was itself to branch out and flourish in the medieval period, as in King Alfred's preface to Augustine's *Soliloquies*, Remigius of Auxerre's commentary on *De Nuptiis Philologiae et Mercurii* and in the well-known work of the aptly named Bernardus Silvestris (*c.*1098–1153), the *Cosmographia.*[23] Bernardus allows Nature to speak of Silva's yearning in her roughness for a tempering power, for cultivation.[24] His word for rough is *hispida*, a term belonging to a word group including *hirtus* and *hirsutus*, meaning shaggy or hairy.[25] Elsewhere Bernardus considers Silva to be both *carens*, 'caring', and *asper*, 'rough'. So Silva is at once rough, many-branched and shaggy: indeed the French *sauvage*, Castilian *salvaje* and Italian *selvaggio* all follow from the term *silva*.[26] We can see how these fundamental notions of matter and becoming have an aesthetic character, a style, which might prove suggestive, especially to those interested in forests and cultivation, cutting and carving.

CULTIVATION: STONE AND WOOD

In writing earlier about the amazing ambivalences of Romanesque sculpted detailing, I noted that it is more open to the game of 'seeing as' than Gothic detailing: we might for instance see the extraordinary scalloped side-shafts of the Apocalypse portal at Moissac as jaw-like, fearsome (see pl. 4). Yet, stricter though Gothic formal language tends to be, it is not for that reason devoid of wit. Wit is often the undoing of expectation, what I have described elsewhere as the 'pleasure of unruling', and it is a fundamental aspect of Gothic visual play.[27] For various forms of gaming or *ludus* to work, some stability must first be in place. Take witty play about the relation of wood and stone. One such is found in the porch of the parish church built around 1170 at Vermenton (pl. 92) where a solid stone Gothic pier has shafts set into its corners carved with woody and gnarly knots as if with an axe not a chisel; the remains of the very finely carved choir enclosure of the priory of Souvigny dating to the 1160s contrast budding shafts and metalwork-derived patterns (pl. 93).[28] The discourse of architectural improvement and upgrading by patrons was already old, indeed ancient, yet at Vermenton the smoothness of Gothic artifice is deliberately teased by a regress to *silva* in a way that resurfaced in late medieval Germany and Iberia. Ambivalence is key: are such 'wooden' shafts a stupid lapse, or a conscious return to virtuous simplicity?

Play of this sort is in fact unusual in the Anglo-French domain of architectural sculpture, where smooth flowing tracery was a fundamental dynamic of invention. In England,

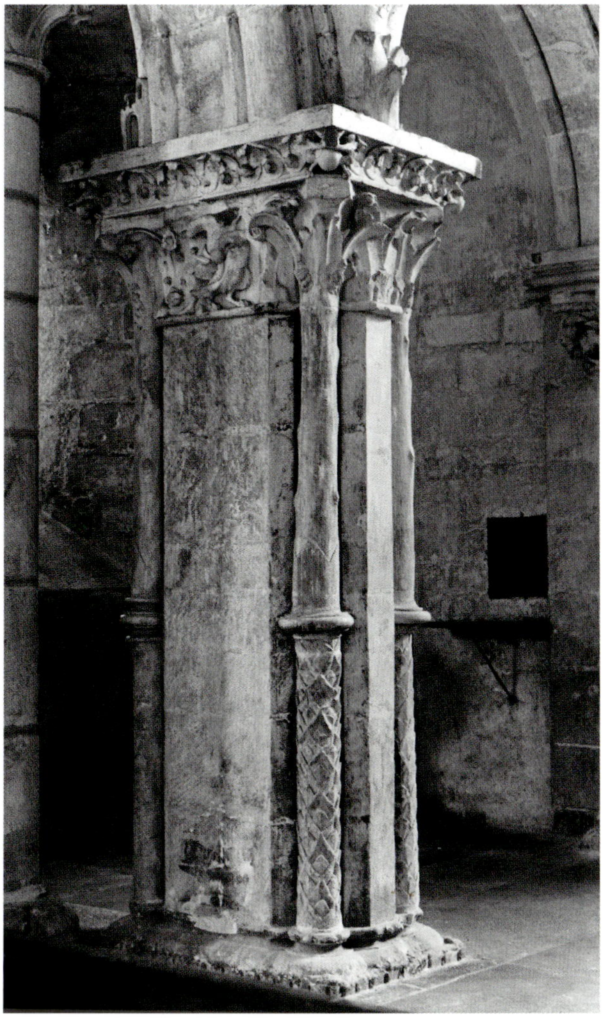

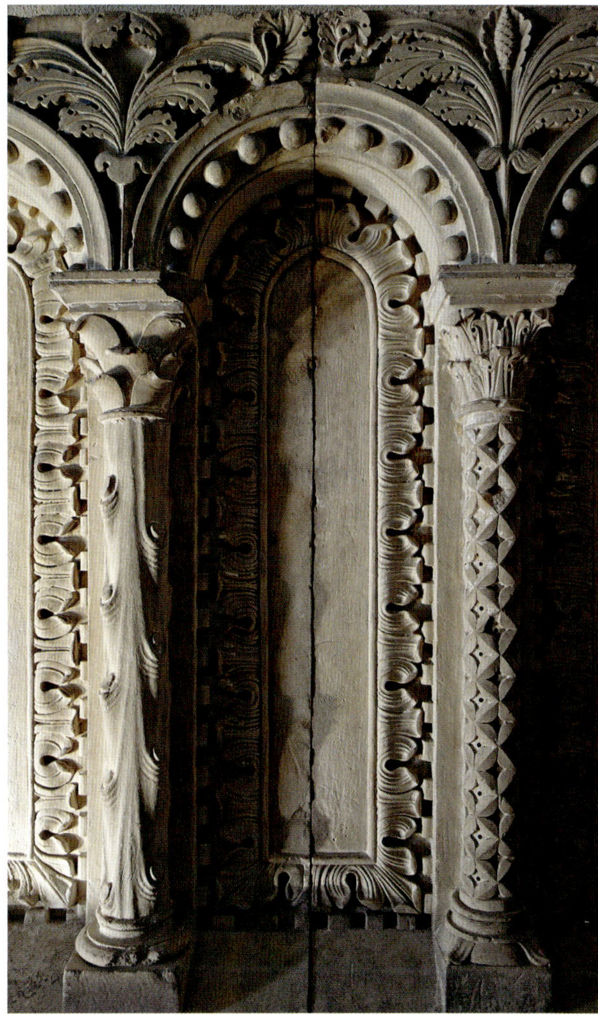

92 Vermenton parish church (Yonne), pier, about 1170

93 Souvigny (Alier), priory church, arcading probably from choir enclosure, third quarter twelfth century

Gothic sculptural practice tended to favour not the illusion of roughness of the sort at Vermenton, but the treatment of leaves and other growing stuff as something imbued with a powerful inner energy which still insisted on its own artificiality. The best examples of this are English so-called 'stiff-leaf' foliage capitals and the extraordinary budding vertical shafts, probably developed from metalwork or the frames of stained-glass windows, which occur from around 1200 at Lincoln (see pl. 48), Ely, St Albans, Peterborough and Wells (see

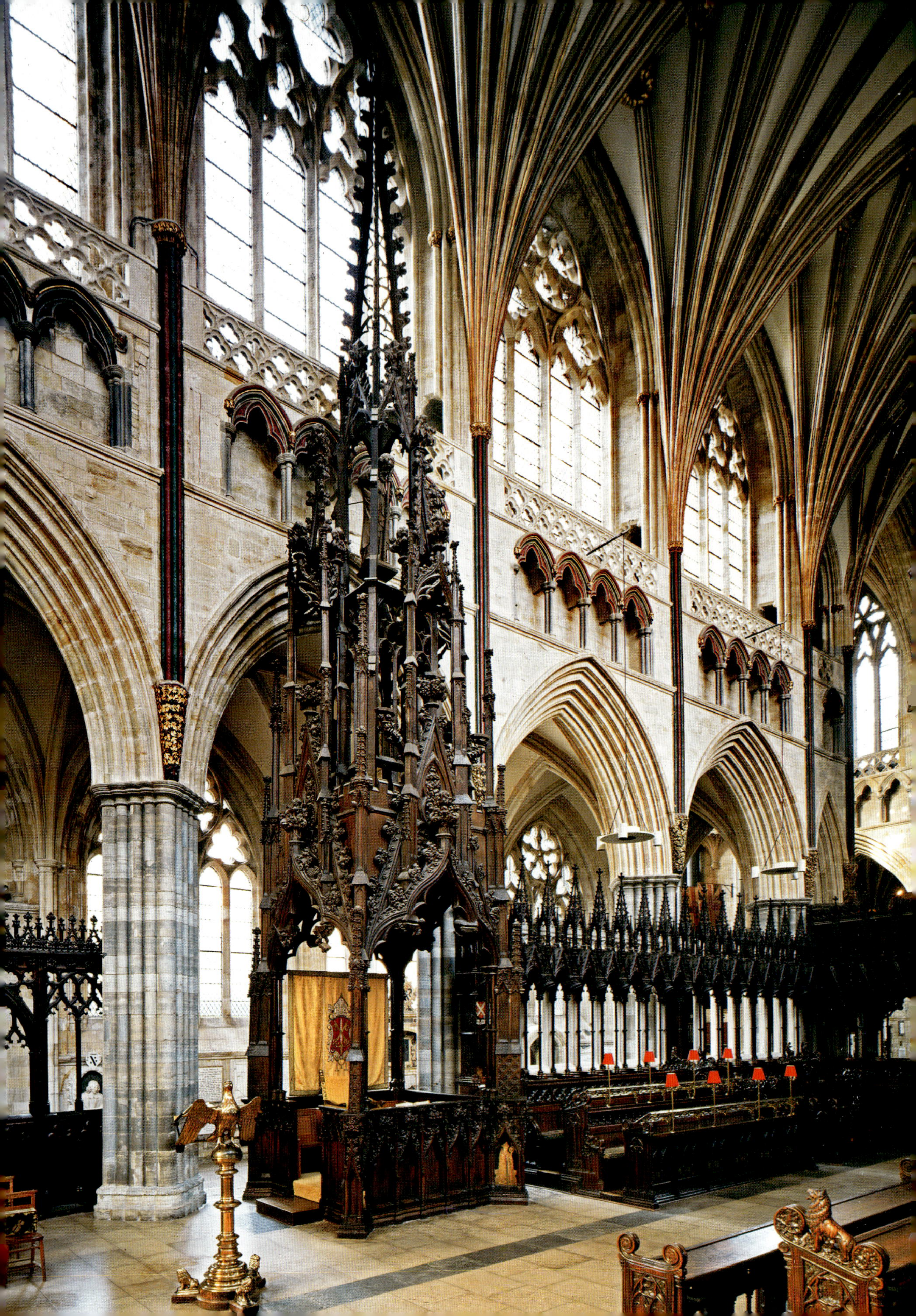

pl. 18) and, in Norway, at Trondheim.[29] The use of these bud-like *gemmae*, foliage 'jewels', on crosses made in the Anglo-Scandinavian domain, we saw earlier, makes perfect theological and imaginative sense (see pl. 62). Foliage in these cases is something wrought rather than strictly mimetic, thereby playing on the relation of the permanent and the impermanent, the precious and base. Within a generation, by the 1240s or so, the English were picking up on the new French method of actually reproducing natural leaf-forms (see pl. 44).[30]

The English, like the French, seem more usually to have taken a comparatively strict view of the boundary between such buds and leaves and the actual tracery lines of architecture. When, in a brilliant insight, Jean Bony pointed to carpentry as a stimulus to English architectural innovation in stone, his objective was to consider structural techniques, technical and visual leaps of the imagination, as much as surface effects.[31] The point is that one can leap both ways. English carvers excelled in a class of objects that seems to test the boundaries between these materials. The best instances are spectacular fourteenth-century carved wooden liturgical furnishings such as the bishop's throne at Exeter Cathedral (pl. 94), in manufacture in the second decade of the century, and the extraordinary sequence of English choir stalls which followed, culminating in the quasi-Flamboyant canopies at Lancaster Priory in the 1340s (pl. 95).[32] In all these cases the imaginary is unquestionably architectural, yet the notion of what architecture can do in different media and at different scales is constantly challenged. These thrones and stalls seem to realise things denied in theory to the weight, granular structure and brittleness of the freestones used by masons. That the masons who produced exceptional feats of risky undercutting and micro-carving at Lincoln or Ely (see pl. 79) were responding to some sort of challenge seems obvious: as Ernst Gombrich in his study of ornament remarks of such feats as the Lancaster stalls, 'the more recalcitrant the material the greater the triumph'.[33]

And yet even at its most luxuriant, English (and ultimately Anglo-Norman) practice in wood or stone was usually to keep the lines of tracery articulating a structure as clean, smooth, ultimately manufactured things, architectural lines not natural lines. This was certainly true of the elaborate vaulting systems in which the English excelled.[34] Where French architects for the whole of the Middle Ages preferred relatively simple quadripartite vaults with few keystones or bosses, in the course of the thirteenth and fourteenth centuries the English developed vaults of prodigious, even breathtaking complexity, consisting of multiple ribs whose intersections burst out into carved bosses of sometimes astonishing beauty, such as those in the aisles of the Angel Choir at Lincoln (pl. 96 and see pl. 48).[35] That such displays of ribs and carved bosses had become a matter of active pride for patrons is shown by the unfolding vista of bosses in the cloister of Norwich Cathedral whose installation began in the first quarter of the fourteenth century, and which eventually extended to the entire cathedral interior like a thousand swallows' nests.[36] The Norwich cloister bosses inserted in the final campaigns of work in the early fifteenth century are among the

94 Exeter Cathedral, choir, with bishop's throne begun in 1313 and completed early 1320s

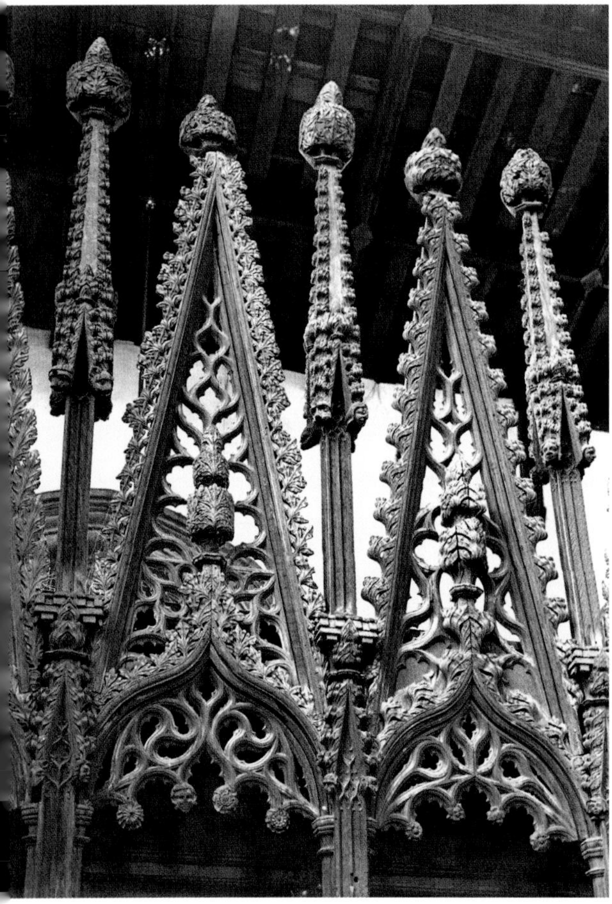

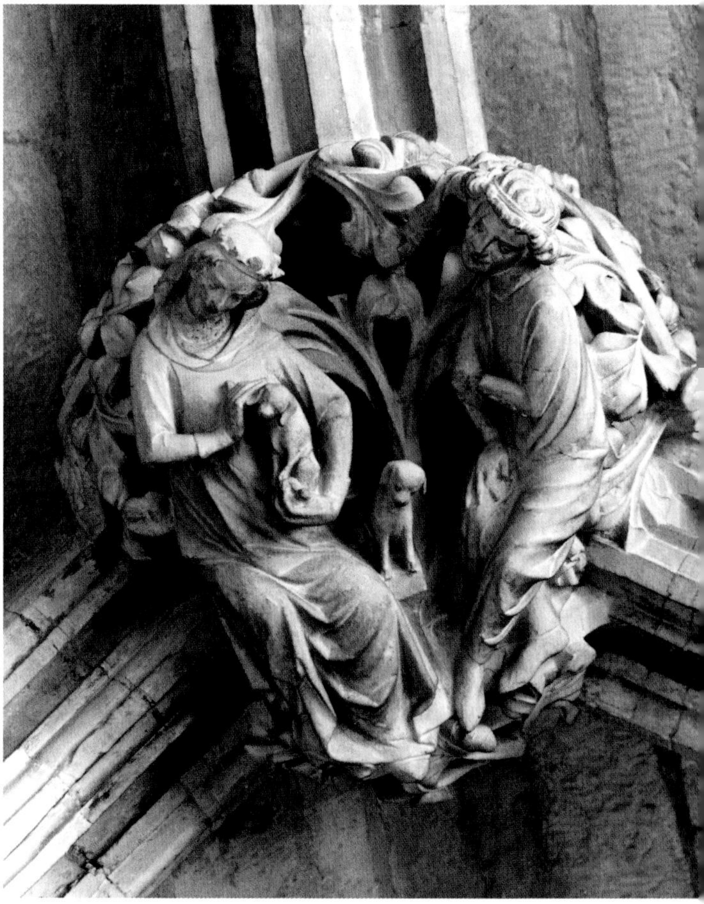

95 Lancaster Priory (Lancashire), choir stall canopies, oak, 1340s

96 Lincoln Cathedral, south choir aisle boss showing Bathsheba and companion, about 1260

most ingenious and entertaining displays of sculptural space ever envisaged in medieval art (pl. 97). Yet English and French vault manufacture tended not to encourage foliage to burst out and alter the appearance of vault ribs, as if from within. In England, such bosses, little knots or pressure-points of eloquence, always served a discursive function, but a function which knew its place.

In other media, however, the English, alert as always to the metaphorical power of nature, showed that the shaggy and rough aesthetic of *silva* could lend bite to the critique of the smooth vanity of academic reasoning. Such is clearly the message of the magnificent figure of the *pilosus*, the hairy man, John the Baptist (Matthew 3:4; pl. 98), added around 1340 at the front of a very academic book owned by St Augustine's Abbey, Canterbury (British Library,

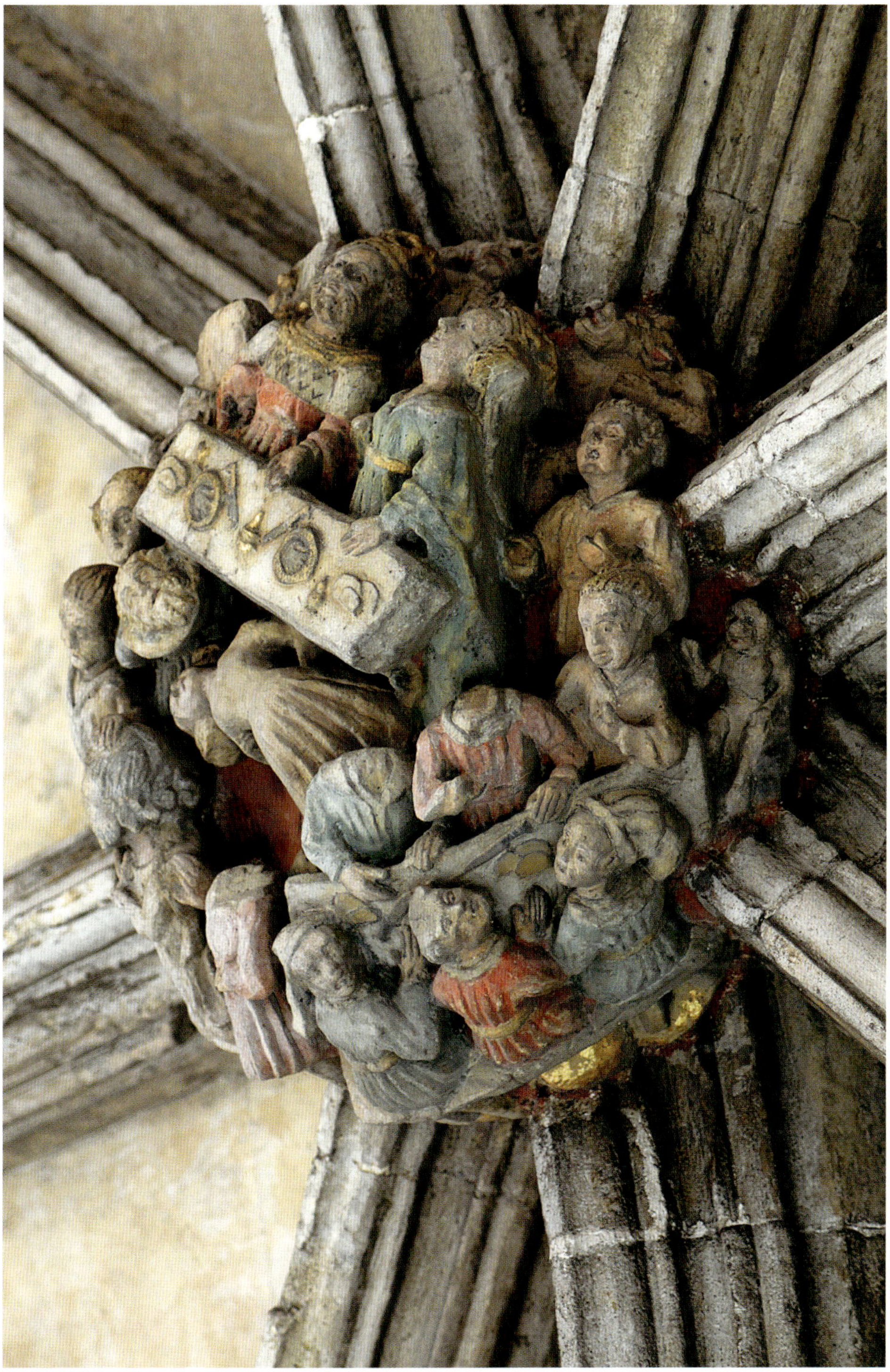

97 Norwich Cathedral, north walk cloister boss, 1420s, showing the Feast of Herod with Salome and the head of St John the Baptist next to the top table. Paintwork modern. Unlike the Green Man in pl. 91, this complex boss is conceived for multiple viewing points.

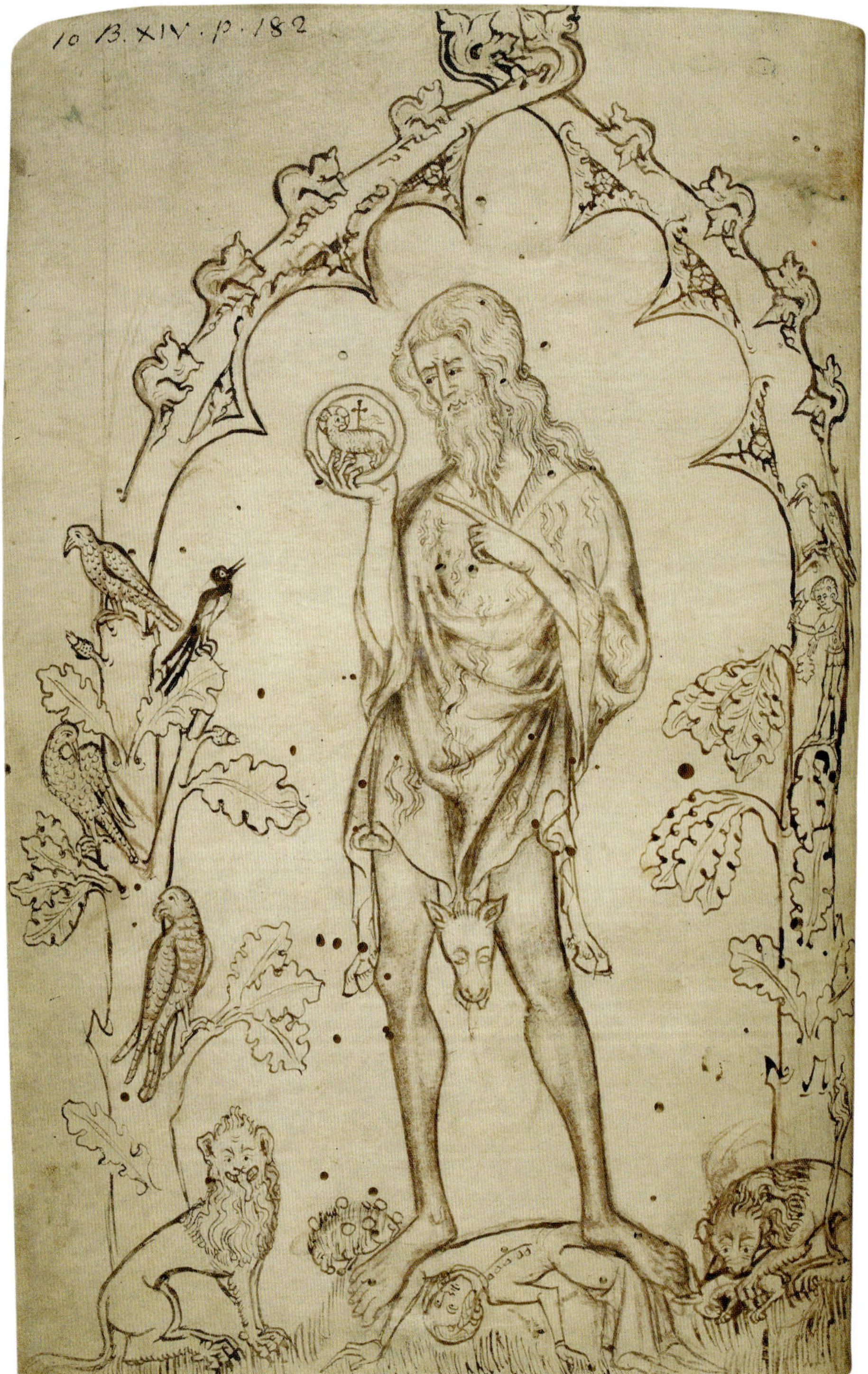

98 St John the Baptist in bower with Salome at his feet, *Summa* of John of Dumbleton, about 1340 (British Library, Ms Royal 10.B.XIV, fol. 3v)

Ms Royal 10.B.XIV, fol. 3v), John of Dumbleton's *Summa*.[37] John of Dumbleton (d. *c.*1349), an Oxford logician and mathematician, was known as one of the 'calculators' favouring rigorous logical disputation.[38] The Baptist's rough wooden bower and camel-hair shirt may well be contrarian ripostes to the vanities of scholastic *a priori* reasoning, as opposed to the asperity and practicality of faith and devotion: presumably the drawing was added as an anti-intellectualist caution for the monks of St Augustine's.[39] The theme of the simplicity of the ancients versus the luxuries of the moderns was Stoic or Senecan in origin, and it had already been turned to new use in the critique of the logic-chopping of scholasticism as opposed to the old-fashioned eloquence of rougher but tougher ages past.[40] So here once again is a form of *oppositio*. In the drawing, St John stands beneath a Gothic arch made of two flexed oak trees, overlapping at the top while yielding crockets above and cusps within; below, it sprouts oak leaves and is inhabited by splendid birds and savage beasts. To the right a tiny woodsman lays the axe to the branches (Matthew 3:10). The seductive power of wordly vanities such as logic is embodied in the tumbling figure of Salome pinned beneath John's feet. The image as a whole has punch and rudeness. An equivalent, if slightly less rustic, St John is sculpted on the grand scale with his oak tree and axe on the interior west end of Reims Cathedral.[41] Our figure's bower unintentionally anticipates the sentiments attributed to Raphael, based on Tacitus and Vitruvius, that the barbarians made huts from trees and branches bent over to form pointed arches when tied together: the picturesque hut of the eighteenth century, a creation of this imaginary, awaits.[42] This remarkable English instance shows that the relation of wood and stone and roughness and smoothness was 'good to think with', and already embedded within the style and body of practices later known as 'Gothic'. Nor, in either the fourteenth or the fifteenth century, was it solely German, as is shown by the extraordinary imitation of forest, wood and garden effects inhabited by full-scale wild men on the portal facade of the Colegio de San Gregorio at Valladolid (pls 99 and 100), of the late 1480s and 90s, described by Pereda as 'a type of vegetal altarpiece': here again, there is a quasi-utopian play with the notion of a prelapsarian state of technological innocence.[43] Medieval art never disappoints in its capacity to produce the weird, one-off wonder.

From a modern German perspective, culture itself either represented the fundamental life-blood of a people or the end result of a process of cultivation. Perhaps the latter was closer to the classical and medieval model. It is of interest that the term *colo*, *cultus*, 'cultivated', was etymologically connected to the term *color* in such a way as to link the eloquent crafting of things, and so aesthetic experience, with cultivation.[44] Yet the idea of an essential identity, and a myth of origin, had already begun to capture the minds of educated Germans in the fifteenth century, just at the time when their arts began to play seriously with the topic of the forest, or at least the relation of stone to wood. In German literature the greatest exploration of what a mighty, indeed almost unimaginably vast, temple is like was already to be found in Albrecht's poem *Der Jüngere Titurel* of around 1270, which conveys the aes-

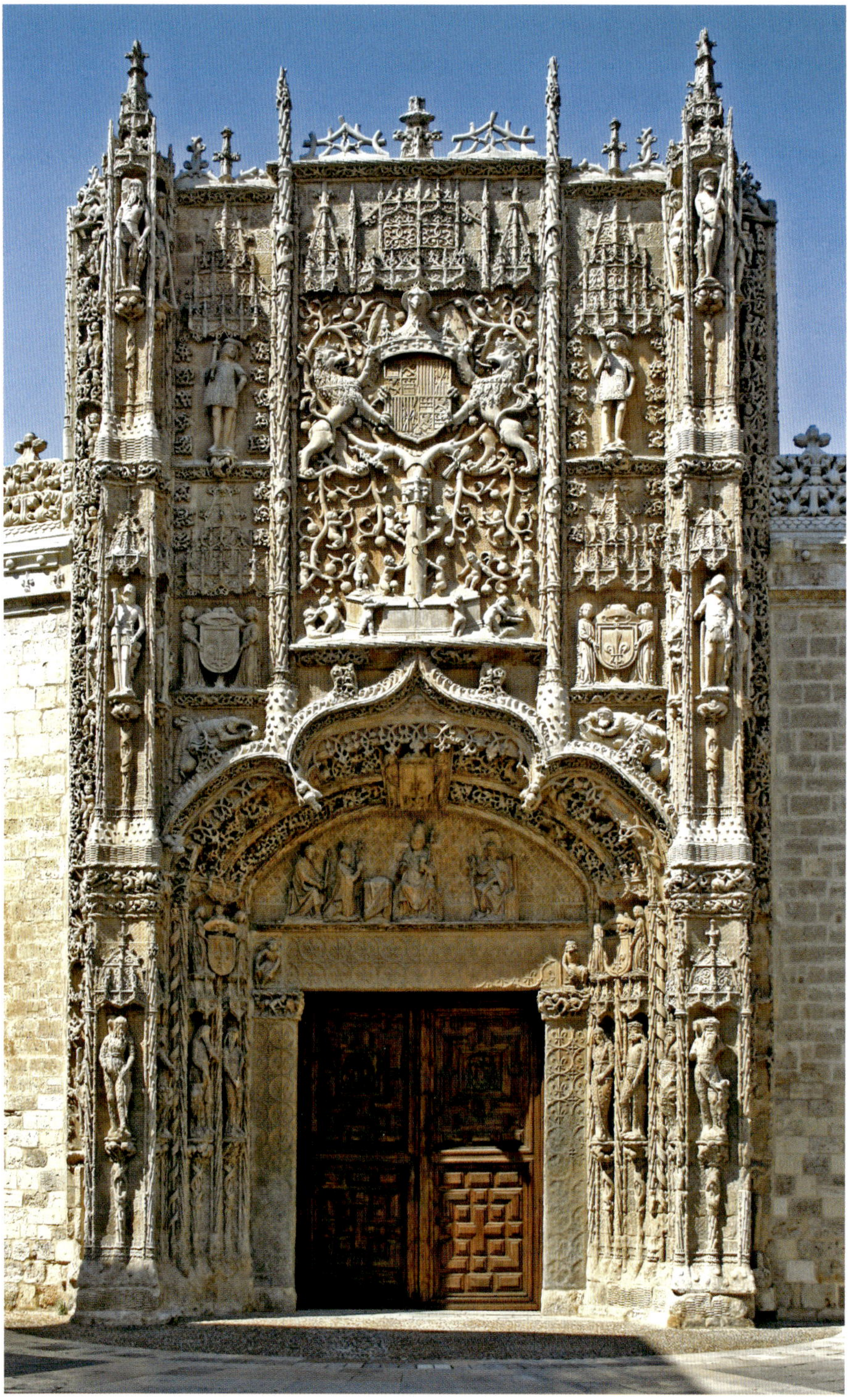

99 Valladolid, Colegio de San Gregorio, portal, late fifteenth century

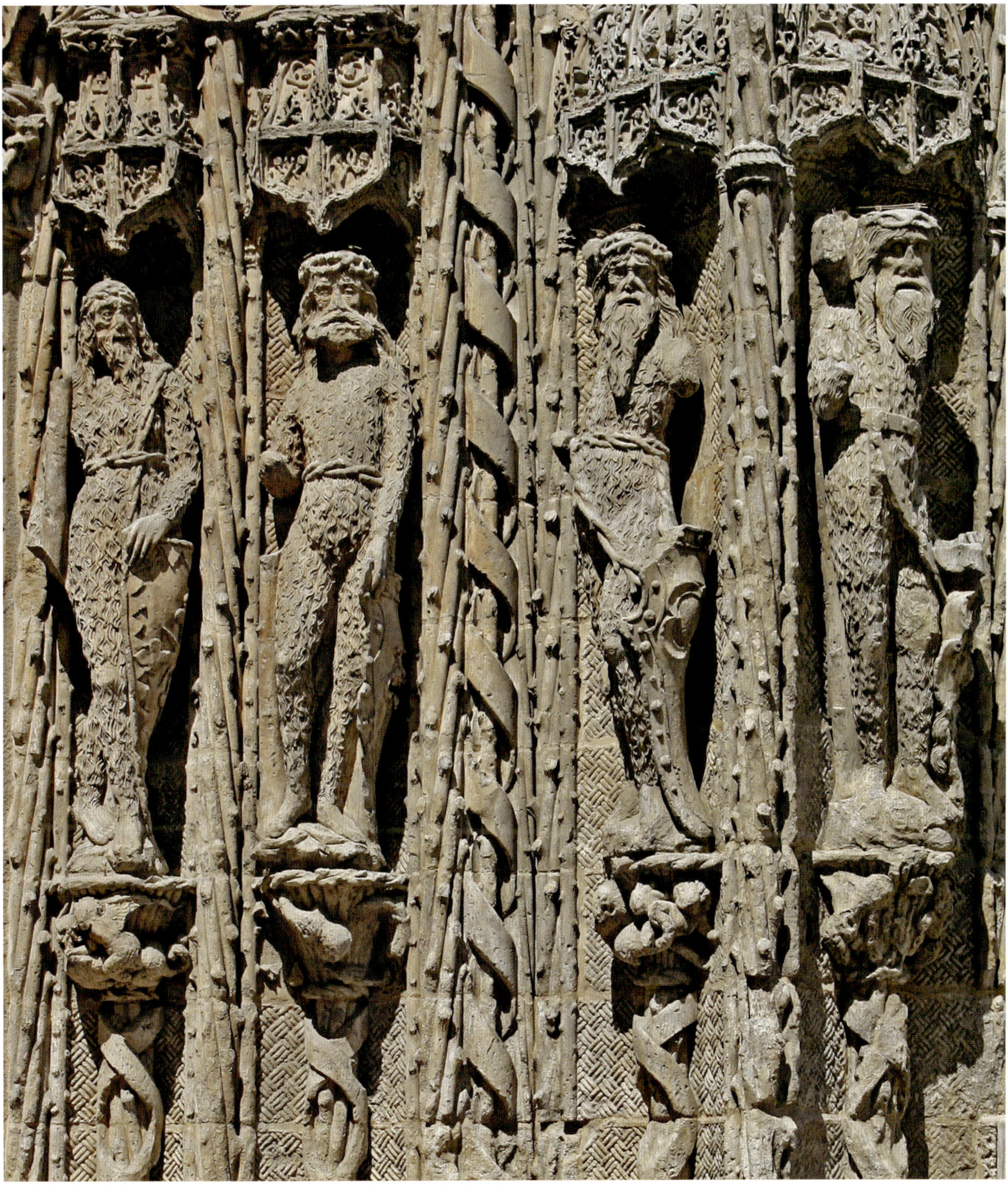

100 Valladolid, Colegio de San Gregorio, portal, Wild Men, late fifteenth century

thetic impact of a great building, the grail temple, through sensory experiences of music and the ringing sound of forest birdsong.[45] Later fifteenth- and early sixteenth-century German carving by such men as Adam Kraft and Tilman Riemenschneider in the service of extraordinary religious paraphernalia such as sacrament houses and retables (see pl. 61), as well as vault design, not only blurred further the already indistinct boundary around animal, vegetable and mineral, but also that of the sculptural and the architectural. Such carving explored positively what it was to work in a medium in such a way as to suggest that medium's possibilities.[46]

In essence, the theme of the forest entered the creative stage of play and illusion to show that stone, like wood, could not only *do* anything but *be* anything by means of wielding a sharp implement. At much the same time the identity issue of Germanness began to surface: so the eventual association of the two ideas, of wood-stone as the occasion for a bravura but also testing play with materiality in the creation of *astwerk* and *laube* (branchwork and arbour), and of the mythical origins of the Germans actually from forests and huts, was perhaps inevitable.[47] In his account of the Silver Age of creation in his *Metamorphoses* (1.113–24), Ovid had related that in response to the rise of the seasons, humankind (in general) moved into houses from caves or dense thickets of branches bound together with bark, and it was at that moment that they began to cultivate the soil as well as themselves.[48] Vitruvius in his books on architecture (2:1–4) had already advanced the notion that once humans had discovered fire they improved their homes, first by erecting wooden structures of a type which, he observed, were still made 'barbarian style' by people in foreign parts (Gaul, Hispania, Lusitania, Aquitania) but also originally by Romans. It was Tacitus in the first century CE who in his *Germania* (chapters 16 and 17) connected this method explicitly with the German tribes' use of unformed and unbeautiful wood (*materia*) to build houses, and of wild animal skins for clothes.[49] And it was comparatively recent art history that associated these idyllic thoughts with the theme of cultural identity: that late medieval German 'forest' Gothic was a sophisticated exploration of Germanness itself through ideas which were by then identifiably humanist and circulated with the printing of the texts of Vitruvius and Tacitus and the writing of Conrad Celtis.[50]

It is not my aim to shed further light on the already considerable debate about this issue of art and identity, so much as on the more specific relation of the natural and the artificial. My point is that the notion of the origination of the powers of cultivation had as much to do with eloquence as with identity.

Although German stone buildings had already amusingly blended the appearance of lopped wood with the smoother cursus of Gothic stone ribs at Ulm and Eichstätt, the architectural climax of these practices is found in the fifteenth-century church of Our Lady at Ingolstadt in Bavaria.[51] Ingolstadt enters the picture not least because its university was witness to Celtis's remarks on German identity, inspired by Tacitus, in 1492.[52] As at

Valladolid, it is tempting to see some link between these accomplishments and the context of education. The vaults of Ingolstadt's nave chapels were added around 1510–20 by Erhard Heydenreich, a mason also responsible for a sculpted cult image of the Virgin Mary at Regensburg.[53] They are some of the most astonishing creations of the Gothic era, testing and dissolving the boundary between architecture and sculpture. The basic conceit is that of an open network of flying ribs suspended beneath upper ribbed vaults in a double-layered effect. In such systems of ribbing the suspended ribs are formed into curves and counter-curves which work deliberately and satisfyingly against the upper linear patterns in contrary motion. At Ingolstadt at least four of the rib vaults add a further dimension to the layering by treating one layer as consisting of smooth moulded ribs in standard if complex Gothic fashion – as found in England and France – and one layer as consisting of rasping lopped branches bent and knotted together in a stable but tensile condition. The effects can be appreciated because the chapel vaults are relatively near the spectator.

How intelligible are these amazing forms? One possible reading has been to see them in binary terms, as a quasi-Platonic contrast of flawlessness and fallenness, involving a 'perverse corruption of divinely ordained matter', a 'descent into the material world' and a nature departing from God's initial imprint.[54] At work is a moral vision of opposing and contrasting order and disorder, waywardness and error, a 'negative becoming' so to speak. But is the narrative one-way? That the direction of process may not be straightforward is indicated by the fact that, while in the first (pl. 101) and second chapel vaults the moulded ribs are on the top surface, in the third chapel (pl. 102) they are suspended beneath the lopped ones.[55] This instantly throws into uncertainty, even confusion – albeit entertaining confusion – any fixed hierarchy of ascent or descent, which in terms of moral exposition would usually be indicated by relative height. At the Marienkirche at Pirna, for instance, the choir vault of about 1540 consists of flying but rough and lopped ribs with clambering Wild Men and demons (pl. 103), all of which evolves upwards into the complex meshed yet smooth vault at the top, in a process of culmination.[56] Nor at Ingolstadt is a typological or dyadic distinction absolute, because while in the first chapel vault the lopped branches grow directly out of, and down from, the moulded top ribs in a continuum (the direction of growth indicated by the angle of the many short stumps), in the third chapel the smooth flying ribs grow out from the rough ones above in a change of pitch. So, while the vault in the first chapel witnesses a change from smooth to rough, in chapel three it is from rough to smooth. This last could admit a second, also 'Platonic', reading drawn from Calcidius on the *Timaeus*

following pages 101 Ingolstadt, Liebfrauenmünster (Bavaria), first chapel vault, north side of nave, around 1510–20

102 Ingolstadt, Liebfrauenmünster (Bavaria), third chapel vault, north side of nave, around 1510–20

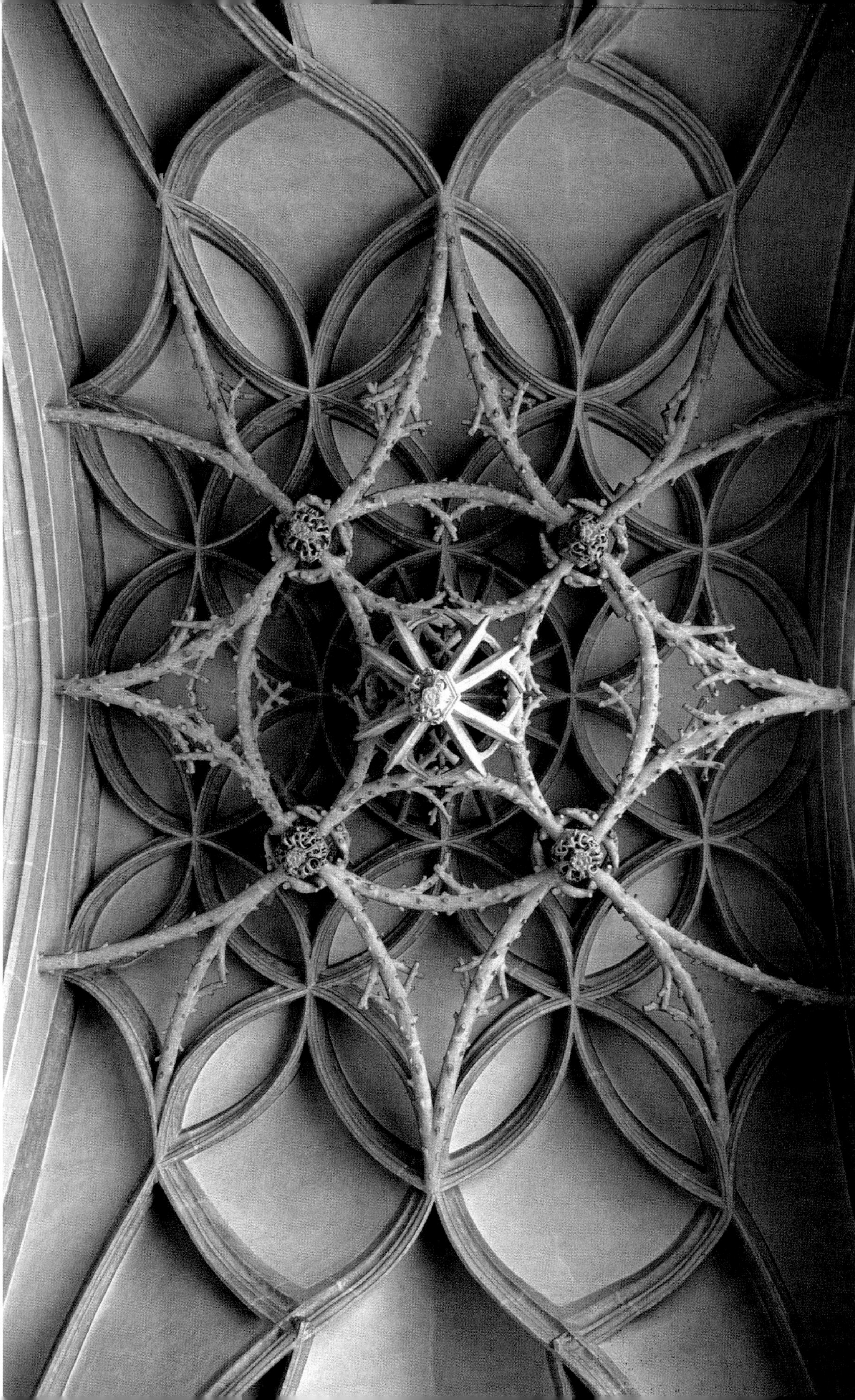

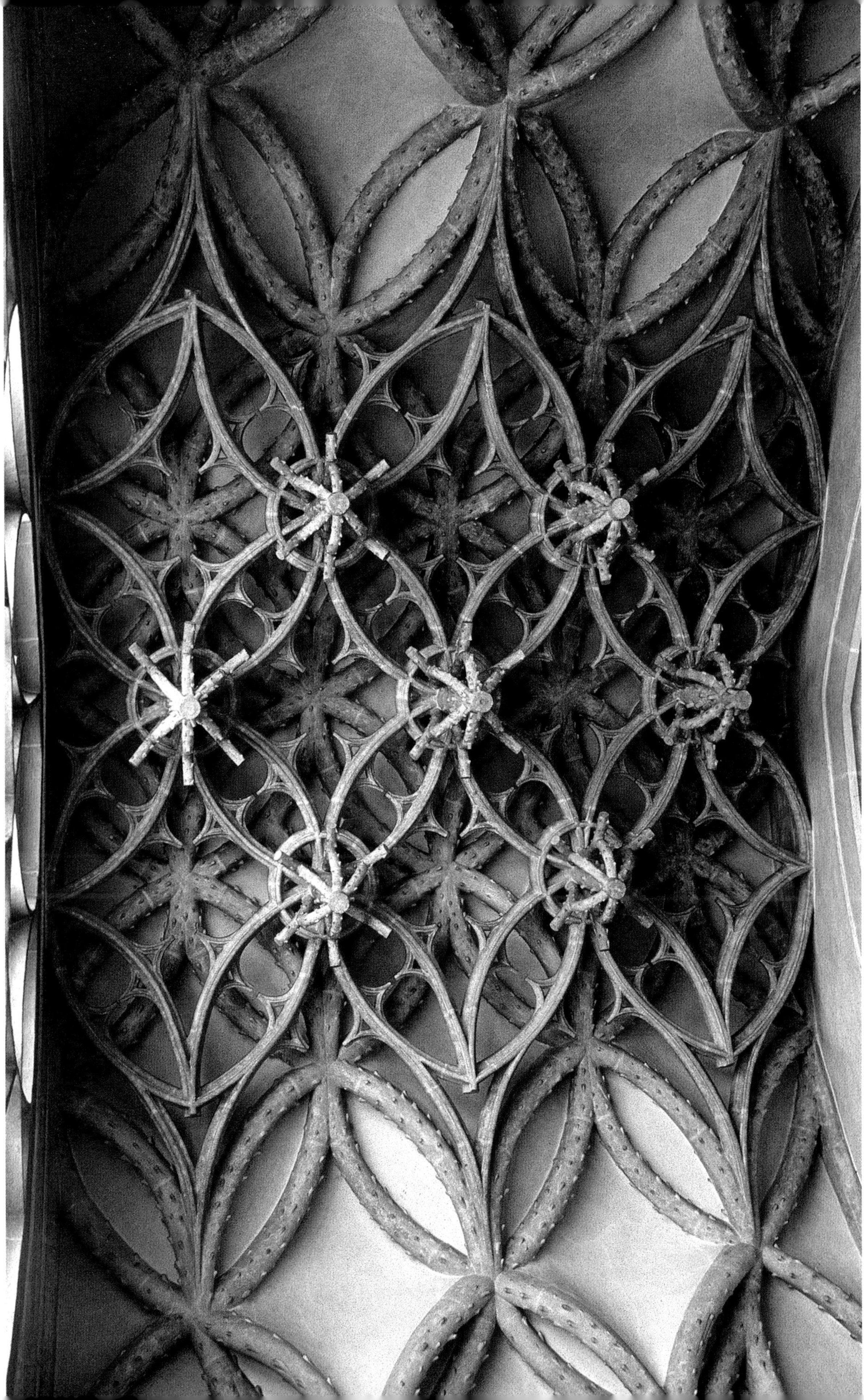

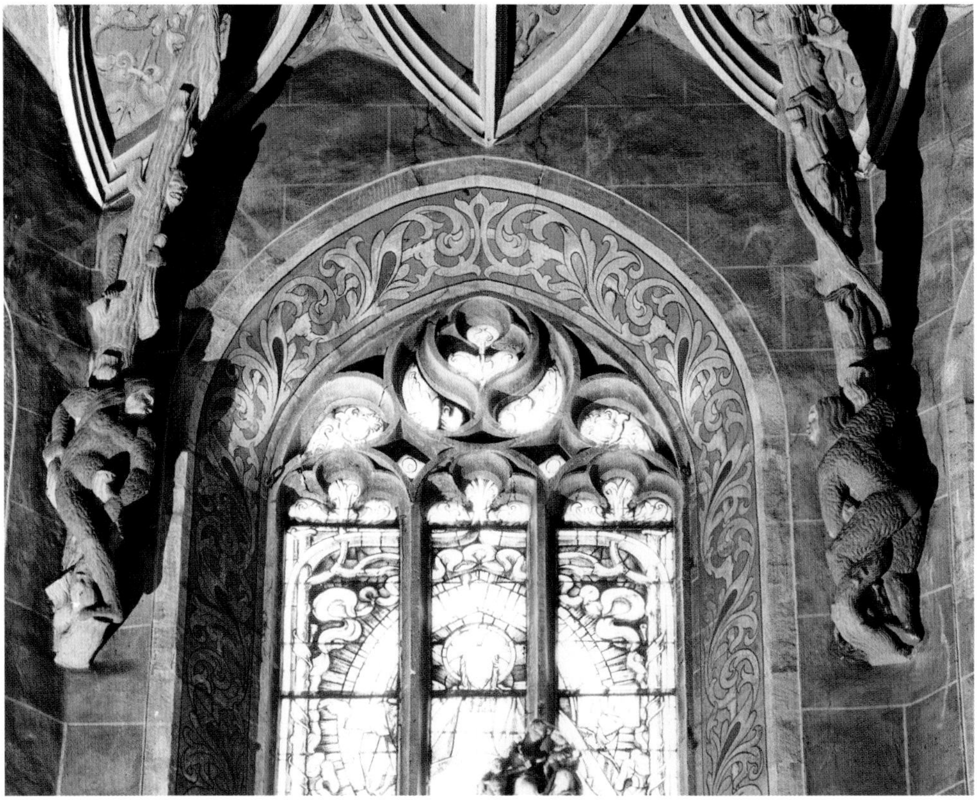

103 Pirna, Marienkirche (Saxony), flying ribs in choir with Wild Men, 1536–46

and commentators on *hyle* and *silva*. The lopped, bent and knotted ribs are not fallen, or for that matter disorderly (they are tightly ordered), but represent the way in which *silva* is drawn out into branches and twigs, figures and modes, through nature's own cultivation as a processual analogy to invention. As Bernardus Silvestris said, *silva* is rude and shaggy. If so, what we witness in at least one vault is not a dyad of the formless and the formed, but a *process* of realisation of matter through form and artifice, a 'becoming' held, like all Creation, in a delicate equilibrium. To get at the smooth ribs, whether above or below, someone somewhere must first have drawn out from the unformed but yearning *silva* those figures which eventually lead to cultivation, smoothness. The same idea might be evident at Pirna. So one reading of one set of ribs at Ingolstadt could be aetiological, a mythical explanation of how things came to be as they are: Heydenreich's art has produced its own origin myth. The eloquence of Gothic is the product of cultivation.

It is hard to escape the conclusion that whoever planned these vaults was involved in a sophisticated form of gamesmanship which eludes one-way readings, but which may nevertheless imply searching intelligence and wit. When viewed as a set, as they were intended to be, the Ingolstadt vaults do not present a single intelligible dynamic, and nor is it clear that they needed to. The to and fro is ludic, a provocation of thought by an initial astonishment and wonder prompted by craft: in that act of provocation, variety, the ability to toy in a protean way with mixed or combined forms, is a central agent. Each vault is different, and within each vault is found satisfying difference. We think back to that expression *Hoc opus eximium vario celamine mirum* – 'this extraordinary work, a marvel of varied relief' at Königslutter (pp. 29–30). Servile mimesis is insufficient. As Harpham says of the ascetic imperative, artificiality itself is insisted on: 'Within the ascetic, art can represent, can mask itself; but it can also refuse to do so: it is not condemned to habitual embarrassment'.[57]

One thing, however, is clear: central to the wit of these vaults is a contrast of eloquent surfaces which returns us to the distinction between the urbane and the rural, to the Ciceronian distinction between rough *sermo rusticus* and sweet and pleasing *sermo urbanus*.[58] In discussing the Cologne horror crosses of about 1300 (see pl. 108), I suggested earlier that they stood in a deliberate relation to the suave sculptural styles of the cathedral in a calculated rhetoric of contrast in which uncraftedness was an admissable aspect of style itself – that styles are antithetical and relational, and can embody *oppositio*. The same relation is at work at Ingolstadt. We might recall just how common in clerical circles in Germany – indeed in Western Europe – had been the contrast of the rural and the urbane, a contrast of style and ethics, in formulating ideals of courtliness and civility.[59] All such ideals are based on the promise of reform and the civilising process and, equally, of the risk of slippage back to simplicity, even wild barbarity. Witty response to this eternal two-way possibility was an aspect of the educated humour of the clerical (and so commissioning) classes. Arguably, it was picked up too by the artificers themselves as part of their conception of professional pride. As Matt Kavaler has demonstrated, German architects of just this generation were given to a range of visual jokes which played on smoothness and roughness or competence and incompetence: to tease their patrons and josh their colleagues, the masons showed tracery tied together ineptly with bits of rope (Utrecht) and vault ribs secured with bolts which split the stone (Wimpfen am Berg) or even pinned together with mock boarding (Salzburg, Stiftskirche).[60] It takes a hard heart not to find these things amusing; but we cannot discount either the possibility that what was at work was also a slightly loftier contrast between the architects as *doctores*, learned and capable in their craft, and *idiotae*, those who had no learning at all.[61] One could always become the other, for we are all fallible, or educable, and ultimately things are only sustained by divine favour.

In this regard the issue at Ingolstadt was not necessarily or solely German identity or *Kultur*. My thought is that it may rather have touched on the notion that crafting, like eloquence, draws order out of chaos in an act which requires eternal vigilance in order for it not to revert. It may therefore have involved another kind of group identity, that of the practitioners of *Kunst*, that word for art deriving from the verb *können*, to know how to do something, and related indirectly to the English 'cunning'. I mean specifically the working and thinking culture of the productive agents of such artworks, and particularly what I infer to have been their jocular mindsets of plaudit and machismo. The jokes about the incompetencies of masoncraft just noted may tell us something deeper about the nature of this mindset, for many a true word is spoken in jest. Within Gothic practice at large I see a connection, in this regard at least, between the bravura representational effects of the sculptures at Reims and the appetite for experiment, risk and provocation apparent at Ingolstadt and more widely in late medieval Germany. Innovation and the attainment of brilliant effect may be understood not by plumbing the depths of a culture as a whole, or indeed the mysteries of *Kunstwollen*, but by considering with greater determination the sheer level of thought involved in craft and process, and with it *ludus*, gamesmanship. This is not a matter of some form of intense intellectualism, but of the practical wit which energises craft and links together crafters.

Ingolstadt also connects with the bravura aesthetics of early modern *Kunst*. The extraordinary combination of fine, involuted winding geometrical forms with surprising juxtapositions of texture, anticipates the virtuosic turned ivory objects known as *Contrefaitkugeln* (polygonal or spherical carvings contained within carvings based on the Platonic solids) that began to feature in the princely *Wunderkammern* (chambers of wonders) of the sixteenth century.[62] Formal differences of Gothic and Renaissance aside, they share an aesthetic of prodigious high-precision strangeness. The ivory objects are far smaller. In the early modern period, such complex works (pl. 104) were considered as part of a genealogy of *Kunst* which stemmed from Dürer and practitioners of the Gothic style such as Adam Kraft.[63] However, any inclination to see the flourishing of the micro-arts solely as an early modern phenomenon can and should be resisted. Minificence, the 'magnificence of the miniature', was as fundamental an aspect of the aesthetics of wonder, and their essentially relativistic sense of scale, in the Gothic era as in the ancient world.[64] The premise of these arts was tremendous discipline. This meant more than fine workmanship, mastery of the difficult to realise. It meant conceptual discipline in the higher understanding of form: the *Contrefaitkugeln* seem to be as much thought-products of Plato's *Timaeus* as the play, if play it be, with *silva* at Ingolstadt. It also implied a larger notion of willed mastery, *enkrasia*, the notion of governance itself, governance of others as of the self. It is unlikely to be coincidental that the *ars tornandi*, the art of lathe turning, was a princely, noble and intellectual occupation in sixteenth-century Germany: in 1518, as the vaults at Ingolstadt were being realised, the Emperor Maximilian was given a lathe by the Tyrolean Diet.[65] The wonder-world of German *Kunst* accompanied the idea of a gubernator, the prince or thinker who by turning gives form to the inchoate and thereby smoothes, stabilises, guards and cultivates that which, in human nature itself, may otherwise be rough and wild.

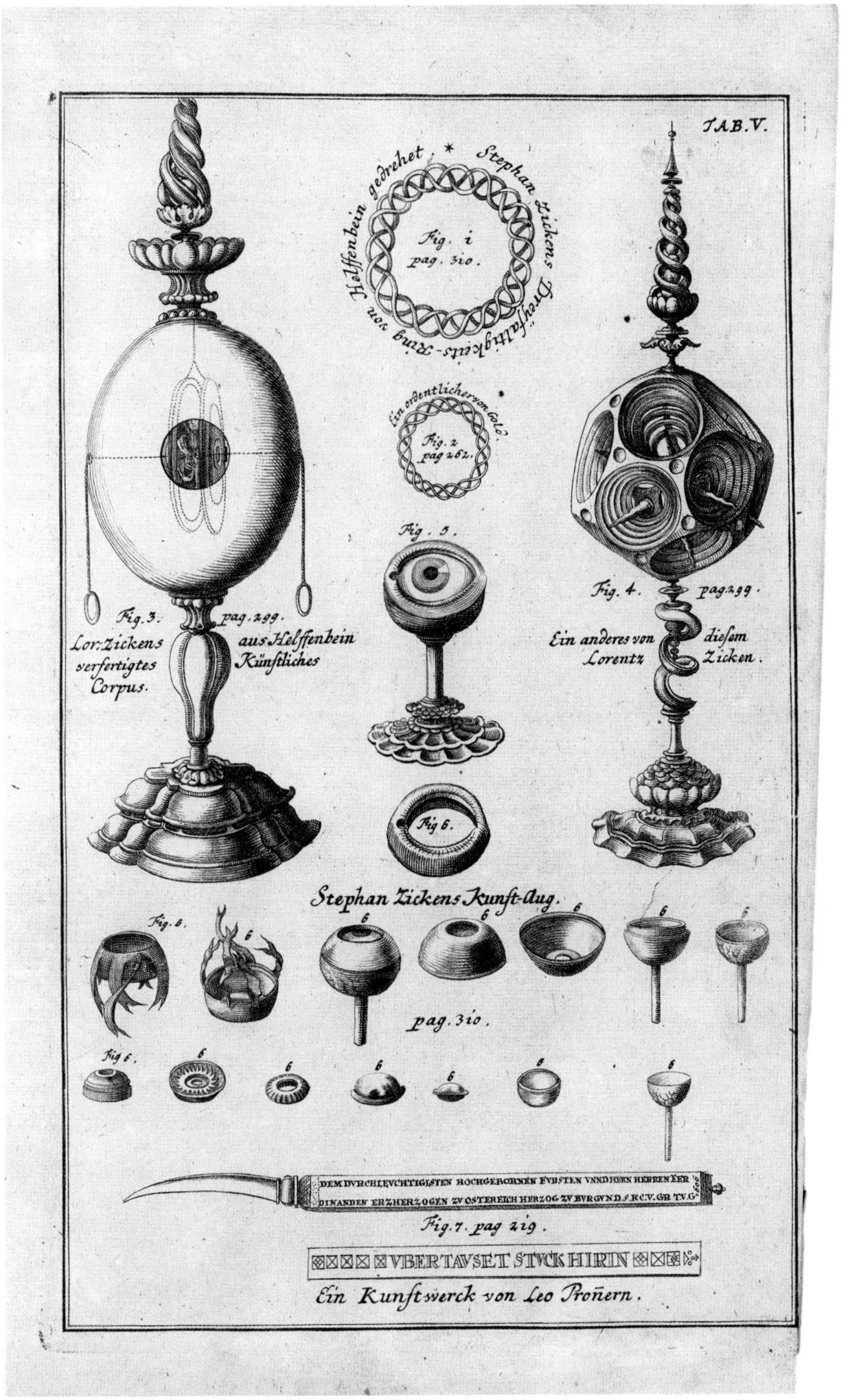

104 *Contrefaitkugeln*, from Johann Gabriel Doppelmayr, *Historische Nachricht von den Nürnbergischen Mathematicis und Künstlern* (Nuremberg, 1730), pl.V

The medieval European imaginary accorded power to those rough beings either cast out into the wild voluntarily or who belonged to the wild by nature.[66] This topic is well beyond the scope of the present book. But it frames our final theme, the rhetoric and aesthetics of death. Asceticism provoked a strong, often heroic, aesthetic and ethos.[67] Foremost were the hermits, those who led asocial, eremitic lives in the desert or forest. Other outsiders, scarcely suitable objects of imitation, were the forest outlaws, the Robin Hoods and particularly the Wild Man – by definition shaggy – who belonged to nature itself, especially that zone of nature near enough to be subject to observation by the civilised, just beyond its portals or *fores*.[68] Our word 'forest' is derived, via later Latin, from *foris*, 'doorway' or 'portal': it designated a boundless outside, a zone either beyond the law or subject to its own special laws. On the foresty facade of the Colegio de San Gregorio at Valladolid (see pl. 100), the portal jambs themselves are occupied by an extraordinary yet conventionalised, almost decorous, array of Wild Men where we might expect the saints of the Church: the ensemble strikes the viewer as a commentary, apparently proper to a university college, on the virtues of cultivation itself.[69] In fact, though separate from the public domain, and despite the biblical association of the wilderness with expulsion, the wild zones were not necessarily spaces of anarchy.[70] For Tacitus the early tribes may have lived outside the portals of cities, but they were not devoid of law or morality. They were firmly within the zone of nature but they were not exactly outside the zone of culture.

In writing about wood sculpture and especially the crosses of the fourteenth century in Germany (see pls 39 and 108), I drew attention to the aesthetics of opposition, of reproach, of the rough versus the smooth, and of the rebuke the rough and ugly offers to the surfaces of beauty. That an urban, mendicant aesthetic was partly at work in this may be suspected. And exactly the same value system emerges in the narrative of virtue, vice and self-denial. Late medieval imagery exploring such themes is copious. It was accompanied by a rich vernacular literature on repentance which thematised eremitic wilderness, the 'desert' of religion conceived as a forest and employing the imagery of the tree to unfold the fundamentals of Christian morality.[71] The moral eloquence of the hair shirt and the Gothic hut has already been encountered in the Dumbleton *Summa* of about 1340 (see pl. 98). Medieval law books as well as religious books were often the site of marginal imagery.[72] One such book, the copiously decorated Smithfield Decretals made for a member of the Batayle family in England towards or around 1340 (British Library, Ms Royal 10.E.IV), includes among the dozens of narrative illustrations in its lower borders stories of hermit saints such as the once promiscuous but now hairy Mary of Egypt (pl. 105), along with wild men, knights and ladies, and the Three Living and the Three Dead.[73] Shagginess in the wild, the quality of *silva*, is also a quality of penance. The south nave aisle of Winchester Cathedral

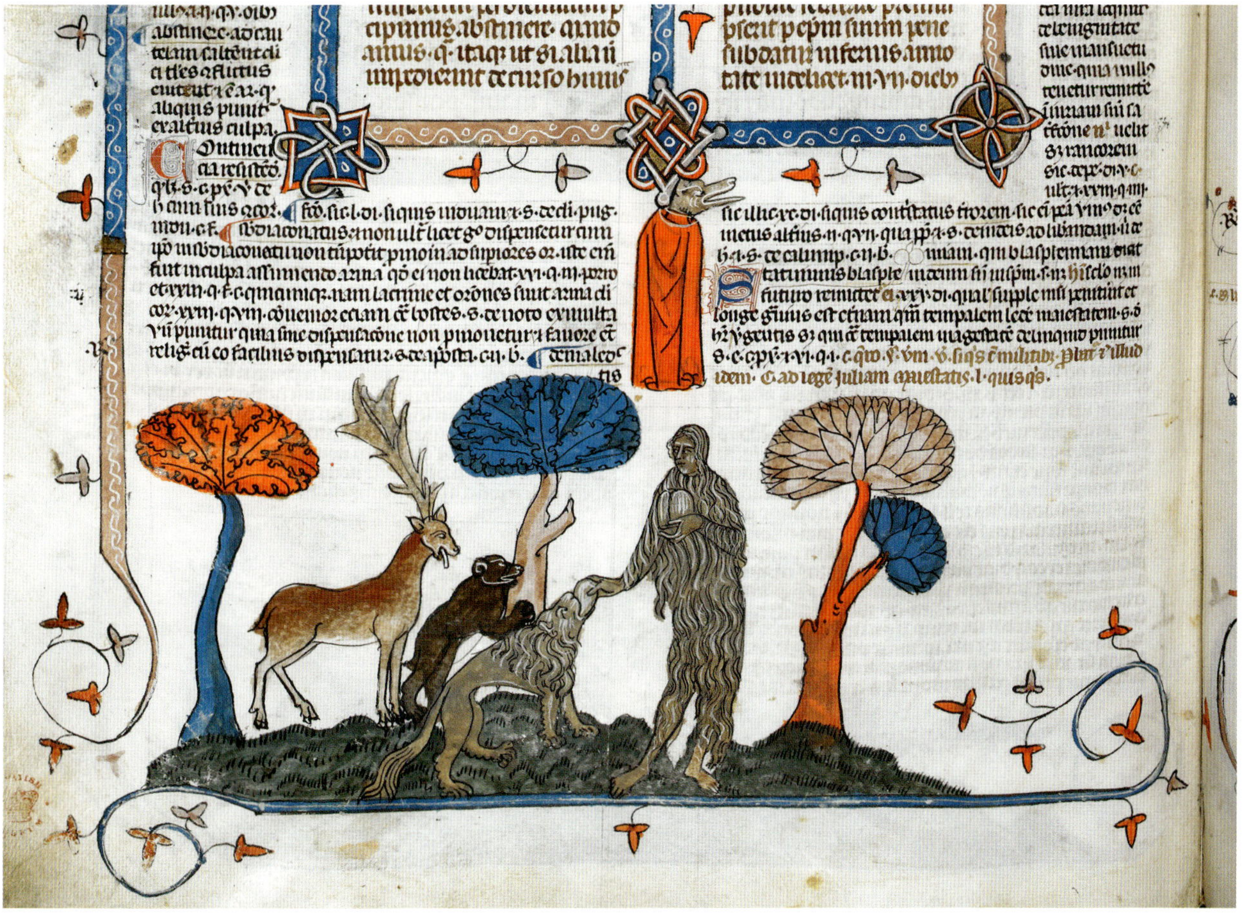

105 St Mary of Egypt feeds the beasts, Smithfield Decretals, around 1340 (British Library, Ms Royal 10.E.IV, fol. 280v)

possesses a late fourteenth-century boss showing Adam and Eve with oundy hair draped in furry animal skin after the Expulsion, Adam still clutching the fateful apple.[74] Many of these slightly bleak tales illustrate the dynamics of repentance and return to God from the exile of sin. Both forest and desert could be a guarantor of spiritual freedom, implicated in the psychological and moral concerns of civilisation itself. Harsh discipline and repentance were their companions; and such things, such technologies of the self, were products of the ordered human search for self-control intensified to the point of self-transcendence by Christian asceticism.[75]

I stress the connection between eremitic discipline, war and aristocratic physical pursuits such as hunting because the forest was shared by the orders of society, those who prayed, those who fought and those who laboured.[76] Knighthood and asceticism formed themselves through harsh, habitual self-discipline or training, askesis. The association of the monastic life with the discipline of the mind and the warfare of the soul, the soldier-monk, was deep-rooted and extremely productive in art and literature, notwithstanding the Church's antipathy to violence.[77] For one thing, the military ideal permitted an extraordinary two-way traffic: just as monks might learn from soldiers, so soldiers could learn from monks or, better, hermits. Both had to restrain appetite, had to prune back the self in order to flourish. One of the most widely influential treatises on chivalry itself was imparted by a hermit, himself a former knight, to a questing youth. This was the work of the Majorcan mystic Ramon Lull (d. 1316), the *Libre del ordre de cavayleria*.[78] Lull's experience had been one of renunciation of court life. His treatise opens with a squire riding through a forest on the way to court, who becomes lost and who encounters an enfeebled hermit, a former warrior, deep in contemplation. The hermit, finding the squire ignorant of the codes and ideals of knighthood, sets them out for him in a little book – to be Lull's *Libre*. Again, the forest is associated with an origin myth, in this case of the codes of knighthood which, like academic disciplines, could be written down because they consisted of a formal and formalising method. Among the knightly practices set out in the *Libre* is continual exercise by hunting wild beasts, jousts and tournaments, which encourage hardiness and prowess.[79] As Alexander Murray says, 'Hunting and religious asceticism play a curious *pas de deux* in sources for monastic history. One reason for their connection was certainly that both took men out to the wilds'.[80] The wilds might occasion conversion or epiphany, as experienced by Saints Hubert, Julian or Eustace. Hunting might reinforce antipathy to violence and cruelty. But it was also an aristocratic pleasure. Lull recommended it for knights and so too did the author of the well-known *Livre de chevalerie*, Geoffroi de Charny, killed at the Battle of Poitiers in 1356, by which time he had become Bearer of the Oriflamme of France.[81]

The tension in the chivalric ethos between the privations of hardiness and their eventual reward is captured by an unusual English tomb executed for a near-contemporary of Geoffroi de Charny who, like him, served in Aquitaine – Sir Oliver de Ingham (d. 1344) in the lofty chancel of the parish church of Ingham on the windy east coast of Norfolk.[82] Unusually, the canopied tomb shows Sir Oliver, a household knight of Edward II and former Seneschal of Aquitaine, lying in effigy in armour on a cobbled bed of rough flints – the flints are beautifully painted – and looking at a mural on the back of the tomb of a hunt (now lost but recorded in the nineteenth century) – truly a *locus amoenus*, happy hunting-ground in the sky (pl. 106).[83] The flints, which the effigy indicates with one gauntletted hand, represent the hardiness and alertness of the knight in the wilds, the privations of chivalry. De Charny had written about these in his *Livre de chevalerie* where he mentions the avoidance by knights of creature comforts, especially the *lit mol*, the soft bed and white sheet.[84] Honour, on the contrary, is to be found in sleeping without a bed and with day clothes on,

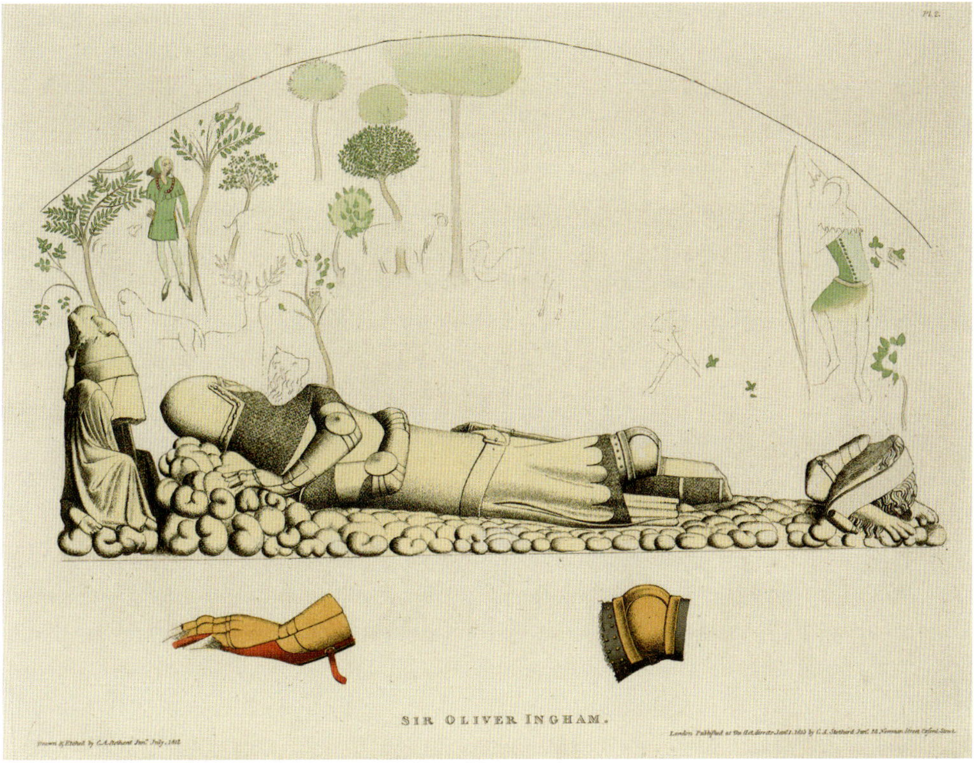

106 Ingham parish church (Norfolk), tomb effigy of Sir Oliver de Ingham (d. 1344) with hunting scene, now lost, state in 1812, from Charles Alfred Stothard, *The Monumental Effigies of Great Britain* (1817)

touz vestus. Of knights 'it can truly be said to them that when they want to sleep, they must keep vigil'.[85] The *Livre* is throughout marked by ascetic restraint. But the tomb's image of the hunt – not a saint's life, or a moralisation, but just a hunt with all its risks and pleasures – beautifully illustrates the rewards of method and self-denial, and the sophisticated character of all indulgence.[86]

MACABRE AESTHETICS: COMPLEX SPECIFICITY AND IMMERSION

The structure and intention of the tomb at Ingham, connecting as it does denial and reward as part of the elaborate incentive system of chivalric ethics, is not directed by narrative so much as by contemplation, itself an active form of discipline. In his *Etymologies* (15.2.27) Isidore for instance sees the gymnasium as a place of 'exercise', which is to say 'meditation'.[87] As an object of contemplation the tomb anticipates the tremendous double-decker *transi* tombs of the next century, minus the incentivising element of fear.[88] Fear was especially manifest in those cases where the happy hunting-ground went terribly wrong, when in a *monde renversé* the hunter became the hunted, as illustrated by the legend of the Three Living and the Three Dead. This popular subject, originating no later than the thirteenth century and common in the visual arts thereafter, was almost certainly courtly in origin, and is encountered first in the vernacular, though it became a common topic for the Office of the Dead in later medieval books of hours.[89] It depicted three young men out hunting or hawking in the wilds who encounter three corresponding figures, as it were their ghastly *doppelgängers*, as images of the decaying dead. Here indeed was a form of *oppositio*. Arranged as a dialogue between the two interdependent teams, the image or image-pairing makes much play with mirroring and doubling effects, prophecy, hesitation and resolution.[90] The aim is to elicit fear, a sensation (in modern parlance) of the uncanny, of defamiliarisation. The aim is to shock the young men, and us, into a change of heart and mind, psychic trauma triggering *metanoia*, the healing process of repentance: hence its legitimacy within the structure of the daily Hours. Italian images, unlike those in north-western Europe, often include the admonitory presence of a hermit such as St Macarius.[91] The hermits were those most likely to lie with the dead, to contemplate immersion in death, a point made by the image of St Macarius, shown in a fourteenth-century French *Miroir historiale* (Paris, Bibliothèque Nationale de France, Ms 5080 réserve, fol. 328v) sleeping with the bones of dead pagans in a terrible rocky tomb.[92] Other images, generally of later date, show the Dead literally in hot and exciting pursuit of the Living as actual quarry.[93]

For our present purposes the issue is precisely the immersive, embodied, aesthetic experience of the Three Living and Three Dead. In this respect macabre aesthetics were not separable from but continuous with the experiences of carved or painted Gothic imagery more generally of the sort which I have discussed throughout these pages, not least in regard to the horror Crucifixions of this very period. I write of 'macabre' aesthetics adjectivally in order to create an opening into the wider possibilities of realist aesthetics more generally. It is too easy to fetishise and isolate 'the macabre' in Romantic fashion, and in effect to model and stiffen it according to ideas of genre which in the Middle Ages were generally suppler: the expression 'macabre' (actually *macabré* in early French and English sources) was not generic but topical, since before the early modern period it applied only to the Dance of Death or *dance macabré*, a theme with a family resemblance to other themes we now designate as the macabre.

Let me therefore emphasise experience rather than topicality. Earlier I drew attention to Mary Carruthers's discussion of the term 'horror' in relation to images or events.[94] Carruthers explains that horror is an imaginative and bodily, sensory, experience of fear in the presence of the unusual, weird or dangerous, associated with trembling and body hair standing on end; the term 'hideous' may itself have arrived in English via the French *hideux*

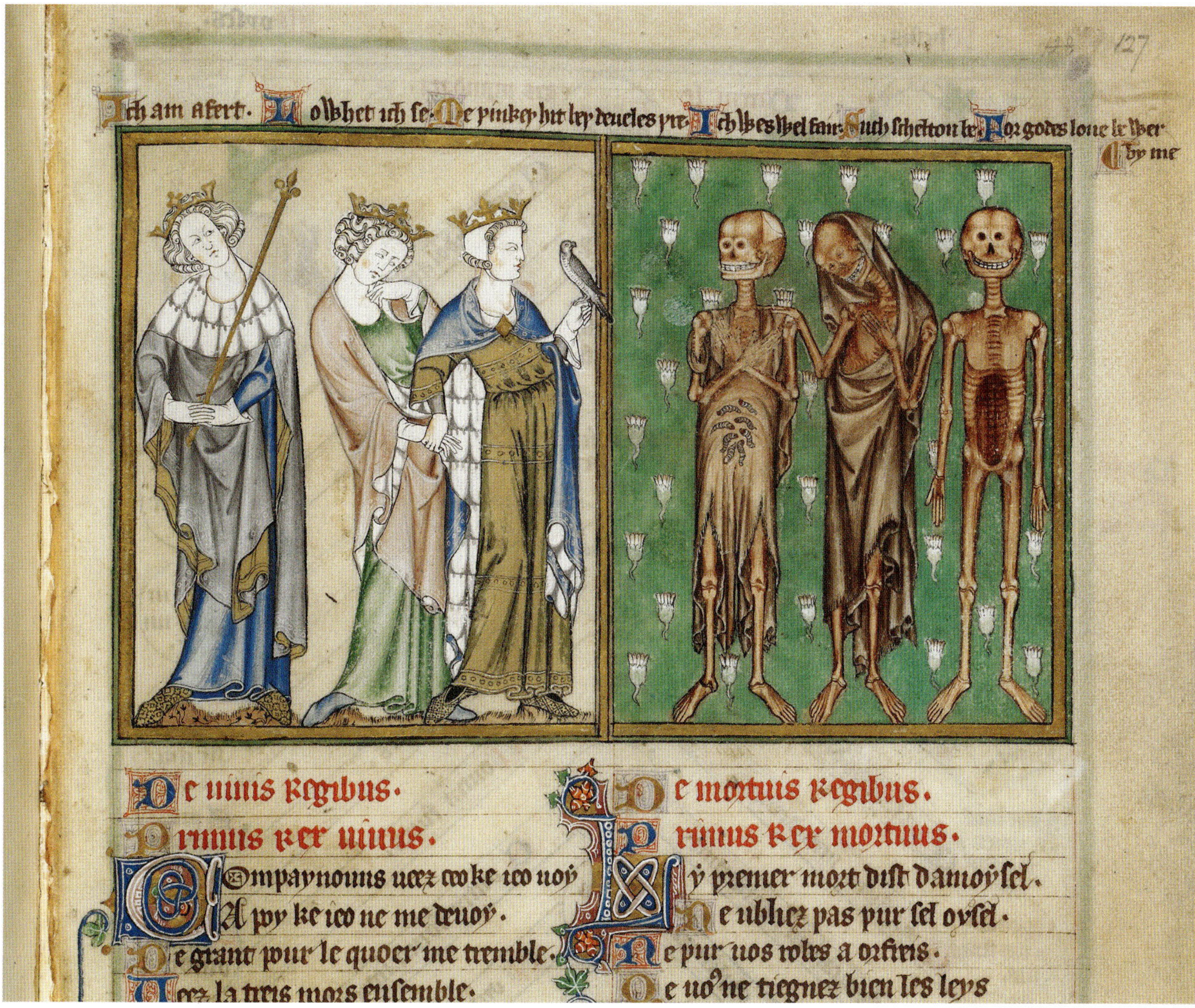

107 The Three Living and the Three Dead, Psalter of Robert de Lisle, around 1310 (British Library, Arundel Ms 83 (II), fol. 127)

from the Latin *hispidus*. The critical usefulness of these observations is exemplified by the language used in the poem accompanying the image of the Three Living and Three Dead. A well-known instance is provided by the version in the so-called Psalter of Robert de Lisle (pl. 107), made to the highest artistic standards of the region of London in the early fourteenth century.[95] This picture, arranged in two frames at the head of the page like a hinged painted diptych, has speech captions in Middle English at the head, the poem beneath being in Anglo-Norman French.[96] Its tropes are familiar and deliberately arresting.

The Living are shown fine-faced with beautifully wrought hair, and arrayed in crowns, fur and gloves. The first king bearing his hawk leads his immediate companion by an ungloved hand – a gesture we have already noted in an encounter with Last Judgement imagery (p. 42). His companion indicates fear or remorse by touching his throat gently with his gloved hand, while the third, facing us and wringing his hands, looks up thoughtfully. The first king begins immediately with the faculty of sight and beholding, often engaged in macabre encounters: 'Friends, can you see what I see?' (*Compaynouns veez ceo ke ieo voy*); the second king raising his hand expresses his desire to amend his life (*amender ma vie*) with eager heart; the third wrings his hands (*destreint ses meins*). Notable is the language of response. The first king says that his heart 'shakes with great fear' (*De grant pour le quoer me tremble*) and, pointing to the Three Dead, comments 'How hideous and strange they are' (*Cum il sunt hidous et divers*). Meanwhile the Third Dead replies that he is so hideous and bare that even the worms will not come near him (*Ore su si hidous et si nuz / Ke moy ver ne deigne nuls*). The term *divers* is rich semantically, including the senses of difference, change, mottling or variegation, connecting an encounter with something at once gripping to the eye but also odd or hard to figure out. It reminds us of the dislocating effect of initial aesthetic encounters with complex or unusual things. But the language in this poem is especially that of horror; indeed the poem is described as 'a most marvellous and horrible history' (*une moult merveilleuse et horrible histoire*) in the Petites Heures of Jean, Duc de Berry (Paris, Bibliothèque Nationale de France, Ms lat. 18014).[97] This horror is not the meta-sensory, desolate otherwordly power of true terror, but a bodily and thoughtful if uncomfortable experience of something complex, odd or amazing which can be acted out in gesture, which can be felt and articulated. The word 'uncanny' (German *unheimlich*) – the sense of something familiar gone terribly wrong – captures its creepiness. A continuum of resemblance between the actors involved, of their typological resemblance, is important no matter how severely tested. That is why this image has utility and serves what I have called the conviction purpose of medieval art.

It will be obvious from the foregoing that I see macabre aesthetics as an intensification of the rhetorical and aesthetic strategies of the sort discussed throughout this study.[98] These strategies can be approached from the angles of identity, aesthetic immersion and rhetorical engagement. As the many illuminations and paintings of subjects such as the Three Living and the Three Dead, or the Dance of Death indicate, this was not solely a sculptural phenomenon.[99] Yet sculpture's ability to capture effects of surface was particularly marked. Macabre images have a particular surface, an aesthetic which is geared not just to producing an emotion but an experience. This is common to all forms of vivid imagination at this time. To understand this we can contrast the distancing effect of symbols. The image of the skull and crossbones has a deathly content, identifiable from afar, unmistakable: it is piratical, poisonous, it signals death or serious danger. But it is not truly macabre, because like all symbols it is a simplified and detached version of a more complex reality. Where symbols may be aesthetically vacuous, macabre things possess aesthetic specificity directing response by means of surface. Macabre images are as they are because they have complex specificity, an eloquence of particularity. The processes of decay revert us to Everyman, the particularity and continuity of identity being annihilated in the generality of death. Its point is conveyed by specifics, by the particular, not the typical: and yet typicality is its aim. This is a central paradox of the loss of self in realism: that personhood itself is challenged as we revert to type. This point was well understood by Julia Kristeva in her study of abjection and the powers of horror. Kristeva argues rightly that the details of flesh do just *signify* (stand in for) death. Corpses actually *show us* what death is, as something to be thrust aside (abjected) in order to live: the abject is the unthinkable threat to identity itself.[100]

The immersive, sensory character of aesthetic experience – particularly unpleasant experience – is fundamental to this. Having established that beauty and pleasure, the praiseworthy and the attractive, have agency, what of the ugly, the repulsive or fearful? What is their eloquence? Aristotle's *Poetics* 1.1448b4 had established the connection between mimesis and the experience of the painful by arguing that we can take a form of pleasure even in the unexpected or unpleasant: 'Though the objects themselves may be painful to see, we delight to view the most realistic representations of them in art, the forms for example of the lowest animals and of dead bodies'.[101] Aristotle is thinking of something like fascination, a powerful, even compulsive, form of attention that simultaneously connects the seemingly opposed powers of attraction and repulsion and to which mimesis is vital. In the case of death images the object of attention is the horrible actuality of the invaded and invasive body, of the boundary breached. The macabre body is invaded by, and produces, decay – worms, snakes, toads emanate, or better go in and out of, the stone cadavers of the great fifteenth-century *transi* tombs of north-western Europe just as they do in the thirteenth century from the moralised body of *Frau Welt* ('Lady World') at Worms Cathedral in the early fourteenth.[102] This aesthetic of penetration and excretion had been captured by sculpture long before, in the infested and crawling surfaces of Romanesque sculptures such as those around Moissac's famous and no less moralising image of *Luxuria* considered earlier in this study. The context, as at Moissac, was conventionally eschatological, concerned with the fate of the body and soul, and the Last Things. Like the hairy, open naked body of the ascetics or the Wild Man, the decaying and vulnerable Gothic body is not separated, sheltered or closed from the world, and so contained, but is open to the forces both of decay and regeneration.[103] This surely is the force of the beautiful image in a fourteenth-century volume of the *Livre des propriétés des choses* (Brussels, Bibliothèque Royale, Ms 9094, fol. 45) showing a corpse laid out amid the Four Elements themselves.[104]

Key to this issue is the two-way nature of invasiveness, for just as the macabre body is open and penetrable so too does it invade our sensibility – this is Aristotle's point about fascination. That invasion is absolutely aesthetic, sensory in character. It means more than simple physical proximity, the wondrous but challenging proximity to the dead captured by the ascetic St Macarius sleeping with corpses. It is an actual taking-in, a form of imitation or *assimilatio*.[105] Caroline Bynum is to my mind right in stating of such experiences that, far from amounting to a rejection of the body, they are not 'flight from' so much as 'submersion in' flesh and decay.[106] This power is typical of the dual ascetic drive both to immerse itself in the world yet also escape from it.[107] This immersion precisely threatens the distancing effect identified, Kantian-fashion, by David Freedberg in his discussion of verisimilitude and resemblance, in which aesthetic attention is premised on distance, detachment.[108] Freedberg notes the emphasis in funerary art throughout the Middle Ages and Renaissance on the commemorative and 'presentist' or tangible use of such substances as hair and wax. We have drawn attention to these materials, hair especially, in discussing and separating representation and substitution. As we saw in the case of Andreas Wunhart, the sculptor who commemorated his dead daughter by using her hair on a Crucified Christ, substitution can be intensely personal and appropriative. Macabre experience is not premised on the total abandonment of imaginative regard typical, for instance, of the fantasy relation; nor is it premised on total detachment. On the contrary, the relation is intensely aesthetic, assimilative, sensory and imaginative. Passion imagery bears this out by providing single, unforgettable images. In her vivid *Revelations* (7:15.23), St Bridget of Sweden (1303–1373) gives an account of the sufferings of the Crucifixion, noting that while stretched in agony on the Cross, Christ had a sunken abdomen that adhered to his back as if he had no guts within (*ventrem submissum coherentem dorso, ac si nulla intus habuisset viscera*).[109] Pickering suggests that this image is uniquely Bridget's, but the evidence of earlier extant German and Scandinavian horror crosses suggests otherwise (pl. 108 and see pl. 39).[110] This eviscerated look recurs on the shrunken *transi* tombs of the fifteenth and sixteenth centuries. Through the immersive, bodily and intellectual powers of aesthesis itself (as understood in the Middle Ages), the spectator is drawn irresistibly to that which belongs to others, but in a way that overcomes distance, provoking wonder and thought as well as pity and remorse.

Macabre aesthetics, in other words, were but one aspect of a rhetorical order within which experience of the particular plays and always played a vital aesthetic and imaginative role. The art of the *transi* tomb and of the represented cadaver in France, England and Germany, of stretched parchment-like skin, the protrusion of bones, the lolling of skulls and jaws, the collapse of stomachs and ribcages and, most horribly, the constant slithering entrance and exit of worms, snakes and other slimy things which eat into and replace the viscera, is an art of penetrable surface (see pl. 111). *Transi* tombs are things infested, paradoxically alive, more alive sometimes than the perfected image of the dead. Indeed, the relation of the horrible or the ugly to the beautiful or perfected in the form of the clothed image often surmounting the corpse in such tombs is a fully structural or relational one, governed throughout by the

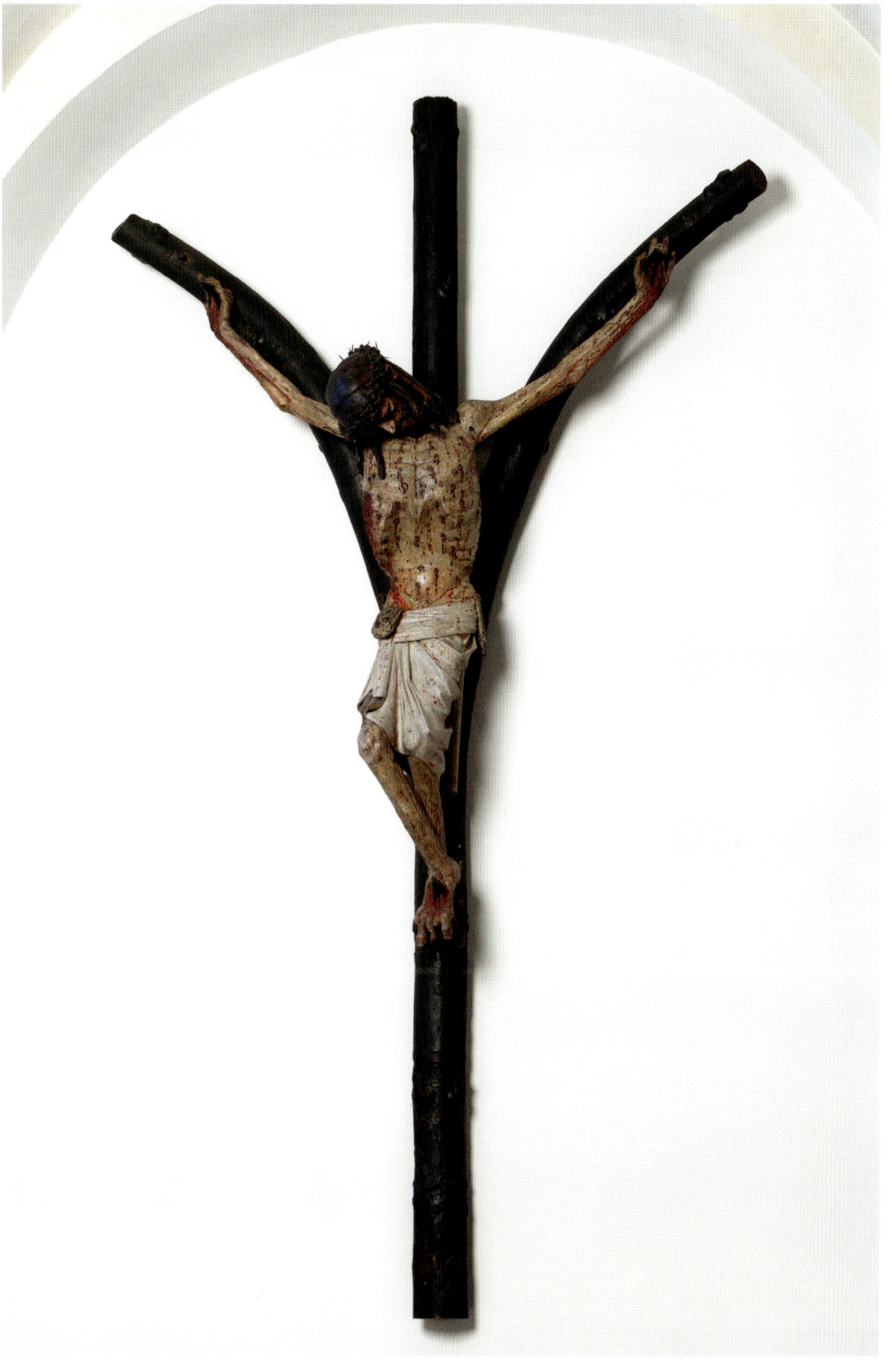

108 Cross, painted wood, S. Maria im Kapitol, Cologne, about 1304

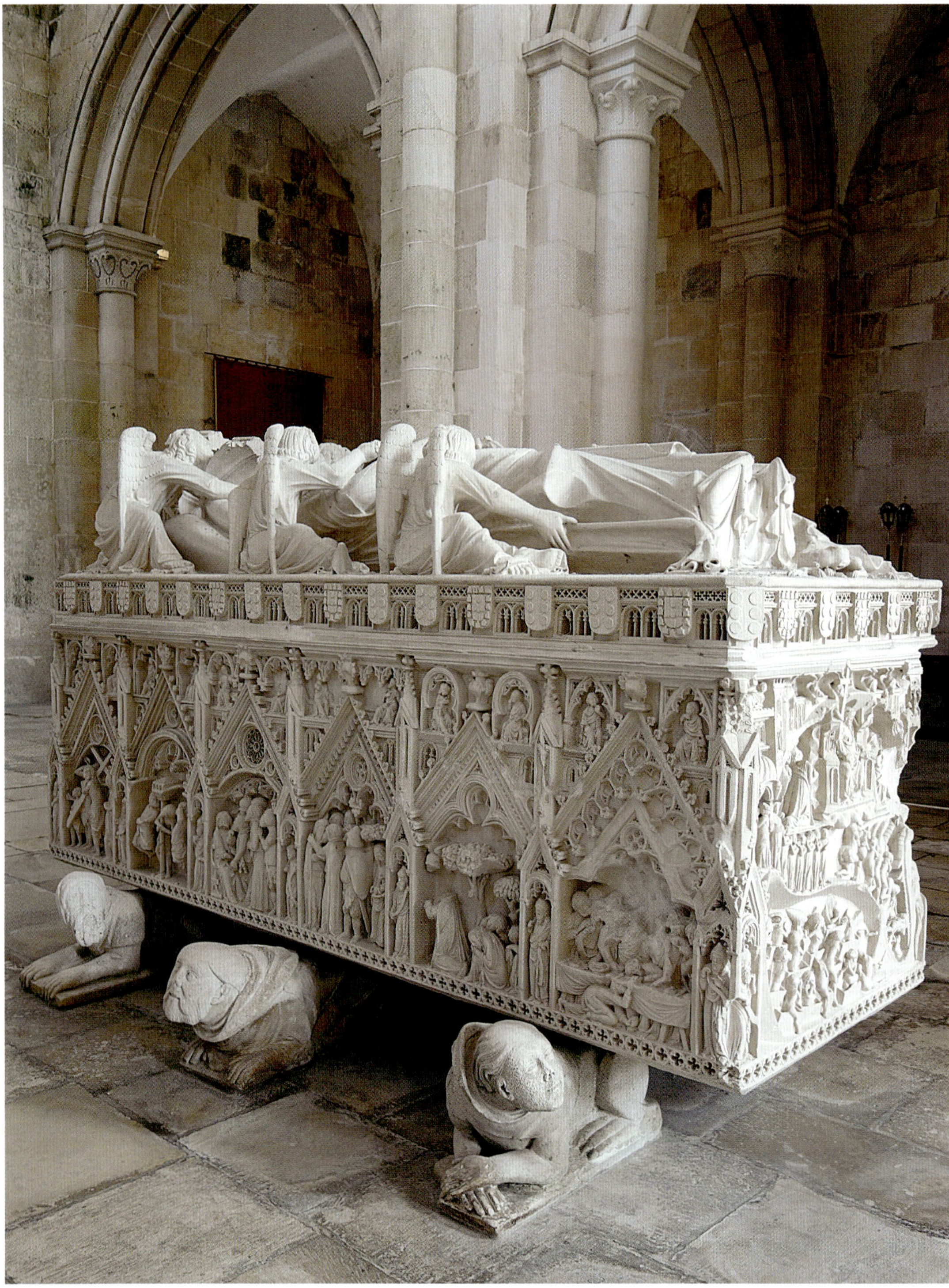

109 Cistercian monastery of Alcobaça (Portugal), tomb of Inês de Castro (murdered 1355), mistress of King Pedro I of Portugal, white marble

skin-depth of beauty, of which the ugly is a deformity, a falling away.[111] St Matthew's Gospel 23:27 captures this relation by likening the hypocrites to 'whited sepulchres' (*sepulchris dealbatis*) which seem beautiful (*speciosa* or *pulchra*) without but are full of dead bones within (pl. 109 and see pl. 113). This entailed a pun on the words *pulchrum* and *sepulchrum* which played straight into the hands of moralists.[112] The treatment of detail is key to the particular fascination with the bones within, their power of gripping the imagination, of standing forth. Following our discussion at the start of this study of the rhetorical nature of larger-scale sculpture, we recall our discussion of that technique of vividness, *enargeia*, which brought the matter to hand, *evidentia*, before the eyes, possessing energy and actuality. This actuality was as much part of the late medieval affective tradition of imagining by homing in on specifics.

Captivating surface detail is central to the literary imagining of things of wondrous appearance such as the fantastic Green Knight in the Middle English poem devoted to him: the knight and his horse is monstrously large and has a prodigious aesthetic of detailed surface.[113] The same highly worked conception of artifice is bodied forth in the gripping and sophisticated over life-size statue of St George in Stockholm's Storkyrkan executed by the sculptor Bernt Notke in the 1480s (pl. 110). This is a nearly four-metre high wooden group showing St George in traditional guise enclosed in sparkling gilded armour, hauling himself up by the stirrups of his no less brightly arrayed charger, while raising a mighty sword as if to strike the huge dragon beneath; this has been pierced by a lance and is surrounded by a grim litter of mangled human remains.[114] Baby dragons peek out gingerly from below the monster, itself rendered incontinent by fear; gold, human hair, leather, parchment and antlers all contribute to the confection, the binding of representation and substitution. Like a 'whited' sepulchre with its vile content, the whole thing is at once fantastic, indeed fascinating, but also absolutely macabre. The Stockholm image was far from isolated in its spiky, sophisticated realism: the St George presented to the London Armourers Company in 1528 and still in their successors' possession has a heart of oak but real iron and leather armour and trappings.[115] Such images are gifts to medieval materiality and 'minificence' studies. And they also illustrate a rhetorical norm (a norm of display rhetoric, anyway): that (probably following Aristotle's *Poetics*) we may be more moved by details than universals, or *particuliers* than *universeles*, as the eminent French theologian Jean Gerson (1363–1429) put it in his *Considerations sur saint Joseph*.[116]

EXIT: FEAR AND THE RHETORICAL ORDER OF DEATH

In this rhetorical order of the dead, fear plays a more explicit part than it had done at any time since the great twelfth-century Last Judgement portals of France. Fear, we recall, is prospective and admonitory, and legitimately plays a part in the function of a monument.

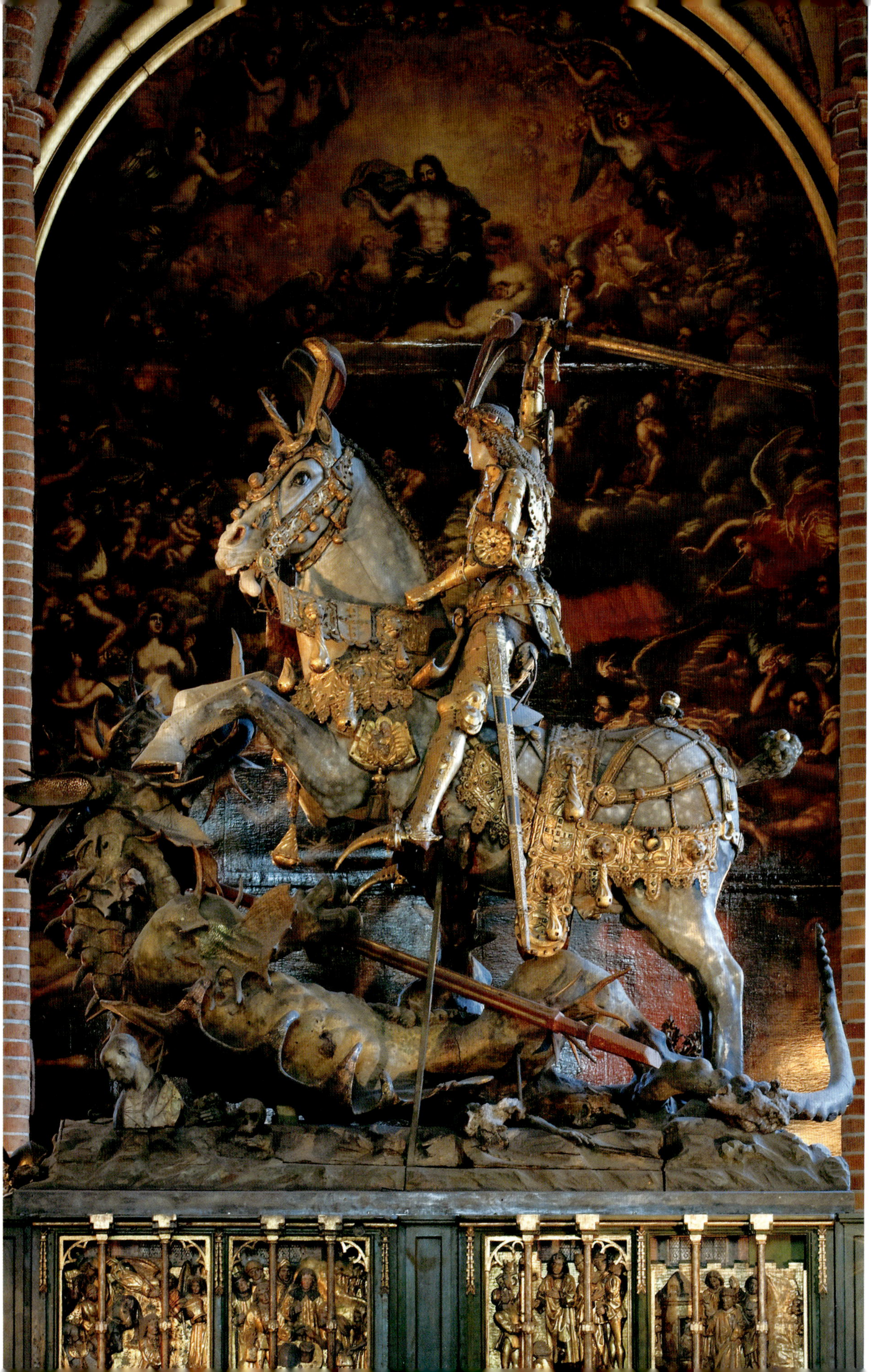

In earlier pages we turned to Isidore of Seville (*Etymologies* 15.11) writing of tombs that a monument is so named because it 'admonishes the mind' (*mentem monere*).[117] By 1400 macabre things had become fear's refuge. What, then, is the role of the unbeautiful in the act of mental admonition and persuasion? Here Augustine guides us. Aristotle had already shown that unpleasant images have captivating power and may give pleasure, and was followed in this by Averroes.[118] Augustine pondered this idea (*Confessions* 10.35) when thinking of the vice of the eyes, or *concupiscentia oculorum* (as in 1 John 2:16), which is to say futile or aimless gratification of the eye, or *curiositas*.[119] He distinguished between looking at something for pleasure and looking at it out of curiosity, because in the latter case unpleasantness provokes the appetite for knowledge; he explicitly cites the example of a mangled corpse the sight of which can only horrify (*quod exhorreas*), pandering to the same sort of titivated appetite as does a freak show. Despite this unlofty view of the impulses resulting from unpleasant spectacles, Augustine took a serious, purposeful view of fear itself. In *De Doctrina Christiana* (2.7), he argued that meditation itself begins in *timor Dei*, fear provoking thought about mortality with a resulting prickle of the flesh which adheres that flesh, as it were, to the Cross.[120] Dread is the beginning of wisdom, and of right action: again, we need to stress that all such imagery served conventional theological purpose, the admonition of mind, the struggle to repent, the attainment of confidence in the Resurrection and so on.[121]

Augustine shows how the essentially prospective emotion of fear had utility, a utility identified with late medieval 'philopassionism' but clearly one embedded in much older beliefs. Philopassionism, the love of suffering, more particularly useful or instructive suffering, is a concept put to significant effect by Esther Cohen.[122] Pain leads us to the good. The notion that the *willed* experience of something ugly or unpleasant (as much as of something beautiful) might affirm the conviction purpose of medieval art – that fear is an instrument with rhetorical and moral ends – is entirely consistent with the larger development of the visual arts, monumental sculpture especially, at this time. Fear as a means (but not as an end) served a practical purpose. Earlier, we examined the utility of the affects in sculpted portals of the Romanesque period, as at Autun, where the point – repentance, amendment of life – is driven firmly by large inscriptions referring to terror and horror. The depiction, or summoning of the image, of death falls into line with this imaginative order. In chapter 23, *De meditatione mortis*, of his *De Disciplina Claustrali*, Peter of Celle, the twelfth-century Bishop of Chartres, states that death is a debt to be paid, and to that end advises the reader to 'paint [*depinge*] Death before your eyes, how horrid is his face, his features so dark and staring'.[123] Peter takes a fundamentally ascetic approach to the role of affliction of the body in the stages of reading, meditation and contemplation; affliction, ascetic discipline, requires self-examination, mortification and also bringing terrible things before the eyes.[124] The notion of something to be painted, or that has been painted actually or in the mind,

110 Storkyrkan, Stockholm, St George and the Dragon, by Bernt Notke, 1480s, painted and gilded wood including human hair, leather, parchment and antlers. Note the remains of the dragon's victims.

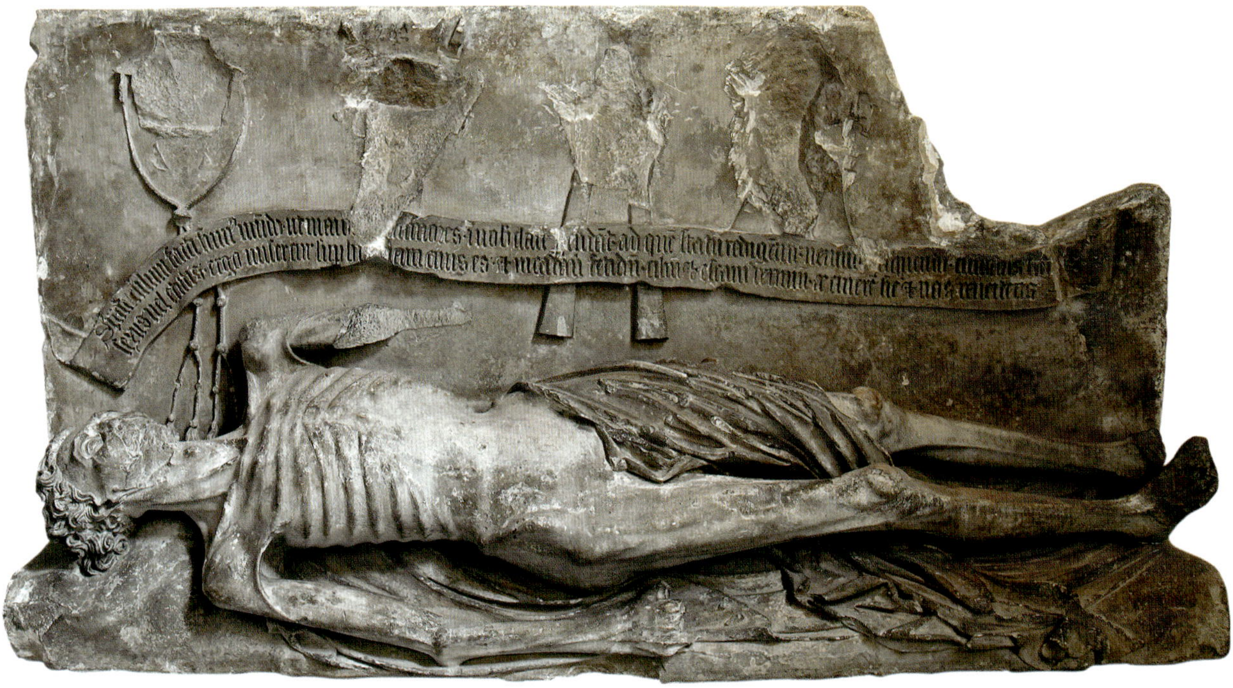

111 Cadaver or *transi* effigy of Cardinal Jean de Lagrange (d. 1402), formerly in Avignon Cathedral (Musée du Petit Palais, Avignon)

is a formula familiar to late antique and medieval literature, mythography especially, which persisted, not suprisingly, in fourteenth-century mendicant writing on such topics as the Roman pictures of Death.[125] In later medieval epitaphs and lyrics Death is overwhelmingly something brought before the eyes by means of such imperatives as *ecce* (behold) and *cerne* (such as, *cerne tuum speculum*, 'see your mirror', on the *transi* tomb of Archbishop Chichele at Canterbury), as well as in the vernacular; at Avignon, Cardinal Jean de Lagrange (d. 1402) was made a 'spectacle' in his pathetic decay according to the epitaph on his towering cadaver tomb (pl. 111).[126] The same language, following the text 'And they have looked and stared upon me' in the so-called Passion Psalm 21:18, was used of beholding the Cross (see pl. 108).

This paradox of the persuasiveness of the fearful, the ugly – its purposefulness – can therefore be illuminated, and shows that the history of the physical representation of death in its many forms participated in the rich rhetorical strategies of Gothic representation at large. As with this larger order, the causality at work remains elusive, for just as affectivity cannot of itself (to my mind) explain the representational accomplishments of Gothic art, so the long-established doctrine of *contemptus mundi*, contempt for the world as articulated by means of the bringing of death before the mind's eye, bore no obvious causal relationship to macabre imagery. In both cases the powers of imagination and of theology had long made apparent that which was to be less quickly articulated by human artifice apparent in the arts. In the first part of this study of the various forms of eloquence of Gothic art, I suggested that this causal disjunct must be understood, if not entirely explained, from within the history of artifice and representation itself, and is not necessarily susceptible to more general cultural explanation.

The binary structure of a topic such as the Three Living and Three Dead is, first, no more than a reiteration, albeit in peculiarly powerful form, of the syncretic method of comparison long exploited in moral exposition in Romanesque and Gothic sculpture, indeed art more generally. In 1408, according to an inscription recorded by Paris antiquarians, this very subject was chosen by Jean, Duc de Berry to adorn a portal of the church of the cemetery of the Innocents in Paris, later the home of the Dance of Death. The topic was executed in relief (*en bosse*) and appears to have comprised two large pictorial fields showing the two teams in woodland, possibly to either side of the doorway, with their dialogue set out below and a memorial inscription giving the date and patron's name on a lintel or cornice (*corniche*) either below the plaques or on the door's lintel; the arms of Berry were at each corner of the ensemble.[127] It is difficult not to see this setting, if not its plaque-like relief presentation, as a continuation of the binary and typological displays at Magdeburg and Strasbourg where the Wise and Foolish Virgins are accompanied by images of the World as seducer or seductress; in the case of Frau Welt at Worms, the two-faced figure is itself a microcosm of syncretic comparison. The arrival of a macabre topic at the Innocents is no more than an extrapolation from the rhetorical, but also theologically orthodox, tradition encountered in the first part of this study of shaping and forming the mysteries of Christian doctrine in terms of dialectical or typological opposition.[128]

This is certainly the logic – though 'logic' is too strong a word – of the fifteenth-century double-decker or *transi* tomb which shares with these sculpted ensembles the binary or mirrored structure of comparison, dialogue and dialectic.[129] It is natural to think of a splendid tomb such as that of Archbishop Henry Chichele (d. 1443) in the choir at Canterbury Cathedral, actually made in the Archbishop's lifetime in *c.*1424–6 and located opposite his throne (pl. 112), as an exemplification of the idea that the cadaver is literally a thing 'fallen' ('cadaver' coming from the Latin *cadere*); ugliness, *deformitas*, may be seen as a falling away from that which is *formosus*, possesses beauty.[130] In a familiar trope, its epitaph describes the prelate as born poor (*pauper natus*), raised (*elevatus*) to be Primate, then laid low (*prostratus*), and so in a sense he is.[131] It might seem more fitting to think of this continuum of rise and fall as an evocation of the Wheel of Fortune, an image also associated with English cathedral choirs, though much less often with tombs (pl. 113).[132] Resolution as such is not wholly the aim of these conceits. Ultimately, such double tombs are orthodox statements of prospective Christian faith in which we are encouraged to have confidence, not least faith in the

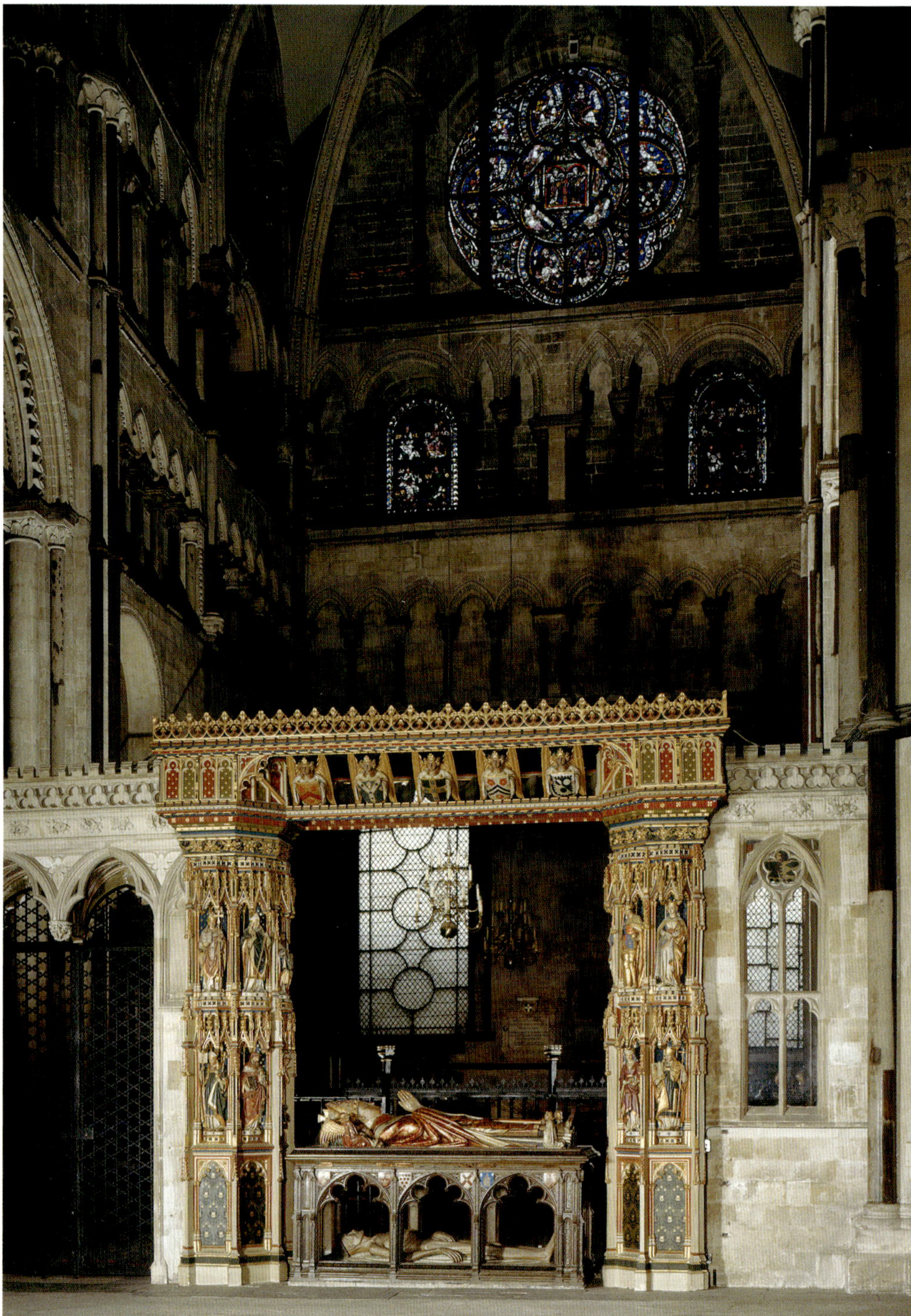

112 Canterbury Cathedral, choir, double-decker tomb of Archbishop Henry Chichele (d. 1443), raised around 1424–6, with north-east transept beyond

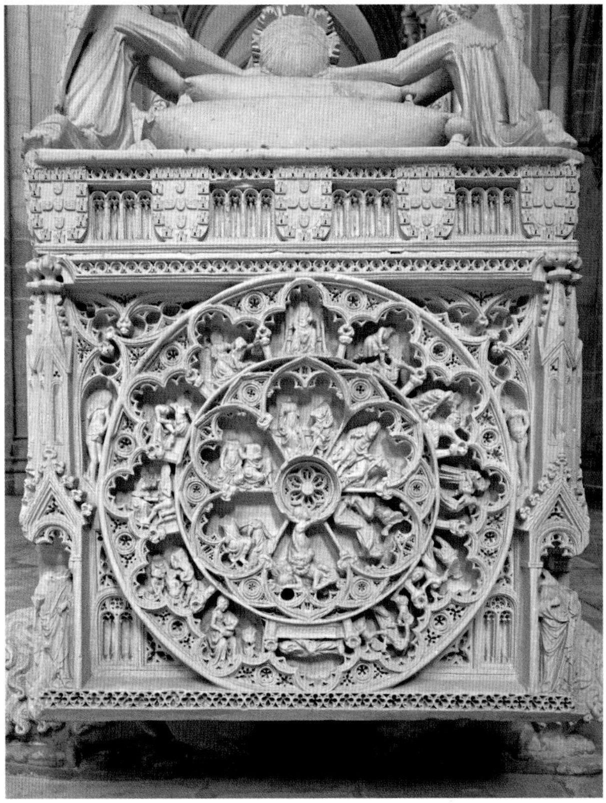

113 Cistercian monastery of Alcobaça (Portugal), tomb of King Pedro I of Portugal (d. 1367), white marble with Wheel of Fortune combined with King Pedro's life

Resurrection. Yet that they are also explorative seems to be arguable, for their images are always held in tension and are not over-determined. They cannot simply be read 'up' from the cadaver or 'down' from the effigy clothed in its finery; rather, they propose to us a state of irresolution between states or possibilities: change is uni-directional whereas the human imaginary is not.[133] At this point we ourselves are required to work. For which here is cause and which effect? In this regard such tombs are really ways of knowing death by obliging us to think: death does not confine meaning, but gathers and harvests it.[134] We still talk of 'turning something over' in our mind, an action captured by the verb *revolvo*, which carried the senses of unravelling, experiencing again, and also to cogitate, brood on or think over.[135] Macabre images are images of contemplation, unsettling or horrifying us, yet never offering the simple satisfaction of closure so much as an experience, almost impossible to fathom, of the rise and fall, the ascent and cadence of all mortal things in which the dread and the beautiful are eternally linked. The only closure is that offered by the final things.

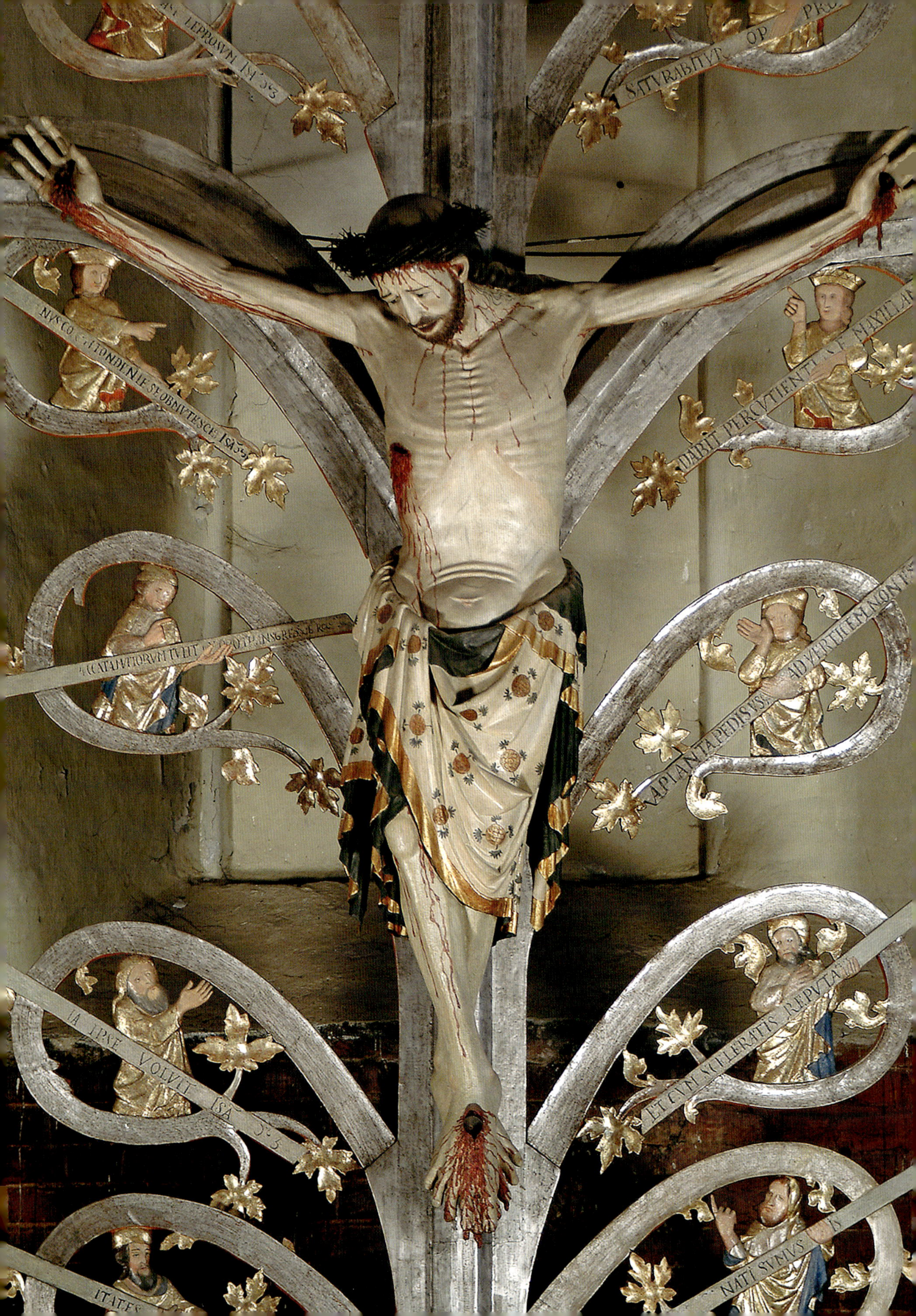
SATVRABITVR OP
DABIT PERCVTIENTI SE
A PLANTA PEDIS VSQ AD VERTICEM
ET CVM SCELERATIS REPVTA
IA IPSE VOLVIT ISA

Epilogue

At the outset of this study I considered the way that sculpture in the public domain – which tomb monuments generally were – often had as its work the dramatising of choice within the frame of an occasion which was public, social, in character. Familiar techniques of rhetorical comparison, *synkresis*, did exactly this work on tombs and portals by confronting the best possible with the worst possible outcomes. Their function was not to prescribe or express so much as to provoke experience, to indicate, move, guide and incentivise. In the Gothic period this work was energised by the capacity of imagery to steer deliberation (for artworks cannot deliberate) and to display through sheer art. In this process, reason and passion were necessarily coupled within that vital part of the equation, the audience. Such artefacts did not fizzle out in a display of emotion: they were more practical and purposeful, and also more artificial. Their affective and artificial powers were directed towards confidence and conviction. To gain these powers required tremendous, and changing, techniques. An important stage in the history of sculpture as an epideictic or 'display' medium was reached when, in the course of the twelfth and thirteenth centuries, tombs were increasingly erected inside churches and furnished with mimetic images of the dead (the privileged dead) in idealised form, as courtly in restraint, beautiful even, as the jamb figures of the portals of the great churches, and as restrained as funerary oration.

Yet beauty and sparkle paved the way for the ugly, the afflicted, the dark yet complicit side of comparison. In the second part of my study, I tried to show how medieval aesthetic language was relational, and how both formal and material causes were tied in to com-

114 Toruń, St James's Church, Tree of Life (detail of pl. 65)

peting patterns of intentionality which required feeling and thinking subjects as well as artefacts. The materials used in artworks were only part of a process of human imaginative experience and reflection. This was a self-aware activity. Between 1200 and 1400 the commemorative art of the tomb as an art of decorum became self-referential (for tombs were often copied from other tombs), self-affirming and stable. The art of the *transi* tomb, which emerged in the second half of the fourteenth century, continued to be referential because it preyed on this stable order by toppling its most cherished conventions. The effect of the *transi* was, doubtless, amplified by the presence within the tomb of a corpse; but the rise of the 'tomb beautiful' and its artful undoing owed much to the power of imagery and its conventions alone.[1] Those conventions had first to be established: once the tomb beautiful spoke with the voice of panegyric, its display became particularly geared to beauty and sparkle, to social nicety, nobility. At exactly that point the sepulchral order of Death could become a self-subverting utterance, a mode of anti-representation. Erwin Panofsky thought that the tomb formerly in Angers Cathedral of René d'Anjou (d. 1480), the titular king of Naples and Sicily, showing the monarch at the top of the tomb as a cadaver crowned in death yet scarcely upright as it collapses pathetically under its own weight, was an 'intentionally and tragically ironic parody' of the much older tomb of Robert the Wise (d. 1343) in S. Chiara in Naples.[2] We might quibble with the exciting words 'tragically ironic' and 'parody': the later tomb affects us and directs us, framing extremes in a method of dialectical opposition with dignified ancestry.

But 'intentionally' we can probably agree with. Although the origins of macabre imagery were probably more diverse than has sometimes been suggested, in this mode of powerful contrast lay a certain pleasure. It might seem glib to connect this tendency to the brilliant self-commentary evident in the sculpted and architectural arts of the later Middle Ages. Yet that there was a connection is apparent. In the to and fro of the Wise and Foolish Virgins, the dazzling vaults of Ingolstadt, the dialogue of the Three Living and Three Dead and the ruminative scanning of the *transi* tomb lay artifice (moral and crafted), a questioning wit, a capacity for enpuzzlement incapable of exact resolution but true, I think, of much in medieval art.

Notes

INTRODUCTION

1 Quintilian, *Institutio Oratoria* 10.3.17 in Russell 2001, vol. 127, 344–5.

2 Stahl and Burge 1977, 65.

3 Plotinus, *Enneads* 1.6.9 in Armstrong 1966, 258–9.

4 Guérin 2013, 65–6 and 76 n. 98.

5 See e.g. the dazzling collection of material in the 2011 Naumburg exhibition: Krohm and Kunde 2012.

1 OCCASION AND AGENCY

1 Ruskin 1960 (1851–3), 161–2, from Book II, ch. 4, 'The Nature of Gothic'. My thanks to Anya Burgon for pointing out this passage to me.

2 Carruthers 2013, 40 and for a general discussion Cosgrove 2008.

3 Panofsky 1979, 62, 64, though I have followed the translation in Carruthers 2013, 39.

4 For a succinct reference for this generalisation see Williamson 1995.

5 Boerner 2006 with bibliography.

6 For French 'harmonic facades' see Erlande-Brandenburg 1994, 204–14 and (in general) Sauerländer and Kroos 1972; Bony 1983a and Kimpel and Suckale 1990 are important general guides to French architecture.

7 For the situation in England see Stone 1972, 93–176 and Williamson 1995, 102–14, 200–18; for the Empire, see *inter alia* Nicolai 2002 and 2011, and for an opinion on a key term in this development, Schurr 2014.

8 The most theoretically well-known discussion of what he called 'intrinsic' as opposed to 'surface' classicism is Panofsky 1960, 55–68.

9 Sauerländer and Kroos 1972, 380–81, pls 1–3.

10 For various overviews, see Stone 1972, 56–92; Zarnecki, Holt and Holland 1984, 146–231 with bibliographies; Williamson 1995, 102–14; also Zarnecki 1953 and 1988 (with bibliography); for York Minster and the question of French-style facades in England, see the judicious study by Norton 1990.

11 Zarnecki 1988, 32–3 and figs 39 and 41 discusses Lincoln and the column figures formerly on the moot hall at Colchester; Williamson 1995, 102.

12 Williamson 1995, 102–3.

13 On this type of screen see McAleer 1988; for Wells, Malone 2004 and Binski 2004, 103–21.

14 Allan and Blaylock 1991. The Exeter facade remains relatively unstudied. Bony 1979, 67 suggested that the screen-like facade of Rouen followed English prototypes.

15 Binski 1995, 69–71, figs 15 and 94 for the state of the facade *c.*1713.

16 Williamson 1995, 206–8 for Westminster and Lincoln.

17 Erlande-Brandenburg 1994, 214.

18 A suggestion in Binski 2014a, 200–01.

19 E.g., Mâle 1919, 1922; Katzenellenbogen 1959; Sauerländer and Kroos 1972; for further remarks see Joubert 2008, 97–138.

20 Here only a selection is feasible. Of these the least developed is the rhetorical and sermonal approach, but see the important studies by Sánchez Ameijeiras 2011 and 2014 which deploy an Auerbachian model (discussed later here) in discussion of levels of style and the *ars predicandi*; Kemp 1997, 102–14 should also be consulted; for sermons, sculpture and rhetorical strategies see S. Murray 2004; for liturgical studies see e.g. Fassler 1993a and Fassler 1993b; a classic of ideological reading is Camille 1989 and see also J. W. Williams 1993; for reform see Castiñeiras 2015; for doctrine and affect, see Boerner 2008, esp. 33–71; for epigraphy on portals, Debiais 2017; for the senses and affects, see the studies by Büchsel in Krohm and Kunde 2012, vol. 1, 177–86 and by Niehr in vol. 3, 154–67; also Jung 2006, 2010, 2013, Guérin 2013, 2016, 2017 and more generally Palazzo 2014 and 2016; a broadly mnemonic position is taken by Recht 1996 and 2008, 195–262.

21 Again, a selection: Kurmann 1987, 1996, 1998; Guillouët 2003 and 2011; a fundamental reassessment of chronology and technique is proposed by J. Wirth 2004 principally in response to the work of Kurmann: see Kurmann 1987 and 1996.

22 A fundamental study is Kimpel 1977.

23 I have enlarged on this in Binski 2014a, 54–7 in response to the work of Hans Belting and the school of *Bild-anthropologie*, and see in particular Barber 1995 (in a volume of *Gesta* devoted to Belting's ideas) and Hamburger 2013. I return to it in the second part of this study.

24 As a judicious exponent of anthropological school, Hamburger 1998, 14–15 remarks: 'The anthropological turn in art history has restored to premodern artifacts something of the immediacy and liveliness that they had lost in intervening centuries'. He continues, wisely, 'despite the convergence of postmodern and premodern, however, there remains the danger of anachronism'. My book continues to alert us to precisely this danger. For ventriloquism, Ginzburg 2013, 105–6.

25 A subtle but important point made by Podro 1982b, 214–15 in regard to the 'retrieval of the past' and wanton anachronism: there is a distinction between accepting that we are historically positioned and refusing to recognise historical difference or the viewpoints of others, indeterminate as the borderlines between the two may be; see also Ginzburg 2013.

26 For the term 'Romanesque' see Bizzarro 1992. For an essay on style see Recht 1993–4.

27 Binski 2010b.

28 Trumbull 1896, 69–74; van Gennep 1960, 20–25; for liminality as a structuring principle of medieval cultural criticism, see Gertsman and Stevenson 2012.

29 Sánchez Ameijeiras 2011, 96–104 and 2014, 96–113.

30 A large topic: in general Debiais 2017 for the period to 1200, with bibliography; see also Kendall 1989; Sauerländer 1992, 19–20; Verzar 1992; J. Wirth 2004, 71–5; Bouché 2006; Castiñeiras 2009; and Stratford 1986–90, 246–9 for medieval mislabelling.

31 Cited Sánchez Ameijeiras 2015, 721 n. 58; Castiñeiras 1999.

32 I refer especially to Carruthers 2013, 13–14, 42, 87, 100, 102.

33 E.g. Margot Fassler's discussion in Fassler 1993a.

34 Brush 2008; Jung 2017.

35 As in Gombrich's 'logic of situations': see Gombrich 1978a, 62 for the structural conditions of communication, and particularly Gombrich 1984, 209–16. For situational agency, Binski 2014a, 180. Bitzer 1968 explores the notion of situation and rhetoric without reference to formal rhetorical writings.

36 For the former, now cut back, see Kahn 1992a, 68–9, figs 32 and 33; for Naumburg, see *inter alia* Kidson 1987, Brush 1993 and Jung 2013, the fullest documentation by far being in Krohm and Kunde 2012.

37 Two foundational studies making 'universalist' claims about ornament are Gombrich 1984 and Grabar 1992, Gombrich's analysis being perceptual or psychological, situational and functional, Grabar's stressing the dialogic or performative character of ornament, its role in creating pleasure through carrying beauty, and its ability to be understood trans-historically and trans-culturally.

38 Henderson 1972, 68–9.

39 For ironwork, Geddes 1999.

40 Thurlby 1999, 37–70.

41 Gell 1992.

42 For *incantatio*, Carruthers 2013, 27; for Idealist transcendentalism, a classic text is Worringer 1912, 48–54, 73–81, 114–18.

43 For *ductus*, Carruthers 1998, 77–81 and 2010, 190–213.

44 Seminal texts of formal analysis of this type begin with the essays collected in Schapiro 1977 and his lectures, Schapiro 2006; for structural analysis of ornament, see Bonne 1996 and for mediation, Grabar 1992; for ornament and ordering, see Gombrich 1984 and Caviness 1983; following Schapiro and others, for dislocation see Carruthers 1998, 261–6, Weinryb 2013 and 2016, 61–2. For insular line, see Ghrádaigh 2012.

45 Doob 1990, 97–8, 207–11.

46 For the trumeau and its context, Schapiro 1977, 102–30 and 2006, 53; for Moissac and Souillac see also the excellent account in Henderson 1972, 90–95; Carruthers 1998, 264–5.

47 Borg 1985.

48 Schapiro 1977, 131–264 for Moissac's cloister and portal; for the date, J. Wirth 2004, 26–7.

49 St Augustine, *Confessions* (10.35), in Migne 1844–64, vol. 32, col. 802, which I owe to Anya Burgon. For 12th-century images of violence and struggle, see Rudolph 1997 and for struggle as a metaphor for spiritual reading, see Kendrick 1999, 110–46. Doob 1990, 145–91 discusses moral labyrinths.

50 Hence 'Manueline' Gothic. For Batalha see Guillouët 2011 and for introductory text and bibliography, Orfão et al. 2014, 88–91.

51 Bynum 2001, 37–75 for a stimulating introduction to the phenomenon of wonder in the Middle Ages, and the (differing) responses of admiration (as it were standing back) and imitation (moving towards) which result from it.

52 Verzar 1992, 128.

53 De Bruyne 1946, 216; principally Carruthers 2013, 135–64.

54 A large topic: see Schapiro 1977, 6–10; Carruthers 1998, 82–7 and 2013, 146–55.

55 Mortet 1911, 166, discussed by Schapiro 1977, 13.

56 Garton 1986, 54 lines 879–80.

57 Ruskin 1849, 23: 'the grace and luxuriance of it all are visible – sensible rather – even to the uninquiring eye'.

58 Quintilian, *Institutio Oratoria*, 8.3.12 in Butler 1921, vol. 126, 216: *Quare, quidquid erit sententiis populare, verbis nitidum, figuris iucundum, translationibus magnificum, compositione elaboratum, velut institor quidam eloquentiae intuendum et paene pertractandum dabit.*

59 Carruthers 2013, 45–6 and for the study of the emotions, see Rosenwein 1998, 2002, 2006 and Boquet 2005. For the distinction between affect and passion, see Tambling 2010. For 'aesthetic-affective styles, and public moods', see e.g. Bennett 2010, xii. For mood and presence, see Gumbrecht 2004 and for mood as a frame for meditation, Carruthers 1998, 264.

60 Van Gennep 1960.

61 For consent and conviction or confident belief (*fides*), starting with Aristotle and the rhetoricians, see Carruthers 2013, 13–15, 38, 42, 84, 102, 119–20. For Joinville and *ferme creance* see Kumler 2011, 75.

62 Carruthers 1998, 221–4; for portals and liturgy, Fassler 1993a.

63 Cicero, *De Inventione*, in Hubbell 2006, 40–41: *Exordium est oratio animum auditoris idonee comparans ad reliquam dictionem; quod eveniet si eum benevolum, attentum, docilem confecerit*; compare Aristotle, *Rhetoric*, II.1378a.5, in J. Barnes 1984, vol. 2, 2194; also Copeland and Sluiter 2009, 627; Carruthers 2013, 54.

64 Bynum 2001, 37–75; for *assimilatio*, see Allen 1982.

65 For such images see Gertsman 2015a.

66 For amplification and abbreviation or diminution in micro-architecture, see Binski 2014a, 140–45 and Binski 2018.

67 Bony 1979, 54.

68 Mary Carruthers drew my attention to Peter of Celle's remarks in her 2016 Clark Lectures; see Feiss 1987, 139.

69 Bernard of Clairvaux, discussed also in Binski 2004, 119–21; Latin original in Leclercq, Talbot and Rochais 1957, 155–6, my translation.

70 Isidore of Seville, *Etymologies* XV.xi in Barney et al. 2006, 313; see also Cahn 1992, 48 and in general Hardison 1992.

71 For the 'Roman' dimensions of the west front of Lincoln, see Quiney 2001 and Heslop 2012, 171–4.

72 Christe 1973.

73 For Wells and related facades, see Sampson 1998, 168–76, also Ayers 2000, 70–82 and Malone 2016 for a full discussion.

74 Carruthers 1990, 223–4.

75 Palazzo 2014, 150; see also Palazzo 2016.

76 Rubinelli 2009, 106–9; Cicero, *De Inventione*, 2.47–8 in Hubbell 2006, 310–12.

77 For the notion of *lieu de mémoire*, see Nora 1996.

78 Schapiro 2006, 3–33.

79 Ibid., 4–6, 19–20, 142–3.

80 Carruthers 2013, 17 and 27–8 for characterisations of ludic spaces as at once privileged yet not 'walled off' from the greater social world. There is a fine line to tread

between this concept and that evolved by Huizinga's *Homo Ludens* (1949) and earlier in Schiller's *Letters on the Aesthetic Education of Man* (1794, nos 14 and 15), in which play is a form of freedom, never in earnest.

81 See also Berliner 1945.

82 Belting 1994, 409, also 262; for a discussion Binski 2004, 175.

83 Beckwith 1993, 40–44.

84 See Cahn 1992, 46–7, discussing *Rezeptionsästhetik* and object-agency versus subject-agency in 'interpretative communities'. For a discussion of Gothic sculpture and public reception, see Jung 2013.

85 Habermas 1992.

86 Hauser 1999, esp. 33–4.

87 For horizons, see Jauss 1982 and for interpretative communities, Fish 1980.

88 Gilbert 2001, 11–12.

89 For the so-called *ratio triplex* (that artworks are didactic, affective and memorable) see *inter alia* the general remarks in Hamburger 1998, 111–14; Boerner 2008, 33–71 is rich in source citation. For the later Middle Ages, see Gayk 2010, 2.

90 Passages from Gregory cited in Chazelle 1990, 139–40, translation however following Carruthers 1990, 222; the notion of burning or inflaming is, like many affective ideas, of great antiquity: Kessler 2006, 152.

91 Carruthers 2013, 79, 116.

92 Binski 2004, 156 citing the Salisbury diocesan statutes of 1238–44.

93 See the (sceptical) discussion in Cahn 1987.

94 For Compostela see Castiñeiras 1999 and for the *visio Thurkilli*, Schmidt 1978a and 1978b; also Plötz 1995, 359–65 and Castiñeiras 2015, 24–5.

95 For such modes see Carruthers 2014b.

96 Douie and Farmer 1985, vol. 2, 137–44 (ch. 2). For interest in visions in Adam's circle, see Munns 2016, 42.

97 Garton 1986, discussed in Binski 2004, 55–62.

98 Douie and Farmer 1985, vol. 2, 140–41 (trans. slightly adapted).

99 This is the moral of the framing anecdotes related at ibid., 138–44.

100 For recollection see Carruthers 1990, 16–32. The expression *cordis oculos* is used, for instance, by Sicard of Cremona for the priest at Mass: Boerner 2008, 40, 252 n. 107.

101 Cahn 1992, 49 asks reasonably: 'How well Romanesque sculpture does these things, however, is open to question'.

102 The literature is extensive but for ekphrasis see *inter alia* James and Webb 1991, 8; Webb 1999 and Debiais 2017, 145–51.

103 Ambrose 2011, fig. 10.

104 Sauerländer and Kroos 1972, ills. 108, 147, 239; Wormald 1973, pl. 37 (Winchester Psalter); Morgan 1982, no. 23 (Munich Psalter); Denny 1984; J. Wirth 2004, 200, 236–42 (Conques); for Mainz, Brush 2008, fig. 1 and Krohm and Kunde 2012, vol. 1, 621–62, items IV.3–4.

105 Joubert 2008, 77–8 and fig. 54, pl. XI; also Pressouyre and Prigent 1989, 807 noting the *Magna Vita* account. The fragments were found in a ditch to the south of the apse, not far from the chapter-house complex. John and Hugh, however, paused *ad porticam ecclesiam*, implying the church itself. The orientation of the blessed, forming a group 130 cm high, would be correct for a position to Christ's right in a Last Judgement but the continuous yet open, almost Baroque, composition and high relief is unusual and not obviously consistent with the arrangement of most French portal voussoirs of this period. The cloth-bearing angel now included with this group is consistent with the angels which carry the Instruments of the Passion on contemporary Judgement portals.

106 For two rhetorical approaches, see Carruthers 2013, Sánchez Ameijeiras 2011 and 2014.

107 See above all Curtius 1990, 154–66; the classical division is given in Aristotle's *Rhetoric*, 1358b in J. Barnes 1984, vol. 2, 2159–61. For a practical exposition, see Cassiodorus, *Expositio Psalmorum* in Copeland and Sluiter 2009, 216–20; Burrow 2008, 6–9. In the 13th century the division was known principally through Cicero's *Ad Herennium*, 1.2.2 in Caplan 1954, 4.

108 For remembering the future, see Carruthers 1998, 66–9.

109 See the discussion in Deimling 1998.

110 Red is a 'visual metaphor of value': Gombrich 1978a, 13.

111 Williamson 1995, 54–7; Nicolai 2002, 112–14.

112 For the English vernacular tradition of praise poetry, see Woolf 1968 and Burrow 2008, 68–70.

113 For a useful consideration of the use of rhetorical style in the transition from antiquity to early Christianity, see Elsner 2014, 338–9. For typology as a form see Auerbach 1953, 73–6, 156–62, 194–202.

114 Draghi et al. 2006 for a discussion of the programme on the Aula Gotica at S. Quattro Coronati, Rome.

115 There is a perceptive discussion of the relationship at Moissac between the parable of Dives and the Apocalypse in Henderson 1972, 90 and for a seminal discussion, see Schapiro 1977, 131–264; for Magdeburg, Jung 2006 and Boerner 2008, 58–62.

116 Elsner 2014, 317, 333–49.

117 Carruthers 1998, 68–9.

118 See Cicero, *De Partitione Oratoria* 2.5 and 3.10 in Rackham 1942, 312–14 and 318: *Nam aut auscultator est modo qui audit aut disceptator, id est, rei sententiaeque moderator.*

119 Here I echo the (Weberian) discussion of instrumental and value rationality in D'Avray, 2010, 19–30, conviction being essentially a manifestation of value rationality shaped by instrumental rationality.

120 Carruthers 2013, 13–15, 38, 42.

121 Boerner 2008, 52–5; for fear Carruthers 1998, 264.

122 Bouché 2006; in general Debiais 2017.

123 See Carruthers 2014b for a bravura discussion of these terms, and for paralysis on portals, Ambrose 2011 and Dale 2010.

124 Cahn 1992, 48, fig. 22.

125 For prophecy see also Sánchez Ameijeiras 2014, 160–64 and 2011, 116–18.

126 Carruthers 1998, 80–81 and for earlier tradition Edsall 2014, 39–41.

127 There are some observations of value on this issue in Gombrich 1978a, 23–7, esp. 25 in which pre-Romantic depictions of the affects are distanced from the 'hydraulic' or naturalistic theory of the emotions discussed below.

128 See e.g. Jung 2006, 136–7 stating of the affective body language at Magdeburg that it would 'allow beholders to understand, through a dynamic process of *empathetic engagement* [my italics], the internal *responses* [author's italics] which that outcome engendered'. Jung develops her position in Jung 2018.

129 Carruthers 2013, 85. For the cognitive model of the emotions see Rosenwein 2002, 836–7.

2 FIGURE AND AFFECT

1 Studies which touch on ethical imitation and visual culture include Jaeger 1985, Schmitt 1990, Jaeger 1994 and Binski 2004. Bynum 1982 frames the history of spirituality partly in the light of these theories of form.

2 Moore 1987.

3 For a Foucauldian perspective, see Kumler 2011, 3–4.

4 Binski 2004, 149–77, and 174 for Grandisson's 1339 remark and its context.

5 A large literature. For 'emotionology', a term coined no later than the 1980s, see Stearns and Stearns 1985; for a range of opinion see de Souza 1987; Reddy 1997, 2001 and 2009; Rosenwein 1998, 2002 and 2006; Corrigan, Crump and Kloos 2000; Knuuttila 2004; Schnell 2004; Arnold 2008; Plamper 2012.

6 The seminal text for constraint and civility is Elias 1982; see Rosenwein 2002 for a critique; for *mimesis* and *zelos* see Elsner and Meyer 2014, 23.

7 See the bravura discussion of the depiction of virtue at Strasbourg Cathedral in Jaeger 1994, 331–48, supported by Binski 2004, 257–9.

8 Allen 1982.

9 Paetow 1927, 174, 243–4, discussed in Binski 2004, 259.

10 Könsgen 2004, 6, lines 58–61, with the variant *animarum* in line 5: *Quid significat porta ecclesia: / Ecclesie porta Ihesus est, qui sidera pandit; / Suppositos aliis doctores dico columpnas / Templi sculpturas morum dic esse figuras / Vivas picturas animarum non perituras.*

11 Le Roux de Lincy and Tisserand 1867, 48; for comment, Perkinson 2009, 86–7.

12 Davril and Thibodeau 1995, 412, I.iii.22: *Ceterum sculpture prominentes de parietibus egredientes ecclesie videntur, quia cum virtutes fidelibus in tantam consuetudinem deveniunt ut eis naturaliter insite videantur, multifariis earum operationibus exercentur.* The first half of the passage derives from 1 Kings 6:29 describing the relief-work in the Temple of Solomon: see also Thibodeau 2007, 38–9, no. 22. Cited by Camille 1989, 45–6; it appears to be alluded to by Bynum 2011, 44.

13 Jaeger 1994, 258–9 and for Alan of Lille, 284–6.

14 Camille 1989, 33–4.

15 Lehmann-Brockhaus 1955–60, vol. 3, no. 587; see Binski 2004, 135.

16 See Kren and Wieck 1990, 53, 57.

17 For metaphor and ornaments of style, see the *Poetria Nova* of Vinsauf in Nims 1967, 42–72.

18 Isidore, *Etymologies*, I.36 in Barney et al. 2006, 58; compare Bede, *De Schematibus et Tropis* in Copeland and Sluiter 2009, 267. For a discussion see Celentano, Chiron and Noel 2004.

19 In the absence of a developed medieval terminology for what we now call 'motifs' I have

borrowed the idea of the topic from the traditional definition of the *topica*, as in Cassiodorus, *Institutiones*, 2.3.14, the topics being the 'seats' or points of origination of arguments, from Carruthers 1998, 23–4 and notes.

20 C. F. Barnes 2009; for further discussion Binski 2012 and J. Wirth 2015.

21 For the colours see Arbusow 1948; Carruthers 2013, 54, 157–8, 186; Tilliette 2013; for clothing, Snyder 2011.

22 Tilliette 2013, 283; Pastoureau 2013, 231.

23 Fuller 2011, 77.

24 This is also discussed in the next chapter. Quintilian, *Institutio Oratoria* 2.17.21 in Russell 2001, vol. 124, 386 expresses suspicion of mimesis; for *color* and glossing see *Institutio Oratoria* 4.2.88–100 in Butler 1921, vol. 125, 98–103; Tilliette 2013, 279–80.

25 Schmitt 1990; Recht 2008, 240; see also Burrow 2002.

26 For liturgical gesture see e.g. Ladner 1961; for gesture and argument, Enders 2001, Otter 2010; for controlled gesture and posture, Binski 2004, 197; for gesture and the courtroom, Schmitt 1990, 59–70 and Brand 2015, 57–8.

27 Verret and Steyaert 2002; see also Joubert 2008, 199–202 and Recht 2008, 239–62. Numerous instances of original polychromy are illustrated in Krohm and Kunde 2012, e.g. vol. 1, 390–94, pls 8–17 (Strasbourg).

28 For reconstructions see Sampson 1998, 113–32; Ayers 2000, 111–30, pls I–VI (by Eddie Sinclair).

29 Castiñeiras 1999.

30 Carruthers 2013, 123–34; the cost of painting is stressed by Pastoureau 2013.

31 Le Roux de Lincy and Tisserand 1867, 46.

32 *Calendar of Close Rolls*, 1929, 165: *depingi faciat de melioribus coloribus quos invenire poterit, ita quod ibi depingatur historia regis Nabugodonosor distincte et aperte*. The expression *distincte et aperte* has liturgical and legal associations: see e.g. Binski 2004, 156–7.

33 Carruthers 2013, 84 and n. 9; Quintilian, *Institutio Oratoria* 6.2.32 in Butler 1921, vol. 125, 434–6.

34 As argued by Quintilian, *Institutio Oratoria*, 8.3.61, in Butler 1921, vol. 126, 244. Here Quintilian contrasts the verbs *pateo* and *ostendo*, the latter having the more active power of reaching outwards. The notion of ostension assists us in understanding what Shearman and others call the 'transitive' mode of engagement: Shearman 1992, 27, 33 derived from the Idealism of Riegl and ultimately Hegel.

35 For further thoughts see James and Webb 1991; compare Roland Barthes's 'reality effect', the basis of which is essentially rhetorical: Barthes 1989.

36 Segré 1957, 4–5 lines 3–5, and 6–7.

37 For indexicality see Turel 2011, which should be read with Snyder 1980.

38 James and Webb 1991; Carruthers 1998, 118–21, 130–35.

39 Sauerländer 1992, 39 and fig. 16; for the date, Cahn 1987, 28–9.

40 See e.g. Pevsner 1945 and Givens 2005.

41 Carruthers 1990, 108; Carruthers 1998, 16; Binski 2014a, 65; for portrayal and counterfeit see e.g. Parshall 1993, Perkinson 2009, 47–61; Turel 2011. The same terms are discussed by J. Wirth 2015, 47–56.

42 Belting 1994, 261–96.

43 Forsyth 2002, following Schapiro 1977; see also Ambrose 2011, 9–12.

44 Above all see Schapiro 2006, 154–84; also Caviness 1983.

45 Williamson 1995 is a good general guide to these developments; for the 'rhetoric' of the broad fold style (a term owed originally to, *inter alia*, Robert Branner), see Jean Wirth in Krohm and Kunde 2012, vol. 2, 1254–62; for the Gothic face in this period, see *inter alia* Jaeger 1994, 331–48 (for *moralitas*); Binski 1997 and 2004, 233–59 (the latter for the ambivalence of facial expressions and the dangers of psychological readings); see also the essays in Jung 2006, Little 2006, Gertsman 2010b, Otter 2010 and Jung 2018.

46 The principal studies of Reims and its diaspora are numerous. The major source for photo-documentation is Hamann-MacLean and Schüssler 1993–2008; Williamson 1995, 47–101, 141–99 gives a fair account of the literature to that point. Kurmann 1987 and 1998 should be read with the revisionist account (i.e. earlier datings) in J. Wirth 2004, 47–9 (Reims), 52–7 (Amiens), 58–9 (Bourges *jubé*), with corresponding re-datings of the German monuments to the 1220s and 30s, for which see also Krohm and Kunde 2012.

47 Lehmann and Schubert 1988.

48 Quintilian, *Institutio Oratoria*, 8.5.34 in Butler 1921, vol. 126, 298–9.

49 Williamson 1995, 193–5; for Basel, Meyer 1945, pls 43–5; for Strasbourg and Freiburg, Boerner 2008, 139–92.

50 Sciurie 1993–4; Williamson 1995, 174, 177; Jung 2006 and 2018.

51 *Calendar of Close Rolls*, 1911, 514: *et capellam regine depingi et lambruscari faciat et inter alias picturas depingi faciat quinque virgines sapientes et quinque fatuas*; but see the re-dating to the 1230s of the Magdeburg figures proposed in J. Wirth 2004, 156–75.

52 Sauerländer 1992, 23 and 25.

53 Munns 2016, 86–9, fig. 14; for such gestures see the classic study by Barasch 1976.

54 'Rationale' as in Schmitt 1990.

55 Barasch 1976, 82, fig. 44.

56 A Panofskian topic: Panofsky 1953, vol. 1, 21–50; for Strasbourg see Gould 1992 and recently Borlée 2014.

57 Documents cited in S. Murray 1987, 188, at 1517–18, payment to Jehan Briaix, *painctre*, for cartoons for sculpted portal images; Kurmann 1998, 23.

58 Panofsky 1979, 25.

59 Compare, however, Jung 2006, 146–7.

60 The classic statement of ratcheting as a reponse to jaded or blunted sensibility is that of Göller, as criticised by Wölfflin: see Gombrich 1984, 201, 212–13; also Wollheim 1980, 136.

61 Schmitt 1981 and 1990.

62 Lucas of Tuy, 1612, 104 (Book II, cap. XI): *Sed dicit aliquis, ad hoc uno pede super alio, uno clavo Dominum dicimus crucifixum, et consuetudines Ecclesiae volumus immutari, ut maiori acerbitate passionis Christi populi devotio excitetur, et novitate in consuetudinibus succedente fastidium relevetur*, 'But someone else says "we say that Christ was crucified with one foot over the other by one nail, and that we wish to change the Church's customs in order that by means of the greater harshness of the passion of Christ the devotion of the people might be stirred up, and boredom assuaged by new customs as a result"'. The underlying notions are certainly rhetorical: for some context see Binski 2004, 221–2.

63 For *varietas* and tedium, see Carruthers 2013, 135–64 and Binski 2004, 222.

64 Rowland 1975, 57, lines 60–76; trans. here mostly after Carruthers 1990, 130–37, 281–8, 349–50 from Cambridge, Fitzwilliam Museum, Ms. McClean 169, fols 254–6.

65 Parshall 1999, 456–8: Bradwardine's emphasis on red is directly indebted to the *Ad Herennium*, a text which stresses the importance of active images (*imagines agentes*).

66 A large subject: for two classic texts see Watson 1930 and Skinner 1974. For the limitations of this type of analysis of emotion, see Kenny 1963, 42–3.

67 For this idea see Ryle 1976.

68 Vinsauf in Nims 1967, 90–91; also Otter 2010.

69 We find this especially in orthodox thinkers such as Lydgate: see Gayk 2010, 84–122, esp. 96–102.

70 Here I allude to Wollheim's discussion (based on Wittgenstein) of intransitive and transitive senses: 'the statue is expressive' (intransitive) and 'the statue expresses grief' (transitive): Wollheim 1980, 93–6 section 41.

71 On the stochastic or rational-estimative character of engagement with represented expression, see Binski 2004, 247–56.

72 Baxandall 1980, 153–63. Baxandall's rhetorical theory claims, I think rightly (158), that represented gesture indicates not the kind but the degree of emotion, because a 'gamut of feeling is not narrowly differentiated'.

73 Maguire 1974, 132–4.

74 For a pluralist (and I think sometimes philosophically ill-defined) discussion of empathy simply as fellow-feeling, see Morrison and Bell 2013. I note, however, Newman 2013 on co-inherence, which nevertheless persists in using the term empathy. For friendship, see Hamburger 2007 and Woolf 1968, 214–17.

75 See Rosenwein 2002, 834–7 and Rosenwein 2006; see also Reddy 2001 and 2009; a useful account is in Arnold 2008. Gombrich 1978a, 23–7 distinguishes between involuntary signs and acculturated symbols in bodily expression; see also 56–69.

76 For a critique of commonsense realist expression, see Belsey 1980.

77 Walton 1990, 195–204 and esp. 214–59.

78 See e.g. Dadlez 1997.

79 See on the contrary Freedberg 1989. Gaiger 2011 is alert to some of these difficulties.

80 Carruthers 1990, 33–4 and 200–01; Carruthers 1998, 64.

81 Forshaw 1973; for the French redaction, Wilshere 1982.

82 Forshaw 1973; see the passage nos 93–103 at 82–93, and for the passage cited next, 83–5. The edition includes a parallel text of the version known as the *Speculum Religiosorum*. See Binski 2004, 193–7 for the impact of this compilation.

83 Forshaw 1973, 18, 19, 20, 32 cap. 2 (*Speculum Religiosorum*), 33 cap. 1 (*Speculum Ecclesie*).

84 Ideas which were not so crisply distinguished that they passed easily into the vernacular, see the notes on vocabulary in Wilshere 1982, xxxv–xxxviii.

85 For critical discussion see e.g. Prinz 2011 and Bloom 2016.

86 Aquinas 1906, 226–7, Qu. 94, art. III. Aristotle, *Rhetoric*, II.2.1378b, 1–5 in J. Barnes 1984, vol. 2, 2195 connects pleasure to the idea of revenge.

87 Discussed by A. Murray 1981.

88 Aristotle, *De Anima*, I.403a, 1–28 in J. Barnes 1984, vol. 1, 642–3; see Fortenbaugh 2002 for the best account; Carruthers 1990, 49, 54, 67–8; Boquet 2005; Knuuttila 2004; Rosenwein 2006; Tambling 2010; Carruthers 2013, 8, 34, 46. In his theological writings Robert Grosseteste, Bishop of Lincoln (d. 1253), uses the term *affectus* as a quality of the soul meaning something like 'desire' or 'affection', as distinguished from *aspectus*, reason or, rather, the way reason 'sees': see Minnis 1988, 119–21; McEvoy 2000, 78; in general Ginther 2016.

89 On which point see R. M. Garnett 1909, 270; McNamer 2010, 119 and for argument see Carruthers 2006c.

90 See e.g. Jung 2006, 153–4.

91 Young 1933, vol. 2, 238: *et tantum quod populus quietetur a risu propter Synagogam expulsam*; see also 406.

92 As per Ambrose: see Auerbach 1965, 68. For *seria* and *ludus*, Carruthers 2013, 141–2.

93 Carruthers 2006a, esp. 1010 for paradox; also Carruthers 2013, 80–107.

94 Reiners-Ernst 1939 is central to this: see pls 12 and 15; see also Hamburger 1997b, 12–13 for a discussion including the 'smiling' Crucifix from Eichstätt, his fig. 4; for mixed affects see Carruthers 2013, 140–46; also Gayk 2010, 101–2 for Lydgate and affects; McNamer 2010, 119–49.

95 Cited Bynum 2001, 71 and 219 n. 76.

96 Compare, however, Jaeger 1994, 331–48.

97 The classic literary investigation is Ménard 1969, and for an empirical overview Svanberg 1993b; Binski 1997 for the smile and metaphysical deportment; Binski 2004, 233–59 (for the Aristotelianised 'superiority' theory – not of course the only way of understanding laughter to anyone with a sense of humour); for Gothic faces more generally, Little 2006. The account in Gertsman 2010b overlooks the discussions of 'emotion' in Baxandall 1980 and Binski 2004, as does the paper by Gesine Mierke in Krohm and Kunde 2012, vol. 3, 180–87; see also Starkey 2003; Wilhelmy 2012 and for medieval English vernacular, Burrow 2002.

98 Vinsauf in Nims 1967, 42 (IV); for another 'whited sepulchre' image, see S. Murray 2004, 91, line 97.

99 Jung 2006, 149–50, though in the context of an argument in favour of empathetic reading; see also Bitzer 1968 for situation.

100 Rowe 2011, 288–90; for repentance and related purposes, Boerner 2008, 52, 58, 109–38; Gayk 2010, 97–8.

101 For 'pointing to' see Carruthers 1998, 121.

102 Arnold 2008, 109–10, 113.

103 Elkins 2001, 70–83; for tears, weeping and their connection (or indeed otherwise) to inner emotional states, see also Carruthers 2006b and 2013, 140–46.

104 For studies of affective piety in later medieval literature and art, see e.g. Woolf 1968; Marrow 1979, 1–32; Kieckhefer 1984; Beckwith 1993; Constable 1995; Aers and Staley 1996; Bestul 1996; Hamburger 1997a, 1997b, 1998; Fulton 2002; Sargent 2004; Kupfer 2008, 1–19; McNamer 2010; Fulton Brown 2013; Lazikani 2015; Mancia 2015; Munns 2016. For 'new emotionalism', Barasch 1976, 87.

105 Raby 1953, 419, cited in Carruthers 2013, 99.

106 Southern 1953, 218–89.

107 Von Simson 1953, 9.

108 As in Auerbach 1965, 67–81.

109 Southern (1963, 37) was an influential spokesman for a position more recently energised, in regard to female influence on the production of affective texts, by McNamer 2010 and by Caroline Walker Bynum, in Bynum 1982 and 1987. But Bynum 2007, xvii fires an important warning shot in avoiding what she calls such 'generalising and merely descriptive categories as "affective" and "expressionist"', rightly seeking to place these in specific historical or circumstantial contexts.

110 Arnold 2008, 107.

111 Boerner 2016, 557.

112 See Pickering 1970 (first published in German in 1966), whose method was elaborated by Marrow 1979.

113 Pickering 1970, 279.

114 Ibid., 244.

115 Ibid., 284.

116 Ibid., 223–4, 279, 284; compare Southern 1953, 211–12.

117 Kidson 1987.

118 Ibid., 143.

119 For an introductory discussion of musical modes, see Sadie 2001, vol. 16, 775–823 ('Mode I–III'); for the doctrine of musical affects, ibid., vol. 1, 186.

120 The term 'beholder's share' was coined for Part Three of *Art and Illusion*, Gombrich 1962, 153.

121 For 'seeing in' and 'seeing as', derived from Wittgenstein, see Wollheim 1980, 205–26 and for a developed view, Wollheim 1987, 46–75; see also Gamboni 2002, 9–41. For further remarks on 'seeing as', see Podro 1982a. For Matthew Paris, Binski 2004, 233–6 and 2006.

122 See Carruthers 1990, 23–4; for blankness and projection see Baxandall 1972, 46–7 and Parshall 1999, 465.

123 Southern 1953, 211, also 218, 220.

124 Panofsky 1960, 55–68.

125 Mâle discussed and contextualised by Gayk 2010, 8–9.

126 Woolf 1968, 13–14, 22. At 184 Woolf remarks that 'Bernardine' doctrine transformed patristic thinking about pictures so that by the later Middle Ages 'their function is now held to be the stirring of emotion rather than the imparting of knowledge'. The choice of the word 'function' as opposed to 'purpose' in this passage is fortunate.

127 Southern 1953, 226.

128 Constable 1995, 180–81; nn. 221, 222 for examples.

129 Ibid., 181–2.

130 Ibid., 221, 230.

131 Ibid., 232.

132 See the numerous citations of imagery in Woolf 1968, 183–273; at 184 Woolf indeed remarks: 'it is a weakness of the fifteenth-century lyric, judged as a whole, that so often it only alludes to this form [the *imago pietatis*] with the intention that the emotive effect should derive from a visual representation external to the poem'. Numerous studies of this relationship have followed, e.g. Hamburger 1998.

133 As in Belsey 1980.

134 Pickering 1970, 284 and 245–6, 275–6, 282–4; see also Gray 1972; Marrow 1979, 7–8; Sargent 2004; Fulton 2002, 3–4, 216–18. An excellent essay on this theme is Edsall 2014, esp. 25–6, 39, 41.

135 For 'living' painting see Belting 1994, 261–96.

136 Baxandall 1980, 153: 'the beholder may project into the figure intimations of character and feeling not so much initiated as admitted by it'.

137 Carruthers 1990, 51–3, also 1–4.

138 Lentes 2006, 363–70.

139 Arnold 2008, 116–18; also Gayk 2010, 4–8 for the reformability of emotions; McNamer 2010, 2–13 157, 162, 174–206 for emotional 'scripting'; de Souza 1987, xv for emotions and salience.

140 The term 'arc of address' is Baxandall's: Baxandall 1980, 166–7.

141 For touch, discussed in the next part of this book, see e.g. Jung 2010 and Guérin 2016.

142 E.g. Binski 2004, 197–20.

143 See e.g. Van Os 1994; Hamburger 1997a and 1998 (for the social context of devotional images of this type); Boerner 2008 for portals.

144 Constable 1988, 249.

145 Fried 1980.

146 For infantilisation, see Gayk 2010, 84–5; also McNamer 2010, 147.

3 EULOGY AND TECHNIQUE

1 Boerner 2008, 109–38, 193–236 enables study of portal forms of emotive response typical of north German religious orders in the 14th century, for which he provides evidence. For the St Paul's rood, see Simpson 1873, lxvi, 91 and Binski 2004, 204; for the Déols Virgin, in the tradition of the *liber miraculorum*, see Hubert 1935 and Smith 2006, 180–82. Camille 1989, 220–41 gives many instances.

2 Shearman 1992, 10–58.

3 Schapiro 1977, 120, 136; on this theme see Hamburger 1994.

4 Harvey 1969, 288–91 for the itinerary of William of Worcestre on Wells, and for a study of the facade, Malone 2004.

5 As with the tomb of Archbishop Siegfried III von Eppstein in Mainz cathedral: Brush 2000.

6 Pinkus 2014 and 2018 for Bremen.

7 Pinkus 2014, 29–70, esp. 60 where the constraints of convention are held to be based on 'modernist and anachronistic assumption'.

8 Camille 1989, 43–4 for the readings of Deleuze and Baudrillard; Pinkus 2014, 1–18.

9 Van Eck 2010, 2013, 2015 for copious instances and literature.

10 Pinkus 2014, 2–7, following the Platonised account in Camille 1989, at 43–4.

11 Pinkus 2014, 15, explicitly sets aside formal, clerical or top-down models in exploring non-religious responses to simulacra, rejecting the arguments in Boerner 2008 for affective devotional readings of portals presumably because of their ultimately clerical origin.

12 For such phraseology see Binski 1997, 350.

13 Freedberg 1989, 215.

14 For Naumburg see Krohm and Kunde 2012 *passim* and esp. vol. 2, 865–958 (by Julia Weiler). In addition to Pinkus 2014, 29–65 and the redaction of his work in Krohm and Kunde 2012, vol. 3, 204–17, see Kidson 1987 and Brush 1993; for screens see Jung 2013.

15 Krohm and Kunde 2012, vol. 2, 1428–43; see also Williamson 1995, 184–6; for Nordhausen, see also Schleif 2013.

16 The deponent form of the verb *miror*, to wonder at, might be recalled: see again Bynum 2001, 37–75 for these stances towards wonders.

17 For ludic space, Carruthers 2013, 17, 28.

18 Pinkus 2014, 105–11; Pinkus 2015; for formal play in architecture and related arts, see Kavaler 2012, 231–42.

19 For the way through, *ductus*, Carruthers 1998, 77–81 and Carruthers 2010, 190–213.

20 Fish 1980 and Jauss 1982.

21 Binski 2004, 236–47.

22 *Calendar of the Liberate Rolls*, 1916, 444.

23 Ibid., 1930, 14–15.

24 I note this because Pinkus 2014, 48 takes Sauerländer to task for claiming that the expressions at Naumburg were explicit commissions, stating that this 'is as fanciful as all the other theses: why should such a stipulation have been inserted into the contract [for Naumburg]?'.

25 Ibid., 62.

26 A distinction developed in modern aesthetics from Coleridge's fancy and imagination posited in his *Biographia Literaria* (Coleridge 1817); see Scruton 1983 for the account drawn on here.

27 Pinkus 2014, 18 and 149–78.

28 Danto 1990, 342; Walton 1990, as discussed earlier.

29 Pinkus 2014, 50, 58.

30 Hauser 1999, 37–8, after MacIntyre 1984, 6–34.

31 See Bedos-Rezak 2000 and 2011. For an essay on individuality, see Bynum 1982, 82–109.

32 MacIntyre 1984, 27–31.

33 Bitzer 1968 wrote: 'Besides exigence and audience, every rhetorical situation contains a set of constraints made up of persons, events, objects, and relations which are parts of the situation because they have the power to constrain decision and action needed to modify the exigence.'

34 Benton 1991, 345–8.

35 Carruthers 2013, 16–18.

36 Ibid., 165–205.

37 See *inter alia* Sauerländer and Kroos 1972; Williamson 1995; Castiñeiras 1999; for Reims, see the prodigious collection of first-class early (pre-1914) photographs in Hamann-MacLean and Schüssler 1993–2008; for a revisionist account of the chronology of the French and German monuments, see J. Wirth 2004 and the papers collected in Krohm and Kunde 2012. For Southwell, the classic study is Pevsner 1945 but for its context see Philip Dixon in Krohm and Kunde 2012, vol. 1, 281–8 and for 'parallels' between England and Europe, see Ute Engel, in Krohm and Kunde 2012, vol. 1, 195–212. For Burgos, see Williamson 1995, 225–30 and figs 332, 335, 336, and for the cathedral as a whole Karge 1995; for later work there and its European relatives, see Krohm and Kunde 2012, vol. 2, 1452–63. For Gothic 'naturalism', start with Givens 2005, 1–36; Perkinson 2009, 27–84.

38 See Karge 2012 for Burgos and the Holy Roman Empire.

39 For science, Pevsner 1945; for physiognomy, see Sauerländer 2003 and the essays in Little 2006 including Sauerländer 2006; Recht 2008, 244–6; for classicism, Panofsky 1960; for the civilising process, Jaeger 1994; for displacement, Camille 1989, 46–7, 199; and for accessibility and the vernacular, Jung 2013.

40 Auerbach 1953, 72–3, 155–6 and Auerbach 1965, 27–66; see e.g. Kidson 1987, Hamburger 1997b and Jung 2013, 171–97, 'Nobles Peasants, and the Vernacular Mode'.

41 Auerbach 1953, 50–76 and Auerbach 1965, 25–66.

42 Auerbach 1953, 155–6.

43 I cite Eagleton 2003 for this insight.

44 For this latter alignment, see Copeland and Sluiter 2009, 552, 554–5. Averil Cameron, in Cameron 1992, 33–4, rightly observes that Auerbach's realism 'is the realism of Huizinga's Late Western Middle Ages, with its earthy juxtaposition of opposites'.

45 See Bäuml 1980, and for related discussions Hamburger 1997b and Jung 2013.

46 For this critique see Dronke 1966, 362–3.

47 Sánchez Ameijeiras 2011, 90–96, 113–18 and Sánchez Ameijeiras 2014; for a version of this, see Sauerländer 1992, 17, 28, 29.

48 Sánchez Ameijeiras 2011, 93.

49 See the essays in Jaeger 2010 including my essay on *magnificentia* and the heroic mode, Binski 2010b. The valuable discussion of level or mode in Jung 2013, esp. 191–7, consciously eschews the 'ancient categories' or *genera dicendi* (194) but nevertheless sets out an argument derived from *exempla*, direct address, simple syntax and so on, which in effect comes closest to *sermo humilis* and an aesthetic of accessible or vernacular naturalism, as set out *inter alia* by Bäuml 1980 but, as noted, above all by Auerbach. See also S. Murray 2004, 37.

50 Curtius 1990, 154–9.

51 Burrow 2008; see also Binski 2014a, 1–9.

52 Elsner 2014 provides a useful essay from the perspective of the ancient world.

53 Panofsky 1964, 39.

54 Panofsky 1964, 67.

55 Curtius 1990, 155.

56 Ibid., 154–9.

57 Ibid., 157; for such writing in England, see Rigg 1992.

58 Binski 2014a, 1–9 and 13–47.

59 Binski 2004, 55–62; Binski 2010b, 140; Binski 2014a, 26–7.

60 Inglis 2003; Binski 2010b, 147; Binski 2014a, 4.

61 Binski 1995, 33–43.

62 Thérel 1984 for Senlis; these general developments may be followed in Sauerländer and Kroos 1972.

63 P. Brown 1981, 69.

64 Sánchez Ameijeiras 2015, fig. 17.15; Sauerländer and Kroos 1972, pl. 206.

65 For blame and invective, see Burrow 2008, 6–28 and Elsner 2014, 317, 336–7, 342.

66 See the discussion in Carruthers 2014b.

67 For zest see Binski 1997; two splendid corbel heads in the north transept at Rochester should be grouped with the Lincoln work: Krohm and Kunde 2012, vol. 1, 484, pls 14 and 15.

68 For a general guide to light, colour and affect, see Gage 1993, 69–78, esp. 69, 77–8; also Binski 1997 for smiling images and illumination. Dante's use (*Purgatorio* XI.79–83) of 'illumination' and 'more smiling' (*più ridon*) painted pages is in this tradition. I refer to the early 15th-century documents for the expertises (professional assessment committees for building works) at Girona Cathedral in which a debate as to whether to choose a giant single or a triple nave was resolved in favour of one nave which would shine 'with much greater brightness, which is happier and delightful' (*tum quia etiam multo maiori claritate fulgebit quod est laetius et jucundum*): Villanueva 1850, vol. 12, 337–8; Street 1865, 513 (app. H); also Freigang 1999, 212.

69 Lewis and Short 1993, 1149: *miror*, from 'Sanscrit smi, smile' (see also Bynum 2001, 209 n.24).

70 Curtius 1990, 159–66.

71 Burrow 2008, 6–28.

72 Ibid., 16–17 for lengthening and heightening in poetry; Binski 2010b, 132 for architectural experience.

73 Caplan 1954, 172–4; Curtius 1990, 179–82.

74 Caplan 1954, 364–6.

75 Nims 1967, 24. For Vinsauf and 13th-century Parisian art see Jordan 2002.

76 Nims 1967, 36–8.

77 For the head of Jeanne, see Williamson 1995, 173 and fig. 257.

78 Bartlett 2008, 92–4; Baxandall 1980, 163 rightly states that while detail may be telling, 'it is the total conformation of the body that carries the main narrative'. For Gothic face and body union, Binski 1997, 353.

79 Nickson 2015, 139–40. On this theme see Smith 2006, 174–9.

80 Robinson 1909, 70.

81 Barthes 1989, 147.

82 Burrow 2008, 16–18.

83 Ruh 1950; Pickering 1970, 256–85. The fullest development of this project with regard to late medieval Passion imagery is Marrow 1979.

84 William Ryding cited in Kemp 1997, 92. For medieval amplification and abbreviation, or diminution, see Vinsauf in Nims 1967, 24–42.

85 Sánchez Ameijeiras 2011, 93, 97, 112–18.

86 Pickering 1970, 228–9.

87 Barthes 1989, 143–4.

88 For Sluter see Morand 1991 and Grandmontagne 2005.

89 Gordon 1979, 9–10; Gross 1992.

90 Belting 1994, 261–96.

91 Turel 2011, 173.

92 The classic study is Panofsky 1964, 39–66.

93 Erlande-Brandenburg 1975 for a study of French examples; Binski 1995 for Westminster.

94 Sauerländer and Kroos 1972, 491–2, pl. 100.

95 For aristocratic self-control and grieving, see Binski 1996, 51–2.

96 Binski 1995, 120 for a brief discussion of the imagery of 'polish' in connection with tombs and court furnishing.

97 Binski 2014a, 185 and also 90–95.

98 Binski 1995, 107–11.

99 The Eleanor Crosses are served by a large literature: e.g. Colvin 1963, 479–85; Bony 1979, 20–22; Parsons 1991; Binski 1995, 118–19; Dilba 2005.

100 Binski 1995, 115–18, figs 160 and 231.

101 See Luxford 2009; Barker 2017; for kinship, Morganstern 2000.

102 Perkinson 2009, esp. 85–134.

103 See Elsner 2014.

104 For *Können* and *Kunstwollen*, see Gombrich 1978b, 1–10 and for the 19th-century antecedents to this thinking, notably Gottfried Semper, see Podro 1982b, 44–58.

105 For the craft metaphor, see Carruthers 2013.

106 For a non-teleological view of Gothic, see Bony 1983b.

107 Joubert 2008, 151 for this timeline.

108 Binski 2014a, 83.

109 Binski 2010a for a discussion of the perception of architects as professionals; for an instance of an architect's fame rising along with his church, see the epitaph of Peter, the master mason of Toledo Cathedral (1291), in Nickson 2015, 95.

110 For great effects and 'heavy' technologies, see Binski 2010b, 136–43; a valuable study of specific sound technologies is J. W. Williams 1993, 314–35.

111 S. Murray 1987, 149 no. 6; Kurmann 1998, 23.

112 S. Murray 1987, 150 no. 2.

113 Useful points of reference are Bony 1983a; Kimpel and Suckale 1990, 277–92, 421–2; Frankl 2000, 114–16; for Villard, see C. F. Barnes 2009; for Westminster, Binski 1995.

114 On which theme see Binski 2014a.

115 Sauerländer and Kroos 1972, 474–88; Williamson 1995, 59–65, 156–60; Hamann-MacLean and Schüssler 1993–2008 is fundamental for close study; J. Wirth 2004 and 283–93 for summary; for the Reims masks, see most recently Schmengler 2016.

116 Abou-el-Haj 1995, 764, 767–9.

117 Ibid., 768.

118 Ibid., 769. For the pre-1918 archive see Hamann-MacLean and Schüssler 1993–2008.

119 J. Wirth 2004, 123.

120 I advance this hypothesis in Binski 2004, 239–41.

121 Kurmann 1987 and 1998; J. Wirth 2004, 175–90 for an alternative chronology.

122 For Naumburg and related European projects, see Krohm and Kunde 2012, vol. 1, 471–520; Pinkus 2014, 43, figs 1.6 and 1.7.

123 Williamson 1995, 62–3; Hamann-MacLean and Schüssler 1993–2008, 1.2, pl. 452; 2.5, pl. 21.

124 S. Murray 1987, 188 under the year 1517–18; Joubert 2008, 199–202.

125 For one version of this idea, 'distributed cognition', owed to Edwin Hutchins, see Binski 2014b, 9–10.

126 Kurmann 2006.

127 Sauerländer 2008, 51.

4 MATERIAL, STYLE, REPRESENTATION

1 Danto 1990, 341. The book under review, Freedberg 1989, repeatedly asserts the importance of the 'look' as opposed to the ontology of images (120, 167), stating (285) that 'I will ... choose to suggest the centrality of the relation between the formal quality and the efficacity of objects'. This relation is not fully explored, however. For a recent account of visions, see Christian 2012; also Warner 2006.

2 Discussed more fully in Danto 1973 (the idea originating in Aristotle's discussion of change in *Metaphysics*, book 9, and eventually developed by Spinoza and Leibniz); see also Stein 2014.

3 Gombrich 1972, 125.

4 A substantial literature: see e.g. Freedberg 1989; Gombrich 1990; Gumbrecht 2004; Maniura and Shepherd 2006; Bredekamp 2010; van Eck 2015.

5 A major theme in Camille 1989: see variously Maniura and Shepherd 2006; García Avilés 2007 (for image miracles in the *Cantigas* of Alfonso X); Sánchez Ameijeiras 2009–10; for movable images, Tripps 1998; for the Virgin Mary, Smith 2006; and for animism, Gertsman 2015b and Pinkus 2018, 411–17. Smith 2006, 178 also rightly warns us that animation 'is rarely spontaneous; images usually come to life in response to an overture on the part of the person' who engages with them.

6 Gayk 2010, 56.

7 D. Cooper 2006, 49.

8 Baxandall 1980, 54; for the Langham image, Alexander and Binski 1987, no. 249; Williamson 1995, 114.

9 The term 'out of bounds' is van Eck's: van Eck 2015.

10 See esp. Belting 1994 for *Kult* or 'operative context' and, for an account of agency which tries to separate from Western-style aestheticism, see Gell 1998; much the same is true of Freedberg 1989; see also the brief remarks in Trilling 1995.

11 The sentiment certainly pre-dates the Enlightenment since the association of old and unattractive images with superstition can be found in Laud and even, by implication, in the writing of the 14th-century Dominican Robert Holcot who noted that old women believed that an image only gained virtue (i.e. power) after 60 years; examples discussed in Aston 2015. Goethe 1996, 594: *Wundertätige Bilder sind meist nur schlechte Gemälde/ Werke des Geists und der Kunst sind für den Pöbel nicht da* (*Venetian Epigrams*, no. 15). Hegel developed this position in his lectures on aesthetics with

regard to the Romantic or Christian form of art in which (in contrast to classical art) aesthetic externals are 'superficial' in regard to inner faith: Knox 1975, 535–9 (Part II, sect. III, ch. 1). A classic expression of this, again stressing the gender divide, is Ruskin 1875, 53–5. A form of this essentially populist theory persists in the work of Auerbach on *sermo humilis* and the social-realist paradoxes of the sublime. Danto 1990, 342 observes: 'aesthetic merit need not be a criterion for immanence'. For an Auerbachian essay on ugliness, see Hamburger 1997b.

12 Coulton and Power 1929, vol. 1, 525–6 (ch. 44). For a discussion, see Freedberg 1989, 312–13.

13 Camille 1989, 78–9.

14 I refer to Gell's (I think non-rhetorical) theory of enchantment: Gell 1992 and 1998, and the discussions in van Eck 2010 and 2013 which concede the difficulty of Gell's marginalisation of *aesthesis*.

15 A point repeatedly and effectively made in Carruthers 2013.

16 A classic study of the valences of the word 'Idea' is Panofsky 1968, esp. 35–43.

17 Compare *Ars auro gemmisque prior*, 'Art comes before gold and gems' on the 'Henry of Blois' plaque; see Stratford 1983, 33 and 37 n. 60.

18 Indeed, for the Stoic-Senecan addition of the Idea or form to Aristotle's four-fold model of causality, including the final cause or purpose, see Panofsky 1968, 21–5.

19 W. J. T. Mitchell 2005, 171.

20 I develop this observation from the fundamental observation in Carruthers 2013, 45 that classical and medieval aesthetic terms are primarily adjectives not nouns.

21 I derive the term 'cognitive map' from Graves 1989, 309; for the way through, *ductus*, see Carruthers 2010, 190–213.

22 For polychrome wood, see e.g. Taubert 2015 and the essays in Nadolny et al. 2006; for stone, Verret and Steyaert 2002 (at Toro, Angers, Senlis, Lausanne); see also Joubert 2008, 199–202, whose figs XL and XLI compare the fine 13th-century murals of St-Maurille in the apse at Angers Cathedral with polychromy at Bourges.

23 See Plahter 2014 for an excellent overview of Scandinavian data, complemented by Nadolny et al. 2006.

24 See the studies by Blindheim 1952 and 2004 (at nos 25 and 63 for Hedalen and Øren), and Plahter 2014; for a full bibliography, see Hohler 2017.

25 For the limewood citation, see Baxandall 1980, 33 after the original text, for which see Salzman 1997, 251.

26 Here I follow the (American wood) data tables in Wangaard 1950, 87–92 (89 for oak, 91–2 for pine).

27 For Ruskin's notion of honesty to materials, see Ruskin 1849, 25–56.

28 See for German examples Kavaler 2005, 2008, 2011, 2012; for English woodwork, Tracy 1987 and Tracy and Budge 2015.

29 For the powers of stone, see Engelen 1978 and J. J. Cohen 2015.

30 See Harris 2014, 22: 'the agency of the hewn object lies in the intention of its objects'. For wood and its powers, see the useful essay by Pastoureau 1993; for recent work on Gothic ivory, see Barnet 1997, Williamson and Davies 2014, Guérin 2017.

31 For 'respect' for the character of materials, see Baxandall 1980, 32.

32 Guérin 2017.

33 For the agency of the otherwise 'transparent' medium, see Carruthers 2013, 15.

34 See the discussion in Hagberg 1995, 109–17.

35 This general issue is usefully discussed in relation to wooden artefacts by D. Cooper 2006. For excellent general studies of Marian imagery in medieval England including sculpture, such as it exists, see Morgan 1991 and 1993.

36 Coulton and Power 1929, vol. 1, 455 (ch. 2), 485–7 (ch. 21), 529 (ch. 46); vol. 2, 23 (ch. 21), 24 (ch. 22), 26 (ch. 25), 84 (ch. 83), 188 (ch. 19); Pinkus 2018, 411–12.

37 St Augustine, *In Ioannis Evangelium Tractatus*, 124.2 (John 1:6–14), in Migne 1844–64, vol. 35, col. 1390: *Sed quare crucifixus est? Quia lignum tibi humilitatis ejus necessarium erat.*

38 Warner 1989, 7.

39 Pickering 1970, 253–6; for a practical discussion of the Cross and tree imagery, see O'Reilly 1987 and 1992; Munns 2016, 116–20; for English Gothic images, Binski 2004, 209–18.

40 E. Evans 1956, 18–19.

41 For ready reference I have used S. A. J. Bradley 1995, 158–63; see also Swanton 1970.

42 S. A. J. Bradley 1995, 161; Warner 1989, 20 for 'hate-dents'.

43 See S. A. J. Bradley 1995, 375–6, no. 30a and O'Reilly 1987, 157.

44 Dronke 1972, 77–88; Binski 2004, 87–101.

45 Binski 2004, 209–18 for English instances.

46 Morris 1875–6, 964–5 for *Cursor Mundi* lines 16,859–68: 'þe rode it was wit leif and bare/ florist ful selcuthli/ Fra þe middai to complin/ þat mani thoght gret ferli/ Bot þof þe Iuus þat it sagh/ thoght selcut noght for-þi/ Noiþer þai gaf man, ne tok/ emsample gode þar-bi/ Bot on þe morn o þat grening/ þe tre als ar was dri'.

47 I cite Bynum 2011, 66.

48 See e.g. Bandmann 1969, and for a theoretical consideration of materiality and its senses, Kumler and Lakey, 2012.

49 Guérin 2013, 62, 65–6; another instance is in the dialogues of Caesarius of Heisterbach: Coulton and Power 1929, vol. 2, 40 (ch. 40).

50 Guérin 2013, 71; for an example see Davies and Townsend 2017, 250–51.

51 E.g. Williamson and Davies 2014, 587, no. 202 and 710, no. 243; also Barnet 1997, 228–9, no. 56. For microarchitecture and *ludus*, see Binski 2018.

52 Carruthers 2013, 106. On this theme see Ohly 1989.

53 For the text of the *Tree of Life*, see Cousins 1978, 119–75.

54 Nims 1967, 18–19; Doob 1990, 205.

55 J. Barnes 1984, vol. 2, 1655.

56 E. Cohen 1995, 52.

57 Pickering 1970, 271–2, 278, 283.

58 Astell 2014, 187–94.

59 L. H. Cooper 2011, 112.

60 Ibid., 93–105.

61 Ibid., 97; also 106–45.

62 The standard survey is Reiss 2000; see also L. H. Cooper 2011, 118–19.

63 Pickering 1970, 270–73; Pickering 1971 for the text; M. P. Brown 2007 for a facsimile.

64 Edsall 2014, 42–6; also Astell 2014.

65 Hesketh 2006, 141, lines 3969–72.

66 As in the *Bibles Moralisées* (e.g., Vienna, Oesterreichische Nationalbibliothek, Codex Vindobonensis 2554; see Guest 1995, fol. 1v).

67 L. H. Cooper 2011, 97–8, 130–36; the notion of confection was drawn to my attention by Eamon Duffy.

68 Carruthers 2013, 21, 205.

69 In general K. A. Wirth 1953 and Thoby 1959–63; for English Gothic material, see Binski 2004, 209–30 and for English Romanesque images, Munns 2016; for the *Crucifixus Dolorosus*, see De Francovich 1938 and Morgan 2006.

70 Blindheim 2004, nos 42, 72; see also nos 50, 52, 59, 74, 75. See also the instances from Gotland in Wolska 1997.

71 De Francovich 1938; Hoffmann, et al. 2006.

72 Pickering 1970, 234–43.

73 De Francovich 1938, fig. 186; Mills 2005, 7–8; Recht 2008, fig. 56.

74 De Francovich 1938, figs 131, 133, 135.

75 *Res multum digna vel vilis, aut vulneratum in vulnere multum patente notabili rivo sanguinis defluente, vel aliter deturpatum*, in Rowland 1975, 57 and Carruthers 1990, 282.

76 For documents and discussion, see Binski 2001 and 2004, 201–5 and Hoffmann, et al. 2006 for the Cologne instance.

77 Carruthers 2014b for a discussion of terror and horror.

78 For two different discussions, see Hamburger 1997b and Carruthers 2013, 175–81.

79 Woolf 1968, 40.

80 Ibid., 41.

81 Ibid., 41–2; for gloves and professional status, see Binski 2010a, 23, 31.

82 Binski 2014a, 348–55.

83 Pickering 1970, 271–3 and Pickering 1971, 10–19.

84 Sargent 2004, 183.

85 Recht 2008, 198–202.

86 Williamson 1995, 195–8, esp. fig. 294.

87 Ramage 1961, 483–5; Jaeger 1985, 113–75. *Oppositio* is discussed by Vinsauf: see Nims 1967, 39–40.

88 Carruthers 2013, 87–8.

89 Westermann-Angerhausen 1996, 25, col. pl. 5.

90 Binski 2004, 226; Morgan 2006 for the Norwegian context.

91 Norton and Park 1986, 318–93 for a table of Cistercian legislation, esp. 324, 368, 374, 378. For a large suspended mid-13th-century Cistercian painted cross, see Krohm and Kunde 2012, vol. 1, pl. 13 (Schulpforte, Germany).

92 Norton and Park 1986, 366.

93 Nyborg 2006, 253 and fig. 10 and Nyborg 2013.

94 The giant cross at Oplinter is poorly published: De Francovich 1938, 161, fig. 102.

95 Mallion 1964; Williamson 1995, 47 and fig. 66; Jung 2013, 179–91.

96 A point stressed throughout Binski 2004.

97 Ibid., 228–9.

98 Cicero, *Ad Familiares*, no. 188: *quin ipsa iudicia non solemus omnia tractare uno modo: privatas causas, et eas tenues, agimus subtilius, capitis aut famae scilicet ornatius;*

in Shackleton Bailey 2001, 184–7. For *subtilitas* see Carruthers 2013, 188–9.

99 Turel 2011, 169–71.

100 For the colours see Arbusow 1948; Carruthers 2013, 54, 157–8, 186; Tilliette 2013.

101 See Hägele 2002 for a specialised study of the depiction of eyes.

102 The expression *varios induta colores* is from Ovid's account (*Metamorphoses* 1) of Iris's garb at the Flood; for the middle style, following Augustine, see Carruthers 2013, 80–107.

103 Ramage 1961, 485.

104 Russell 2001, vol. 124, 354–5.

105 Quintilian, *Institutio Oratoria* 2.17.21 in ibid., 386 expresses suspicion of mimesis; for *color* and glossing see *Institutio Oratoria* 4.2.88–100 in Butler 1921, vol. 125, 98–103; Tilliette 2013, 279–80; for Lollard and anti-fraternal language, see Gayk 2010, 15–44, and for the commonplace of paint and deceit in Lydgate, see Reynolds 2007, 12–13.

106 For 'honest' taste see Carruthers 2013, 112–25.

107 Sears 2006.

108 Blindheim 1952, 87–108.

109 Accounts of particulars for painters at Westminster Palace in the 1290s include the purchase of candles in the darker winter months: National Archive (NA, formerly PRO), E 101/468/6 rots 17b–27 (October 1292–January 1293).

110 Sears 2006, 231.

111 Binski and Massing 2009 for a full technical and historical account.

112 Ibid., figs 21 and 24.

113 Sears 2006.

114 For illusion see Carruthers 2013, 188–92, esp. 190 n. 17.

115 For *venustas* see ibid., 182–3 and 184 for Isidore.

116 I cite the discussion in Bynum 2011, 53–8.

117 Panofsky 1953.

118 Garnett and Rosser 2013.

119 For an acceptance of Belting's views, see Bynum 2011, 120–21; yet she devotes only 25 lines to 'viewer response' largely in connection with the tactility of sculpture (ibid., 65). For critiques and qualifications of Belting's work, see the remarks of Jeffrey Hamburger in Hamburger and Bouché 2006, 12–13, 14, 16–17; Hamburger 2013; Binski 2014a, 55–6.

120 Aristotle, *De Memoria*, 450b21–451a2 in J. Barnes 1984, vol. 1, 716.

121 Camille 1989, 206–7; D. Cooper 2006, 49–50; for the related theory of imagination, Carruthers 1990, 23–4.

122 D. Cooper 2006, 47–9 and n. 4.

123 J. Barnes 1984, vol. 1, 332–4 and vol. 2, 1600–01.

124 Panofsky 1968, 41: 'The fact was therefore well established in medieval thought that the artist worked, even if not from an Idea in the real, metaphysical sense, at least from an inner notion of form, or "quasi idea", that preceded the work'. For preconception in the artist's mind, see Carruther's thoughts on *ductus* in Carruthers 2010, 199–206 and Binski 2010a for the related group of concepts auxillary to theology; also Taubert 2015, 31.

125 I paraphrase a thought from Durkheim (1995, 122) used by W. J. T. Mitchell 2005, 123.

126 For a devotional-functional account of this process, see Hoeniger 1995; see also Tångeborg 2006.

127 Compare, however, Bynum 2011, 61–2: 'The point of the flesh on a medieval painted Madonna was not to be fleshlike'. This is surely contestable. Michael Psellos writing in the 11th century about an icon of the Virgin Mary states of it that 'the layering of paints reproduces the nature of flesh'; see Jaeger 2012, 119–21.

128 Carruthers 2013, 1–3.

129 *Libri Carolini* IV, c. 16, in Bastgen 1924, 204.

130 Bynum 2011, 53–61.

131 Spencer 1977, 85.

132 Eco 1986, 68–9.

133 For Moissac see Schapiro 1977, 131–264 and fig. 114; Dale 2010, 66, 73–4.

134 Schapiro 1977, 139–53 and 102–30 for Souillac.

135 Zarnecki 1961 for the image and its context.

136 Cahn 1992, 58 and fig. 26; Castiñeiras 2015, 16–19.

137 Binski 1996, 52; for formalised grieving see also Valdez del Alamo 1996; for gestures of despair, Barasch 1976.

138 For drilling at Reims, see Williamson 1995, 62–3; for related reception of classical statuary, see the comments in Heslop 1998, 129–31.

139 For the Douce Apocalypse, see Klein 1981, 1983; for Strasbourg, Williamson 1995, fig. 288; for the Toulouse St Paul see Chaumet 1998, 32–3.

140 Joubert 2008, 190, fig. 164.

141 Binski 1997, 367–9.

142 Gillerman 1994, 109–10 and fig. 45, 188–9, no. 6. Gillerman identifies the image as St Mary of Egypt, but the discussion in Gaborit-Chopin et al. 1998, no. 54, accepting it as Mary Magdalen, carries greater conviction.

143 Gillerman 1994, fig. 43 and 187, no. 5; Gaborit-Chopin et al. 1998, no. 53; compare Turel 2011, fig. 9 for another instance.

144 Gillerman 1994, fig. 120; in limewood, Baxandall 1980, figs 23 and 67.

145 Yamamoto 2000, 164–5.

146 For a subtle account of the utility of stirring mixed affects, see Koerner 1985. For pre-Reformation 'whorish' images such as those of Magdalen, and their powers of insinuation, see Baxandall 1980, 89–90.

147 Bartlett 1994; Yamamoto 2000, 161–6; Milliken 2012.

148 W. J. T. Mitchell 2005, 59–60; for line and hair in the Renaissance, Saviello 2012.

149 Binski 2014a, 207–9.

150 Gombrich 1984, 213–15.

151 For the rear view see Gaborit-Chopin et al. 1998, 107; Baert 2011, 11–34.

152 Tripps 1998, 149–52, 160, 166, fig. 10e–f (Bad Wimpfen); see the discussion of verisimilitude in Freedberg 1989, 192–245.

153 Recht 2008, 214.

154 Tångeborg 2006; Bynum 2011, 53.

155 Knuuttila 2004, 47–71, 152–76, 195–212.

156 Binski 2014a, 205–9.

5 THE POETICS OF MATERIALS

1 For vibrancy see Jane Bennett 2001.

2 Bynum 2011 and 2013.

3 Kessler 2004, 19, followed by Bynum 2011, 53, 58, 70, 121 for 'per se living'.

4 Bynum 2011, 25; see also 121: understanding of the materiality of images 'involves a sense that matter is per se living'; also Bynum 1990, 332, in review of Michael Camille: 'I suspect that images simply were powerful to medieval people because images were in a sense that which they were "like".... It is also to suggest that "being" and "being like" may be closer to each other than many modern theorists are comfortable admitting.'

5 Baxandall 1980, esp. 27–48.

6 Scribner 1987, 14.

7 Baxandall 1980, 93.

8 Ibid., 78–93.

9 Ibid., 32.

10 Nims 1967, 41–2.

11 Wetherbee 2013, 300–01 (*Anticlaudianus*, 3.95–8): *nunc ignis demollit eam, nunc malleus ipsam flectit et ad cultum ferri suspirat uterque; sic ferrum ferro contendit, ut excolat illud, ut socium venerans sese veneretur in illo* ('Now the fire makes it hotter, then the hammer bends it, and both strive to mould the metal. Thus iron struggles with iron in an attempt to work it, so that by honouring its comrade it may thereby do hono[u]r to itself'). For conquest see 292–3 (2.483–5). I am indebted to Anya Burgon for drawing my attention to these passages.

12 Doob 1990, 213–14.

13 Carruthers 2013, 43, 187–93.

14 J. Mitchell 2012, 17–18, drawing on the work of James Trilling.

15 A large topic: see e.g. James and Webb 1991; Webb 1999; Bartsch and Elsner 2007.

16 De Stefani 2011, 76–7, lines 79f; Mango 1972, 92–3 for what follows; also Barry 2007 and J. Mitchell 2012.

17 Carruthers 2013, 165–205.

18 Economou 1972 and Hadot 2006.

19 As Podro 1982a, 100 puts it, '*Seeing in* allows for "two-fold seeing" which *seeing as* excludes'.

20 For the alabaster industry, see Ramsay 1991; see also A. Gardner 1940; Cheetham 1984 and 2003; Williamson 2010; Woods 2011 and 2017. For the Swansea Altarpiece illustrated here, Cheetham 1984, 70–71.

21 Pliny, *Historia Naturalis* in Rackham 1968, 107–8: *unguenta optime servantur in alabastris, odores in oleo, quod diuturnitati eorum tanto utilius est quanto pinguius, ut ex amygdalis; et ipsa unguenta vetustate meliora.*

22 Ramsay 1991, 29–30.

23 Grand-Clément 2015; also Carruthers 2013, 135, 137.

24 Thomas 2015, 286–7. For marble see the prodigious study in Greenhalgh 2009.

25 Garton 1986 and Binski 2004, 53–62.

26 The critical passage of the *Metrical Life* is at Garton 1986, 54–5; for honey and rock, see Deuteronomy 32:13.

27 For Tutbury see Cheetham 1984, 12; for onyx at Canterbury, see Fergusson 2011, 113, 128, 156–60.

28 Binski 1990, 30–32. The notion of *silva* is defined by, among others, Bernardus Silvestris in his *Cosmographia*; see Wetherbee 1973. I return to *silva* in Ch. 6 (pp. 197–8).

29 The evidence for Henry's request is an account rendered by the Sheriff of Nottingham (a common source of alabaster) in 1269 of £2 10s to Peter of Lincoln, king's mason, *ad albam petram frangendam et reparandam ad pavimentum ecclesie Beati Edwardi Westmonasterii*: Colvin 1963, 147 n. 2.

30 See Binski 2014a, 22–30 for a discussion; for *venustas*, Carruthers 2013, 182–3.

31 Binski 2004, 3–12; for the exegesis which follows, see O'Reilly 1981; for commentary on the symbolism of the column and its apostolic associations, see J. Mitchell 2017.

32 Ramsay 1991, 29.

33 Ibid., 30.

34 E.g. C. Wilson in Alexander and Binski 1987, 416–17, no. 497. For complexion see Carruthers 2013, 45–79.

35 Northamptonshire Record Office, Stopford Sackville Collection, no. 4239: *de pierre appellee alabastre bon fyn et pure*; see F. H. Crossley 1921, 30 for a translation.

36 Marks 2004, 154, 156. For the Flawford Virgin illustrated here, Alexander and Binski 1987, no. 699.

37 For a useful practical discussion of the devotional contexts and significations of alabaster devotional images in England, see ibid., 86–156, especially 'Alba Maria', 154–6.

38 Discussed in Binski 2014a, 353; see Luxford 2011, 271–2 for this aesthetic within the monastic orders.

39 For an overview and bibliography, see Hahn 2006; also Hahn 2000.

40 See e.g. Kumler and Lakey 2012.

41 See e.g. Jane Bennett 2001, Harris 2014 and J. J. Cohen 2015.

42 For balance see Kaye 2016; for the balance of the body and humours, see Carruthers 2013, 29–31, also 57, 59–60.

43 A large topic: Bynum 2011 (e.g. at 66) connects materiality and tactility; see also the essays in Dent 2014. For other studies see Jung 2010, Kingsley 2010, Guérin 2013 and 2016; for different perspectives on the senses, see Turner 1995, 220; Palazzo 2014 and 2016.

44 See McLuhan 1964 and Ong 1967: versions of this include the haptic–optic transition (Reigl, Wölfflin) and the oral–written transition in modernity.

45 Hamburger 1998, 187.

46 Ibid., 435–40 and figs 9.5 and 9.6; Jung 2010.

47 Johnson 2014.

48 Ibid; see also Kingsley 2010.

49 Compare Luke 24:39, *palpate et videte*. The Lichfield document was passed to me by Julian Luxford, from Lichfield Record Office, D30/10/4/1 fol. 38; see Luxford 2017, pl. 1.

50 A. Murray 2006, 41–2; on this theme see Hamburger 2000.

51 A. Murray 2006, 51.

52 See Sullens 1983.

53 For the mindful hand, see Roberts, Schaffer and Dear 2007; for chiromancy, Baxandall 1980, 27–49.

54 Carruthers 1990, 54–5.

55 Jonathan Bennett 1971 for a discussion of primary and secondary qualities: 'the sense of touch – or rather of touch-and-movement – is involved in all the primary qualities in a way in which it isn't with any of the secondary. But that is only a suspicion. Someone should write a book on the epistemology of the sense of touch' (101).

56 See Carruthers 2010, 199–200; also 1–2.

57 Carruthers 2013, 9–10.

58 L. H. Cooper 2011, 146.

59 See the discussion in Muratova 1986, and following it Camille 1989, 47.

60 Carruthers 2013, 16–17. For the distinction between rightness and the 'tremendous', begin with Wittgenstein 1978, 7–8, no. 23.

61 Binski 2010a.

62 L. H. Cooper 2011, 106–45.

63 For an essay on the connection between ethical and aesthetic shaping in this period, see Binski 2004.

64 Bertinetto 2012, 119–20.

65 Carruthers 2013, 16–44.

66 E.g. Reynolds 2007, 8–9; for proportion and honesty, see Carruthers 2013, 46, 47 and 112–18, 120–23.

67 Reynolds 2007, 8. For notes on the history of the *Pietà* in England, see Morgan 1993, 53–7 and Marks 2004, 123–43.

68 Reiners-Ernst 1939.

69 Reynolds 2007, 7–8.

70 Ibid., 14; also 7 for weight.

71 Carruthers 2013, 29–31, 59–60; Kaye 2016.

72 Carruthers 2013, 57; for equity and beauty, see Scarry 2000.

73 Barney 2006, 39. See also Copeland and Sluiter 2009, 385, 412, 471; also 234.

74 Copeland and Sluiter 2009, 471.

6 THE WILD AND THE DEAD

1 I am indebted for this to Harpham 1987.

2 See Wölfflin 1935; Frankl 1950, 619.

3 Goethe in Gage 1980, 105–6.

4 Lee 1977, 40–42 (sections 27–9); also Curtius 1990, 544.

5 For 'tensive' biology see Carruthers 2013, 31–5.

6 Ibid., 29, 31–5, 80–107.

7 Camille 1989, 199.

8 For one view of medieval metamorphosis, see Bynum 2001.

9 Harpham 1987.

10 As set out in Aristotle's *Ethics* 1117b24–1118a35, in J. Barnes 1984, vol. 2, 1764–5.

11 Harpham 1987; for the commonplace of imitation and admiration, see Vauchez 1991.

12 Carruthers 2013, 48–53, 167–72.

13 Pliny, *Historia Naturalis* in Rackham 1968, 438–9.

14 Ramage 1961, 483–5 and C. Connors 1997.

15 Cicero, *De Oratore* 3.12.44 in Rackham 1942, 34–7.

16 Quintilian, *Institutio Oratoria* 10.3.17 in Russell 2001, vol. 127, 344–5.

17 Ibid., 8.3.9–10 in Butler 1921, 214–17; see also Carruthers 2013, 120–21.

18 Stahl and Burge 1977, 65. I am especially indebted to Anya Burgon for her insights into these passages and the material following.

19 Artifice like nature has been usefully discussed by Pereda 2010.

20 Aristotle, *Metaphysics* 1032a12–25 in J. Barnes 1984, vol. 2, 1629–30.

21 Cicero, *De Inventione* in Hubbell 2006, 4–9.

22 See e.g. Saunders 1993, 20; for invention, van Deusen 2003–8 and 2011, 83–104. For Calcidius see Dutton 2003 and Waszink 1975. Weinryb 2016, 65–73 provides a rare instance of the use of Calcidius in the criticism of medieval art.

23 Van Deusen 2003–8 for a discussion.

24 Bernardus Silvestris in Wetherbee 1973, 67: *Turbida temperium, formam rudis, hispida cultum optat.*

25 Carruthers 2014b.

26 Pereda 2010, 307.

27 Binski 2014a, 283–305. For *ludus* see Carruthers 2013, 16–44.

28 For Vermenton, Binski 2004, 97 and fig. 76; for Souvigny, Stratford et al. 2002, 123–64.

29 Stone 1972, 102–3; two classic English studies of foliage sculpture are S. Gardner 1927 and Pevsner 1945; for vertical budding, Binski 2004, 87–95.

30 Pevsner 1945; Givens 2005.

31 Bony 1979, 21–2, 60.

32 For the Exeter throne, see the full study in Tracy and Budge 2015; also Binski 2014a, 134–9; for English choir stalls, see Tracy 1987, 40–43 for Lancaster Priory.

33 Gombrich 1984, 65.

34 English vaults plotted most systematically by Bock 1962, 44–70 and Bony 1979, 43–56.

35 Cave 1948, figs 121–33; Binski 2004, 273–6, figs 219–23.

36 Rose 1997 and 1999. For a discussion of the cloister's 14th-century work, see Binski 2014a, 101–14. The cloister bosses are currently the subject of PhD research by Robert Hawkins.

37 Luxford 2010.

38 Weisheipl 1959; Pasnau and van Dyke 2010, 904.

39 Pantin 1955, 132–5 on reactions to scholasticism in this period in England; also Tachau 1998.

40 On this theme and the arts in England, see Binski 2004, 45; for Seneca, Pereda 2010, 339–42.

41 Sauerländer and Kroos 1972, pl. 230; Sadler 2012, 84–94.

42 On the primitive hut theory, see Rykwert 1972, esp. 82f; P. Crossley 1993, 71; Schama 1995, 226–39.

43 Pereda 2010, 281; Kavaler 2012, 218, pl. 224.

44 Carruthers 2013, 65–6, 188.

45 Binski 2010b, 141–3.

46 Baxandall 1980; Kavaler 2005, 2008, 2011, 2012; Timmermann 2009.

47 Germanness, the hut and the forest are large topics: see e.g. Oettinger 1962; Rykwert 1972; Baxandall 1980; Silver 1983; Le Goff 1988; Baltrušaitis 1989; Crossley 1993; Schama 1995; Howe and Wolfe 2002; Kavaler 2005, 2008, 2011, 2012; Timmermann 2009; Pereda 2010.

48 Ovid, *Metamorphoses* in Miller 1916, 10–11.

49 Rykwert 1972 for the various sources; also Schama 1995, 76–134, esp. 81–100.

50 See esp. Crossley 1993 and Kavaler 2005, 238–43.

51 See esp. Kavaler 2005; also 2012, 153, 211–20.

52 Crossley 1993; Schama 1995, 92–3; Kavaler 2005, 238–9.

53 Baxandall 1980, 83–4, fig. 52.

54 Kavaler 2005, 230 and 241; also 2012, 211–20.

55 Here I follow Kavaler's enumeration and images at Kavaler 2005 figs 1–9.

56 Ibid., 243–4, fig. 26; Kavaler 2012, 212.

57 Harpham 1987, 198–200.

58 Ramage 1961, 481, 483–4.

59 Jaeger 1985, 113–75.

60 Kavaler 2008 and 2012, 231–42, figs 236, 239–42.

61 On this theme in the early modern period, see Oosterhoff 2014.

62 Diemer 1985; J. Connors 1990; Laue 2004; for the culture of wonder, see Evans and Marr 2006.

63 E.g. Doppelmayr 1730, 177–314, esp. 299 and 310 and pls II and V as illustrated here; for German art, see Ashcroft 2012.

64 On minificence see Carruthers 2013, 172–3; Binski 2014a, 7, 144; for Gothic micro-aesthetics, Binski 2018; also Levy 2002 and Payne 2009.

65 J. Connors 1990, 219–20.

66 For the forest and identity, see Schama 1995, 142–53.

67 Harpham 1987.

68 In a large literature on Wild Men, see e.g. Bernheimer 1952; Dudley and Novak 1972; Husband 1980; Le Goff 1988; Yamamoto 2000, 144–96; for outlawry see Keen 1977; Holt 1982; Pollard 2004.

69 Pereda 2010.

70 Yamamoto 2000, 150 after the original text, for which see Le Goff 1988, 115.

71 See the studies by Hogg 1981, Gray 2005 and Brantley 2007.

72 Binski 2014a, 302–4.

73 Sandler 1986, vol. 2, no. 101; Bovey 2002; for Mary of Egypt, see Yamamoto 2000, 198–9.

74 Cave 1948, fig. 259.

75 Harpham 1987, 19–44.

76 Yamamoto 2000, 151.

77 Carruthers 1998, 105–7.

78 Keen 1984, 8–9; for editions of Lull, see Ramón de Luanco 1901; Byles and Milford 1926; Fellows 2013.

79 Keen 1984, 9–10. For hunting, see variously Thiebaux 1967; Cummins 1988; Rooney 1993; Yamamoto 2000, 99–131.

80 A. Murray 1986, 379–80.

81 Keen 1984, 12–15; Kaeuper and Kennedy 1996, 4–6.

82 Binski 2017a for a discussion and bibliography; for earlier observations, Badham 2007.

83 On the *locus amoenus*, see Curtius 1990, 194–200.

84 Kaeuper and Kennedy 1996, 122–5.

85 Ibid., 176–7.

86 On rewards, see Winbush and Valantasis 1995, 357–68.

87 Barney 2006, 307.

88 K. Cohen 1973; King 1990; Binski 1996, 139–52; Kinch 2013, 171–81.

89 See e.g. Binski 1996, 134–8; for books of hours and the Office of the Dead, see Wieck 1988, 124–36, 133 for the Three Living and Three Dead; Kinch 2013, 109–44, 149–71.

90 For doubling and the uncanny, see Binski 1996, 138; also Kinch 2013, 109–44.

91 As in Glixelli 1914, 17 and 92 (poem 5); Kinch 2013, 123–7.

92 Camille 1996, 82–3, fig. 42.

93 E.g. for the Hours of Mary of Burgundy, see Boase 1972, 106 and fig. 91, where the reference may be to her fatal hunting accident.

94 Carruthers 2014b.

95 Sandler 1983, 42 and pl. 5.

96 Compare the variants in Glixelli 1914, 4–5, esp. Paris, Arsenal, Ms 3142 (poem 1), as well as poem 4, as in Paris, BNF, Ms fr. 378 in ibid., 83–91; for diptych renditions, see Kinch 2013, 115, 122–3.

97 Glixelli 1914, 83; Kinch 2013, 135 and fig. 6.

98 A point anticipated, though with a marked gender bias, in Ruskin's Oxford Lectures: Ruskin 1875, 53–4.

99 For the Dance of Death, see Gertsman 2010a and Kinch 2013, 185–259.

100 Kristeva 1982, 3–4.

101 Aristotle, *Poetics* in J. Barnes 1984, vol. 2, 2318; see Binski 1996, 149.

102 For the allegory of Frau Welt, see Stammler 1959.

103 Yamamoto 2000, 166, 170–71.

104 Camille 1996, 172–4, fig. 124.

105 For different readings of *assimilatio* or imitation, see Allen 1982 and Bynum 2001, 37–75.

106 Bynum 1995, 14–15.

107 Gott 2013, 3.

108 See Freedberg 1989, 200.

109 See Bergh 1967, 166–7.

110 Morgan 2006; see Pickering 1970, 280–81. This observation has been made before, as in Sari 2015, 21–2, knowledge of which I owe to Fernando Gutiérrez Baños.

111 For a discussion of the surface values of beauty and ugliness, see Carruthers 2013, 175–81.

112 Ibid., 184; for related moralising images about 'whitewash', see Nims 1967, 42 and S. Murray 2004, 91, line 97.

113 Carruthers 2013, 175–6.

114 Svanberg 1993a, 43–4, 45–66, 132–40.

115 Marks 2004, 114–20 and col. pl. XIII.

116 See Glorieux 1960–73, vol. 7, pt 1, 65, discussed by Mary Carruthers in her 2016 Clark Lectures in Cambridge.

—, 2004. *Gothic Painted Wooden Sculpture in Norway 1220–1350*, Oslo

Bloom, P., 2016. *Against Empathy: The Case for Rational Compassion*, London

Boase, T., 1972. *Death in the Middle Ages: Mortality, Judgment and Remembrance*, London

Bock, H., 1962. *Der Decorated Style: Untersuchungen zur englischen Kathedralarchitektur der ersten Hälfte des 14. Jahrhunderts*, Heidelberg

Boerner, B., 2006. 'Sculptural Programs', in *A Companion to Medieval Art*, ed. C. Rudolph, Oxford, 557–76

—, 2008. *Bildwirkungen: Die kommunikative Funktion mittelalterliche Skulpturen*, Berlin

—, 2016. 'Les cinq sens et la sculpture Gothique', in Palazzo, 547–58

Boffey, J., and A. S. G. Edwards, eds, 2005. *A New Index of Middle English Verse*, London

Boldrick, S., D. Park and P. Williamson, 2003. *Wonder: Painted Sculpture from Medieval England*, Leeds

Bonne, J.-C., 1996. 'De l'ornemental dans l'art médiéval: VIIe–XIIe siècle; le modèle insulaire', in *L'Image: fonctions et usages des images dans l'Occident médiéval*, ed. J. Baschet and J.-C. Schmitt, Paris, 207–49

Bony, J., 1979. *The English Decorated Style: Gothic Architecture Transformed, 1250–1350*, Oxford

—, 1983a. *French Gothic Architecture of the 12th and 13th Centuries*, Berkeley and London

—, 1983b. 'La Genèse de l'architecture gothique: accident ou necessité?', *Revue de l'art ancien et moderne*, 58/9: 9–20

Boquet, D., 2005. *L'Ordre de l'affect au Moyen Age: autour de l'anthropologie affective d'Aelred de Rievaulx*, Caen

Borg, A., 1985. 'The Gloucester Candlestick', in *Medieval Art and Architecture at Gloucester and Tewkesbury*, British Archaeological Association Conference Transactions, 7: 84–92

Borlée, D., 2014. 'Transferts stylistiques et iconographiques au tympan du portail central de la cathédrale de Strasbourg', in *Les Transferts artistiques dans l'Europe gothique*, ed. J. Dubois et al., Paris, 275–87

Bouché, A.-M., 2006. '*Vox Imaginis*: Anomaly and Enigma in Romanesque Art', in Hamburger and Bouché, 306–35

Boucheron, P., and N. Offenstadt, eds, 2011. *L'espace public au Moyen Age: débats autour de Jürgen Habermas*, Paris

Bovey, A., 2002. 'A Pictorial *ex libris* in the Smithfield Decretals: John Batayle, Canon of St Bartholomew's, and his Illuminated Law Book', in *Decoration and Illustration in Medieval English Manuscripts,* ed. A. S. G. Edwards, English Manuscript Studies, 1100–1700, 10, London, 60–82

Bradley, J., 2008. *You Shall Surely not Die: The Concepts of Sin and Death as expressed in the Manuscript Art of Northwestern Europe, c.800–1200*, 2 vols, Leiden

Bradley, S. A. J., ed. and trans., 1995. *Anglo-Saxon Poetry*, London

Brand, P., 2015. 'The Languages of the Courtroom in England, *c.*1300', in *Language in Medieval Britain: Networks and Exchanges*, ed. M. Carruthers, Harlaxton Medieval Studies, 25, Donington, Lincolnshire, 48–58

Brantley, J., 2007. *Reading in the Wilderness: Private Devotion and Public Performance in Late Medieval England*, Chicago

Bredekamp, H., 2010. *Theorie des Bildakts*, Berlin

Brown, M. P., 2007. *The Luttrell Psalter*, London

Brown, P., 1981. *The Cult of the Saints: Its Rise and Function in Latin Christianity*, Chicago

—, 1988. *The Body and Society: Men, Women, and Sexual Renunciation in Early Christianity*, New York

—, 1995. *Authority and the Sacred: Aspects of the Christianisation of the Roman World*, Cambridge

Brush, K., 1993. 'The Naumburg Master: A Chapter in the Development of Medieval Art History', *Gazette des Beaux-Arts*, 122: 109–22

—, 2000. 'The Tomb Slab of Archbishop Siegfried III von Eppstein in Mainz Cathedral: A Thirteenth-Century Image and its Interpretative Context', in *Grabmäler: Tendenzen der Forschung an Beispielen aus Mittelalter und früher Neuzeit*, ed. W. Maier, W. Schmid and M.V. Schwarz, Berlin, 33–5

—, 2008. 'Screening, Sculpture, and the Structuring of Viewer Experience in Thirteenth-Century Mainz', in *Reading Gothic Architecture*, ed. M. M. Reeve, Turnhout, 25–36

Bruyne, E. de, 1946. *Etudes d'esthétique médiévale*, vol. 2, Bruges

Burrow, J., 2002. *Gestures and Looks in Medieval Narrative*, Cambridge

—, 2008. *The Poetry of Praise*, Cambridge

Butler, H. E. R., trans., 1921. *Quintilian: Institutio Oratoria*, Loeb Classical Library, vols 125, 126, Cambridge, MA

Byles, A. T. P., and H. Milford, eds, 1926. *The Book of the Ordre of Chyvalry*, Early English Text Society, London

Bynum, C. W., 1982. *Jesus as Mother: Studies in the Spirituality of the High Middle Ages*, Berkeley and London

—, 1987. *Holy Feast and Holy Fast: The Religious Significance of Food to Medieval Women*, Berkeley and London

—, 1990. Review of Camille 1992, *Art Bulletin*, 72/2: 331–2

—, 1995. 'Why all the Fuss about the Body? A Medievalist's Perspective', *Critical Enquiry*, 22: 1–33

—, 2001. *Metamorphosis and Identity*, New York

—, 2007. *Wonderful Blood: Theology and Practice in Late Medieval Northern Germany and Beyond*, Philadelphia, PA

—, 2011. *Christian Materiality: An Essay on Religion in Late Medieval Europe*, New York

—, 2013. 'Notes from the Field: Materiality', *Art Bulletin*, 95/1: 12–13

Cahn, W., 1987. 'Heresy and the Interpretation of Romanesque Art', in *Romanesque and Gothic: Essays for George Zarnecki*, ed. N. Stratford, 2 vols, Woodbridge, vol. 1, 27–33

—, 1992. 'Romanesque Sculpture and the Spectator', in Kahn 1992b, 45–60

Caillet, J.-P., 2013. 'Retour sur les grands portails Romans: essai sur les causes et leur essoir', in *L'Image en questions: pour Jean Wirth*, ed. F. Elsig et al., Geneva and Paris, 34–41

Calendar of Close Rolls, Henry III, 1911. Vol. 4: *1237–42*, ed. H. C. Maxwell Lyte, London

Calendar of Close Rolls, Henry III, 1929. Vol. 8: *1253–4*, ed. A. E. Stamp, London

Calendar of the Liberate Rolls, Henry III. 1916. Vol. 1: *1226–40*, ed. W. H. Stevenson, London

Calendar of the Liberate Rolls, Henry III. 1930. Vol. 2: *1240–45*, ed. W. H. Stevenson, London

Cameron, A., 1992. 'The Language of Images: The Rise of Icons and Christian Representation', in *The Church and the Arts*, ed. D. Wood, Studies in Church History, 28, Oxford, 1–42

Camille, M., 1989. *The Gothic Idol: Ideology and Image Making in Gothic Art*, Cambridge

—, 1990. 'The *Très Riches Heures*: An Illuminated Manuscript in the Age of Mechanical Reproduction', *Critical Enquiry*, 17/1: 72–107

—, 1992. Review of Belting 1994, *Art Bulletin*, 74/3: 514–17

—, 1996. *Master of Death: The Lifeless Art of Pierre Remiet*, New Haven and London

Caplan, H., trans., 1954. *Cicero: Rhetorica ad Herennium*, Loeb Classical Library, vol. 403, Cambridge

Carruthers, M., 1990. *The Book of Memory: A Study of Memory in Medieval Culture*, Cambridge

—, 1998. *The Craft of Thought: Meditation, Rhetoric and the Making of Images, 400–1200*, Cambridge

—, 2006a. 'Sweetness', *Speculum*, 81: 999–1013

—, 2006b. 'On Affliction and Reading. Weeping and Argument: Chaucer's Lachrymose Troilus in Context', *Representations*, 93: 1–21

—, 2006c. 'Moving Images in the Mind's Eye', in Hamburger and Bouché, 287–305

—, 2013. *The Experience of Beauty in the Middle Ages*, Oxford

—, 2014a. 'The Sociable Text of the "Troilus Frontispiece": A Mode of Textuality', *English Literary History*, 81/2: 423–41

—, 2014b. '*Terror, Horror*, and the Fear of God, or why there is no Medieval Sublime', in *'Truthe is the Beste': A Festschrift in Honour of A. V. C. Schmidt*, ed. N. Jacobs and G. Morgan, Oxford, 17–36

—, ed., 2010. *Rhetoric Beyond Words: Delight and Persuasion in the Arts of the Middle Ages*, Cambridge

Castiñeiras, M. A., 1999. *El Pórtico de la Gloria*, Madrid

—, 2009. 'Da Conques a Compostela: retorica e performance nell'era dei portal parlanti', in *Medioevo: Immagine e memoria. Atti del Convergo internazionale di studi, Parma, 23–28 septembre 2008*, ed. A. Carlo Quintavalle, Milan, 233–51

—, 2015. 'The Romanesque Portal as Performance', *Journal of the British Archaeological Association*, 68: 1–33

Cave, C. J. P., 1948. *Roof Bosses in Medieval Churches*, Cambridge

Caviness, M., 1983. 'Images of Divine Order and the Third Mode of Seeing', *Gesta*, 22/2: 99–120

—, 1991. '"The simple perception of matter" and the Representation of Narrative, ca. 1180–1280', *Gesta*, 30/1: 48–64

Celentano, M. S., P. Chiron and M.-P. Noel, eds, 2004. *Skhèma/ Figura: formes et figures chez les anciens. Rhétorique, philosophie, littérature*, Etudes de Littérature Ancienne, 13, Paris

Chaumet, M.-P., 1998. *Gothic Sculpture (13th–15th centuries)*, Musée des Augustines, Toulouse

Chazelle, C. M., 1990. 'Pictures, Books, and the Illiterate: Pope Gregory I's Letters to Serenus of Marseilles', *Word & Image*, 6/1: 138–53

Cheetham, F., 1984. *English Medieval Alabasters*, Oxford

—, 2003. *Alabaster Images of Medieval England*, Woodbridge

Christe, Y., 1973. *La vision de Matthieu (Matth. XXIV–XXV): origines et développement d'une image de la Seconde Parousie*, Paris

Christian, W. A., Jnr, 2012. *Divine Presence in Spain and Western Europe 1500–1960: Visions, Religious Images and Photographs*, Budapest and New York

Cohen, E., 1995. 'Towards a History of European Physical Sensibility: Pain in the Later Middle Ages', *Science in Context*, 8/1: 47–74

—, 2000. 'The Animated Pain of the Body', *American Historical Review*, 105/1: 36–68

Cohen, J. J., 2015. *Stone: An Ecology of the Inhuman*, Minneapolis

Cohen, K., 1973. *Metamorphosis of a Death Symbol: The Transi Tomb in the Late Middle Ages and the Renaissance*, Berkeley, CA

Coleridge, S. Taylor, 1817. *Biographia Literaria*, London

Colvin, H. M., ed., 1963. *The History of the King's Works*, vol. 1, London

Connors, C., 1997. 'Field and Forum: Culture and Agriculture in Roman Rhetoric', in *Roman Eloquence: Rhetoric in Society and Literature*, ed. W. Dominik, London, 71–89

Connors, J., 1990. '*Ars Tornandi*: Baroque Architecture and the Lathe', *Journal of the Warburg and Courtauld Institutes*, 53: 217–36

Constable, G., 1988. *Monks, Hermits, and Crusaders in Medieval Europe*, London

—, 1995. *Three Studies in Medieval Religious and Social Thought*, Cambridge

Cooper, D., 2006. 'Projecting Presence: The Monumental Cross in the Italian Church Interior', in *Presence: The Inherence of the Prototype within Images and Other Objects*, ed. R. Maniura and R. Shepherd, Aldershot, 47–69

Cooper, L. H., 2011. *Artisans and Narrative Craft in Late Medieval England*, Cambridge

—, and A. Denny-Brown, eds, 2014. *Arma Christi: Objects, Representation and Devotional Practice in Medieval and Early Modern Culture*, Farnham

Copeland, R., and I. Sluiter, eds, 2009. *Medieval Grammar and Rhetoric: Language Arts and Literary Theory, AD 300–1475*, Oxford

Corrigan, J., 1997. 'Against Constructionism: The Historical Ethnography of Emotions', *Current Anthropology*, 38: 327–52

—, with E. Crump and J. Kloos, 2000. *Emotion and Religion: A Critical Assessment and Annotated Bibliography*, Westport, CT, and London

Cosgrove, D., 2008. *Geography and Vision: Seeing, Imagination and Representing the World*, London and New York

Coulton, G. G., and E. Power, eds, 1929. *The Dialogue of Miracles: Caesarius of Heisterbach*, 2 vols, London

Cousins, E., trans., 1978. *Bonaventure: The Soul's Journey into God, the Tree of Life, the Life of St Francis*, New York and Toronto

Cronan, T., 2013. *Against Affective Formalism: Matisse, Bergson, Modernism*, Minneapolis

Crossley, F. H., 1921. *English Church Monuments A.D. 1150–1550*, London

Crossley, P., 1993. 'The Return to the Forest: Natural Architecture and the German Past in the Age of Dürer', in *Kunstlerischer Austausch: Artistic Exchange. Akten des XXVIII. Internationalen Kongresses für*

Kunstgeschichte, ed. T. W. Gaehtgens, vol. 2, Berlin, 71–80

Cummins J., 1988. *The Hound and the Hawk: The Art of Medieval Hunting*, London

Curtius, E. R., 1990. *European Literature and the Latin Middle Ages*, trans. W. R. Trask, Bollingen Series, 36, Princeton, NJ

Dadlez, E. M., 1997. *What's Hecuba to Him? Fictional Events and Actual Emotions*, University Park, PA

Dale, T., 2010. 'The Nude at Moissac: Vision, *Phantasia* and the Experience of Romanesque Sculpture', in *Current Directions in Eleventh- and Twelfth-Century Sculpture Studies*, ed. R. Maxwell and K. Ambrose, Turnhout, 61–76

Dalston, L., and K. Park, 1998. *Wonders and the Order of Nature 1150–1750*, New York

Danto, A. C., 1973. *Analytical Philosophy of Action*, London

—, 1990. review of Freedberg 1989, *Art Bulletin*, 72/2: 341–2

Davies, G., and E. Townsend, eds, 2017. *A Reservoir of Ideas: Essays in Honour of Paul Williamson*, London

D'Avray, D. L., 2010. *Medieval Religious Rationalities: A Weberian Analysis*, Cambridge

Davril, A., and T. M. Thibodeau, eds, 1995. *Guillelmi Durandus Rationale Divinorum Officiorum I–IV*, vol. 1, Corpus Christianorum, 140, Turnhout

Debiais, V., 2017. *La Croisée des signes: l'écriture et les images médiévales (800–1200)*, Paris

De Francovich, G., 1938. 'L'origine e la diffusione del crocifisso gotico doloroso', *Römisches Jahrbuch für Kunstgeschichte*, 2: 143–261

Deimling, B., 1998. '*Ad Rufam Ianuam*: Die rechtsgeschichtliche Bedeutung von "roten Türen" im Mittelalter', *Zeitschrift der Savigny-Stiftung für Rechtsgeschichte: Germanistische Abteilung*, 115: 498–513

Denny, D., 1984. 'The Date of the Conques Last Judgement and its Compositional Analogues', *Art Bulletin*, 66/1: 7–14

Dent, P., ed., 2014. *Sculpture and Touch*, Farnham

Deusen, N. van, 2003–8. 'In and Out of a Latin "Forest": The *Timaeus latinus*, its Concept of Silva, and Music as a Discipline in the Middle Ages', *Musica Disciplina*, 53: 51–70

—, 2011. *The Cultural Context of Medieval Music*, Santa Barbara, CA

Diemer, D., 1985. 'Giovanni Ambrogio Maggiore und die Anfänge der Kunstdrechselei um 1570', *Jahrbuch des Zentralinstituts für Kunstgeschichte*, 1: 295–341

Dilba, C., 2005. 'Das Memorialprogramm für Eleanore von Kastilien: Manifestation königlichen Selbstanspruchs Edwards I. von England 1290–1300', PhD diss., University of Bonn

Dinzelbacher, P., 1996. *Angst im Mittelalter. Teufels-, Todes- und Gotteserfahrung: Mentalitätsgeschichte und Ikonographie*, Paderborn, 1996

Doob, P. B., 1974. *Nebuchadnezzar's Children: Conventions of Madness in Middle English Literature*, New Haven, CT

—, 1990. *The Idea of the Labyrinth from Classical Antiquity through the Middle Ages*, Ithaca, NY

Doppelmayr, J. G., 1730. *Historische Nachricht von den Nürnbergischen Mathematicis und Künstlern*, Nuremberg

Douie, D. L., and Hugh Farmer, eds, 1985. *The Life of St Hugh of Lincoln*, 2 vols, Oxford

Draghi, A., et al., 2006. *Gli affreschi dell'Aula Gotica nel Monastero dei Santi Quattro Coronati*, Milan

Dronke, P., 1966. Review of Auerbach 1965, *Classical Review*, n.s. 16: 362–4

—, 1972. 'Tradition and Innovation in Medieval Western Colour-Imagery', *Eranos-Jahrbuch*, 41: 51–106

Dudley, E., and M. E. Novak, eds, 1972. *The Wild Man Within: An Image in Western Thought from the Renaissance to Romanticism*, Pittsburgh, PA

Durkheim, E., 1995. *The Elementary Forms of Religious Life*, trans. K. E. Fields, New York and London

Dutton, P. E., 2003. 'Medieval Approaches to Calcidius', in *Plato's Timaeus as Cultural Icon*, ed. G. J. Reydams-Schils, Notre Dame, IN, 183–205

Eagleton, T., 2003. Review of Auerbach 1965, *London Review of Books*, 25/20: 17–19

Eck, C. van, 2010. 'Living Statues: Alfred Gell's Art and Agency, Living Presence Response and the Sublime', *Art History* 33/4: 643–59

—, 2013. 'Groaning Paintings and Weeping Viewers: A Gellian Perspective on Visual Persuasion', in

Speaking to the Eye: Sight and Insight through Text and Image (1150–1650), ed. T. de Hemptinne, V. Fraeters and M. E. Góngora, Turnhout, 259–83

—, 2015. *Art, Agency and Living Presence: From the Animated Image to the Excessive Object*, Leiden

Eco, U., 1986. 'Dreaming of the Middle Ages', in *Travels in Hyper Reality*, trans. W. Weaver, San Diego, CA, 61–72

Economou, G. D., 1972. *The Goddess Natura in Medieval Literature*, Cambridge, MA

Edsall, M. A., 2014. 'The *Arma Christi* before the *Arma Christi*: Rhetorics of the Passion in Late Antiquity and the Early Middle Ages', in *Arma Christi: Objects, Representation, and Devotional Practice in Medieval and Early Modern Culture*, ed. A. Denny-Brown and L. H. Cooper, Farnham, 21–52

Elias, N., 1982. *The Civilizing Process*, trans. E. Jephcott, 2 vols, Oxford

Elkins, J., 2001. *Pictures and Tears: A History of People Who Have Cried in Front of Paintings*, New York and London

Elsner, J., 2014. 'Rational, Passionate and Appetitive: The Psychology of Rhetoric and the Transformation of Visual Culture from non-Christian to Christian Sarcophagi in the Roman World', in Elsner and Meyer, 316–49

—, and M. Meyer, eds, 2014. *Art and Rhetoric in Roman Culture*, Cambridge

Enders, J., 2001. 'Of Miming and Signing: The Dramatic Rhetoric of Gesture', in *Gesture in Medieval Drama and Art*, ed. C. Davidson, Kalamazoo, 1–25

Engelen, U., 1978. *Die Edelsteine in der deutschen Dichtung des 12. und 13. Jahrhunderts*, Munich

Erlande-Brandenburg, A., 1975. *Le Roi est mort: étude sur les funérailles, les sépultures et les tombeaux des rois de France jusqu'à la fin du 13e siècle*, Geneva

—, trans. M. Thom, 1994. *The Cathedral: The Social and Architectural Dynamics of Construction*, Cambridge

Evans, E., ed. and trans., 1956. *Tertullian's Treatise on the Incarnation*, London

Evans, R. J. W., and A. Marr, eds, 2006. *Curiosity and Wonder from the Renaissance to the Enlightenment*, Aldershot

Even-Ezra, A., 2013. 'The Conceptualization of Charisma in the Early Thirteenth Century', *Viator*, 44/1: 151–68

Fassler, M., 1993a. 'Liturgy and Sacred History: The Twelfth-Century Tympana at Chartres', *Art Bulletin*, 75/3: 499–520

—, 1993b. *Gothic Song: Victorine Sequences and Augustinian Reform in Twelfth-Century Paris*, Cambridge

Feiss, H., trans., 1987. *Peter of Celle: Selected Works*, Cistercian Studies, 100, Kalamazoo

Fellows, N., trans., 2013. *The Book of the Order of Chivalry*, Woodbridge

Fergusson, P., 2011. *Canterbury Cathedral Priory in the Age of Becket*, New Haven and London

Fish, S., 1980. *Is There a Text in this Class? The Authority of Interpretative Communities*, Cambridge, MA

Fisher, P., 1998. *Wonder, the Rainbow, and the Aesthetics of Rare Experiences*, Cambridge, MA

Forshaw, H. P., ed., 1973. *Edmund of Abingdon: Speculum Religiosorum and Speculum Ecclesie*, London

Forsyth, I., 2002. 'Narrative at Moissac: Schapiro's Legacy', *Gesta*, 41/1: 71–93

Fortenbaugh, W. W., 2002. *Aristotle on Emotion: A Contribution to Philosophical Psychology, Rhetoric, Poetics, Politics, and Ethics*, 2nd edn, London

Frankl, P., 1950. *The Gothic: Literary Sources and Interpretations through Eight Centuries*, Princeton, NJ

—, 2000. *Gothic Architecture*, rev. P. Crossley, New Haven and London, 2000

Freedberg, D., 1989. *The Power of Images: Studies in the History and Theory of Response*, Chicago and London

Freigang, C., 1999. 'Die Expertisen zum Kathedralbau in Girona (1386 und 1416/17): Ammerkungen zur mittelalterlichen Debatte um Architektur', in *Gotische Architektur in Spanien*, ed. C. Freigang, Frankfurt-am-Main and Madrid, 203–26

Fried, M., 1980. *Absorption and Theatricality: Painting and Beholder in the Age of Diderot*, Berkeley and London

Fuller, S., 2011. 'Concerning Gendered Discourse in Medieval Musical Theory: Was the Semitone "Gendered Feminine"?', *Music Spectrum Theory*, 33/1: 65–89

Fulton, R., 2002. *From Judgment to Passion: Devotion to Christ and the Virgin Mary*, New York

Fulton Brown, R., 2013. 'Anselm and Praying with the Saints', in Morrison and Bell, 115–38

Gaborit-Chopin, D., et al., eds, 1998. *L'Art au temps des rois maudits: Philippe le Bel et ses fils 1285–1328*, Paris

Gage, J., 1993. *Colour and Culture: Practice and Meaning from Antiquity to Abstraction*, London

—, 1999. *Colour and Meaning: Art, Science and Symbolism*, London

—, ed. and trans., 1980. *Goethe on Art*, London

Gaiger, J., 2011. 'Participatory Imagining and the Explanation of Living-Presence Response', *British Journal of Aesthetics*, 51:363–81

Gamboni, D., 2002. *Potential Images: Ambiguity and Indeterminacy in Modern Art*, London

García Avilés, A., 2007. 'Imágenes 'vivientes': idolatría y herejía en las *Cantigas* de Alfonso X el Sabio', *Goya*, 321: 324–42

Gardner, A., 1937. *A Handbook of English Medieval Sculpture*, Cambridge

—, 1940. *Alabaster Tombs*, Cambridge

Gardner, S., 1927. *English Gothic Foliage Sculpture*, Cambridge

Garnett, J., and G. Rosser, 2013. *Spectacular Miracles: Transforming Images in Italy, from the Renaissance to the Present*, London

Garnett, R. M., 1909. 'De arte lacrimandi', *Anglia*, 32: 269–94

Garton, C., ed. and trans., 1986. *The Metrical Life of St Hugh*, Lincoln

Gayk, S. N., 2010. *Image, Text, and Religious Reform in Fifteenth-Century England*, Cambridge

Geddes, J., 1999. *Medieval Decorative Ironwork in England*, London

Gell, A., 1992. 'The Technology of Enchantment and the Enchantment of Technology', in *Anthropology, Art and Aesthetics*, ed. J. Coote and A. Shelton, Oxford, 40–63

—, 1998. *Art and Agency: An Anthropological Theory*, Oxford

Gennep, A. van, 1960. *The Rites of Passage*, trans. M. B. Vizedon and G. L. Caffee, Chicago

Gertsman, E., 2010a. *The Dance of Death in the Middle Ages: Image, Text, Performance*, Turnhout

—, 2010b. 'The Facial Gesture: Misreading Emotion in Gothic Art', *Journal of Medieval Religious Cultures*, 36/1: 28–46

—, 2015a. *Worlds Within: Opening the Medieval Shrine Madonna*, University Park, PA

—, 2015b. 'Introduction: Bewilderment overwhelms Me', *Preternature*, 4/1: 1–12

—, and J. Stevenson, eds, 2012. *Thresholds of Medieval Culture: Liminal Spaces*, Woodbridge

Ghrádaigh, N., 2012. 'Otherworldly Gesturing? Understanding Linear Complexity in Medieval Insular Art', in *Linea II: Giochi, metamorfosi, seduzioni della linea*, ed. M. Faietti and G. Wolf, Florence, 77–97

Gilbert, C., 2001. *The Saints' Three Reasons for Paintings in Churches*, Ithaca, NY

Gillerman, D., 1994. *Enguerran de Marigny and the Church of Notre-Dame at Ecouis: Art and Patronage in the Reign of Philip the Fair*, University Park, PA

Ginther, J. R., 2016. *Master of the Sacred Page: A Study of the Theology of Robert Grosseteste ca. 1229/30–1235*, London

Ginzburg, C., 2013. 'Our Words and Theirs: A Reflection on the Historian's Craft, Today', *Cromohs*, 18: 97–114

Givens, J. A., 1991. 'The Fabric Accounts of Exeter Cathedral as a Record of Medieval Sculptural Praxis', *Gesta*, 30/2: 112–18

—, 2005. *Observation and Image Making in Gothic Art*, Cambridge

Glixelli, S., 1914. *Les cinq poèmes des trois morts et des trois vifs*, Paris

Glorieux, P., ed., 1960–73. *Jean Gerson: oeuvres complètes*, 10 vols, Paris

Goethe, J. W. von, 1996. *Werke, I: Gedichte und Epen*, vol. 1, ed. E. Trunz, Munich

Gombrich, E. H., 1962. *Art and Illusion: A Study in the Psychology of Pictorial Representation*, 2nd edn, London

—, 1970. *Aby Warburg: An Intellectual Biography*, Chicago and Oxford

—, 1972. *Symbolic Images: Studies in the Art of the Renaissance*, London

—, 1978a. *Meditations on a Hobby Horse and Other Essays on the Theory of Art*, 3rd edn, London
—, 1978b. *Norm and Form: Studies in the Art of the Renaissance*, 3rd edn, London
—, 1984. *The Sense of Order: A Study in the Psychology of Decorative Art*, 2nd edn, London
—, 1990. 'The Edge of Delusion', review of Freedberg 1989, *New York Review of Books*, 15: 6–9
Gordon, R. L., 1979. 'The Real and the Imaginary: Production and Religion in the Graeco-Roman World', *Art History*, 2/1: 5–34
Gott, H. M., 2013. *Ascetic Modernism in the Work of T. S. Eliot and Gustave Flaubert*, London
Gould, K., 1992. 'Jean Pucelle and Northern Gothic Art: New Evidence from Strasbourg Cathedral', *Art Bulletin*, 74/1: 51–74
Grabar, O., 1992. *The Mediation of Ornament*, Princeton and Oxford
Grand-Clément, A., 2015. 'Poikilia', in *The Blackwell Companion to Ancient Aesthetics*, ed. P. Destrée and P. Murray, Chichester, 406–21
Grandmontagne, M., 2005. *Claus Sluter und die Lesbarkeit mittelalterliche Skulptur: das Portal der Kartause von Champmol*, Worms
Graves, P., 1989. 'Social Space in the English Medieval Parish Church', *Economy and Society*, 18: 297–322
Gray, D., 1972. *Themes and Images in the Medieval English Religious Lyric*, London
—, 2005. 'London, British Library, Additional Ms 37049: A Spiritual Encyclopedia', in *Text and Controversy from Wyclif to Bale*, ed. H. Barr and A. M. Hutchinson, Turnhout, 99–116
Greenhalgh, M., 2009. *Marble Past, Monumental Present: Building with Antiquities in the Mediaeval Mediterranean*, Leiden and Boston
Gross, K., 1992. *The Dream of the Moving Statue*, Ithaca, NY
Guérin, S. M., 2013. 'Meaningful Spectacles: Gothic Ivories staging the Divine', *Art Bulletin*, 95/1: 53–77
—, 2016. 'Saisir le Sens', in Palazzo 2016, 589–611
—, 2017. 'Synergy across Media: Gothic Sculptors in Wood and Ivory', in Davies and Townsend, 124–36
Guest, G. B., 1995. *Bible Moralisée: Codex Vindobonensis 2554, Vienna Oesterreichische Nationalbibliothek*, London
Guillouët, J.-M., 2003. *Les portails de la cathédrale de Nantes: un grand programme sculpté du XVe siècle et son public*, Rennes
—, 2011. *Le portail de Santa Maria da Vitória Batalha et l'art européen de son temps*, Leiria
Gumbrecht, H. U., 2004. *The Production of Presence: What Meaning Cannot Convey*, Stanford, CA
Habermas, J., 1992. *The Structural Transformation of the Public Sphere: An Inquiry into a Category of Bourgeois Society*, trans. T. Burger and F. Lawrence, Cambridge
Hadot, P., 2006. *The Veil of Isis: An Essay on the Idea of Nature*, trans. P. Chase, Cambridge, MA, and London
Hagberg, G., 1995. *Art as Language: Wittgenstein, Meaning and Aesthetic Theory*, Ithaca, NY, and London
Hägele, H., 2002. 'In the Eye of the Beholder: The Depiction of the Eye in Western Sculpture with Special Reference to the Period 1350–1700 and to Colour in Sculpture', PhD diss., University of Cambridge, 2002
Hahn, C., 2000. 'Visio Dei: Changes in Medieval Visuality', in *Visuality before and beyond the Renaissance: Seeing as Others Saw*, ed. R. S. Nelson, Cambridge, 169–96
—, 2006. 'Vision', in *A Companion to Medieval Art*, ed. C. Rudolph, Oxford, 44–64
Hamann-MacLean, R., and I. Schüssler, 1993–2008. *Die Kathedrale von Reims*, 8 vols, Stuttgart
Hamburger, J. F., 1994. 'Medieval Studies and Medieval Art History', in *The Past and Future of Medieval Studies*, ed. J. van Engen, Notre-Dame, IL, 383–400
—, 1997a. *Nuns as Artists: The Visual Culture of a Medieval Convent*, Berkeley and Los Angeles
—, 1997b. '"To make women weep": Ugly Art as "Feminine" and the Origins of Modern Aesthetics', *Res*, 31: 9–33
—, 1998. *The Visual and the Visionary: Art and Female Spirituality in Late Medieval Germany*, New York
—, 2000. 'Seeing and Believing: The Suspicion of Sight and the Authentication of Vision in Late Medieval Art and Devotion', in *Imagination und Wirklichkeit: zum Verhältnis von mentalen und realen Bildern in der Kunst der frühen Neuzeit*, ed. K. Krüger and A. Nova, Mainz, 47–69

—, 2007. 'Visible, yet Secret: Images as Signs of Friendship in Seuse', *Oxford German Studies*, 36/2: 141–62
—, 2013. 'Hans Belting. Bild und Kult: Eine Geschichte des Bildes vor dem Zeitalter der Kunst, 1990', in *The Books that Shaped Art History: From Gombrich and Greenberg to Alpers and Krauss*, ed. R. Shone and J. P. Stonard, London, 203–30
—, and A.-M. Bouché, eds, 2006. *The Mind's Eye: Art and Theological Argument in the Middle Ages*, Princeton
Hardison, O. B., 1992. *The Enduring Monument*, Chapel Hill, NC
Harpham, G. G., 1987. *The Ascetic Imperative in Culture and Criticism*, Chicago and London
Harris, A. F., 2014. 'Hewn', in *Ecologies of the Inhuman*, ed. J. J. Cohen and L. Duckert, Washington, DC, 17–38
Hartsock, C., 2008. *Sight and Blindness in Luke – Acts: The Use of Physical Features in Characterization*, Leiden and Boston
Harvey, J. H., ed., 1969. *William Worcestre: Itineraries*, Oxford
Hauser, G. A., 1999. *Vernacular Voices: The Rhetoric of Publics and Public Spheres*, Columbia, SC
Hearn, M. F., 1981. *The Revival of Monumental Stone Sculpture in the 11th and 12th Centuries*, Oxford
Henderson, G., 1972. *Early Medieval*, Harmondsworth
Hesketh, G., ed., 2006. *Rossignos by John of Howden*, Anglo-Norman Text Society, 63, Oxford
Heslop, T. A., 1998. 'Late Twelfth-Century Writing about Art, and Aesthetic Relativity', in *Medieval Art: Recent Perspectives. A Memorial Tribute to C. R. Dodwell*, ed. G. R. Owen-Crocker and T. Graham, Manchester and New York, 129–41
—, 2012. 'Constantine and Helena: The Roman in English Romanesque', in *Architecture and Interpretation: Essays for Eric Fernie*, ed. J. A. Franklin, T. A. Heslop and C. Stevenson, Woodbridge, 163–75
Hirsh, J. C., 1996. The *Boundaries of Faith: The Development and Transmission of Medieval Spirituality*, Leiden, 1996
Hoeniger, C., 1995. *The Renovation of Paintings in Tuscany, 1250–1500*, Cambridge
Hoffmann, G., et al., 2006. *Das Gabelkreuz in St. Maria im Kapitol zu Köln und das Phänomen der Crucifixi dolorosi in Europa*, Worms
Hogg, J., ed., 1981. *An Illustrated Yorkshire Carthusian Religious Miscellany: British Library London, Additional Ms. 37049*, vol. 3, *Analecta Cartusiana*, 95, Salzburg
Hohler, E., 1999. *Norwegian Stave Church Sculpture*, 2 vols, Oslo and Oxford
—, 2017. 'Medieval Wooden Sculptures in Norway', *Collegium Medievale*, 30: 33–84
Holt, J., 1982. *Robin Hood*, 2nd edn, London
Howe, J. M., and M. Wolfe, eds, 2002. *Inventing Medieval Landscapes: Senses of Place in Western Europe*, Gainesville, FL
Hubbell, H. M., trans., 2006. *Cicero: De Inventione*, Loeb Classical Library, vol. 386, Cambridge, MA
Hubert, J., 1935. 'Le miracle de Déols et la trêve conclue en 1187 entre les rois de France et d'Angleterre', *Bibliothèque de l'Ecole des chartes*, 96: 285–300
Hunzinger, C., 2015. 'Wonder', in *The Blackwell Companion to Ancient Aesthetics*, ed. P. Destrée and P. Murray, Chichester, 422–37
Husband, T., 1980. *The Wild Man: Medieval Myth and Symbolism*, New York
Inglis, E., 2003. 'Gothic Architecture and a Scholastic: Jean de Jandun's *Tractatus de laudibus Parisius* (1323)', *Gesta*, 42/1: 63–85
Jaeger, C. S., 1985. *The Origins of Courtliness: Civilizing Trends and the Formation of Courtly Ideals 939–1210*, Philadelphia, PA
—, 1994. *The Envy of Angels: Cathedral Schools and Social Ideals in Medieval Europe, 950–1200*, Philadelphia, PA
—, 1997. 'Charismatic Body – Charismatic Text', *Exemplaria*, 9/1: 117–37
—, 2012. *Enchantment: On Charisma and the Sublime in the Arts of the West*, Philadelphia, PA
—, ed., 2010. *Magnificence and the Sublime in Medieval Aesthetics*, New York
James, L., and R. Webb, 1991. '"To Understand Ultimate Things and Enter Secret Places": Ekphrasis and Art in Byzantium', *Art History*, 14/1: 1–17

Jauss, H. R., 1982. *Towards an Aesthetic of Reception*, trans. T. Bahti, Minneapolis

Johnson, G. A., 2014. 'A Taxonomy of Touch: Tactile Encounters in Renaissance Italy', in Dent, 91–106

Jordan, A., 2002. *Visualizing Kingship in the Windows of the Sainte-Chapelle*, Turnhout

Joubert, F., 2008. *La sculpture gothique en France XIIe–XIIIe siècles*, Paris

Jung, J. E., 2000. 'Beyond the Barrier: The Unifying Role of the Choir Screen in Gothic Churches', *Art Bulletin*, 82: 622–57

—, 2006. 'Dynamic Bodies and the Beholder's Share: The Wise and Foolish Virgins of Magdeburg Cathedral', in *Bild und Körper im Mittelalter*, ed. Kristin Marek et al., Munich, 135–60

—, 2010. 'The Tactile and the Visionary: Notes on the Place of Sculpture in the Medieval Religious Imagination', in *Looking Beyond: Visions, Dreams, and Insights in Medieval Art and History*, ed. C. Hourihane, Index of Christian Art Occasional Papers, 11, Princeton, NJ, 203–40

—, 2013. *The Gothic Screen: Space, Sculpture, and Community in the Cathedrals of France and Germany, ca. 1200–1400*, Cambridge

—, 2017. 'Moving Pictures on the Gothic Choir Screen', in *The Art and Science of the Church Screen in Medieval Europe*, ed. S. Bucklow, R. Marks and L. Wrapson, Woodbridge, 176–94

—, 2018. 'Compassion as Moral Virtue: Another Look at the Wise and Foolish Virgins in Gothic Sculpture', in *Faces of Charisma. Image, Text, Object in Byzantium and the Medieval West*, ed. B. M. Bedos-Rezak, M. D. Rust, Leiden and Boston, 76–127

Kaeuper, R. W., and E. Kennedy, 1996. *The* Book of Chivalry *of Geoffroi de Charny: Text, Context, and Translation*, Philadelphia, PA

Kahn, D., 1992a. 'Anglo-Saxon and Early Romanesque Frieze Sculpture in England', in Kahn 1992b, 61–74

—, ed., 1992b. *The Romanesque Frieze and its Spectator*, London

Karge, H., 1995. *La Catedral de Burgos y la arquitectura del siglo XIII en Francia y España*, trans. C. A. Corredor, Valladolid

—, 2012. 'From Naumburg to Burgos: European Sculpture and Dynastic Politics in the Thirteenth Century', *Hispanic Research Journal*, 13/5: 434–48

Karnes, M., 2011. *Imagination, Meditation, and Cognition in the Middle Ages*, Chicago

Katzenellenbogen, A., 1959. *The Sculptural Programs of Chartres Cathedral*, Baltimore, MD

Kavaler, E. M., 2005. 'Nature and the Chapel Vaults at Ingolstadt: Structuralist and Other Perspectives', *Art Bulletin*, 87/2: 230–48

—, 2008. 'Architectural Wit: Playfulness and Deconstruction in the Gothic of the Sixteenth Century', in *Reading Gothic Architecture*, ed. M. M. Reeve, Turnhout, 139–50

—, 2011. 'On Vegetal Imagery in Renaissance Gothic', in *Le Gothique de la Renaissance*, ed. M. Chatenet et al., Paris, 297–312

—, 2012. *Renaissance Gothic: Architecture and the Arts in Gothic Europe 1470–1540*, New Haven, CT

Kaye, J., 2016. *A History of Balance, 1250–1375: The Emergence of a New Model of Equilibrium and its Impact on Thought*, Cambridge

Keen, M., 1977. *The Outlaws of Medieval Legend*, 2nd edn, London

—, 1984. *Chivalry*, New Haven and London

Kemp, W., 1997. *The Narratives of Gothic Stained Glass*, Cambridge

Kendall, C. B., 1989. 'The Voice in the Stone: The Verse Inscriptions of Ste-Foy of Conques and the Date of the Tympanum', in *Hermeneutics and Medieval Culture*, ed. P. J. Gallacher and H. Damico, Albany, NY, 163–182

Kendrick, L., 1999. *Animating the Letter: The Figurative Embodiment of Writing from Late Antiquity to the Renaissance*, Columbus, OH

Kenny, A., 1963. *Action, Emotion and Will*, London

Kessler, H. L., 2004. *Seeing Medieval Art*, Peterborough, Ontario, and Plymouth

—, 2006. 'Gregory the Great and Image Theory in Northern Europe during the Twelfth and Thirteenth Centuries', in *A Companion to Medieval Art*, ed. C. Rudolph, Oxford, 151–72

Kidson, P., 1987. 'A Note on Naumburg', in *Romanesque and Gothic: Essays for George Zarnecki*, ed. N. Stratford, 2 vols, Woodbridge, vol. 1, 143–6

Kieckhefer, R., 1984. *Unquiet Souls: Fourteenth-Century Saints and their Religious Milieu*, Chicago and London

Kimpel, D., 1977. 'Le développement de la taille en série dans l'architecture médiévale et son rôle dans l'histoire économique', *Bulletin Monumental*, 135/3: 195–222

—, and R. Suckale, 1990. *L'Architecture gothique en France 1130–1270*, trans. F. Neu, Paris

Kinch, A., 2013. *Imago Mortis: Mediating Images of Death in Late Medieval Culture*, Boston, MA

King, P., 1990. 'The Cadaver Tomb in England: Novel Manifestations of an Old Idea', *Church Monuments*, 5: 26–38

Kingsley, J. P., 2010. 'To Touch the Image: Embodying Christ in the Bernward Gospels', *Peregrinations*, 3/1: 138–73

Klein, P., 1981, 1983. *Vollständige Faksimile-Ausgabe im Originalformat der Handschrift Ms. Douce 180, Apokalypse, aus dem Besitz der Bodleian Library, Oxford*, 2 vols, Graz, Paris

Knox, T. M., trans., 1975. *Hegel's Aesthetics: Lectures on Fine Art, I*, Oxford

Knuuttila, S., 2004. *Emotions in Ancient and Medieval Philosophy*, New York

Koerner, J. L., 1985. 'The Mortification of the Image: Death as a Hermeneutic in Hans Baldung Grien', *Representations*, 10: 52–101

Könsgen, E., ed. and trans., 2004. *Iohannes de Garlandia: Carmen de Misteriis Ecclesie*, commentary by P. Dinter, Mittellateinische Studien und Texte, 32, Leiden

Kren, T., and R. S. Wieck, 1990. *The Visions of Tondal from the Library of Margaret of York*, Malibu, CA

Kristeva, J., 1982. *Powers of Horror: An Essay on Abjection*, trans. L. S. Roudiez, New York

Krohm, H., and H. Kunde, eds, 2012. *Der Naumburger Meister: Bildhauer und Architekt im Europa der Kathedralen*, 3 vols, Petersberg

Kumler, A., 2011. *Translating Truth: Ambitious Images and Religious Knowledge in Late Medieval France and England*, New Haven and London

—, and C. R. Lakey, 2012. 'The Material Sense of Things in the Middle Ages', *Gesta*, 51/1: 1–17

Kupfer, M., ed., 2008. *The Passion Story: From Visual Representation to Social Drama*, University Park, PA

Kurmann, P., 1987. *La Façade de la cathédrale de Reims*, 2 vols, Paris and Lausanne

—, 1996. 'Un Collose aux pieds d'argile: la chronologie de la sculpture française du XIIIe siècle repose-t-elle sur des dates assurées?' in *Epigraphie et iconographie: actes du colloque tenu à Poitiers*, ed. R. Favreau, Poitiers, 143–51

—, 1998. 'Mobilité des artistes ou mobilité des modèles? A propos de l'atelier des sculpteurs rémois au XIIIe siècle', *Revue de l'art*, 120/2: 23–34

—, 2006. 'Jedem Meister seinem Stil: Zur Herstellungsproblematik französischer Monumentalskulptur in den grossen Bauhutten des 13. Jahrhunderts', in *Stilfragen zur Kunst des Mittelalters: Eine Einführung*, ed. B. Klein and B. Boerner, Berlin, 137–49

Ladner, G. B., 1961. 'The Gestures of Prayer in Papal Iconography of the Thirteenth and Early Fourteenth Centuries', in *Didascaliae: Studies in Honor of Anselm M. Albareda*, ed. S. Prete, New York, 245–75

Laue, G., ed., 2004. *Gedrehte kostbarkeiten: Turned Treasuries*, Munich

Lazikani, A. S., ed., 2015. *Cultivating the Heart: Feeling and Emotion in Twelfth- and Thirteenth-Century Religious Texts*, Cardiff

Leach, E. A., 2006. 'Gendering the Semitone, Sexing the Leading Tone: Fourteenth-Century Music Theory and the Directed Progression', *Music Theory Spectrum*, 28: 1–21

Leclercq, J., C. H. Talbot and H. M. Rochais, eds, 1957. *S. Bernardi: Opera Omnia*, vol. 2: *Sermones super Cantica Canticorum, 36–86*, Rome

Lee, D., trans., 1977. *Plato: Timaeus and Critias*, London

Le Goff, J., 1988. 'The Wilderness in the Medieval West', in *The Medieval Imagination*, trans. Arthur Goldhammer, Chicago, 47–59

Lehmann, E., and E. Schubert, 1988. *Dom und Severikirche zu Erfurt*, Stuttgart

Lehmann-Brockhaus, O., ed., 1955–60. *Lateinische Schriftquellen zur Kunst in England, Wales und Schottland vom Jahre 901 bis zum Jahre 1307*, 5 vols, Munich

Lentes, T., 2006. '"As Far as the Eye can See ...":

Rituals of Gazing in the Late Middle Ages', in Hamburger and Bouché, 360–734

Le Roux de Lincy, A., and L. M. Tisserand, 1867. *Paris et ses historiens aux XIVe et XVe siècles, documents et écrits originaux*, Paris

Levy, E., 2002. 'Ottaviano Jannella: Micro-Sculptor in the Age of the Microscope', *Burlington Magazine*, 144/2 no. 1192: 420–28

Lewis, C. S., 1964. *The Discarded Image: An Introduction to Medieval and Renaissance Literature*, Cambridge

Lewis, C. T., and C. Short, 1993. *A Latin Dictionary*, Oxford

Lindley, P. G., 1995. *Gothic to Renaissance: Essays on Sculpture in England*, Stamford

—, ed., 2003. *Making Medieval Art*, Donington, Lincolnshire

Little, C. T., ed., 2006. *Set in Stone: The Face in Medieval Sculpture*, New Haven and London

Longinus, 1995. *On the Sublime*, trans. W. Hamilton Fyfe, rev. D. A. Russell, Loeb Classical Library, vol. 199, Cambridge, MA

Lucas of Tuy, 1612. *Lucae Tudensis Episcopi de Altera Vita Fidei*, Ingolstadt

Luxford, J., 2009. 'Tombs as Forensic Evidence in Medieval England', *Church Monuments*, 24: 7–25

—, 2010. 'Out of the Wilderness: A Fourteenth-Century English Drawing of John the Baptist', *Gesta*, 49/2: 137–50

—, 2011. 'The Space of the Tomb in Carthusian Consciousness', in *Ritual and Space in the Middle Ages*, ed. F. Andrews, Harlaxton Medieval Studies, 21, Donington, Lincolnshire, 259–81

—, 2017. 'The Nature and Purpose of Medieval Relic-Lists', in *Saints and Cults in Medieval England*, ed. S. Powell, Harlaxton Medieval Studies, 27, Donington, Lincolnshire, 58–79

MacIntyre, A. C., 1984. *After Virtue: A Study in Moral Theory*, 2nd edn, London

Maguire, H., 1974. 'Truth and Convention in Byzantine Descriptions of Works of Art', *Dumbarton Oaks Papers*, 28: 113–40

Mâle, E., 1919. *Art religieux du XIIIe siècle en France: étude sur l'iconographie du Moyen Age et sur ses sources d'inspiration*, Paris

—, 1922. *Art religieux du XIIe siècle en France: études sur les origines de l'iconographie du Moyen Age*, Paris

Mallion, J., 1964. *Le Jubé de la Cathédrale de Chartres*, Luisant-Chartres

Malone, C. M., 2004. *Facade as Spectacle: Ritual and Ideology at Wells Cathedral*, Boston, MA

—, 2016. 'Architecture as Evidence for Liturgical Performance', in *Understanding Medieval Liturgy: Essays in Interpretation*, ed. H. Gittos and S. Hamilton, London and New York, 207–37

Mancia, L. E., 2015. 'John of Fécamp and Affective Reform in Eleventh-Century Normandy', *Anglo-Norman Studies*, 37: 161–80

Mango, C., ed., 1972. *The Art of the Byzantine Empire 312–1453: Sources and Documents*, Englewood Cliffs, NJ

Maniura, R., and R. Shepherd, eds, 2006. *Presence: The Inherence of the Prototype within Images and Other Objects*, Aldershot

Marks, R., 2004. *Image and Devotion in Late Medieval England*, Stroud

Marrow, J. H., 1979. *Passion Iconography in Northern European Art of the Late Middle Ages and Early Renaissance*, Kortrijk

McAleer, J. P., 1988. 'Particularly English? Screen Facades of the Type at Salisbury and Wells Cathedral', *Journal of the British Archaeological Association*, 141, 124–58

McEvoy, J., 2000. *Robert Grosseteste*, Oxford

McLuhan, M., 1964. *Understanding Media: The Extensions of Man*, London

McNamer, S., 2010. *Affective Meditation and the Invention of Medieval Compassion*, Philadelphia, PA

Ménard, P., 1969. *Le Rire et le sourire dans le roman courtois en France au Moyen Age*, Geneva

Merleau-Ponty, M., 1989. *The Phenomenology of Perception*, trans. C. Smith, London, 1989

Meyer, P., 1945. *Schweizerische Münster und Kathedralen des Mittelalters*, Zurich

Migne, J.-P., ed. 1844–64. *Patrologia Latina: Cursus Completus*, 221 vols, Paris

Miller, F. J., 1916. *Ovid: Metamorphoses, I*, trans. and rev. G. P. Good, Loeb Classical Library, vol. 42, Cambridge, MA

Milliken, R., 2012. *Ambiguous Locks: An Iconology of Hair in Medieval Art and Literature,* Jefferson, NC

Mills, R., 2005. *Suspended Animation: Pain, Pleasure and Punishment in Medieval Culture*, London

Minnis, A. J., 1988. *Medieval Theory of Authorship*, 2nd edn, Aldershot

Mitchell, J., 2012. 'Believing is Seeing: The Natural Image in Late Antiquity', in *Architecture and Interpretation: Essays for Eric Fernie*, ed. J. A. Franklin, T. A. Heslop and C. Stevenson, Woodbridge, 16–41

—, 2017. 'Lively Columns and Living Stones: The Origins of the Constantinian Church Basilica', in *Encounters, Excavations and Argosies: Essays for Richard Hodges*, ed. J. Moreland, J. Mitchell and B. Leal, Oxford, 190–207

Mitchell, W. J. T., 2005. *What Do Pictures Want? The Lives and Loves of Images*, Chicago and London

Moore, R. I., 1987. *The Formation of a Persecuting Society: Power and Deviance in Western Europe, 950–1250*, Oxford

Morand, K., 1991. *Claus Sluter: Artist at the Court of Burgundy*, London

Morgan, N. J., 1982. *Early Gothic Manuscripts (I), 1190–1250*, Survey of Manuscripts Illuminated in the British Isles, 4, Oxford

—, 1991. 'Texts and Images of Marian Devotion in Thirteenth-Century England', in *England in the Thirteenth Century*, ed. W. M. Ormrod, Harlaxton Medieval Studies, 1, Stamford, 69–104

—, 1993. 'Texts and Images of Marian Devotion in Fourteenth-Century England', in *England in the Fourteenth Century*, ed. N. J. Rogers, Harlaxton Medieval Studies, 3, Stamford, 34–57

—, 2006. 'The Norwegian and Swedish *Crucifixi Dolorosi c.*1300–50 in their European Context', in Nadolny et al., 266–78

Morganstern, A. M., 2000. *Gothic Tombs of Kinship in France, the Low Countries, and England*, University Park, PA

Morris, R., ed., 1875–6. *Cursor Mundi*, vol. 2, Early English Text Society, London

Morrison, K. F., and R. M. Bell, eds, 2013. *Studies on Medieval Empathies*, Turnhout

Mortet, V., 1911. *Recueil de textes relatifs à l'histoire de l'architecture et à la condition des architectes en France au Moyen Age, XIe–XIIe siècles*, Paris

Munns, J., 2016. *Cross and Culture in Anglo-Norman England*, Woodbridge

Muratova, X., 1986. 'Vir quidem fallax et falisidicus, sed artifex praeelectus: remarques sur l'image sociale et littéraire de l'artiste au Moyen Âge', in *Artistes, artisans et production artistique au Moyen Age*, ed. X. Barral I Altet, Paris, 53–72

Murray, A., 1981. 'Confession as a Historical Source in the Thirteenth Century', in *The Writing of History in the Middle Ages: Essays presented to Richard William Southern*, ed. R. H. C. Davis and J. M. Wallace-Hadrill, Oxford, 275–322

—, 1986. *Reason and Society in the Middle Ages*, Oxford

—, 2006. 'Doubting Thomas in Medieval Exegesis and Art', *Unione internazionale degli Istituti di archeologia storia e storia dell'arte in Roma*, Conferenze 22, Rome, 21–75

Murray, S., 1987. *Building Troyes Cathedral: The Late Gothic Campaigns*, Bloomington and Indianapolis

—, 2004. *A Gothic Sermon: Making a Contract with the Mother of God, Saint Mary of Amiens*, Berkeley and London

Nadolny, J., et al., eds, 2006. *Medieval Painting in Northern Europe: Techniques, Analysis, Art History. Studies in Commemoration of the 70th Birthday of Unn Plahter*, London

Newman, B., 2013. 'Indwelling: A Meditation on Empathy, Pregnancy, and the Virgin Mary', in Morrison and Bell, 189–212

Nickson, T., 2015. *Toledo Cathedral: Building Histories in Medieval Castile*, University Park, PA

Nicolai, B., 2002. 'Orders in Stone: Social Reality and Artistic Approach: The Case of the Strasbourg South Portal', *Gesta*, 41/2, 111–28

—, 2011. 'Transformation and Innovation of Rising Gothic in the Northern Holy Roman Empire: Transferring Gothic', in *Gothic Art and Thought in the Later Medieval Period*, ed. C. Hourihane, Index of Christian Art Occasional Papers, 12, Princeton, NJ, 119–33

Nims, M. F., trans., 1967. *Poetria Nova of Geoffrey of Vinsauf*, Toronto

Nora, P., 1996. *Realms of Memory: Rethinking the French Past*, trans. A. Goldhammer, New York

Nordenfalk, C., 1990. 'The Sense of Touch in Art', in *The Verbal and the Visual: Essays in Honor of William Sebastian Heckscher*, ed. K.-L. Selig and E. Sears, New York, 109–20

Norton, C., 1990. 'Figure Sculpture from the Twelfth Century Minster', *Friends of York Minster Annual Report*, 11–30

— and D. Park, eds, 1986. *Cistercian Art and Architecture in the British Isles*, Cambridge

Nyborg, E., 2006. 'Danish Panel Painting until *c.*1300', in Nadolny, 248–65

—, 2013. 'Das ältere Sorø-Kruzifix: Ein Versuch zisterziensische Traditionen für die Gestaltung monumentaler Kruzifixe zu umreissen', *Spiritualität und Baukunst: Leben und Wirken der Zisterzienser im Kloster Doberan*, Convent, Beiträge zur Geschichte des Klosterwesens in Mecklenburg und Vorpommern, 5, Weimar and Rostock, 22–68

Oettinger, K., 1962. 'Laube, Garten und Wald: Zu einer Theorie der süddeutschen Sakralkunst 1470–1520', in *Festschrift für Hans Sedlmayr*, ed. K. Oettinger and M. Rassem, Munich, 201–28

Ohly, F., 1989. *Süsse Nägel der Passion: Ein Beitrag zur theologischen Semantik*, Baden-Baden

Ong, W. J., 1967. *The Presence of the Word: Some Prolegomena for Cultural and Religious History*, New Haven, CT

Oosterhoff, R. J., 2014. 'Idiotae, Mathematics, and Artisans: The Untutored Mind and the Discovery of Nature in the Fabrist Circle', *Intellectual History Review*, 24/3: 301–19

O'Reilly, J., 1981. '"Candidus et Rubicundus": An Image of Martyrdom in the "Lives" of Thomas Becket', *Analecta Bollandiana*, 99: 303–14

—, 1987. 'The Rough-Hewn Cross in Anglo-Saxon Art', in *Ireland and Insular Art AD 500–1200*, ed. M. Ryan, Dublin, 153–8

—, 1992. 'The Trees of Eden in Mediaeval Iconography', in *A Walk in the Garden: Biblical, Iconographical and Literary Images of Eden*, ed. P. Morris and D. Sawyer, *Journal for the Study of the Old Testament*, Supplement Series, 136, Sheffield, 167–204

Orfão, J., et al., 2014. *Monastery of Batalha: Interpretation Centre*, Lisbon

Osborne, J., trans., 1987. *Master Gregorius: The Marvels of Rome*, Toronto

Otter, M., 2010. 'Vultus adest (*the face helps*): Performance, Expressivity and Interiority', in Carruthers, 151–72

Paetow, L. J., ed. and trans., 1927. 'Morale Scolarium of John of Garland', *Memoirs of the University of California*, 4: 69–273

—, 1928. 'The Crusading Ardor of John of Garland', in *The Crusades and Other Historical Essays presented to D. C. Munro by his Former Students*, ed. L. J. Paetow, New York, 207–22

Palazzo, E., 2014. *L'Invention chrétienne des cinq sens dans la liturgie et l'art au Moyen Age*, Paris

—, ed., 2016. *Les cinq sens au Moyen Age*, Paris

Palmer, N. F., 1983. '"Antiquitus depingebatur": The Roman Pictures of Death and Misfortune in the *Ackermann aus Böhmen* and *Tradleček*, and in the Writings of the English Classicizing Friars', *Deutsche Vierteljahrsschrift für Literaturwissenschaft und Geistesgeschichte*, 57/2: 171–239

Panofsky, E., 1953. *Early Netherlandish Painting: Its Origin and Character*, 2 vols, Princeton, NJ

—, 1960. *Renaissance and Renascences in Western Art*, Stockholm

—, 1964. *Tomb Sculpture: Four Lectures on its Changing Aspects from Ancient Egypt to Bernini*, New York

—, 1968. *Idea: A Concept in Art History*, trans. J. J. S. Peake, New York

—, ed., 1979. *Abbot Suger on the Abbey Church of St.-Denis and its Art Treaures*, 2nd edn, Princeton, NJ

Pantin, W. A., 1955. *The English Church in the Fourteenth Century*, Cambridge

Parshall, P., 1993. '*Imago contrafacta*: Images and Facts in the Northern Renaissance', *Art History*, 16/4: 554–79

—, 1999. 'The Art of Memory and the Passion', *Art Bulletin*, 81/3: 456–72

Parsons, D., ed., 1991. *Eleanor of Castile 1290–1990: Essays to Commemorate the 700th Anniversary of her Death: 28 November 1290*, Stamford

Pasnau, R., and C. van Dyke, eds, 2010. *The Cambridge History of Medieval Philosophy*, vol. 2, Cambridge

Pastoureau, M., 1993. 'Introduction à la symbolique médiévale du bois', in *L'arbre: histoire naturelle et symbolique de l'arbre, du bois et du fruit au Moyen-Age*, ed. M. Pastoureau, vol. 2, Paris, 25–40

—, 2013. 'Quand les carottes étaient blanches: les pièges de l'anachronisme dans l'étude des couleurs médiévales', in *L'Image en questions: pour Jean Wirth*, ed. F. Elsig et al., Geneva and Paris, 224–36

Payne, A., 2009. 'Materiality, Crafting and Scale in Renaissance Architecture', *Oxford Art Journal*, 32/3: 365–86

Pereda, F., 2010. 'The "Shelter of the Savage": From Valladolid to the New World', *Medieval Encounters*, 19: 268–359

Perkinson, S., 2009. *The Likeness of the King: A Prehistory of Portraiture in Late Medieval France*, Chicago and London

—, ed., 2017. *The Ivory Mirror: The Art of Mortality in Renaissance Europe*, Brunswick, ME

Pevsner, N., 1945. *The Leaves of Southwell*, London and New York

Pickering, F. P., 1970. *Literature and Art in the Middle Ages*, Coral Gables, FL

—, 1971. *The Anglo-Norman Text of the Holkham Bible Picture Book*, Anglo-Norman Texts, 23, Oxford

Pinkus, A., 2014. *Sculpting Simulacra in Medieval Germany, 1250–1380*, Farnham and Burlington, VT

—, 2015, 'Lost in Symulachra: The Living Statues on the Imperial Balcony in Mülhausen', *Neue Frankfurter Forschungen zur Kunst*, 16: 384–400

—, 2018. 'The Giant of Bremen: Roland and the "Colossus Imagination"', *Speculum*, 93/2: 387–419

Plahter, U., 2014. 'Norwegian Art Technology in the Twelfth and Thirteenth Centuries: Materials and Techniques in a European Context', *Zeitschrift für Kunsttechnologie und Konservierung*, 28/2: 298–332

Plamper, J., 2012. *Geschichte und Gefühl: Grundlagen der Emotionsgeschichte*, Munich

Plötz, R., 1995. 'Visión y realidad', *Compostellanum*, 40: 339–65

Podro, M., 1982a. Review of Wollheim 1980, *Burlington Magazine*, 124/947: 100–02

—, 1982b. *The Critical Historians of Art*, New Haven and London

Pollard, A. J., 2004. *Imagining Robin Hood: The Late Medieval Stories in Historical Context*, Abingdon

Pressouyre, L., and D. Prigent, 1989. 'Un jugement dernier retrouvé à Fontevraud', *Comptes rendus des séances de l'année Académie des inscriptions et belles lettres*, 3: 804–9

Prinz, J., 2011. 'Against Empathy', in 'Spindel Supplement: Empathy and Ethics', *Southern Journal of Philosophy*, 49, suppl. 1: 214–33

Prior, E. S., and A. Gardner, 1912. *An Account of Medieval Figure-Sculpture in England*, Cambridge

Quiney, A., 2001. '*In Hoc Signo*: The West Front of Lincoln Cathedral', *Architectural History*, 44: 162–71

Raby, F. J. E., 1953. *A History of Christian-Latin Poetry from the Beginnings to the Close of the Middle Ages*, Oxford

Rackham, H., trans., 1942. *Cicero: De Oratore: De Partitione Oratoria*, Loeb Classical Library, vol. 349, Cambridge, MA

—, 1968. *Pliny: Historia Naturalis*, Loeb Classical Library, vol. 370, London and Cambridge, MA

Ramage, E. S., 1961. 'Cicero on Extra-Roman Speech', *Transactions and Proceedings of the American Philological Association*, 92: 481–94

Ramón de Luanco, J., ed. and trans., 1901. *Libre del ordre de cavayleria*, Barcelona

Ramsay, N. J., 1991. 'Alabaster', in *English Medieval Industries: Craftsmen, Techniques, Products*, ed. N. Ramsey and J. Blair, London and Rio Grande, 29–40

Recht, R., 1993–4. 'Du style en général et du Moyen Age en particulier', *Wiener Jahrbuch für Kunstgeschichte*, 46–7: 577–93

—, 1996. 'Un Bible pour illettrés? Sculpture gothique et "theâtre de mémoire"', *Critique*, 586: 188–206

—, 2008. *Believing and Seeing: The Art of Gothic Cathedrals*, Chicago

Reddy, W. M., 1997. 'Against Constructionism: The Historical Ethnography of Emotions', *Current Anthropology*, 38: 327–52

—, 2001. *The Navigations of Feeling: A Framework for the History of Emotions*, Cambridge

—, 2009. 'Historical Research on the Self and Emotions', *Emotion Review*, 1/4: 302–15

Reiners-Ernst, E., 1939. *Das freudvolle Vesperbild und die Anfänge der Pieta-Vorstellung*, Munich

Reiss, A., 2000. *The Sunday Christ: Sabbatarianism in English Medieval Wall Painting*, BAR British Series, 292, Oxford

Reynolds, C., 2007. '"In ryche colours delytethe the peyntour": Painting and the Visual Arts in the Poems of John Lydgate', in *Late Gothic England: Art and Display*, ed. R. Marks, Donnington, Lincolnshire, 1–15

Rigg, A. G., 1992. *A History of Anglo-Latin Literature, 1066–1422*, Cambridge

Roberts, L., S. Schaffer and P. Dear, eds, 2007. *The Mindful Hand: Inquiry and Invention from the Late Renaissance to Early Industrialization*, Amsterdam

Robinson, J. A., ed., 1909. *The History of Westminster Abbey by John Flete: Notes and Documents relating to Westminster Abbey, no. 2*, Cambridge

Rooney, A., 1993. *Hunting in Middle English Literature*, Woodbridge

Rose, M., 1997. *Stories in Stone: The Medieval Roof Carvings of Norwich Cathedral*, London

—, 1999. *The Norwich Apocalypse: The Cycle of Vault Carvings in the Cloisters of Norwich Cathedral*, Norwich

Rosenwein, B., 1998. *Anger's Past: The Social Uses of an Emotion in the Middle Ages*, Ithaca, NY, and London

—, 2002. 'Worrying about Emotions in History', *American Historical Review*, 107: 821–45

—, 2006. *Emotional Communities in the Early Middle Ages*, Ithaca, NY

Rosewell, R., 2008. *Medieval Wall Paintings in English and Welsh Churches*, Woodbridge

Rowe, N., 2011. 'Rethinking Ecclesia and Synagoga in the Thirteenth Century', in *Gothic Art and Thought in the Later Medieval Period*, ed. C. Hourihane, Index of Christian Art Occasional Papers, 12, Princeton, NJ, 265–91

Rowland, B., 1975. 'Bishop Bradwardine, the Artificial Memory, and the House of Fame', in *Chaucer at Albany*, ed. R. H. Robbins, New York, 41–62

Rubinelli, S., 2009. *Ars Topica: The Classical Technique of Constructing Arguments from Aristotle to Cicero*, Argumentation Library, 15, online https://dblp.org/db/series/argulib

Rudolph, C., 1997. *Violence and Daily Life: Reading, Art, and Polemics in the Cîteaux Moralia in Job*, Princeton

Ruh, K., 1950. 'Zur Theologie des mittelalterlichen Passionstraktats', *Theologische Zeitschrift*, 6: 17–39

Ruskin, J., 1849. *The Seven Lamps of Architecture*, London

—, ed. J. G. Links, 1960 (1851–3). *The Stones of Venice*, London

—, *Lectures on Art*, 1875. 2nd edn, Oxford

Russell, D. A., 1964. *Longinus on the Sublime*, Oxford

—, trans., 2001, *Quintilian: Institutio Oratoria*, Loeb Classical Library, vols 124, 127, 494, Cambridge, MA

Rykwert, J., 1972. *On Adam's House in Paradise: The Idea of the Primitive Hut in Architectural History*, New York

Ryle, G., 1976. *The Concept of Mind*, Harmondsworth

Sadie, S., ed., 2001. *The New Grove Dictionary of Music and Musicians*, 2nd edn, 29 vols, London

Sadler, D. L., 2012. *Reading the Reverse Facade of Reims Cathedral: Royalty and Ritual in Thirteenth-Century France*, Farnham

Salzman, L. F., 1997. *Building in England down to 1540: A Documentary History*, Oxford

Sampson, J., 1998. *Wells Cathedral West Front: Construction, Sculpture and Conservation*, Stroud

Sánchez Ameijeiras, R., 2009–10. '"Como a Virgen santa paresceu, paresçia": las empresas marianas alfonsíes y la teoría neoplatónica de la imagen sagrada', in *Alfonso X el Sabio*, ed. T. López de Guereño Sanz and I. G. Bango Torviso, Murcia, 357–65

—, 2011. 'The Faces of the Words: Aesthetic Notions and Artistic Practices in the Thirteenth Century', in *Gothic Art and Thought in the Later Medieval Period*, ed. C. Hourihane, Index of Christian Art Occasional Papers, 12, Princeton, NJ, 90–118

—, 2014. *Los Rostros de las palabras: imágenes y teoria literaria en el Occidente medieval*, Madrid

—, 2015. 'Dreams of Kings and Buildings: Visual and Literary Culture in Galicia (1175–1230)', in *Culture and Society in Medieval Galicia: A Cultural Crossroads at the Edge of Europe*, ed. and trans. J. d'Emilio, Leiden and Boston, 695–764

Sandler, L. F., 1983. *The Psalter of Robert de Lisle in the British Library*, Oxford
—, 1986. *Gothic Manuscripts, 1285–1385*, 2 vols, Survey of Manuscripts Illuminated in the British Isles, 5, Oxford
Sargent, M. G., 2004. *Nicholas Love. The Mirror of the Blessed Life of Jesus Christ: A Reading Text*, Exeter
Sari, A., 2015. *Crocifissi dolorosi della Sardegna: Il Nicodemo di Oristano*, Ghilarza
Sauerländer, W., 1992. 'Romanesque Sculpture and its Architectural Context', in Kahn 1992b, 17–43
—, 2003. '*Phisionomia est doctrina salutis*: Über Physiognomik und Porträt im Jahrhundert Ludwigs des Heligen', in *Das Poträt vor der Erfindung des Porträts*, ed. M. Büchsel, P. Schmidt, Mainz, 101–21
—, 2006. 'The Fate of the Face in Medieval Art', in Little, 3–17
—, 2008. 'Romanesque Art 2000: A worn out Notion?' in *Romanesque Art and Thought in the Twelfth Century*, ed. C. Hourihane, Index of Christian Art Occasional Papers, 10, Princeton, NJ, 40–56
—, and R. Kroos, 1972. *Gothic Sculpture in France, 1140–1270*, trans. J. Sondheimer, London
Saunders, C. J., 1993. *The Forest of Medieval Romance: Avernus, Broceliande and Arden*, Cambridge
Saviello, J., 2012. 'Haarkunst als Linienspiel im 15. und 16. Jahrhundert', in *Linea II: Giochi, metamorfosi, seduzioni della linea*, ed. M. Faietti and G. Wolf, Florence, 52–73
Scarry, E., 1985. *The Body in Pain: The Making and Unmaking of the World*, New York
—, 2000. *On Beauty and being Just*, London
Schama, S., 1995. *Landscape and Memory*, London
Schapiro, M., 1977. *Romanesque Art: Selected Papers*, London
—, 2006. *Romanesque Architectural Sculpture: The Charles Eliot Norton Lectures*, ed. L. Seidel, Chicago
Schleif, C., 2013. 'Seeking Patronage: Patrons and Matrons in Language, Art and Historiography', in *Patronage: Power and Agency in Medieval Art*, ed. C. Hourihane, Index of Christian Art Occasional Papers, 15, Princeton, NJ, 119–33, 206–32
Schmengler, D., 2016. *Die Masken von Reims: Zur Genese negativer Ausdrucksformen zwischen Tradition und Innovation*, Berlin
Schmidt, P. G. 1978a. 'The Vision of Thurkill', *Journal of the Warburg and Courtauld Institutes*, 41: 40–64
—, ed., 1978b. *Visio Thurkilli*, Leipzig
Schmitt, J.-C., 1981. '"*Gestus*" – "*gesticulatio*": contribution à l'étude du vocabulaire latin médiéval des gestes', in *La Lexicographie du latin médiéval et ses rapports avec les recherches actuelles sur la civilisation du Moyen-Age*, ed. Y. Lefebvre, Paris, 377–90
—, 1990. *La Raison des gestes dans l'occident médiéval*, Paris
Schnell, R., 2004. 'Historische Emotionsforschung: Eine mediävistische Standortsbestimmung', *Frühmittelalterliche Studien*, 38: 173–276
Scholar, R., 2005. *The Je-ne-Sais-Quoi in Early Modern Europe: Encounters with a Certain Something*, Oxford
Schuller, M., 1993. *Das Fürstenportal des Bamberger Domes*, Bamberg
Schurr, M. C., 2014. 'L'opus francigenum de Wimpfen im Thal: transfert technologique ou artistique?' *Les Transferts artistiques dans l'Europe gothique: repenser la circulation des artistes, des oeuvres, des thèmes et des savoir-faire (XXe–XVIe siècle)*, ed. J. Dubois, Paris, 45–55
Sciurie, H., 1993–4. 'Ecclesia und Synagoge an den Domen zu Strassburg, Bamberg, Magdeburg und Erfurt: Körpersprachliche Wandlungen im gestalterischen Kontext', *Wiener Jahrbuch für Kunstgeschichte*, 46–7: 679–87
Scribner, R., 1987. *Popular Culture and Popular Movements in Reformation Germany*, London
Scruton, R., 1983. 'Fantasy, Imagination and the Screen', *Grazer Philosophische Studien*, 19: 35–46
Searle, J. R., 1983. *Intentionality: An Essay on the Philosophy of Mind*, Cambridge
Sears, E. S., 2006. 'Craft Ethics and the Critical Eye in Medieval Paris', *Gesta*, 45/2: 221–38
Segré, C., ed., 1957. *Richart de Fournival: Li Bestiaires d'Amours*, Milan
Shackleton Bailey, D. R., trans., 2001. *Cicero: Letters to Friends*, vol. 2, Loeb Classical Library, vol. 216, Cambridge, MA
Shearman, J., 1992. *Only Connect: Art and the Spectator in the Italian Renaissance*, Princeton

Silver, L., 1983. 'Forest Primeval: Albrecht Altdorfer and the German Wilderness Landscape', *Simiolus* 13/1: 4–43

Simson, O. von, 1953. 'Compassion and Co-Redemption in Roger Van der Weyden's Descent from the Cross', *Art Bulletin*, 35/1: 9–16

Simpson, W. S., ed., 1873. *Registrum statutorum et consuetudinem Ecclesiae Cathedralis Sancti Pauli Londinensis*, London

Skinner, B. F., 1974. *About Behaviourism*, London

Smith, K. A., 2006. 'Bodies of Unsurpassed Beauty: Living Images of the Virgin in the High Middle Ages', *Viator*, 37/1: 167–87

Snyder, J., 1980. 'Picturing Vision', *Critical Enquiry*, 6/3: 499–526

—, 2011. *Early Gothic Column-Figure Sculpture in France: Appearance, Materials and Significance*, Farnham

Southern, R. W., 1953. *The Making of the Middle Ages*, London

—, 1963. *Saint Anselm and his Biographer: A Study of Monastic Life and Thought, 1059–c.1130*, Cambridge

Souza, R. de, 1987. *The Rationality of Emotions*, Cambridge, MA

Spencer, J. R., trans., 1977. *Leon Battista Alberti: On Painting*, New Haven and London

Stahl, W. H., and E. L. Burge, ed. and trans., 1977, *Martianus Capella and the Seven Liberal Arts*, vol. 2, New York

Stammler, W., 1959. *Frau Welt: Eine mittelalterliche Allegorie*, Freiburg

Starkey, K., 2003. 'Brunhild's Smile: Emotion and the Politics of Gender in the Niebelunglied', in *Codierungen von Emotion im Mittelalter*, ed. C. S. Jaeger and I. Kasten, Berlin, 159–73

Stearns, P. N., and Carol Z. Stearns, 1985. 'Emotionology: Clarifying the History of Emotions and Emotional Standards', *American Historical Review*, 90/4: 813–36

Stefani, C. de, ed., 2011. *Paulus Silentarius: Descriptio Sanctae Sophiae, Descriptio Ambonis*, Bibliotheca Scriptorum Graecorum et Romanorum Teubneriana, Berlin

Stein, N., 2014. 'Immanent and Transeunt Potentiality', *Journal of the History of Philosophy*, 52/1: 33–60

Stock, B., 1972. *Myth and Science in the Twelfth Century: A Study of Bernard Silvester*, Princeton, NJ

Stone, L., 1972. *Sculpture in Britain: The Middle Ages*, 2nd edn, Harmondsworth

Stratford, N., 1983. 'The "Henry of Blois Plaques" in The British Museum', *Medieval Art and Architecture at Winchester Cathedral: British Archaeological Association Conference Transactions*, 6: 28–37

—, 1986–90. 'Romanesque Sculpture in Burgundy: Reflections on its Geography, on Patronage, on the Status of Sculpture and on the Working Methods of Sculptors', in Barral I Altet, vol. 3, 235–50

—, Chevalier, P. and A. Moquet, 2002. *La frise monumentale romane de Souvigny*, Souvigny

Street, G. E., 1865. *Some Account of Gothic Architecture in Spain*, London

Sullens, I., ed., 1983. *Robert Mannyng of Brunne: Handlyng Synne*, Binghamton, NY

Svanberg, J., 1993a. *Sankt Göran och draken*, Stockholm

—, 1993b. 'The Gothic Smile', in *Künstlerischer Austausch-Artistic Exchange: Akten des XXVIII. Internationalen Kongresses für Kunstgeschichte*, ed. T. W. Gaethgens, vol. 2, Berlin, 357–70

Swanton, M. J., ed. and trans., 1970. *The Dream of the Rood*, Manchester

Tachau, K. H., 1998. 'God's Compass and *vana curiositas*: Scientific Study in the Old French *Bible Moralisée*', *Art Bulletin*, 80/1: 7–33

Tambling, J., 2010. *Dante in Purgatory: States of Affect*, Turnhout

Tångeborg, P., 2006. 'The Enthroned Virgin of Stora Malm, Södermanland, Sweden', in Nadolny et al., 59–75

Taubert, J., 2015. *Polychrome Sculpture: Meaning, Form, Conservation*, ed. M. D. Marincola, Los Angeles

Thénard-Duvivier, F., 2011. 'Construction et fonctions d'un récit hagiographique sculpté: le portail mériodional de Saint-Ouen de Rouen (XIVe siècle)', in *L'image médiévale: fonctions dans l'espace sacré et structuration de l'espace cultuel*, ed. C. Voyer and E. Sparhubert, Turnhout, 239–98

—, 2012. *Images sculptées au seuil des cathédrales: les portails de Rouen, Lyon et Avignon (XIIIe–XIVe siècles)*, Rouen

Thérel, M.-L., 1984. *Le Triomphe de la Vierge-Eglise: à l'origine du décor du portail occidental de Nôtre-Dame de Senlis: sources historiques, littéraires et iconographiques*, Paris

Thibodeau, T. M., trans., 2007. *The Rationale Divinorum Officiorum of William Durand of Mende: A New Translation of the Prologue and Book One*, New York

Thiebaux, M., 1967. 'The Medieval Chase', *Speculum*, 42: 260–74

Thoby, P., 1959–63. *Le Crucifix des origines au Concile de Trente*, 2 vols, Nantes

Thomas, E., 2015. 'The Beauties of Architecture', in *The Blackwell Companion to Ancient Aesthetics*, ed. P. Destrée and P. Murray, Chichester, 274–90

Thompson, F. H., ed., 1983. *Studies in Medieval Sculpture*, Society of Antiquaries Occasional Papers, 3, London

Thurlby, M., 1999. *The Herefordshire School of Romanesque Sculpture*, Logaston, Herefordshire

Tilliette, J.-Y., 2013. '*Color*: petite histoire d'une notion rhétorique', in *L'Image en questions: pour Jean Wirth*, ed. F. Elsig et al., Geneva and Paris, 278–84

Timmermann, A., 2009. *Real Presence: Sacrament Houses and the Body of Christ, c. 1270–1400*, Turnhout

Toman, R., 1997. *Romanesque: Architecture, Sculpture, Painting*, Cologne

Tracy, C., 1987. *English Gothic Choir Stalls 1200–1400*, Woodbridge

—, and A. Budge, 2015. *Britain's Medieval Episcopal Thrones*, Oxford and Philadelphia

Trilling, J., 1995. 'Medieval Art without Style? Plato's Loophole and a Modern Detour', *Gesta*, 34/1: 57–62

Tripps, J., 1998. *Das handelnde Bildwerk in der Gotik*, Berlin

Trumbull, H. C., 1896. *The Threshold Covenant: The Beginning of Religious Rites*, 2nd edn, New York

Turel, N., 2011. 'Living Pictures: Rereading "au vif", 1350–1550', *Gesta*, 50/2: 163–82

Turner, D., 1995. *The Darkness of God: Negativity in Christian Mysticism*, Cambridge

Valdez del Alamo, E., 1996. 'Lament for a Lost Queen: The Sarcophagus of Doña Blanca in Nájera', *Art Bulletin*, 78/2: 311–33

Van Os, H., et al., eds, 1994. *The Art of Devotion in the Late Middle Ages in Europe 1300–1500*, London and Amsterdam

Vauchez, A., 1991. 'Saints admirables et saints imitables: les fonctions de l'hagiographie ont-elles changé aux derniers siècles du Moyen Âge?', in *Les Fonctions des saints dans le monde occidental (IIIe–XIIIe siècles)*, Collection de l'Ecole Française de Rome, 149, Rome, 161–72

Venturi, R., 1966. *Complexity and Contradiction in Architecture*, New York

Verret, D., and D. Steyaert, 2002. *La Couleur et la pierre: polychromie des portails gothiques*, Paris

Verzar, C. B., 1992. 'Text and Image in North Italian Romanesque Sculpture', in Kahn 1992b, 121–40

Villanueva, J., 1850. *Viage literario a las iglesias de España*, vols 11 and 12, Madrid

Walton, K., 1990. *Mimesis as Make-Believe: On the Foundations of the Representational Arts*, Cambridge, MA

Wangaard, F. F., 1950. *The Mechanical Properties of Wood*, New York and London

Warner, M., 1989. 'Signs of the Fifth Element', in *The Tree of Life: New Images of an Ancient Symbol*, ed. R. Malbert, London

—, 2006. *Phantasmagoria: Spirit Visions, Metaphors and Media into the Twenty-First Century*, Oxford

Waszink, J. H., ed., 1975. *Timaeus a Calcidio translatus commentarioque instructus*. Plato latinus, vol. 4, London and Leiden

Watson, J. B., 1930. *Behaviorism*, Chicago

Webb, R., 1999. 'The Aesthetics of Sacred Space: Narrative, Metaphor, and Motion in "Ekphraseis" of Church Buildings', *Dumbarton Oaks Papers*, 53: 59–74

Weinryb, I., 2013. 'Living Matter: Materiality, Maker and Ornament in the Middle Ages', *Gesta*, 52/3: 113–32

—, 2016. *The Bronze Object in the Middle Ages*, Cambridge

Weisheipl, J., 1959. 'The Place of John Dumbleton in the Merton School', *Isis*, 50: 439–54

Westermann-Angerhausen, H., ed., 1996. *Schatz aus den Trümmern: Der Silberschrein von Nivelles und die europäische Hochgotik*, Cologne

Wetherbee, W., trans., 1973. *The Cosmographia of Bernard Silvestris*, New York

— and trans., 2013. *Alan of Lille: Literary Works*, Dumbarton Oaks Medieval Library, 22, Cambridge, MA

Wieck, R. S., ed., 1988. *Time Sanctified: The Book of Hours in Medieval Art and Life*, New York and Baltimore

Wilhelmy, W., ed., 2012. *Seliges Lächeln und höllisches Gelächter: Das Lachen in Kunst und Kultur des Mittelalters*, Mainz and Regensburg

Williams, J. W., 1993. *Bread, Wine and Money: The Windows of the Trades at Chartres Cathedral*, Chicago and London

Williams, P., 1993. *The Organ in Western Culture 750–1250*, Cambridge

Williamson, P., 1995. *Gothic Sculpture, 1140–130*, New Haven and London

—, ed., 2010. *Object of Devotion: Medieval English Alabaster Sculpture from the Victoria and Albert Museum*, Alexandria, VA

—, and G. Davies, eds, 2014. *Medieval Ivory Carvings, 1200–1550*, 2 vols, London

Wilshere, A. D., ed., 1982. *Mirour de Seinte Eglise*, Anglo-Norman Text Society, 40, London

Wilson, C., 1995. 'The Medieval Monuments', in *A History of Canterbury Cathedral*, ed. P. Collinson, N. Ramsay and M. Sparks, Oxford, 451–510

Winbush, V. L., and R. Valantasis, eds, 1995. *Asceticism*, New York

Wirth, J., 2004. *La Datation de la sculpture médiévale*, Geneva

—, 2015. *Villard de Honnecourt: architecte du XIIIe siècle*, Geneva

Wirth, K. A., 1953. 'Die Entstehung des Dreinagelkruzifixus', diss., Frankfurt-am-Main

Wittgenstein, L., 1978. *Lectures and Conversations on Aesthetics, Psychology and Religious Belief*, ed. C. Barrett, Oxford

Wölfflin, H., 1935. 'Prolegomena zu einer Psychologie der Architectur' (1886), repr. in *Kleine Schriften*, Basel, 13–47

Wollheim, R., 1980. *Art and its Objects*, 2nd edn, Cambridge

—, 1987. *Painting as an Art*, London

Wolska, J., 1997. *Ringkors från Gotlands Medeltid: En iconografisk och stilistik studie*, Stockholm

Woods, K., 2011. 'The Fortunes of Art in Alabaster: A Historiographical Analysis', in *Gothic Art and Thought in the Later Medieval Period*, ed. C. Hourihane, Index of Christian Art Occasional Papers, 12, Princeton, NJ, 82–102

—, 2017. *Cut in Alabaster: A Material of Sculpture 1330–1530*, Brepols

Woolf, R., 1968. *The English Religious Lyric in the Middle Ages*, Oxford

Wormald, F., 1973. *The Winchester Psalter*, London

Worringer, W., 1912. *Formprobleme der Gotik*, 2nd edn, Munich

Yamamoto, D., 2000. *The Boundaries of the Human in Medieval English Literature*, Oxford

Young, K., 1933. *The Drama of the Medieval Church*, 2 vols, Oxford

Zarnecki, G., 1951. *English Romanesque Sculpture, 1066–1140*, London

—, 1953. *Later English Romanesque Sculpture, 1140–1210*, London

—, 1958. *The Early Sculpture of Ely Cathedral*, London

—, 1961. *Gislebertus: Sculptor of Autun*, London

—, 1970. *Romanesque Sculpture at Lincoln Cathedral*, Lincoln

—, 1979. *Studies in Romanesque Sculpture*, London

—, 1988. *Romanesque Lincoln: The Sculpture of the Cathedral*, Lincoln

—, J. Holt and T. Holland, eds, 1984. *1066: English Romanesque Art 1066–1200*, London

Photograph credits

Photo © Bednorz Images / Bridgeman Images: 4, 5, 6, 10, 12, 16, 19, 21, 24, 31, 36, 41, 46, 47, 50, 61, 81, 90 (De Agostini Picture Library / Bridgeman Images); © Conway Library, the Courtauld Institute of Art, London: 7, 15 (A. F. Kersting), 17, 23 (James Austin), 30 (James Austin), 74 (James Austin), 92, 95, 96; Paul Binski: 8, 32, 33, 34, 55, 71, 73, 79, 83, 84, 85, 87, 91, 93, 109, 111, 113; John Crook: 9, 14, 18, 20, 25, 28, 43, 44, 48, 49, 94; © Kulturhistorisk museum, UiO, lisens CC BY-SA 4.0: 13, 59 (photo Eirik Irgens Johnsen), 62 (photo Restaureringsatelieret); Jean-Claude Bonne: 22; The J. P. Getty Museum Open Content Program: 26, 27; Tom Nickson: 29, 45, 52, 99, 100; Metropolitan Museum, New York, OA Public Domain: 35, 63; Bildarchiv photo Marburg: 37, 56; The Parker Library, Corpus Christi College, Cambridge: 38; Alamy Stock Photo: 39 (Bildarchiv Monheim GmbH), 51 (funkyfood London – Paul Williams), 53 (funkyfood London – Paul Williams) 69 (Angelo Hornak), 88 (Prisma Archivo), 108 (Bildarchiv Monheim GmbH), 112 (Angelo Hornak); Dean and Chapter of Westminster: 42, 57; Getty Images: 54 (Angelo Hornak), 78 (De Agostini Picture Library); © Victoria and Albert Museum, London: 60, 82; Photograph © The State Hermitage Museum / photo by Vladimir Terebenin: 64; Juliusz Raczkowski: 65; © The British Library Board, reproduced by permission: 66, 98, 105, 107; Muzeum Narodowe w Warszawie: 67 © National Museum of Denmark, Copenhagen, photo: Sofus Bengtsson: 68; The Hamilton Kerr Institute, Cambridge: 70; Poitiers (© CESCM Photothèque, Eva Michaud-Avril 2013): 72; The Bodleian Library, University of Oxford: 75; Musée des Augustins, Toulouse: 76; photo © RMN-Grand Palais / Jean-Gilles Berizzi: 77, 78; Image © Nottingham City Museums: 86; Robert Hawkins: 97; Matt Kavaler: 101, 102, 103; © By Permission of the Syndics of Cambridge University Library: 104; Richard Maack: 110

Index

Note: page numbers in *italics* refer to illustrations.